THE BEST TEST PREPARATION FOR THE

CLEP

COLLEGE-LEVEL EXAMINATION PROGRAM

SPANISH
LANGUAGE

Featuring the Latest on the CLEP Computer-Based Test (CBT)

Lisa J. Goldman
B.A. Spanish Language

And the Staff of
Research & Education Association
Dr. M. Fogiel, Director

Research & Education Association
61 Ethel Road West
Piscataway, New Jersey 08854

**The Best Test Preparation for the
CLEP SPANISH LANGUAGE**

Year 2004 Printing

Copyright © 2003, 2002, 1999 by Research &
Education Association, Inc. All rights reserved.
No part of this book may be reproduced in any form
without permission of the publisher.

Printed in the United States of America

Library of Congress Control Number 2002116330

International Standard Book Number 0-87891-221-5

REA® is a registered trademark of Research & Education Association, Inc.,
Piscataway, New Jersey 08854.

REA supports the effort to conserve and
protect environmental resources by
printing on recycled papers.

About Research & Education Association

Founded in 1959, Research & Education Association is dedicated to publishing the finest and most effective educational materials—including software, study guides, and test preps—for students in middle school, high school, college, graduate school, and beyond.

REA's Test Preparation series includes study guides for all academic levels in almost all disciplines. Research & Education Association publishes test preps for students who have not yet completed high school, as well as high school students preparing to enter college. Students from countries around the world seeking to attend college in the United States will find the assistance they need in REA's publications. For college students seeking advanced degrees, REA publishes test preps for many major graduate school admission examinations in a wide variety of disciplines, including engineering, law, and medicine. Students at every level, in every field, with every ambition can find what they are looking for among REA's publications.

Unlike most test preparation books—which present only a few practice tests that bear little resemblance to the actual exams—REA's series presents tests that accurately depict the official exams in both degree of difficulty and types of questions. REA's practice tests are always based upon the most recently administered exams, and include every type of question that can be expected on the actual exams.

REA's publications and educational materials are highly regarded and continually receive an unprecedented amount of praise from professionals, instructors, librarians, parents, and students. Our authors are as diverse as the fields represented in the books we publish. They are well-known in their respective disciplines and serve on the faculties of prestigious high schools, colleges, and universities throughout the United States and Canada.

Acknowledgments

In addition to our author, we would like to thank Larry B. Kling, Manager, Editorial Services, for his direction of the editorial development of this revised edition; Project Managers Diane Goldschmidt and Mike Sedelmaier for coordinating revisions; Cristina Bedoya for her editorial contributions and voice-over work; Jannette Ball and Lucio Nava for their voice-over work; Paul Sukovich at Suite 16 Studios, Piscataway, N.J., for recording and editing the audio material; and Paula Musselman for typesetting the manuscript. Development of the book was coordinated by Nicole Mimnaugh. Press readiness was ensured by Pam Weston, Production Manager.

CONTENTS

CHAPTER 1

PASSING THE CLEP SPANISH LANGUAGE CBT

Chapter 1

PASSING THE CLEP SPANISH LANGUAGE CBT

ABOUT THIS BOOK

This book provides you with an accurate and complete representation of the CLEP Spanish Language Computer-Based Test, or CBT. Inside you will find a concise Spanish Language subject review with drills, as well as tips and strategies for test-taking. We give you three full-length practice tests—along with audio CDs for the Listening portion of the test—all based on the official CLEP subject exam. Our practice tests contain every type of question that you can expect to encounter on the computer-based CLEP. Following each practice test you will find an answer key with detailed explanations designed to help you more completely absorb the test material.

All 34 CLEP exams are computer-based. As you can see, the practice tests in our book are presented as paper-and-pencil exams. While our printed tests provide slightly more questions than the CBT, the content and format of the actual CLEP subject exam are otherwise faithfully mirrored. We detail the format and content of the CLEP Spanish Language CBT on pages 5–6.

ABOUT THE EXAM

Who takes the CLEP Spanish Language CBT and what is it used for?

CLEP (College-Level Examination Program) examinations are usually taken by people who have acquired knowledge outside the classroom and wish to bypass certain college courses and earn college credit. The CLEP Program is designed to reward students for learning—no matter where or how that knowledge was acquired. With more than 2,900 colleges that grant credit and/or advanced standing for CLEP exams, CLEP is the most widely accepted credit-by-examination program in the country.

Although most CLEP examinees are adults returning to college, many graduating high school seniors, enrolled college students, and international students also take the exams to earn college credit or to demonstrate their ability to perform at the college level. There are no prerequisites, such as age or educational status, for taking CLEP examinations. You must, however, meet any specific requirements of the particular institution from which you wish to receive CLEP credit.

There are 34 CLEP examinations. Of these, five—English Composition (with or without essay), Humanities, Mathematics, Natural Sciences, and Social Sciences and History—cover material usually taken as requirements during the first two years of college.

Who administers the exam?

The CLEP CBT is developed by the College Board, administered by Educational Testing Service (ETS), and involves the assistance of educators throughout the United States. The test development process is designed and implemented to ensure that the content and difficulty level of the test are appropriate.

When and where is the exam given?

The CLEP Spanish Language CBT is offered each month of the year at some 1,400 test centers in the United States and can be arranged for candidates abroad on request. To find the test center nearest you and to register for the exam, you must obtain a copy of the free booklets *CLEP Colleges* and *CLEP Information for Candidates and Registration Form*, which are available at most colleges where CLEP credit is granted, or by contacting:

CLEP Services
P.O. Box 6600
Princeton, NJ 08541-6600
Phone: 800-257-9558 (8 a.m. to 6 p.m. ET)
Website: www.collegeboard.com/clep

HOW TO USE THIS BOOK

What do I study first?

Read over the course review and the suggestions for test-taking, take the first practice test to determine your area(s) of weakness, and then go back and focus your study on specific problems. Studying the review material thoroughly will reinforce the basic skills you will need to do well on the exam. Make sure to take the practice tests to become familiar with the format and procedures involved with taking the actual exam.

To best utilize your study time, follow our Independent Study Schedule at the end of this section. The schedule is based on a six-week program, but can be condensed to three weeks, if necessary, by collapsing each two-week study session into a one-week period.

When should I start studying?

It is never too early to start studying for the CLEP Spanish Language CBT. The earlier you begin, the more time you will have to sharpen your skills. Do not procrastinate! Cramming is *not* an effective way to study, since it does not allow you the time needed to learn the test material. The sooner you learn the format of the exam, the more time you will have to familiarize yourself with it.

FORMAT OF THE CLEP SPANISH LANGUAGE CBT

The CLEP Spanish Language CBT assumes you'll have a level of mastery that would equate to skills normally achieved during two to four semesters of college-level work. The exam tests basic vocabulary and word usage, as well as the ability to understand oral and written Spanish.

There are approximately 120 multiple-choice questions on the test, each with four possible answer choices, to be answered in three separately timed sections. You will be allotted a total of approximately 30 minutes for the Listening portion of the test (which comprises Sections I and II) and 60 minutes for the Reading portion of the test (which comprises Section III).

The approximate breakdown of topics is as follows:

Section I – Listening[†]: Rejoinders (15%)

Section II – Listening[†]: Dialogues and narratives (25%)

Section III – Reading

> **Part A (16%): Discrete sentences (vocabulary and structure)**
>
> **Part B (20%): Short cloze passages (vocabulary and structure)**
>
> **Part C (24%): Reading passages and authentic stimulus materials (reading comprehension)**

SCORING YOUR PRACTICE TEST vs. THE CLEP CBT

How do I score my practice test?

The CLEP Spanish Language CBT is scored somewhat differently than our printed practice tests. Again, note that we give you about 10 additional questions per practice test to hone your test-taking skills. To score your practice tests, count the number of correct answers and enter the result on the scoring worksheet below. Next, total your incorrect answers, multiply this number by one-third and enter the result on the worksheet. Subtract the number of incorrect responses from the number of correct ones; this will yield your total raw score. Finally, convert your raw score to a scaled score using the conversion table on page 7.

PRACTICE-TEST SCORING WORKSHEET

Raw Score: _____ – (1/3 x _____) = _____

                  # correct   *# incorrect*

Scaled Score: _____

Caution: The conversion table on page 7 provides only an estimate of your scaled score. Since scaled scores vary from one form of a test to another, your score on the actual exam may be higher or lower than what our table indicates. Also, be aware that you will suffer no penalty for incorrect guesses on the CLEP CBT.

---

† The audio portions of the Listening sections will be presented only once. In Section I, you will be given 10 seconds to click on your response before the next conversation begins. In Section II, you will be given a total of nine minutes to register all your responses. The timer will run only when you are answering questions.

SCALED-SCORE CONVERSION TABLE

Raw Score	Scaled Score	Course Grade	Raw Score	Scaled Score	Course Grade
100 & up	80	A	48	54	B
99	80	A	32	47	B
98	80	A	46	52	B
97	79	A	45	51	B
96	79	A	44	51	B
95	78	A	43	50	B
94	78	A	42	50	B
93	77	A	41	50	B
92	77	A	40	50	B
91	76	A	39	50	B
90	76	A	38	49	B
89	75	A	37	48	B
88	74	A	36	48	B
87	74	A	35	47	B
86	73	A	34	46	B
85	72	A	33	46	B
84	72	A	32	45	C
83	71	A	31	45	C
82	71	A	30	45	C
81	70	A	29	45	C
80	69	A	28	45	C
79	69	A	27	44	C
78	68	A	26	44	D
77	67	A	25	43	D
76	67	A	24	42	D
75	66	A	23	41	D
74	66	A	22	41	D
73	65	A	21	40	F
72	64	A	20	40	F
71	64	A	19	40	F
70	63	A	18	40	F
69	62	A	17	39	F
68	62	A	16	39	F
67	61	A	15	38	F
66	61	A	14	37	F
65	60	A	13	36	F
64	60	A	12	35	F
63	60	A	11	34	F
62	60	A	10	33	F
61	59	B	9	32	F
60	58	B	8	31	F
59	58	B	7	30	F
58	57	B	6	29	F
57	57	B	5	28	F
56	56	B	4	26	F
55	56	B	3	24	F
54	55	B	2	23	F
53	55	B	1	22	F
52	55	B	0	21	F
51	55	B	-1	20	F
50	55	B	-2	20	F
49	54	B	and below	20	F

*This table is provided for scoring REA practice tests only. The American Council on Education recommends that colleges use a single across-the-board credit-granting score of 50 for all 34 CLEP computer-based exams. Nonetheless, on account of the different skills being measured and the unique content requirements of each test, the actual number of correct answers needed to reach 50 will vary. A "50" is calibrated to equate with performance that would warrant the grade C in the corresponding introductory college course. Furthermore, for the Spanish Language exam, ACE recommends that a score of 50 should earn two semesters of credit, and a score of 54 should earn four semesters of credit.

When will I receive my score report and what will it look like?

The test administrator will print out a full Candidate Score Report for you immediately upon your completion of the CBT (except for CLEP English Composition with Essay). Your scores are reported only to you, unless you ask to have them sent elsewhere. If you want your scores reported to a college or other institution, you must indicate this when you sit for the exam. Since your scores are kept on file for 20 years, you can also request transcripts from Educational Testing Service at a later date.

STUDYING FOR THE CLEP SPANISH LANGUAGE CBT

It is crucial for you to choose the time and place for studying that works best for you. Some students set aside a certain number of hours every morning, while others choose to study at night before going to sleep. Only you can determine when and where your study time will be most effective. But be consistent and use your time wisely. Work out a study routine and stick to it!

When you take our practice tests, try to make your testing conditions as much like the actual test as possible. Turn off the television or radio, and sit down at a quiet table or desk free from distraction. Use a timer to ensure that each section is accurately clocked.

As you complete each practice test, score it and thoroughly review the explanations for the questions you answered incorrectly; but don't review too much at one sitting. Concentrate on one problem area at a time by reviewing the question and explanation, and by studying our review until you are confident that you completely understand the material.

Keep track of your scores and mark them on the scoring worksheet. By doing so, you will be able to gauge your progress and discover general weaknesses in particular sections. You should carefully study the review sections that cover your areas of difficulty, as this will build your skills in those areas.

TEST-TAKING TIPS

You may never have taken a standardized computer-based test like the CLEP Spanish Language exam, but it's not hard to learn the things you need to know to be comfortable on test day.

Know the format of the CBT. CLEP CBTs are *not adaptive* but rather fixed-length tests. In a sense, this makes them kin to the familiar paper-and-pencil exam in that you have the same flexibility to go back and review your work in each section. Moreover, the format hasn't changed a great deal from the paper-and-pencil CLEP. For this exam, you can expect to encounter 120 questions that need to be answered within 90 minutes. You are likely to see some so-called pretest (experimental) questions as well, but you won't know which ones they are and they won't be scored.

Use the process of elimination. If you don't immediately see the correct answer among the choices, go down the list and eliminate as many as you can. Confidently casting aside choices will help you isolate the correct response, or at least knock your choices down to just a few strong contenders. This approach has the added benefit of keeping you from getting sidetracked and distracted by what in fact may be just an occasional tricky question. Importantly, your score is based only on the number of questions you answer *correctly*.

Work quickly and steadily. You will have a total of about 30 minutes for the two Listening sections and 60 minutes for the reading section. Taking our practice tests—which, again, have a few more questions than the actual test—will help you learn to budget your time. Count on 40% of your total exam time being spent listening to the material in Section I and Section II.

Learn the directions and format for each section of the test. This will put extra time on your side that you can use to review your work.

Acquaint yourself with the CBT screen. Familiarize yourself with the CLEP CBT screen beforehand by logging on to the College Board Website. Waiting until test day to see what it looks like in the pretest tutorial risks injecting needless anxiety into your testing experience.

Be sure that your answer registers before you go to the next item. Look at the screen to see that your mouse-click causes the pointer to darken the proper oval. This takes far less effort than darkening an oval on paper, but don't lull yourself into taking less care!

THE DAY OF THE EXAM

On the day of the test, you should wake up early (after a decent night's rest, one would hope) and have a good breakfast. Dress comfortably so that you are not distracted by being too hot or too cold while taking the test. Arrive at the test center early. This will allow you to collect your thoughts and relax before the test, and will also spare you the anxiety that comes with being late.

No one will be allowed into the test center after the test session has begun.

Before you set out for the test center, make sure that you have your admission form, Social Security number, and a photo ID with your signature (e.g., driver's license, student identification card, or current alien registration card). You need proper ID to get into the test center.

You may wear a watch to the test center, but it cannot make any noise, which could disturb your fellow test-takers. No calculators, computers, dictionaries, textbooks, notebooks, scrap paper, briefcases, or packages will be permitted; drinking, smoking, and eating are prohibited.

Finally, be assured that any time you spend on taking tutorials or giving personal information will not be metered by the test clock. Also, while you may encounter occasional sluggishness in the operation of your computer, this won't affect timing, as the clock won't run until each question or set of questions is fully loaded.

Good luck on the CLEP Spanish Language CBT!

INDEPENDENT STUDY SCHEDULE
CLEP SPANISH LANGUAGE CBT

The following study schedule allows for thorough preparation for the CLEP Spanish Language CBT. Although this schedule has been designed for six weeks, the schedule can be condensed into a three-week course by condensing each two-week activity into a one-week plan. Be sure to set aside enough time—at least two hours a day—to study. No matter which study schedule works best for you, the more time you spend studying, the more prepared and relaxed you will feel on the day of the examination.

Week	Activity
1–2	Read and study Chapter 1, which introduces you to the CLEP Spanish Language CBT. Then take Practice Test 1 to determine your strengths and weaknesses. Score the test by using the scoring table in Chapter 1. You can then determine the areas in which you need to strengthen your skills.
3–4	Carefully study the review material for the CLEP Spanish Language CBT. Be sure to take the drills that follow each section.
5	Take Practice Test 2. After scoring your exam, review all incorrect answer explanations. If there are any types of questions or particular areas that seem difficult to you, review those subjects by studying the appropriate section of the review.
6	Take Practice Test 3. After scoring your exam, review all incorrect answer explanations. If there are any types of questions or particular areas that seem difficult to you, review those subjects by studying the appropriate section of the review.

CHAPTER 2

CLEP SPANISH REVIEW

Chapter 2

CLEP SPANISH REVIEW

THE ALPHABET

Spanish uses the same Latin alphabet as English except for the addition of three letters:

ch pronounced like "ch" in "chief"

ll pronounced like the "y" in "beyond"

ñ pronounced like "ni" in "opinion" or "ny" in "canyon"

Some consonants have different pronunciation:

c sounds like "s" before "e" and "i," and like "k" in all other cases.

g sounds like the "h" in "humid" before "e" and "i," and like the "g" in "go" or "get" in front of "a," "o," and "u." In order to obtain the hard sound before "e" and "i," Spanish interpolates the vowel "u": *guerra, guión.* In these cases the "u" is silent; a dieresis indicates that it must be pronounced: *vergüenza, güero.*

h is always silent: *ahora, húmedo, horrible.*

v is pronounced like "b" in all cases.

y sounds like "ll" at the beginning of a word or syllable. When it stands alone or comes at the end of a word, it is equivalent to the vowel "i."

z is pronounced like "s."

(This pronunciation guide follows Latin American usage. In Castilian Spanish the soft "c" and the "z" are pronounced like "th" in "thin.")

Letter		Spanish Example	English Example
b	[b]	*bomba*	boy
c	[k]	*calco*	keep
	[T]	*cero*	same
ch	[+S]	*mucho*	chocolate
d	[d]	*andar*	dog
f	[f]	*fama*	fake
g	[x]	*general*	humid
	[g]	*rango*	get
h	always silent	*hombre*	honor
j	[x]	*justo*	humid
k	[k]	*kilogramo*	kite
l	[l]	*letra*	light
ll	[¥]	*ella*	beyond
m	[m]	*mano*	mad
n	[n]	*pan*	no
ñ	[ñ]	*uña*	onion
p	[p]	*padre*	poke
q	[k]	*que*	kite
r	[r]	*rápido*	(this is a trilled or "rolling" sound with no English equivalent)
s	[s]	*casa*	some
	[z]	*mismo*	rose
t	[t]	*patata*	tame
v	[b]	*vamos*	boy
x	[ks]	*máximo*	fox
y	[j]	*yo*	yes
z	[T]	*zapato*	same

The sounds of the Spanish vowels are invariable.

a sounds approximately like "a" in "ah."
e sounds approximately like "e" in "men."
i sounds approximately like "ee" in "eel."
o sounds approximately like "o" in "or."
u sounds approximately like "oo" in "moon."

Letter		Spanish Example	English Example
a	[a]	*pata*	father
e	[e]	*pelo*	men
i	[i]	*filo*	eel
o	[o]	*poco*	or
u	[u]	*luna*	moon

A combination of one strong (a, e, o) and one weak vowel (i, u) or of two weak ones is a diphthong and counts as one syllable:

ai, ay	*aire, hay*	pronounce like "eye"
ei, ey	*reino, ley*	pronounce like "may"
oi, oy	*oigo, hoy*	pronounce like "toy"
iu	*triunfo*	pronounce like "you"
ui, uy	*cuidar, muy*	pronounce like "Louie"
ue	*hueso, muerde*	pronounce like "west"

RULES FOR STRESS IN SPANISH

There are two rules that indicate stress in Spanish. If either of these two rules is broken, a written accent mark will appear on the word.

1. If a word ends in a vowel, *–n,* or *–s,* the **normal** stress is on the penultimate (next to last) syllable.

mano (over the *–a*)	*tribu* (over the *–i*)
esposa (over the *–o*)	*hablan* (over first *–a*)
clase (over the *–a*)	*tomaban* (over first *–a*)

2. If the word ends in any other letter (than those mentioned above), the **normal** stress will fall on the last syllable.

hablar (over the *–a*)	*papel* (over the *–e*)
comer (over the *–e*)	*ejemplar* (over the *–a*)
vivir (over the *–i*)	*nivel* (over the *–e*)

3. Spanish words will have an accent for the following specific reasons:

    a. There is another identical word and the accent distinguishes the one from the other.

de (of, from)	vs.	*dé* (give—formal command)
se (reflexive pronoun)	vs.	*sé* (I know, verb)
el (article)	vs.	*él* (he, pronoun)

tu (yours possessive adj.)	vs.	*tú* (you, pronoun)
mas (but, conjunction)	vs.	*más* (more, adverb)
si (if)	vs.	*sí* (yes)

b. A pronoun has been added to a verb form.

diciéndolo	saying it
diciéndomelo	saying it to me
explíquelo	explain it
explíquemelo	explain it to me

Note: *decírselo* (to say it to him). Infinitives require two pronouns before an accent is necessary.

c. The accent is the result of a stem change.

reunir (ú) — The *ú* will appear in the first, second, and third person singular and third person plural of the present indicative/subjunctive.

Other examples:

continuar (ú),   *enviar (í)*
graduarse (ú)

d. There may be a diphthong (two weak vowels or a weak with a strong) where the weak vowel (*u* or *i*) needs to be stressed.

Examples:

divertíos	Enjoy yourselves!
creíste	you believed

SYLLABIC DIVISION

A consonant between two vowels joins the second vowel to form a syllable: *li-te-ra-tu-ra, e-ne-mi-go, a-ho-ra.*

- Two consonants together must be separated: *cuer-no, pac-to.*

- "ch," "ll," and "rr" are considered one letter and are not separated.

- "l" or "r" preceded by "b," "c," "d," "f," "g," "p," and "t" are not separated: *ha-blar, a-brup-to, te-cla, pul-cri-tud, me-lo-dra-ma, in-flu-jo, a-gra-de-cer.*

- "ns" and "bs" are not separated in groups of three or four consonants: *ins-cri-bir, obs-tá-cu-lo.*

- In words formed with prefixes, the prefix stands alone as one syllable: *sub-ra-yar, in-ú-til, des-a-gra-dar.*

ARTICLES

The forms of the definite article are:

	Masculine	Feminine
Singular	*el*	*la*
Plural	*los*	*las*

El is used instead of *la* before feminine nouns beginning with stressed "a" or "ha": *el agua,* **el** *hacha,* **el** *alma,* **el** *hambre.*

El contracts to *al* when the article follows the preposition *a* (*a + el*) and to *del* when the article follows the preposition *de* (*de + el*).

Uses of the Definite Article

The definite article is used in Spanish (but not in English):

- when the noun represents an abstraction: **life** is short; **time** is money; **freedom** is worth fighting for; **politics** is a practical art. (In Spanish: *la vida, el tiempo,* **la** *libertad,* **la** *política.*);

- when the noun includes the totality of a category: **books** are good; **man** is mortal; the Incas were acquainted with **gold**; **bread** is a staple. (In Spanish: *los libros, el hombre, el oro, el pan.*);

- with the days of the week (except after a form of the verb *ser*) and the seasons of the year: *el lunes* (but *hoy es lunes*), *la primavera, el otoño;*

- with the hours of the day: *son* **las** *tres de la tarde; a* **las** *doce* **del** *día* (or *al mediodía*);

- with personal or professional forms of address in the third person: *el señor Jiménez, la señorita Méndez, el doctor Márquez, el licenciado Vidriera.* (It is omitted when the individual is directly addressed and in front of titles such as *Don, Doña, San,* or *Santo[a]: venga, señor Jiménez; no se preocupe, señorita Méndez;*

- with the parts of the body or articles of clothing instead of the possessive adjective: I brushed **my** teeth. *Me cepillé* **los** *dientes.* I put on **my** shirt. *Me puse* **la** *camisa;*

- with the names of languages except after the prepositions *en* and *de* and the verb *hablar: el francés es difícil* (but *no hablo francés; ese texto está en francés*);

- with weights and measures: *un dólar la libra,* one dollar per pound; *diez pesos la docena,* ten pesos per dozen;

- with infinitives used as nouns (gerunds): Lying is a vice. *El mentir es un vicio.* (This use is optional, especially in proverbs.) Seeing is believing. *Ver es creer;*

- with names of "generic" places: jail, *la cárcel;* class, *la clase;* church, *la iglesia;* market, *el mercado;*

- with family names: The García's, *los García;*

- with adjectives to make them nouns: the pretty one, *la bonita;* the poor, *los pobres;* the old man, *el viejo;*

- with nouns in apposition with a pronoun: We Americans . . . *Nosotros los americanos . . .*

Omission of the Definite Article in Spanish

The definite article in Spanish is omitted in the following cases:

1. With fields of knowledge, in general, one needs an article unless one . . .

   a. gives a **definition**

   ¿Qué es astronomía?
   Astronomía es una ciencia.

   b. uses *estudiar* or *examinar*

   Estudiamos química.

2. With the expressions *de . . . a*

   En casa comemos *de seis a ocho.*
   At home we eat from 6:00 to 8:00.

3. With expressions such as

   por primera vez   for the first time
   por segunda vez   for the second time
   en primer lugar   in the first place

4. With *con* and *sin* before an unmodified abstract noun.

   No puedo vivir sin libertad.
   I cannot live without liberty.

   Con amor la vida tiene sentido.

With love, life has meaning.

5. With a numeral that denotes the order of a monarch.

    Carlos Quinto   Charles the Fifth

The Neuter Article *Lo*

This article is used exclusively in the singular as follows:

1. *Lo* + adjective = **part/thing**

    Examples: *lo importante*   the important thing/part
                lo mejor   the best thing/part

2. *Lo* + adj/adv + *que* = **how**

    Examples: *Tú no sabes lo importante que es.*
                You don't know **how** important it is.

                Él no entiende lo despacio que va.
                He doesn't know **how** slowly it goes.

3. *Lo de* = All that or everything that (happened)

    Example: *Vamos a cubrir lo de ayer.*
                We'll cover everything we did yesterday.

4. *Lo* is used in sentences with the pronoun ***todo*** as the direct object.

    Example: *Lo entiendo todo.*
                I understand everything.

5. *Todo lo que* = All that

    Example: *Todo lo que oí no es verdad.*
                All that I heard isn't true.

6. *Lo* is used as a complement to replace adjectives, pronouns, or nouns with ***ser***, ***estar,*** and ***parecer***.

    Examples: *Pareces enojada.* [adj-*enojada*]
                You seem angry.

                —Quizás **lo** parezca, pero no **lo** estoy.
                Perhaps I seem it, but I'm not.

                ¿Estas llaves son tuyas? [noun-*llaves*]

Are these keys yours?

—*No, no **lo** son.*
No, they're not.

Forms of the Indefinite Article

The indefinite article must agree in gender and number with the noun it modifies. Its forms are the following:

	Masculine	Feminine
Singular	*un*	*una*
Plural	*unos*	*unas*

Examples: *un perro* – a dog
unos perros – some dogs

Note: feminine nouns beginning with a stressed "a" or "ha" take *un* instead of *una:* **un** *alma,* **un** *hacha,* **un** *hada madrina.* This rule only applies if the noun is singular.

Uses of the Indefinite Article

Spanish *omits* the indefinite article (but not English) as follows:

- after the verb *ser* with nouns denoting profession, religion, or nationality: *soy professor, son católicos, es española.* (This rule does not apply when the noun is followed by an adjective or some other modifier: *soy **un** profesor exigente* (I'm a demanding teacher)).

- with words such as *otro* (other), *medio* (half), *cien* (one hundred or a hundred), *mil* (one thousand or a thousand), *tal* (such a), *cierto* (a certain), and *qué* (what a): *cierta mujer* (a certain woman), *¡qué día! (What a day!),* cien libros (a hundred books), *mide un metro y medio* (it measures one and one-half meters), *otra respuesta* (another answer), *tal hombre* (such a man).

- after **sin**:
  Salío sin abrigo.   He left without a coat.

- after **haber** used impersonally, **buscar,** and **tener** (otherwise it means **one**)*:*

  No hay respuesta.   There isn't **an** answer.
  Estoy buscando trabajo.   I'm looking for **a** job.
  No tiene coche.   He doesn't have **a** car.

GENDER

In Spanish most nouns are either masculine or feminine. Most nouns ending in *-o* or *-or* are masculine and most of those ending in *-a* , *-d*, *-ión*, *-umbre*, *-ie*, *-sis*, *-itis* are feminine.

Masculine	Feminine
el dinero – money	*la muchedumbre* – crowd
el otoño – autumn	*la serie* – series
el amor – love	*la crisis* – crisis
	la presencia – presence
	la bronquitis – bronchitis
	la acción – action

Note: Drop the accent on *–ión* words when made plural: *nación, naciones*

Many masculine nouns become feminine by changing the *-o* ending to *-a* or by adding an *-a* if the word ends in a consonant:

Masculine	Feminine
el escritor – the writer	*la escritora* – the woman writer
el doctor – the doctor	*la doctora* – the woman doctor
el hijo – the son	*la hija* – the daughter
el muchacho – the young man	*la muchacha* – the young woman

Exceptions

A few common words ending in *-o* are feminine:

la mano – the hand
la foto (la fotografía) – the photo, picture
la moto (la motocicleta) – the motorcycle

There is a large number of words ending in *-ma*, *-pa*, and *-ta* that are masculine. For the most part, if these are easily identifiable in English, they are probably masculine.

el clima – climate	*el problema* – problem
el diploma – diploma	*el sistema* – system
el drama – drama	*el mapa* – map
el poema – poem	*el profeta* – prophet
el tema – theme	*el aroma* – aroma

There are also other ways of forming the feminine than by adding an -*a* ending:

Masculine	Feminine
el rey – the king	*la reina* – the queen
el poeta – the poet	*la poetisa* – the woman poet
el gallo – the rooster	*la gallina* – the hen

Sometimes the masculine and feminine words corresponding to a matched pair of concepts are different:

Masculine	Feminine
el yerno – the son-in-law	*la nuera* – the daughter-in-law
el macho – the male	*la hembra* – the female
el toro – the bull	*la vaca* – the cow

Masculine words that appear to be feminine:

el día – day	*el césped* – turf
el sofá – sofa	*el colega* – colleague
el ataúd – coffin	*el tranvía* – trolley

Nouns of Invariable Gender

Some nouns can be either masculine or feminine depending on their content or reference, without undergoing any formal alterations.

Masculine	Feminine
el artista – the male artist	*la artista* – the woman artist
el estudiante – the student	*la estudiante* – the female student
el joven – the young man	*la joven* – the young woman

Gender and Meaning Change

There are nouns that have different meanings depending on whether they are used as masculine or feminine:

el policía – the policeman	*la policía* – the police (force)
el Papa – the Pope	*la papa* – the potato
el cometa – the comet	*la cometa* – the kite
el orden – order (as in public order)	*la orden* – the order (to do something)
el cura – the priest	*la cura* – the cure

el guía – the guide (person)	*la guía* – the guide (book, as in *guía de teléfonos*)
el frente – the front	*la frente* – the forehead

Use of *El* Before a Feminine Noun

If the feminine noun begins with a stressed *a* or *ha*, the singular forms of the article used are *el* or *un*. If anything intercedes between these two items, use the normal *la* or *una*.

el águila (eagle)	*las águilas*	*la gran águila*
un hacha (hatchet)	*unas hachas*	*una gran hacha*

Other examples: *el alma* – soul, *el aula* – classroom. *el agua* – water, *el ala* – wing, *el alba* – dawn, *el hada* – fairy, *el hambre* – hunger.

Note: On exams, this concept is tested by asking students to write the correct form of an adjective that follows, as in these examples. Observe that the adjective is feminine because the noun is, despite the masculine article.

el agua tibia	the warm water
el alba bonita	the pretty dawn
el águila maravillosa	the marvelous eagle

Other Feminine Words (Often Used on Exams)

la pirámide – pyramid	*la vez* – time
la torre – tower	*la razón* – reason
la leche – milk	*la imagen* – image
la carne – meat	*la luz* – light
la gente – people	*la catedral* – cathedral
la frase – sentence	*la suerte* – luck

NUMBER

In Spanish, as in English, nouns can be singular or plural. The most common way to form the plural is by adding the *-s* ending to the singular form of the word. (Note that the following examples are of words ending in an unstressed vowel.)

Singular	Plural
hombre – man	*hombres* – men
niño – boy	*niños* – boys
perro – dog	*perros* – dogs

Formation of the Plural by Addition of *-es*

In other cases (words ending in a consonant or in a stressed vowel other than *-é*), the plural is formed by adding an *-es* ending to the singular form of the word:

Singular	Plural
mujer – woman	*mujeres* – women
razón – reason	*razones* – reasons
jabalí – boar	*jabalíes* – boars

Exceptions: *mamá* (mother), pl. *mamás; ley* (law), pl. *leyes.*

Nouns of Invariable Number

Nouns ending in *-s* are the same in the singular and the plural if the final syllable is unstressed:

el (los) rascacielos – the skyscraper(s)
el (los) paraguas – the umbrella(s)
el (los) lunes – Monday(s)

Diminutives

The Spanish endings *-ito, -cito*, and their feminine forms are used to indicate affection or to emphasize smallness of size:

*Tú eres mi **amor.***
You are my **love.**

*Tú eres mi **amorcito.***
You are my **sweetheart.**

*Quiero chocolate. Dame un **poco.***
I want chocolate. Give me **some.**

*Quiero chocolate. Dame un **poquito.***
I want chocolate. Give me **a little.**

*Ese **hombre** tiene buen aspecto.*
That **man** is good looking.

*Ese **hombrecito** debe ser muy desgraciado.*
That **poor man** must be very unfortunate.

Augmentatives

The endings *-ote, -ón,* and *-ona* are added to express increased size:

hombre – man	*hombrón* – big man
mujer – woman	*mujerona* – big woman
casa – house	*casona* – big house

ADJECTIVES

Adjectives agree in gender and number with the noun they modify.

a) Adjectives ending in *-o* change their ending to *-a* when they modify a feminine noun:

bueno, buena – good; *malo, mala* – bad; *bello, bella* – beautiful

b) Adjectives ending in *-or* (or *-ón* or *-án*) add an *-a* to become feminine:

hablador, habladora – talkative

Exceptions:

mejor – better	*peor* – worse
superior – upper, superior	*inferior* – lower, inferior
exterior – outer, external	*interior* – inner, internal
anterior – earlier, anterior	*posterior* – later, posterior

c) Most other adjectives have the same ending for both genders:

verde – green	*grande* – big, great
azul – blue	*soez* – mean, vile
cortés – courteous	

d) Adjectives of nationality have four forms. If they end in *-o*, they follow the normal pattern of change. All others may be changed by adding *-a* to make them feminine and *-as* to make them feminine plural.

inglés, inglesa, ingleses, inglesas
alemán, alemana, alemanes, alemanas
español, española, españoles, españolas

Number

a) Adjectives ending in a vowel add an *-s* to form the plural:

bello, bellos – beautiful; *grande, grandes* – big, great

b) Adjectives ending in a consonant add *-es* to form the plural:

azul, azules – blue; *débil, débiles* – weak; *vulgar, vulgares* – vulgar

c) If an adjective modifies more than one noun and one of those nouns is masculine, the adjective must be **masculine** and **plural:**

*Mis tíos y tías eran **ricos.*** My uncles and aunts were **rich.**
*Los hombres y las mujeres son **viejos.*** **The** men and women are old.

Shortening of Adjectives

Some adjectives that directly precede the noun lose their final vowel or syllable:

ciento → cien	*grande → gran**
bueno → buen**	*malo → mal***
Santo → San**	*primero → primer***
tercero → tercer**	*alguno→ algún***
ninguno→ ningún**	*cualquiera→ cualquier**

* The shortening of this adjective only happens in front of singular nouns, either masculine or feminine. Compare:

*El acontecimiento fue **grande.***
The event was **big.**

*el **gran** acontecimiento* – the **big** event

** These adjectives only shorten in front of masculine singular nouns. Compare:

*El hombre es **bueno.***
The man is **good.**

*el **buen** hombre* – the **good** man

Qualifying Adjectives

Qualifying adjectives usually follow the noun:

*un día **frío*** – a **cold** day
*unas sábanas **limpias*** – some **clean** sheets

Change of Meaning with Location

Some common adjectives change their meaning with their location:

*el hombre **pobre*** – the poor man (impecunious)
*el **pobre** hombre* – the poor man (pitiable)

un cuadro **grande** – a large painting
un **gran** *cuadro* – a great painting

el policía **mismo** – the policeman himself
el **mismo** *policía* – the same policeman

ciertas *palabras* – certain words (specific words from among many)
palabras **ciertas** – certain (sure)

nueva *casa* – new house (different)
casa **nueva** – new house (brand new)

un **simple** *empleado* – a mere employee
un empleado **simple** – a simple-minded employee

COMPARISON OF ADJECTIVES AND ADVERBS

Adverbs modify verbs, adjectives, and other adverbs and are invariable. The following is a list of frequently used adverbs:

bien – well	*mal* – badly
más – more	*menos* – less
siempre – always	*nunca* – never
cerca – near	*lejos* – far
antes – before	*después* – afterwards
bastante – enough	*demasiado* – too much
temprano – early	*tarde* – late
así – thus, so	*casi* – almost
entonces – then	*luego* – later, afterward
todavía – still	

Aún is a common adverb whose meaning depends on whether the sentence is affirmative or negative:

Aún *quiere trabajar.*
He **still** wants to work.

Aún *no está despierta.*
She's not **yet** awake.

Aun (no accent) normally has the meaning **even** and commonly precedes the word it modifies.

¿Aun no ha llegado Juan?
Juan hasn't **even** arrived?

Adverbs Ending in *-mente*

Many adverbs are derived from the **feminine** form of the adjective (when such a form is available) by the addition of *-mente:*

> *claro/claramente* – clearly
> *rápido/rápidamente* – quickly
> *feliz/felizmente* – happily
> *hábil/hábilmente* – skillfully
> *dulce/dulcemente* – sweetly

When two or more adverbs are used in a sequence, only the last adverb ends in *–mente*. All others are written as feminine adjectives (if they have a feminine form).

> *Habla lenta y elocuente**mente**.*
> He speaks slowly and eloquently.

> *Juan corre rápida y hábil**mente**.*
> Juan runs rapidly and skillfully.

Con, Sin + Noun

At times an adverb can be formed by using the preposition *con* (with) or *sin* (without) + a noun.

> *con cuidado* – carefully
> *sin cuidado* – carelessly
> *con rapidez* – rapidly

Recientemente vs. *Recién*

Recientemente becomes *recién* before a past participle.

> *los recién llegados* – the recent arrivals
> *los recién casados* – the newlyweds

Adverbs Replaced by Adjectives

Adverbs may be replaced by adjectives with verbs of motion.

> *Ellos van y vienen silenciosos.*
> They come and go silently.

Comparison of Equality

This is constructed in the following ways:

> ***Tanto, a, os, as*** + (noun) + ***como***

Tan + (adverb or adjective) + *como*

*Tuve **tantas** deudas **como** el mes pasado.* I had **as many** debts **as** last month.

*Su música es **tan** clara **como** el agua.*
Her music is **as** clear **as** water.

*Llegué **tan** tarde **como** ayer.*
I arrived **as** late **as** yesterday.

Tanto como (without intervening expressions) means "as much as."

*Tu amigo estudia **tanto como** yo.*
Your friend studies **as much as** I [do].

Comparison of Inequality

The formula for describing levels of superiority is:

más + (noun, adjective, or adverb) + *que*

*Tengo **más** dinero **que** tú.*
I have **more** money **than** you.

*Su auto es **más** caro **que** el mío.*
His car is **more** expensive **than** mine.

*Me levanto **más** temprano **que** ella.*
I get up earli**er than** she does.

The above formula changes to *más de* if a numerical expression is involved and the sentence is in the affirmative:

*Vimos **más de** mil estrellas en el cielo.*
We saw **more than** a thousand stars in the sky.

But:

*No tengo **más que** cinco dólares en el bolsillo.*
I don't have **more than** five dollars in my pocket.

The formula for describing levels of inferiority is:

menos + (noun, adjective, or adverb) + *que*

*Nos dieron **menos** tiempo **que** a ustedes para completar el examen.*
They gave us **less** time **than** they gave you to finish the exam.

*Eres **menos** pobre **que** ella.*

You are **less** poor **than** she is.

*Tiene **menos** problemas **que** su madre.*
She has **fewer** problems **than** her mother.

The same change applies to the comparison of inferiority **except** that even in negative sentences *de* is used instead of *que:*

*No eran **menos de** cinco los asaltantes.*
The assailants were no **fewer than** five.

If the second part of the comparison has a different verb from the first, **than** is expressed in one of five ways: *del que, de la que, de los que, de las que* (which all have gender and refer to nouns that are objects of both verbs), and *de lo que* (which is used when adjectives or adverbs are being compared).

*Ella gasta más dinero **del que** gana su esposo.* [*dinero*]
She spends more money **than** her husband earns.

*Tengo más coches **de los que** puedo contar.* [*coches*]
I have more cars **than** I can count.

*Es más fácil **de lo que** crees.* [*fácil*]
It is easier **than** you believe.

*Anda más despacio **de lo que** corre.* [*despacio*]
He walks more slowly **than** he runs.

Special Comparatives

Adjective (Adverb)	Comparative
bueno (bien) – good, well	*mejor* – better
malo (mal) – bad, badly	*peor* – worse
grande – big	*mayor** – older
pequeño – small	*menor** – younger

* *Mayor* and *menor* only refer to age; otherwise, *más (menos) grande (pequeño) que* is used.

*Mi padre es **mayor** que yo; mi hijo es **menor**.*
My father is **older** than I; my son is **younger**.

*Esta ciudad es **más grande que** la capital.*
This city is **bigger than** the capital.

Superlatives

In English the true or relative superlative is rendered by **the most (least) of** a category:

El, la, los, las + *más (menos)* + (adjective) + *de*
Lo + *más (menos)* + (adverb) + *de*

*Estos anillos son **los más** caros **de** la tienda.*
These rings are **the most** expensive **in** the store.

*Tienes **los** ojos **más** lindos **del** mundo.*
You have **the prettiest** eyes **in** the world.

*Corre **lo más** rápidamente **de** todos.*
He runs **the most** quickly **of** all.

The special comparatives previously noted have a superlative form:

El, la, los, las + (special comparatives) + *de*
*Mi hijo es **el mayor de** la clase.* My son is **the oldest in** the class.

Absolute Superlative

Superlatives can also be formed by adding the *-ísimo(a)* ending to adjectives and adverbs. (Some spelling adjustments may be necessary.)

The absolute superlative is usually rendered in English as "very pretty," "very ugly," etc.

lindo/lindísimo – very pretty
feo/feísimo – very ugly
tarde/tardísimo – very late
cerca/cerquísimo – very near
rico/riquísimo – very rich
fácil/facilísimo(a) – very easy

The adjective *malo* has the special superlative *pésimo* in addition to the more informal *malísimo*. The adjective *bueno* has the special superlative *óptimo* in addition to *buenísimo*.

☞ Drill 1

1. Ramiro es más guapo _____ Felipe.

   (A) que   (C) de

   (B) como   (D) tan

2. _____ arma de fuego es peligrosa.

   (A) El   (C) Los

   (B) La   (D) Las

3. Mercedes lavó los platos _____.

   (A) rápidamente y cuidadosamente   (C) rápida y cuidadosamente

   (B) rápida y cuidadosa   (D) rápidamente y cuidadosa

4. Los explicaron _____ nosotros.

   (A) menor que   (C) mayor que

   (B) tanto   (D) mejor que

5. Elena tiene más amigas _____ puede contar.

   (A) de los que   (C) de las que

   (B) que   (D) de lo que

6. Pablo trabaja mejor _____ usted cree.

   (A) que   (C) del que

   (B) de lo que   (D) de la que

7. Anita es menos alta _____ Elena

   (A) tan   (C) como

   (B) de   (D) que

8. Estas películas son _____ interesantes como ésas.

   (A) tan   (C) tantas

   (B) tantos   (D) como

9. Roberto y Ana son _____ inteligentes de la clase.

   (A) las más   (C) más

   (B) los más   (D) menos

10. Ellos corren _____ y hábilmente.

    (A) rápida   (C) rápidamente

    (B) rápido   (D) rápidos

11. Las chicas hablan _____ lentamente de todos.

    (A) el más   (C) lo más

    (B) las más   (D) más

12. Hay _____ torres como palacios en aquel país.

    (A) tan   (C) tan muchos

    (B) tantos   (D) tantas

13. _____ persona puede estudiar este curso.

    (A) Algún   (C) Ningún

    (B) Cualquier   (D) Cualquiera

14. Juan y María son chicos _____.

    (A) alemanas   (C) alemanes

    (B) de alemanes   (D) alemanos

15. Isabela I fue _____.

    (A) una gran mujer   (C) una mujer gran

    (B) una grande mujer   (D) mujer grande

16. Mis notas son _____ las de Juan.

    (A) mayor que   (C) mejores que

    (B) mayores de   (D) mejores de

17. Tú no sabes _____ importante _____ son las tareas.

   (A) los . . . que   (C) lo . . . que

   (B) las . . . que   (D) lo . . . de

18. ¿Estas llaves son tuyas? —No, no _____ son.

   (A) las   (C) ellas

   (B) lo   (D) nothing needed

19. Juan lo hizo _____ ayer.

   (A) para primera vez   (C) por primera vez

   (B) por primer vez   (D) por la primera vez

20. Todo _____ oí ayer no es verdad.

   (A) que   (C) la que

   (B) lo que   (D) de

Drill 1—Detailed Explanations of Answers

1. **(A)** The most common pattern to express a **comparison** of superiority (i.e., to show that one thing or person is superior to another in some respect) is "más . . . que" (more than); for example, "Yo soy más delgado que tú" (I am thin**er than** you); "Hablas español más fácilmente que yo" (You speak Spanish more easily than I); "Tengo más años que ella" (I am older than she). Notice from these three examples that we may use either adjectives, adverbs, or nouns between the words "más" and "que." The only time we use "de," as in (C), after "más" is when there is a number immediately afterwards: "Tenemos más de tres pesos" (We have more than three pesos).

2. **(A)** "Arma de fuego" means "firearm." Of the possible choices, we can immediately eliminate (C) and (D) because they are plural definite articles and cannot be placed before a singular noun such as "arma." This reduces our choices to "El" or "La." We know that most nouns that end in -*a* are feminine. By looking at the sentence carefully, we also see that the adjective "peligrosa" (dangerous) is feminine and most certainly modifies "arma." Therefore, you might have been tempted to choose (B), "La."

This is not correct, however. Feminine singular nouns which end in -*a* but begin with "a" or "ha" and have their **stress** on the **first syllable**, as in "arma," require that we use the masculine singular definite article in front of them. This does not change the gender of the noun, however. It still stays feminine. We can see this in our sentence because we used the feminine adjective "peligrosa" to describe "arma." Remember that this rule applies only to feminine **singular** nouns. In the plural, we use the feminine plural definite article: "Las armas de fuego son peligrosas."

3.   **(C)**   When two or more adverbs are used together to refer to the same verb, the last one is the only one with the –*mente* ending.

4.   **(D)**   The verb "explicaron" in our sentence means "they explained." Comparisons of superiority, i.e., comparisons which show that in some respect someone or something is superior to someone or something else, are usually formed according to the following pattern: "más" + adjective or adverb or noun + "que." Example: "Enrique es **más rico que** yo." (Enrique is richer than I). There are some adjectives and adverbs which have irregular comparatives. For example, "menor," which appears in (A), is the comparative form of "pequeño." "Mayor," in (C), is the comparative for "grande." Neither of these could be used in the blank because we are not talking about size. On the other hand, "mejor que" would mean "better than" and makes sense in our sentence. The word "tanto," in (B), means "as much" or sometimes "so much." It is usually followed by "como" to form comparisons of equality, i.e., to show that two persons or things are equal in some respect: "Tengo **tanto dinero como** tú" (I have as much money as you). In (B), however, we have omitted the word "como," which is obligatory in comparisons of equality.

5.   **(C)**   When the verbs in each half of the comparison are both referring to the same noun ("amigas"), the longer form of **than** is required. Because "amigas" is a feminine noun, "de las que" is used. For this reason (A) would be incorrect because it is masculine plural, and (D) is also incorrect because it is neuter. Answer (B) would be used in a simple comparison where the verb is not repeated in the second half.

6.   **(B)**   Because an adjective is the point of comparison for each verb ("trabaja" and "cree"), the neuter form of **than** is used. Therefore, (C), the masculine form, and (D), the feminine form, are not correct. Answer (A) would be used in a simple comparison where the verb is not repeated in the second half.

7. **(D)** This is a simple comparison where the verb in the second half of the comparison is not stated but understood to be from the same infinitive (**ser** in this case). Choice (A) is used in the first half of an equal comparison and means **as**. Choice (C) is used in the second half of an equal comparison to mean **as**. Choice (B) is used in an unequal comparison when followed by a number.

8. **(A)** When there is an equal comparison that involves using an adjective or adverb, the word preceding this adjective or adverb is **tan**, meaning **as**. The second half of this comparison requires using **como**, which is already in the sample. Therefore, choice (D) cannot be used to precede the adjective. Choices (B) and (C) each have gender and would precede nouns.

9. **(B)** Superlative statements require the use of the definite article and are followed by **de**. In this sample, because Roberto is masculine and Ana is feminine, the masculine plural "los" is required. Therefore, choice (A), the feminine plural, is incorrect. In order to use either choice (C) or (D), the sentence would need to be in the comparative form (not the superlative) and **que** would then need to follow the adjective.

10. **(A)** Whenever there are two or more adverbs modifying a verb, only the last adverb ends in -*mente*. The other must be written in the feminine form of the adjective (if there is one). This would eliminate choice (B), which is a masculine adjective, and (D), which is a masculine plural adjective. Choice (C) is incorrect because it ends in -*mente*.

11. **(C)** When dealing with the superlative forms of adverbs, instead of using the definite article, which has gender, **lo** is used with **más** or **menos**. Therefore, (A), which is masculine, and (B), which is feminine plural, are incorrect. Choice (D) is incomplete because **lo** is needed.

12. **(D)** Because "torres" is a feminine plural noun, the feminine plural form of **tanto** is required. Choice (A) means **as** and does not translate correctly with a noun after it. Choice (C) is a completely incorrect form since forms of **tanto** mean **as much** or **as many**.

13. **(B)** Before any singular noun, "cualquiera" apocopates (drops the -a). Therefore, (D) is incorrect. Choices (A) and (C), although apocopated, are used with masculine singular nouns. To be correct, each would need to end in -a.

14. **(C)**   Adjectives of nationality have four forms. The masculine plural form is required here because the adjective is modifying both a masculine and feminine subject. Because the masculine singular form is **alemán**, the plural adds **-es** to that form. (Note that the accent is dropped on the plural form.) This would eliminate (A), which is feminine plural, and (D), which is nonexistent. Choice (B) is incorrect because adjectives of this sort are not preceded by **de**.

15. **(A)**   There are two grammatical points here: "grande" becomes "gran" before any singular noun and means **great**; the indefinite article ("una") is required before predicate nouns of occupation that are modified (have adjectives). Choice (B) is incorrect because "grande" is not apocopated, and (C) is incorrect because the apocopated form precedes, not follows, the noun. Choice (D) requires an indefinite article.

16. **(C)**   This answer requires knowing the meaning of "mejor" (better) and "mayor" (older). Also, a comparison is followed by **que** not **de**. "Mejor" must be plural in this sample to match "notas." Although choices (B) and (D) are plural, they are followed by **de**. Choices (A) and (B) also mean "older," which doesn't make sense in this context. Although (D) is plural, it is also followed by **de** and is, therefore, incorrect.

17. **(C)**   To express **how** followed by an adjective or adverb, use **lo** before that adjective/adverb and follow it with **que**. This would eliminate (A), (B), and (D) as correct choices.

18. **(B)**   **Lo** is used as a complement to replace adjectives, pronouns, or nouns used with **ser, estar,** and **parecer**. In this sample, the noun "llaves" (keys) is being replaced in the answer with **lo**. *Lo* used in this sense is invariable and will not, therefore, have the same gender and number as the noun it replaces.

19. **(C)**   The definite article is omitted with expressions such as this one (por primera vez, en primer lugar, etc.) Also, "vez" is feminine.

20. **(B)**   "Todo lo que" is an expression meaning "all that."

PRESENT INDICATIVE

	amar **to love**	*comer* **to eat**	*vivir* **to live**
yo	amo	como	vivo
tú	amas	comes	vives
él/ella/Ud.	ama	come	vive
nosotros, −as	amamos	comemos	vivimos
vosotros, −as*	amáis	coméis	vivís
ellos/ellas/Uds.	aman	comen	viven

* This pronoun and corresponding forms of the verb are used in Spain only.

Verbs irregular in **yo** form only:

caber	to fit	quepo	saber	to know	sé
caer	to fall	caigo	salir	to leave	salgo
dar	to give	doy	traer	to bring	traigo
hacer	to make/do	hago	valer	to be worth	valgo
poner	to put	pongo	ver	to see	veo

Verbs irregular in more than one form:

decir **to tell or say**	*estar* **to be**	*haber* **to have (auxiliary)**	*ir* **to go**
digo	estoy	he	voy
dices	estás	has	vas
dice	está	ha	va
decimos	estamos	hemos	vamos
decís	estáis	habéis	vais
dicen	están	han	van

oír **to hear**	*ser* **to be**	*tener* **to have**	*venir* **to come**
oigo	soy	tengo	vengo
oyes	eres	tienes	vienes
oye	es	tiene	viene
oímos	somos	tenemos	venimos
oís	sois	tenéis	venís
oyen	son	tienen	vienen

Verbs Ending in *-cer, -cir*

The *yo* form ends in *–zco* if preceded by a vowel. If the ending is preceded by a consonant, the form ends in *–zo*.

conocer	to know	*cono**zco***
*tra**duc**ir*	to translate	*tradu**zco***
*ven**cer***	to conquer	*ven**zo***

Others:

merecer – to deserve   *crecer* – to grow
carecer – to lack   *convencer* – to convince
aparecer – to appear   *nacer* – to be born
parecer – to seem

Verbs that Have Stem Changes

There are five types of stem changes that may occur in the present tense: *(ie)*, *(ue)*, *(i)*, *(ú)*, *(í)*. This will occur in all forms except nosotros/vosotros and appears in the stressed syllable.

ie *pensar* **to think**	ue *dormir* **to sleep**	i *pedir* **to ask for**	ú *actuar* **to act**	í *enviar* **to send**
pienso	*duermo*	*pido*	*actúo*	*envío*
piensas	*duermes*	*pides*	*actúas*	*envías*
piensa	*duerme*	*pide*	*actúa*	*envía*
pensamos	*dormimos*	*pedimos*	*actuamos*	*enviamos*
pensáis	*dormís*	*pedís*	*actuáis*	*enviáis*
piensan	*duermen*	*piden*	*actúan*	*envían*

Other examples:

ie: *comenzar/empezar* – to begin, *nevar* – to snow, *cerrar* – to close, *apretar* – to tighten, *perder* – to lose, *querer* – to want, *mentir* – to lie, *sentir* – to feel, *herir* – to wound

ue: *morir* – to die, *dormir* – to sleep, *volar* – to fly, *poder* – to be able, *volver* – to return, *rogar* – to beg, *jugar* – to play

i: *elegir* – to elect, *repetir* – to repeat, *servir* – to serve, *corregir* – to correct

ú: *graduarse* – to graduate, *continuar* – to continue

í: *confiar* – to confide, *guiar* – to guide, *variar* – to vary

Verbs Ending in *-ger, -gir*

In the *yo* form there will be a spelling change because the *-go* combination will produce a *g* sound and the infinitive has an *h* sound.

coger	to catch	*cojo*
elegir	to elect	*elijo*

Others:

escoger	to choose	*recoger*	to gather
corregir	to correct		

Verbs Ending in *-uir*

All forms except *nosotros/vosotros* have a *y*.

huir **to flee**	**construir** **to build**
huyo	*construyo*
huyes	*construyes*
huye	*construye*
huimos	*construimos*
huís	*construís*
huyen	*construyen*

Verbs Ending in *-guir*

The *yo* form drops the *u*.

seguir (i) – to follow	*sigo*
perseguir (i) – to pursue	*persigo*

Uses of the Present Indicative

There are three possible translations for the present tense as expressed below with the verb to eat (*comer*).

I eat./I do eat./I am eating. = *Como.*

Immediate Future

The present tense is commonly used to express the immediate future.

Mañana voy a casa.
Tomorrow I will go home.

The "*Hace*" Sentence

When an action began in the past and is still continuing in the present, the Spanish sentence is rendered with the following formula:

hace + time + *que* + Present/Present Progressive

Hace dos horas que comemos/estamos comiendo.
We have been eating for two hours.

¿Cuánto tiempo hace que ella canta/está cantando?
How long has she been singing?

PRETERITE AND IMPERFECT

Preterite Indicative—Regular: *-ar, -er, -ir*

	amar to love	comer to eat	vivir to live
yo	amé	comí	viví
tú	amaste	comiste	viviste
él/ella/Ud.	amó	comió	vivió
nosotros, –as	amamos	comimos	vivimos
vosotros, –as	amasteis	comisteis	vivisteis
ellos/ellas/Uds.	amaron	comieron	vivieron

Preterite Indicative—Irregular

The following group of preterites shares the same set of irregular endings: *–e, –iste, –o, –imos, –isteis, –ieron.*

andar to walk	caber to fit	estar to be	haber to have	hacer to make/do
anduve	cupe	estuve	hube	hice
anduviste	cupiste	estuviste	hubiste	hiciste
anduvo	cupo	estuvo	hubo	hizo
anduvimos	cupimos	estuvimos	hubimos	hicimos
anduvisteis	cupisteis	estuvisteis	hubisteis	hicisteis
anduvieron	cupieron	estuvieron	hubieron	hicieron

poder* to be able	poner to put	querer* to want
pude	puse	quise
pudiste	pusiste	quisiste
pudo	puso	quiso
pudimos	pusimos	quisimos
pudisteis	pusisteis	quisisteis
pudieron	pusieron	quisieron

venir to come	saber* to know	tener* to have
vine	supe	tuve
viniste	supiste	tuviste
vino	supo	tuvo
vinimos	supimos	tuvimos
vinisteis	supisteis	tuvisteis
vinieron	supieron	tuvieron

* These verbs have an altered translation in the preterite and will be discussed later in this chapter.

Irregular Preterites with a –j

decir to say/tell	traer to bring	–ducir types conducir to drive
dije	traje	conduje
dijiste	trajiste	condujiste
dijo	trajo	condujo
dijimos	trajimos	condujimos
dijisteis	trajisteis	condujisteis
dijeron	trajeron	condujeron

Note: The third plural does not have an i after the j.

Irregulars of Dar, Ir, Ser

   Dar is irregular in that it takes the endings of the -er/-ir verbs (without accents). Ser and ir are identical in this tense.

dar to give	*ir/ser* to go/to be
di	*fui*
diste	*fuiste*
dió	*fue*
dimos	*fuimos*
disteis	*fuisteis*
dieron	*fueron*

Stem-Changing Verbs

Stem changes commonly occur in the preterite for *–ir* verbs that have a stem change in the present. These changes have a pattern (*ue/u*), (*ie/i*), and (*i/i*). The second vowel in parenthesis will surface in the preterite third person singular and plural.

dormir (ue, u) to sleep	*sentir* (ie, i) to regret or feel	*pedir* (i, i) to ask for
dormí	*sentí*	*pedí*
dormiste	*sentiste*	*pediste*
durmió	*sintió*	*pidió*
dormimos	*sentimos*	*pedimos*
dormisteis	*sentisteis*	*pedisteis*
durmieron	*sintieron*	*pidieron*

Others:

morir — to die	*divertirse* — to enjoy oneself *herir* — to wound *mentir* — to lie	*servir* — to serve *repetir* — to repeat *seguir* — to follow

Verbs ending in *–car, –gar, –zar*

Verbs ending in *–car*, *–gar*, and *–zar* are affected in the **yo** form of the preterite by the final *–é*. This vowel will cause the consonants before it (*c, g, z*) to change in sound. To maintain the original sound of the infinitive, these verbs will require a spelling change in that form as follows.

–car = qué	*–gar = gué*	*–zar = cé*

Examples:

	atacar = ataqué	I attacked.
	entregar = entregué	I delivered.
	rezar = recé	I prayed.

Verbs that Change I to Y

All *–er* and *–ir* verbs with double vowels in the infinitive (with the exception of *traer/atraer*) will require this change in the third person singular and plural.

oír **to hear**	*creer* **to believe**	*leer* **to read**
oí	*creí*	*leí*
oíste	*creíste*	*leíste*
oyó	*creyó*	*leyó*
oímos	*creímos*	*leímos*
oísteis	*creísteis*	*leísteis*
oyeron	*creyeron*	*leyeron*

An added requirement for these verbs is the accent mark over the *i* in the *tú*, *nosotros*, and *vosotros* forms to split the diphthong.

Verbs Ending in *–ller, –llir, –ñir, –ñer*

Although these verbs are used with less frequency, they can surface on an exam. Because of the double *l* and the tilde over the *n,* these verbs in the third person singular and plural do not need the *i* of those endings.

bruñir **to polish**	*bullir* **to boil**
bruñí	*bullí*
bruñiste	*bulliste*
bruñó	*bulló*
bruñimos	*bullimos*
bruñisteis	*bullisteis*
bruñeron	*bulleron*

Verbs Ending in *–uir*

Just like the present tense of these verbs, the preterite also needs a *y*. It will occur in the third person singular and plural only.

huir	construir
to flee	**to build**
huí	construí
huiste	construiste
huyó	construyó
huimos	construimos
huisteis	construisteis
huyeron	construyeron

Verbs Ending in *–guar*

In this particular combination of letters, the *u* is heard as a separate letter, not treated as a diphthong with the *a* that follows. This sound will be altered in the *yo* form because of the final *–é*. To maintain the sound of the *u*, a dieresis mark is placed over it.

   averiguar (to verify) = *averigüé*

Note: This also occurs in other Spanish words:

   la vergüenza (shame), *el agüero* (omen)

Imperfect Indicative–Regular: *–ar*, *–er*, *–ir*

This tense may be translated as "used to + verb," "was" or "were + ing", or the normal past tense ending "–ed."

	amar	comer	vivir
	to love	**to eat**	**to live**
yo	amaba	comía	vivía
tú	amabas	comías	vivías
él/ella/Ud.	amaba	comía	vivía
nosotros, –as	amábamos	comíamos	vivíamos
vosotros, –as	amabais	comíais	vivíais
ellos/ellas/Uds.	amaban	comían	vivían

Imperfect Indicative–Irregulars

There are only three irregular verbs in this tense.

ser	ir	ver
to be	to go	to see
era	iba	veía
eras	ibas	veías
era	iba	veía
éramos	íbamos	veíamos
erais	ibais	veíais
eran	iban	veían

Continuation vs. Completion of an Action

The imperfect is used for an action **continuing** in the past; the preterite designates a **finished** action or an action whose beginning, duration, or end is emphasized by the speaker.

> *Estaba nublado.* (Imperfect)
> It was cloudy. (No indication of when it got that way.)

> *Estuvo nublado.* (Preterite)
> It was cloudy. (But now it has changed.)

> *Ella quería a su marido.* (Imperfect)
> She loved her husband. (Indefinitely in the past.)

> *Ella quiso a su marido.* (Preterite)
> She loved her husband. (While he was alive, while she was married
> to him, etc.)

Description vs. Narration

The imperfect is used to **describe** a quality or a state in the past; the preterite is used to **narrate** an action.

> *Los soldados* **marcharon** (pret.) *toda una mañana y* **llegaron** (pret.)
> *al fuerte enemigo al mediodía cuando* **hacía** (imp.) *mucho calor.*
> *Se* **sentían** (imp.) *cansados y* **necesitaban** (imp.) *descansar. Se*
> **sentaron** (pret.) *a la sombra de un árbol.*
> The soldiers marched one full morning and arrived at the enemy fort
> at noon when it was very hot. They were tired and needed to rest.
> They sat down in the shade of a tree.

"Used to" Followed by Infinitive

The English expression **used to** followed by an infinitive is rendered by the imperfect, as this is the tense that designates a habitual action in the past.

Pasábamos las vacaciones en la costa.
We **used to spend** the holidays on the shore.

Eran amigos.
They **used to be** friends.

Alternatively, the verb *soler* (to be in the habit of) may be used in the imperfect to render the sense of "used to." *Soler* must be accompanied by an infinitive: *solíamos pasar las vacaciones en la costa; solían ser amigos,* etc.

"Was" or "Were" plus Present Participle

Expressions formed with the past tense of "to be" followed by the present participle of another verb (**was** or **were** doing, singing, studying, etc.) are rendered by the imperfect.

*El **conducía** cuando ocurrió el accidente.*
He **was driving** when the accident occurred.

Pensaban visitarnos ese verano.
They **were thinking** of visiting us that summer.

Telling Time in the Past

The imperfect (of *ser*) is used to tell time in the past.

Eran las tres.
It was 3 o'clock.

Era tarde cuando se fueron los invitados.
It was late when the guests left.

Special Preterites

The preterite of some verbs (such as *conocer, saber, poder, poner, tener,* and *querer*) has a special meaning:

*Yo la **conocí** el año pasado.*
I **met** her last year.

*Cuando **supimos** la noticia nos pusimos tristes.*
When we **learned/found out** the news we felt sad.

*El fugitivo **pudo** abandonar el país a última hora.*
The fugitive **managed to** abandon the country at the last minute.

*Jamás **tuvo** noticias de su familia.*
She never **received** news of her family.

*El ladrón **quiso** abrir la puerta con una barra.*
The thief **tried to** open the door with a bar.

*Juan no **quiso** pagar la cuenta.*
Juan **refused** to pay the bill

States of Mind

Normally verbs indicating state of mind (*saber, creer, pensar, comprender, convencerse*, etc.) are expressed using the imperfect unless there is an indication of change in that state. Look for words to indicate this change like *de pronto* (soon), *de repente* (suddenly), *luego que* (as soon as), *cuando* (when), *al + infinitive* (upon + ing).

Juan creía la verdad.
Juan believed the truth.

But:

***De pronto** Juan la creyó.*
Suddenly Juan believed it.

"Ago" Statements

Ago statements are normally expressed with this formula:

Hace + time + *que* + preterite

Hace dos años que fuimos allí.
We went there two years ago.

"*Hacía*" Statements

To express "had been + ing," use the formula:

hacía + time + *que* + imperfect past progressive

Hacía dos horas que cantaba/estaba cantando.
He had been singing for two hours.

FUTURE AND CONDITIONAL

Future/Conditional Indicative–Regular: *–ar, –er, –ir*

Since these two tenses use the entire infinitive as their stem, only two examples are given here.

	amar **to love**	**comer** **to eat**
yo	*amaré/ía*	*comeré/ía*
tú	*amarás/ías*	*comerás/ías*
él/ella/Ud.	*amará/ía*	*comerá/ía*
nosotros, –as	*amaremos/íamos*	*comeremos/íamos*
vosotros, –as	*amaréis/íais*	*comeréis/íais*
ellos/ellas/Uds.	*amarán/ían*	*comerán/ían*

Future/Conditional Indicative–Irregulars

Verbs that drop the *–e* of the infinitive.

caber **to fit**	**haber** **to have–** **auxiliary**	**poder** **to be able**
cabré/ía	*habré/ía*	*podré/ía*
cabrás/ías	*habrás/ías*	*podrás/ías*
cabrá/ía	*habrá/ía*	*podrá/ía*
cabremos/íamos	*habremos/íamos*	*podremos/íamos*
cabréis/íais	*habréis/íais*	*podréis/íais*
cabrán/ían	*habrán/ían*	*podrán/ían*

querer **to want**	**saber** **to know**
querré/ía	*sabré/ía*
querrás/ías	*sabrás/ías*
querrá/ía	*sabrá/ía*
querremos/íamos	*sabremos/íamos*
querréis/íais	*sabréis/íais*
querrán/ían	*sabrán/ían*

Verbs that change the vowel (*e* or *i*) to a *d*.

poner **to put**	**salir** **to leave**	**tener** **to have**
pondré/ía	*saldré/ía*	*tendré/ía*
pondrás/ías	*saldrás/ías*	*tendrás/ías*

pondrá/ía	*saldrá/ía*	*tendrá/ía*
pondremos/íamos	*saldremos/íamos*	*tendremos/íamos*
pondréis/íais	*saldréis/íais*	*tendréis/íais*
pondrán/ían	*saldrán/ían*	*tendrán/ían*

valer **to be worth**	**venir** **to come**
valdré/ía	*vendré/ía*
valdrás/ías	*vendrás/ías*
valdrá/ía	*vendrá/ía*
valdremos/íamos	*vendremos/íamos*
valdréis/íais	*vendréis/íais*
valdrán/ían	*vendrán/ían*

Verbs that drop the *e* and *c* of the infinitive.

decir **to tell/say**	**hacer** **to make/do**
diré/ía	*haré/ía*
dirás/ías	*harás/ías*
dirá/ía	*hará/ía*
diremos/íamos	*haremos/íamos*
diréis/íais	*haréis/íais*
dirán/ían	*harán/ían*

Note: Compounds of the above words are conjugated in the same manner (*proponer, detener, contener*). However, **maldecir** and **bendecir** are conjugated as regular verbs in these two tenses and do not follow the pattern for **decir**.

Uses of Future/Conditional

Common translations include **will/shall** for the future and **would** for the conditional.

Saldré en seguida.	I shall leave immediately.
Me gustaría saberlo.	I would like to know it.
Juan vivirá conmigo.	Juan will live with me.

Probability Statements or Conjecture

The future tense is used to express **present** probability statements, while the conditional expresses **past** probability. These statements in

English may be expressed a number of ways.

Present Probability	Past Probability
He **is** probably ill.	He **was** probably ill.
Estará enfermo.	*Estaría enfermo.*
*[Debe de estar enfermo.]**	*[Debía de estar enfermo.]*
It **must** be 1:00.	It **must have been** 1:00.
Será la una.	*Sería la una.*
[Debe de ser la una.]	*[Debía de ser la una.]*
Where **can** he be?	Where **could** he be?
¿Dónde estará?	*¿Dónde estaría?*
I wonder who he **is**?	I wonder who he **was**?
¿Quién será?	*¿Quién sería?*

* *Deber de + infinitive* is another way to express probability statements.

Expressing "Would," "Wouldn't" with the Past Tense

When **would** means **used to**, the imperfect tense is used.

When **wouldn't** means **refused**, the negative preterite of *querer* is used.

Cuando era joven, iba al cine a menudo.
When he was young, he would go to the movies often.

No quiso verme.
He wouldn't (refused to) see me.

☞ Drill 2

1. Ninguna de las ventanas está sucia porque la criada las
   _____ ayer.

   (A) limpio   (C) limpió

   (B) limpiaba   (D) limpian

2. Ayer, al levantarme por la mañana, vi que _____ un día
   estupendo.

   (A) hacía   (C) hizo

   (B) hará   (D) había hecho

3. Durante mi niñez siempre _____ a la casa de mis tíos.

    (A) iría   (C) fui

    (B) iba   (D) iré

4. Cuando tropezaron conmigo, _____ de salir del cine.

    (A) acabaron   (C) acabé

    (B) acababa   (D) acaban

5. Los jugadores no _____ jugar más.

    (A) tuvieron   (C) quisieron

    (B) trataron   (D) iban

6. Esta tarde mientras _____ el periódico, sonó el teléfono.

    (A) miraré   (C) leía

    (B) busqué   (D) estudio

7. Aunque ella vino temprano, no la _____.

    (A) vi   (C) vea

    (B) viera   (D) veré

8. Al despertarse Ramón se dio cuenta de que _____.

    (A) llovió   (C) llovido

    (B) llovía   (D) había llover

9. El ladrón entró por la ventana que _____ abierta.

    (A) estuvo   (C) estará

    (B) estaba   (D) estaría

10. La guerra de Vietnam _____ varios años.

    (A) duraba   (C) duró

    (B) durará   (D) hubo durado

11. _____ tres horas que regresó de su viaje.

   (A) Hacen   (C) Hace

   (B) Ha   (D) Desde

12. Yo _____ el colegio a los 10 años.

   (A) dejé   (C) dejara

   (B) dejaba   (D) dejase

13. Yo _____ dormido cuando me llamaste.

   (A) estaba   (C) estoy

   (B) estuve   (D) estaré

14. Lo _____ la semana que viene.

   (A) hicimos   (C) haremos

   (B) hacíamos   (D) habíamos hecho

15. Si yo fuera al centro, te _____ algo.

   (A) compraría   (C) compre

   (B) compré   (D) compraré

16. Cuando era niño, me _____ viendo pasar a la gente por las calles.

   (A) divertí   (C) divertiría

   (B) divertía   (D) divirtiera

17. ¿Cuánto tiempo _____ que hablabas cuando entraron?

   (A) hacía   (C) hacían

   (B) hizo   (D) había sido

18. Hacía dos horas que ellos _____ cuando sonó el teléfono.

   (A) charlaron   (C) habían charlado

   (B) charlan   (D) estaban charlando

19. Ayer al oír al testigo, el juez lo _____.

    (A) crea   (C) creyó

    (B) creía   (D) creerá

20. _____ las tres cuando el tren partió.

    (A) Eran   (C) Fue

    (B) Era   (D) Fueron

21. _____ dos años que terminó la guerra.

    (A) Hizo   (C) Hace

    (B) Hacía   (D) Hacen

22. Ayer yo _____ a Juan por primera vez.

    (A) conocía   (C) supe

    (B) conocí   (D) sabía

23. Hace dos semanas que no he visto a Ana. ¿_____ enferma?

    (A) Estará   (C) Va a estar

    (B) Esté   (D) Estás

24. Cuando Juan era joven, _____ al cine a menudo.

    (A) va   (C) iba

    (B) iría   (D) irá

25. Si tengo el tiempo, _____ el museo.

    (A) visitaría   (C) visitaré

    (B) visite   (D) visitaba

26. ¿Cuánto tiempo _____ que andas sin coche?

    (A) hacía   (C) hizo

    (B) haces   (D) hace

Drill 2—Detailed Explanations of Answers

1. **(C)** We know that a past tense is needed in this sentence because of the word "ayer" (yesterday). We must then choose between the two past tenses given among the choices: preterite and imperfect. The imperfect tense is often used to imply that a past action was incomplete, i.e., that it had not come to an end, that it was not concluded. In this sentence however, we know that the maid finished her task of cleaning the windows because we are told that for that very reason the windows are now clean. The preterite tense is used to show that a past action, as viewed by the speaker, is considered completed, over and done with.

2. **(A)** The use of the preterite of the verb "ver" tells us that we are talking about the past. In our sentence, we are describing what the weather was like yesterday morning. The imperfect tense, rather than the preterite, is most frequently used in sentences which describe the past, particularly if we do not wish to place undue emphasis on the idea that the situation described came to an end. This use of the imperfect tense is especially evident in contexts in which one is setting up the scene or describing the background against which other major events will take place, for example: "Era una tarde triste y lluviosa. No había nadie en la calle." (It was a sad and rainy afternoon. There was no one in the street.)

3. **(B)** In the sentence where you are to fill in the blank, the adverb "siempre" (always) is important. When we are talking about the past and we are referring to a customary or habitual action, as is the case in our sentence, we use the imperfect tense to place emphasis on the idea that the action was performed repeatedly (for an unspecified number of times). In (A), however, the verb "ir" is used in the conditional tense, not the imperfect. English speakers sometimes erroneously use the conditional tense in Spanish to express the idea of "would" in the sense of "used to," simply because English uses the word "would" both as a conditional and also to convey the concept of repeated and habitual past action. This cannot be done in Spanish. Compare the following two English sentences: If he were here, I would know it; Every Saturday when we were at the beach I would swim. Notice that only the second example has to do with a customary and habitual past action. It is in such a case that Spanish would use the imperfect tense instead of the conditional. Choice (C) is wrong because although the sentence refers to the past, it is in the preterite tense. Choice (D) is incorrect also because it is in the wrong tense, the future.

4. **(B)** The verb "tropezar" means "to stumble." The expression "tropezar **con**" means "to meet or encounter." Notice how the preposition "con," when followed by the prepositional pronoun "mí," results in the special form "conmigo." The same thing happens in the second person singular (the familiar form) to produce the word "contigo." The expression "acabar de" + infinitive signifies "to have just" done something. This expression is normally only used in two tenses, the simple present and the imperfect. In the present it means "have or has just." In the imperfect it means "had just." Since our sentence contains a verb in the preterite tense, "tropezaron," we know that we are talking about the past. Therefore, we must logically use the only form of the imperfect that appears among the choices, "acababa."

5. **(C)** (A) is incorrect because "to have to" do something is "tener que" + infinitive, but we have omitted the "que." (B), "trataron," is wrong because we have not included the "de" from the expression "tratar de" + infinitive (to try to do something). In (D), "iban," the preposition "a" is lacking. Remember, "ir a" + infinitive means "to be going to" do something. (C), "quisieron," is the only answer which fits grammatically in our sentence. Try to recall the special meanings which the verb "querer" may have in the preterite tense. If the sentence is affirmative, it may be a synonym for "tratar de" (to try to). "Quisieron venir" would mean "They tried to come." If we simply mean "They wanted to come," we would use the imperfect tense: "Querían venir." If the sentence is negative, then "querer" in the preterite can mean "refused to," as is the case in our sentence. If we simply mean "They didn't want to come," then we would use the imperfect tense again: "No querían venir."

6. **(C)** In our sentence, "mientras" means "while," and "sonó" is the third person singular of the verb "sonar" (to ring—what a telephone does). Do not confuse "sonar" with "soñar" (to dream). Because "sonó" is a past tense, we know that neither (A), "miraré," the first person singular of the future of "mirar" (to look at), nor (D), "estudio" (I study), the first person singular of the present, can be used. Then we are faced with a choice between the first person singular of the preterite of "buscar" (to look for), in (B) "busqué," and "leía," the first person singular of the imperfect of "leer" (to read), in (C), which are both past tenses. When we are talking about the past and we wish to show that an action which was in progress was interrupted by another action, the action in progress is given the imperfect tense and the interrupting action appears in the preterite. In our sentence, the action which was in progress when something else cut across it or interrupted is "I was reading" ("leía"). The action which caused the interruption is "rang" ("sonó").

7. **(A)** After **aunque,** if the present tense is used, the independent clause is generally in the future. In this case, since it is in the past, the preterite indicative is correct. This sentence does not express any uncertainty, but fact. She did arrive, and early. Another statement of fact is that "I did not see her." Therefore, the subjunctive is not needed.

8. **(B)** The correct choice is "llovía" since the imperfect translates a sense of an ongoing event in the past (sometimes, as in this phrase, "intersected" by another discrete event, namely, "se dio cuenta"). The preterite, on the other hand, marks the start, end, or completed duration of an event. In this context such an event is the realizing and not the raining, which had already started outside the enunciation, so to speak. This is why choice (A) is incorrect. (As a rule of thumb, if a Spanish verb in the past can be translated into English by means of was + ing, then the Spanish verb can be rendered in the imperfect.) Choices (C) and (D) are wrong for other reasons: "llovido" is a past participle that requires an auxiliary verb ("haber") to function in the present context; and "había llover" is ungrammatical since compound tenses cannot be formed with the infinitive of the main verb.

9. **(B)** The window was already open. The real action of the phrase is the entering. By comparison, the reference to the window is in the mode of a **state** of things or in the mode of a **description**. This is why the correct answer involves an imperfect tense and not a preterite. Choices (C) and (D) do not correlate temporally with "entró."

10. **(C)** Again, the right answer is the preterite because the temporal function of the verb is to designate a duration. Choice (D) is a rarely used formation mostly reserved for literary style. It means the same as the preterite.

11. **(C)** The formula for this kind of expression is **hace** (never in the plural) + **time** + **que** + **preterite** (or **preterite** + **hace** + **time**). In English, this formula translates the particle "ago."

12. **(A)** Choices (C) and (D), both in the subjunctive, are ungrammatical, and (B) is not a good choice in view of the fact that the sentence is about temporal circumscription: the action of quitting school is "bound" by the point in time designated by "ten years." Remember that "imperfect" means incomplete and that an imperfect action is one that the sentence does not mark as ending (or beginning) in the past. The action described in this question, however, is complete; it is a point in time and not an open-ended line.

13. **(A)** Both (C) and (D) make no sense in terms of the temporal frame of the question. Now, the action of calling is in the preterite, which means it did not go on in time and that it is limited and complete in itself. But this is not true of sleeping, which becomes the temporal background for the instance of calling. And here we run into another criterion for learning the difference between preterite and imperfect: when there is a description in the past (as opposed to a main action), the verb used is in the imperfect.

14. **(C)** This item simply tests your understanding that the future tense must be used in the sentence and your recognition of the future tense form of the verb "hacer" (to make or do), "haremos." We know that we must use the future because of the expression "la semana que viene" (next week) in our sentence. (A) "hicimos," is the first person plural of the preterite of "hacer." (B) and (D) give us, respectively, the first person plural of the imperfect, "hacíamos," and of the pluperfect, "habíamos hecho," of the same verb.

15. **(A)** In an "if" clause in the past, using the subjunctive, the conditional is the appropriate form to follow.

16. **(B)** You should first recognize the different forms of "divertirse" given as options and realize, for example, that "divirtiera" is a subjunctive form with no place in the sentence (because there is no "que" followed by a dependent verb). You can also eliminate (C) in order to avoid the contradiction in tense that would result if you put together an imperfect ("era") and a conditional. So the final choice boils down to a choice between the preterite form (A) and the imperfect one (B). The latter is correct because the action of having fun is not circumscribed temporally by any semantic element of the sentence. In other words, you may translate the second part of the sentence with "used to," and being able to do this automatically signals the use of the imperfect.

17. **(A)** In time phrases that use the imperfect tense (hablabas), the third singular of the imperfect of "hacer" is needed. This would eliminate (C) because it is plural and (B) because it is preterite. Answer (D) is a form of the verb **ser**.

18. **(D)** In time phrases beginning with "hacía," in either the imperfect tense or, in this case, the past progressive is correct. This would eliminate (A) the preterite and (B) the present tense of charlar. Choice (C) could be used if it were negative.

19. **(C)** Because the action occurred yesterday and "upon hearing" the witness, the preterite of the verb is necessary. If the sentence does not have any indications of past completion, the imperfect answer (B) would be preferred. This would eliminate (A) the subjunctive and (D) the future.

20. **(A)** To express time in the past, the imperfect tense is used. Because it is "three" o'clock and, therefore, plural in Spanish, the plural form of the verb is required. Therefore, choice (B), which is singular, is incorrect. Because both (C) and (D) are in the preterite tense, they are incorrect.

21. **(C)** In order to express **"ago"** in Spanish, an "hace" statement of time will be followed by the preterite tense (in this case "terminó"). "Hace" will be written in the third person singular of the present tense in these statements. Therefore, choices (A), in the preterite, (B), in the imperfect, and (D), in the plural are all incorrect.

22. **(B)** Certain verbs change meaning in the preterite. "Conocer" means "met" in this tense. Because this happened yesterday (ayer) for the first time (por primera vez), we know that the preterite is necessary. This would make choice (A) in the imperfect incorrect. Also, to "meet or know" people requires the use of the verb **conocer**. Therefore, choices (C) "I found out" and (D) "I knew" for the verb **saber** are incorrect in this context.

23. **(A)** This question intimates probability in that it has been two weeks since Ana was seen last. To express present probability, the future tense is used. This may be translated a number of ways: I wonder if she is ill?; Can she be ill?; Is she probably ill? Choices (B), the present subjunctive, and (C), the immediate future, make no sense in this context. Choice (D) is the second singular to refer to Ana, but the third singular is required here.

24. **(C)** In English we often use "would" to refer to something we "used to" do in the past. In Spanish, however, this must be expressed with the imperfect tense, not the conditional. Choices (A), the present tense, (B), the conditional tense, and (D), the future tense, are incorrect in this context.

25. **(C)** In this question an understanding of **if** clauses is needed. Commonly when the **if** clause is in the present tense, the other clause will be written in the future tense. Choice (A) is conditional and would call for a past subjunctive to be used in the **if** clause. Choice (B), the present subjunctive, and (D), the imperfect, make no sense when translated in this context.

26. **(D)** Time expressions with **hace** have a certain formula. When asking "how long something **has been** going on," **hace** is paired up with the present tense (or present progressive tense). The other possible time expression would have **hacía** coupled with the imperfect (or past progressive tense). Since "andas" follows **que** and is in the present tense, "hace" must be used in the time expression. Choices (A), the imperfect, and (C), the preterite, are incorrect here. Choice (B) is in the wrong person to be used in an **hace** sentence.

FORMATION OF COMPOUND TENSES

Compound tenses are formed by adding an invariable past participle to the different forms of the auxiliary verb *haber*.

The Past Participle

The past participle in Spanish is formed by appending *–ado* to the stem of an *–ar* verb or *–ido* to the stem of an *–er* or *–ir* verb,

jugar – jugado (played)   *comer – comido* (eaten)
recibir – recibido (received)

The Irregular Past Participle

There are 12 irregular past participles.

abrir — abierto (opened)   *morir — muerto* (died)
cubrir — cubierto (covered)   *poner — puesto* (put)
decir — dicho (said)   *resolver— resuelto* (solved)
escribir — escrito (written)   *romper — roto* (broken)
hacer — hecho (done)   *ver — visto* (seen)
imprimir — impreso (printed)   *volver — vuelto* (returned)

Past Participles Ending in *–ido*

Most double-voweled infinitives will require an accent mark over the participle ending to separate the diphthong created when the weak vowel **i** follows the strong vowel of the stem.

oír – oído (heard)   *caer – caído* (fallen)   *leer – leído* (read)

Note: Verbs ending in *–uir* do not require accents in this form.

huir – huido (fled)   *construir – construido* (built)

Conjugation of *Haber*: Indicative Mood*

	Present	Preterite*	Imperfect	Future	Conditional
yo	*he*	*hube*	*había*	*habré*	*habría*
tú	*has*	*hubiste*	*habías*	*habrás*	*habrías*
él/ella/Ud.	*ha*	*hubo*	*había*	*habrá*	*habría*
nosotros, –as	*hemos*	*hubimos*	*habíamos*	*habremos*	*habríamos*
vosotros, –as	*habéis*	*hubisteis*	*habíais*	*habréis*	*habríais*
ellos/ellas/Uds.	*han*	*hubieron*	*habían*	*habrán*	*habrían*

* The preterite perfect is a literary tense not commonly used in everyday speech. It is always preceded by a conjunction of time:

luego que	as soon as	*apenas*	hardly, scarcely
en cuanto	as soon as	*cuando*	when
así que	as soon as	*después que*	after
tan pronto como	as soon as	*no bien*	no sooner

Conjugation of *Haber*: Subjunctive and Imperative Moods

	Present	Imperfect
yo	*haya*	*hubiera/hubiese*
tú	*hayas*	*hubieras/hubieses*
él/ella/Ud.	*haya*	*hubiera/hubiese*
nosotros, –as	*hayamos*	*hubiéramos/hubiésemos*
vosotros, –as	*hayáis*	*hubierais/hubieseis*
ellos/ellas/Uds.	*hayan*	*hubieran/hubiesen*

Names of Compound Tenses

Compound tenses are formed by combining different tenses of verbs to create a new one.

Perfect

The present indicative of *haber* with a past participle forms the **present perfect** tense:

He amado.
I **have** loved.

Han partido.
They **have** left.

Note: Only *haber* is conjugated. *Amado* and *partido* do not have to agree in gender and number with their respective subjects.

Pluperfect

The imperfect indicative of *haber* with a past participle forms the **pluperfect** or **past perfect** tense. This tense is used for a past action that precedes another past action:

Había amado.
I **had** loved.

Habíais comido.
You **had** eaten.

Habían partido.
They **had** left.

Future Perfect

The future of *haber* with a past participle forms the **future perfect**:

Habré amado.
I **will have** loved.

Habrán partido.
They **will have** left.

Note: This tense expresses an action that will take place **before** another. But very commonly the future perfect denotes probability in the past. Compare the following examples:

a) *¿**Habrán partido** antes de que comience a llover?*
    Will they **have left** before it starts to rain?

b) *Ya **habrán partido.***
    They **probably left** already.

Conditional Perfect

The conditional of *haber* with a past participle forms the **conditional perfect**:

Habría amado.
I **would have** loved.

Habrían partido.
They **would have** left.

Perfect Subjunctive

The present subjunctive of *haber* with a past participle forms the **present perfect subjunctive**:

*Es increíble que no **haya amado** a nadie en su vida.*
It's incredible that he **has** not **loved** anyone in his life.

*Los extrañaremos cuando **hayan partido.***
We'll miss them when they **have left.**

Pluperfect Subjunctive

The imperfect subjunctive of *haber* with a past participle forms the **pluperfect** or **past perfect subjunctive**:

*Yo no habría conocido la felicidad si no **hubiera amado**.*
I would not have known happiness if I **had** not **loved.**

*Él siempre había dudado de que sus amigos **hubieran partido** sin despedirse.*
He had always doubted that his friends **had left** without saying goodbye.

Past Participle as Adjective

When the past participle is used with *haber* to form the perfect tenses it is invariable. When not accompanied by some form of *haber*, it functions as an adjective and has four possible forms.

He roto la taza.	I have broken the cup.	[perfect]
La taza está rota.	The cup is broken.	[adjective]
Una ventana abierta	An open window	[adjective]

THE PRESENT PARTICIPLE

The present participle is formed by appending *-ando* to the stem of *–ar* verbs and *-iendo* to the stem of *–er* and *–ir* verbs.

andar–andando (walking)   *escribir–escribiendo* (writing)
vivir–viviendo (living)

Present Participles with a *y*

Double-voweled infinitives ending in *–er* and *–ir* (*creer, leer, oír, caer*, etc.) have a *y* in the present participle. It replaces the *i* of the participle ending.

caer–cayendo   leer–leyendo   oír–oyendo   traer–trayendo

Exception: *reír–riendo* (laughing)

Present Participles with Stem Changes

Verbs ending in *–ir* that have preterite tense stem changes use the same stem change in the present participle.

dormir–durmiendo	*pedir–pidiendo*	*servir–sirviendo*
(ue, **u**)	(i, **i**)	(i, **i**)

Irregular Present Participles

There are four irregular present participles.

ir–yendo   *poder–pudiendo*   *venir–viniendo*   *decir–diciendo*

The Present Formation of Compound Tenses Participle with *Estar*

The present participle denotes an action in progress and commonly follows the verb *estar*. It corresponds to the "-ing" form of the verb in English. In Spanish it is always invariable. These are called progressive tenses.

Estoy comiendo.	I am eating.
Estaban leyendo.	They were reading.
Estaremos jugando al tenis.	We will be playing tennis.

The Present Participle with Motion Verbs

The present participle may also follow verbs of motion: *ir* (to go), *venir* (to come), *andar* (to walk), *entrar* (to enter), *salir* (to go out), etc.

Ella va corriendo por la calle.
She goes running down the street.

Juan entró riendo pero salió llorando.
Juan entered laughing but left crying.

The Present Participle with *Seguir/Continuar*

Present participles also follow forms of *seguir* (i, i) (to keep on) and *continuar* (ú) (to continue). In English, "to continue" is often followed by an infinitive. This will **not** occur in Spanish.

Siga leyendo.	Keep on reading.
Ellos continúan hablando.	They continue talking.
	They continue to talk.

The Present Participle Used Alone

The present participle does not need a helping verb to exist. It is often used alone.

Andando por la calle, se cayó.
Walking down the street, he fell down.

No conociendo bien la ciudad, se perdieron.
Not knowing the city well, they got lost.

When Not to Use the Present Participle

Never use the present participle as an **adjective**. Use a clause instead.

a crying child   *un niño que llora*
a frightening event   *un asunto que aterroriza*

Never use the present participle as a **noun** (gerund). Use the infinitive instead.

Seeing is believing.   *Ver es creer.*

Never use the present participle after a **preposition**. Use the infinitive instead.

después de comer   after eating

Never use the present participle of *ir* with the verb **estar**. Use *voy a, vas a, iba a,* etc.

Voy a salir.   I am going to leave.
Iban a comer.   They were going to eat.

REFLEXIVE PRONOUNS

Verbs whose action reflects back upon the subject are called reflexive. Infinitives of reflexive verbs in Spanish end in *–se*. Verbs of this type require the use of the reflexive pronoun group (*me, te, se, nos, os, se*). English uses pronouns such as myself, herself, themselves, etc. to designate reflexive actions. There are a number of reasons why a verb is reflexive.

1. The verb actually has a "reflexive" translation. I bathe "myself." = *Me baño*.

2. The pronoun is an inherent part of the verb and has no English translation: *atreverse a* (to dare to), *quejarse de* (to complain about), etc.

3. The pronoun alters the meaning of the verb in some way, other than reflexively: *irse* = to go **away**, *caerse* = to fall **down**, etc.

4. To render the meaning "get or become": *enfermarse* (to get ill), *casarse* (to get married), *enojarse* (to get angry), etc.

5. The pronoun is used with the verb when the subject is performing an action **on** his/her own body. *Me rompí la pierna.* = I broke my leg.

Placement of the Pronouns with Verbs

After selecting the pronoun that matches the subject of the verb, it will be placed either **before** the verb or **after** and **attached** to the verb. The following samples demonstrate the placement.

Quiero bañarme.	I want to bathe.	[infinitive]
¡Levántese!	Get up!	[+ command/formal]
¡No te sientes!	Don't sit down!	[– command/familiar]
Estás lavándote.	You are washing up.	[present participle]
Me llamo Juana.	I am called Juana.	[conjugated]

Uses of *Se*

The reflexive pronoun *se* is used in a number of ways.

1. To express the impersonal **one/people/they** statement with the third person singular of the verb.

   se dice = one says/people say/they say

2. To render "non-blame" statements when used with certain verbs: *perder* (to lose), *olvidar* (to forget), *romper* (to break), *quemar* (to burn). With statements such as these the speaker is indicating that something happened that was unintentional on his/her part. The *se* will precede the indirect object pronoun (which replaces the subject in English), and the verb will match the noun that follows it.

*se **me** rompió el vaso.*	**I** broke the glass.
*se **nos** perdió el dinero.*	**We** lost the money.
*se **le** olvidaron los libros.*	**He** forgot the books.

Reciprocal Actions

The plural reflexive pronouns (*nos, os, se*) are used to express "each other" in Spanish.

Se escriben.	They write to each other (to themselves).
Nos amamos.	We love each other (ourselves).

Note: Because the above statements could have a reflexive meaning (in parenthesis) as well, one may add the following phrase to clarify:

Se escriben uno a otro	or	*el uno al otro*
una a otra	or	*la una a la otra*
unos a otros	or	*los unos a los otros*
unas a otras	or	*las unas a las otras*

This additional clarifying statement is especially useful with verbs that are already reflexive. In those cases the reflexive pronoun cannot have dual meanings—it must act as a reflexive. As is often the case with these types, there is an accompanying preposition to be dealt with. This preposition is placed in the clarifying statement.

casarse con	to get married to
*Se casan uno **con** otro.*	They get married to each other.
burlarse de	to make fun of
*Se burlan uno **de** otro.*	They make fun of each other.

Reflexive Substitute for the Passive Voice

It is more idiomatic to replace the passive construction with a reflexive construction using the pronoun *se* and the verb in the third person singular or plural. This is especially true of passive sentences that have no expressed agent.

Aquí se habla español.	Spanish is spoken here.

☞ Drill 3

1. Después de dos horas el orador siguió _____.

    (A) hablar   (C) habla

    (B) hablaba   (D) hablando

2. _____ olvidó lavar la ropa por la manaña.

    (A) Me   (C) Se me

    (B) Se   (D) Me lo

3. Los alumnos están _____ la composición.

    (A) escrito   (C) analizando

    (B) leen   (D) escriben

4. Los vampiros no _____ en el espejo.

    (A) lo ven   (C) le ven

    (B) se ven   (D) les ven

5. Los trabajadores han _____ su labor.

   (A) terminaron   (C) terminados

   (B) terminando   (D) terminado

6. Hace mucho tiempo que yo no _____ con mi mamá.

   (A) he hablado   (C) estaba hablando

   (B) había hablado   (D) hablado

7. _____ el trabajo, pudo salir a tiempo.

   (A) Haber terminado   (C) Al terminando

   (B) Estar terminando   (D) Habiendo terminado

8. Los problemas _____ , cerró el libro y salió.

   (A) resueltos   (C) resolvidos

   (B) resueltas   (D) resuelven

9. Para este viernes ellos _____ la película.

   (A) habían visto   (C) habrán visto

   (B) habrían visto   (D) han visto

10. Ellos vinieron _____ por la calle.

    (A) andando   (C) andado

    (B) andar   (D) andados

11. _____ , salió del cuarto.

    (A) Decírmelo   (C) Diciéndomelo

    (B) Me lo decir   (D) Deciéndomelo

12. Juan entró _____ después de oír el chiste.

    (A) reír   (C) reyendo

    (B) riendo   (D) riyendo

13. No continúes _____ en la iglesia por favor.

    (A) hablar

    (B) a hablar

    (C) hablado

    (D) hablando

14. Un niño _____ me causa pena.

    (A) que llora

    (B) llorando

    (C) llorar

    (D) a llorar

15. Esto es _____.

    (A) vivido

    (B) vivir

    (C) viviendo

    (D) viva

16. Los chicos _____ por la calle cuando vieron al policía.

    (A) eran yendo

    (B) estaban yendo

    (C) yendo

    (D) iban

17. Al _____ el ruido, todos corrieron.

    (A) oír

    (B) oyeron

    (C) oído

    (D) oyendo

18. ¡Ay de mí! ¡ _____ el vaso!

    (A) se me rompió

    (B) me rompí

    (C) se me rompieron

    (D) me rompieron

19. ¿Quieres _____ antes de ir?

    (A) bañarse

    (B) báñate

    (C) bañarte

    (D) bañándote

20. Es importante _____ la mano antes de hablar.

    (A) levantarse

    (B) que levanta

    (C) que te levantes

    (D) levantar

21. El sacerdote _____ la pareja.

    (A) se casó   (C) casó a

    (B) se casó a   (D) casó con

22. Aunque vivimos en distintos lugares, _____ uno a otro cada semana.

    (A) nos escribimos   (C) escribimos

    (B) se escriben   (D) nos escriben

Drill 3—Detailed Explanations of Answers

1.   **(D)**   The gerund in Spanish may be used after a conjugated verb, as in this case. The only answer which is correct is **hablando. The siguió** is translated as "kept on" or "continued," i.e., verbs of motion.

2.   **(C)**   There are three different forms in which the verb "olvidar" (to forget) may be used. The simplest of these is "olvidar" used non-reflexively and followed by a noun or an infinitive, for example, "Olvidé lavar la ropa" (I forgot to wash the clothes). Another form is "olvidar**se de**" + noun or infinitive: "**Me** olvidé **de** lavar la ropa." The third form is also reflexive but does not use the preposition "de." It is always accompanied by an indirect object pronoun in addition to the reflexive pronoun: "**Se me** olvidó lavar la ropa." Notice that in this sentence the verb and the reflexive pronoun both are used in the third person singular. This is because the subject of the Spanish sentence is **not** "yo" (I), but rather the infinitive "lavar." In other words, the Spanish literally says "Washing forgot itself." In this sentence, "me" is an indirect object pronoun and means "to me." Therefore, "Se me olvidó lavar la ropa" literally means "Washing the clothes forgot itself to me." One would never say that in English. Instead, we would simply say "I forgot to wash the clothes." The indirect object pronoun, when used this way with the reflexive form of "olvidar," simply shows who is affected by the action of the verb. (A) "Me" will not work here. For it to be correct, we would have to change the verb to "olvidé" and then add the preposition "de."

3.   **(C)**   In order to form the present progressive tense, we use "estar" + –*ndo* verb form, meaning "to be doing (something)." Hence, we must say "están analizando" (are analyzing). The progressive tenses place very

special emphasis on the fact that the action is (was, etc.) in progress or is (was, etc.) happening at a particular moment. If we do not wish to give that decided emphasis, we just use the simple tenses (present, imperfect, etc.) We can use the progressive form in all of the tenses simply by changing the tense of "estar," for example, "estaban analizando" (they were analyzing), etc. Choice (A) "escrito" is wrong because it is the past participle, not the present participle, of "escribir" (to write). (B) "leen" will not function in our sentence because we cannot have two conjugated verbs, one immediately after the other ("están" and "leen"). The same is true for (D) "escriben."

4.   **(B)**   "Espejo" indicates that the pronoun needed is reflexive, and the only such pronoun among the choices is (B). The rest are direct object pronouns (A) or indirect, (C) and (D).

5.   **(D)**   What is needed to fill in the blank is a past participle, which eliminates the first two choices. You also must know that a past participle in a compound tense (following "haber") is invariable in person, gender, and number.

6.   **(A)**   "Time" statements beginning with **hace** are normally written using the present indicative or the present progressive tenses. Only in the case where the main verb is negative can a perfect tense be used. Choice (B) would be correct if the verb were negative and followed "hacía." Choice (C) also would be found in an "hacía" statement. Choice (D) makes no sense since it is the past participle by itself.

7.   **(D)**   The translation of this sentence indicates that a participle is required ("Having finished the work,") to make sense. In order for (A) to be correct in the infinitive form, it would have to act as a gerund (i.e., be the subject or object of the verb). Choice (C) is incorrect because **al** must be followed by an infinitive. Choice (B) makes no sense when translated and used in this context.

8.   **(A)**   The past participle may act as an adjective and in that capacity must match the noun it modifies. Because this noun is masculine and this participle is irregular, (A) is the correct answer. Choice (B) is feminine and (C) is an incorrect form of the past participle. Choice (D) is a conjugated verb and makes no sense in this context.

9.   **(C)**   By translating this sentence (By this Friday they will have seen the movie.) the proper perfect tense surfaces. Choice (A) "they had

seen, (B) "they would have seen," and (D) "they have seen" make no sense in this context.

10. **(A)**   Verbs of motion ("vinieron") can be followed by present participles, in this case "andando." They cannot, however, be followed by an infinitive (B) or the past participle (C) and (D).

11. **(C)**   This sentence begins with the participial phrase meaning "Saying it to me." Because "Saying" is not the subject of the sentence, it will not be written as a gerund (the infinitive form in Spanish). Therefore, choice (A) is incorrect. Choice (B) is incorrect not only because it is in the infinitive form but also because pronouns must be after and attached to infinitives. Choice (D) is misspelled.

12. **(B)**   Again, verbs of motion may be followed by present participles. Choices (C) and (D) appear to be written in the present participle but are misspelled. Choice (A) is an infinitive and is, therefore, incorrect.

13. **(D)**   Unlike English, the verb **continue** (continuar) in Spanish cannot be followed by either the infinitive or the present participle. In Spanish, only the present participle is correct with this verb. This would eliminate (A), the infinitive, (B), the infinitive preceded by an "a," and (C) the past participle.

14. **(A)**   The present participle in Spanish may not act as an adjective. Phrases such as these must be converted to clauses such as the one found in this sample. Therefore, "a crying child" becomes "a child that cries" in the Spanish sentence. Therefore, (B), the present participle, (C), the infinitive, and (D), the infinitive with "a," are all incorrect.

15. **(B)**   In Spanish, a verb used as a gerund, either as a subject or the object of the verb, must be in the infinitive form. Therefore, (A), the past participle, (C), the present participle, and (D), the present subjunctive, are all incorrect.

16. **(D)**   "Ir" may not be used in the progressive tense in Spanish. In order to say that one "is or was doing something," a form of **ir a** (either in the present or in the imperfect tense) is used with the infinitive. Choice (B) is in the progressive tense and choice (A) is a form of **ser** with a present participle, which is never correct. Choice (C) is the present participle alone and makes no sense in the context of this sentence.

17. **(A)** The idiom **al + infinitive** means **upon + –ing**. Because choices (B), the preterite, (C), the past participle, and (D), the present participle, are not in the infinitive form, they are all incorrect.

18. **(A)** This sentence is considered a "non-blame" statement. Certain verbs (such as *perder*, *dejar*, *caer*, *romper*, etc.) are used in this manner so as to indicate that the subject did not commit the action on purpose. These sentences require using the reflexive pronoun **se**, the **indirect object** pronoun for the subject, and the verb in either the third person singular or plural depending on what follows it. In this case "vaso" is singular and requires a singular verb. Choice (C) is, therefore, incorrect because the verb is plural. Choice (D) is plural and the reflexive pronoun is missing. Choice (B) would be correct if written as "rompí" alone but would then mean that this action occurred on purpose.

19. **(C)** After a conjugated verb the infinitive is necessary. In this case the subject (tú) requires adjusting the reflexive pronoun to match it. For this reason choice (A) is incorrect because the pronoun (se) does not match the subject (tú). Choice (B) is the familiar singular command and (D) is the present participle, neither of which would follow the conjugated verb in this sample.

20. **(D)** In order to answer this question, one must know the difference between "levantar" and "levantarse." The former means "to raise" while the latter means "to get up." This would then eliminate both (A) and (C). While choice (B) appears to be correct in that it is **not** reflexive, the verb form would need to be subjunctive to fit this particular sentence since it begins with an impersonal expression and there is a change in subject. "Levanta" in this sample is the present indicative.

21. **(C)** This sentence requires knowing the difference between "casarse con" (to get married) and "casar" (to marry). Because the priest is performing the ceremony, choice (C) is correct. The personal **a** precedes the direct object "pareja." Choice (A) is incorrect because it is reflexive and the meaning would not fit this sentence and (B), which is also reflexive, is followed by the wrong preposition. Choice (D) is not correct with "con."

22. **(A)** This is a statement calling for an "each other" translation. The phrase "uno a otro" also indicates this. In Spanish the plural reflexive pronouns are used in these statements. The phrase "uno a otro" is an additional piece so that the translation of the verb will not be confused for

"we write to ourselves." Choice (B) is incorrect because the subject in this sentence is **we** (intimated in the first part of the sentence with "vivimos"). Choice (C) requires the matching reflexive pronoun "nos." Choice (D) means "they write to us" and doesn't fit the meaning implied by this sentence.

THE INFINITIVE

The Infinitive as the Subject of the Sentence

When the infinitive is used as the subject of the sentence (gerund) in English, it may be written in the infinitive form or end in "–ing." In Spanish this is written only in the infinitive form.

Seeing is believing.   *Ver es creer.*
Eating is important.   *Comer es importante.*

The Infinitive After Prepositions

In Spanish the only correct verb form that can follow a preposition is the infinitive.

antes de salir	before leaving
después de comer	after eating
al entrar	upon entering

The Infinitive with Verbs of Perception

The infinitive is used with verbs of perception *ver* (to see) and *oír* (to hear) when the sentence has a noun object.

Oí llorar al niño.	I heard the child cry.
Ella vio salir a Juan.	She saw Juan leave.

Verbs Requiring a Preposition Before the Infinitive

Certain verbs require an *a, en, de, por,* or *con* before the infinitive.

Verbs Requiring NO Preposition Before the Infinitive

aconsejar	advise to	*pensar (ie)*	think, intend to
deber	ought to	*permitir*	allow to
dejar	let, allow to	*poder (ue)*	be able to
desear	desire to	*prometer*	promise to
esperar	hope to	*querer (ie)*	wish to
impedir (i, i)	prevent from	*recordar (ue)*	remember to
lograr	succeed in	*rehusar*	refuse to

necesitar	need to	*saber*	know how to
oír	hear	*soler (ue)**	be accustomed to
pedir (i, i)	ask to	*temer*	be afraid to

* This verb is defective and commonly used in two tenses only—the present and the imperfect.

☞ Drill 4

1. Lavé la ropa después de _____ .

   (A) cenar (C) comida

   (B) comiendo (D) había almorzado

2. Al _____ la alarma, todos abandonaron el hotel.

   (A) oyen (C) oír

   (B) oyendo (D) oído

3. Orlando oyó _____ a la puerta.

   (A) tocó (C) tocando

   (B) tocar (D) tocándola

4. El respirar no es _____ .

   (A) vivir (C) la vida

   (B) viviendo (D) vive

5. Al _____ , le dije adiós.

   (A) salir (C) salí

   (B) saliendo (D) salido

6. _____ es bueno para el cuerpo.

   (A) Corriendo (C) Correr

   (B) Corrido (D) Fumar

7. _____ es bueno para la salud.

    (A) Dormir   (C) Dormido

    (B) Durmiendo   (D) Dormí

8. Sin _____ , no puedo recomendar la película.

    (A) ver   (C) verla

    (B) veo   (D) verlo

9. Antes de _____ del autobús, Juan pagó el pasaje.

    (A) bajando   (C) bajar

    (B) el bajar   (D) baje

10. El policía vio _____ al ladrón del banco.

    (A) salida   (C) saliendo

    (B) salir   (D) salió

Drill 4—Detailed Explanations of Answers

1. **(A)** "Después de" (after) is a preposition. The only form of the verb we use directly following a preposition is the infinitive. Therefore, we cannot use the present participle, as in (B), "comiendo." The present participle in English is the verbal form ending in "–ing": for example, "eating." In English, this form may be used as a noun, in which case we call it a gerund. In a phrase such as "after eating," "eating" is a gerund and means "the act of eating." In Spanish, the form which corresponds to the "–ing," i.e., words ending in *–ando* and *–iendo*, do not follow a preposition. This is a mistake often made in Spanish by English speakers. Choice (C) is incorrect. If we want to say "after the meal" or "after the afternoon meal," we would have to use the definite article: "después de **la** comida." Choice (D) is also wrong. In Spanish, a conjugated form of the verb does not immediately follow a preposition. We could say, however, "después de haber almorzado" (after **having eaten** lunch). Then the verb is not in a conjugated form.

2. **(C)** Syntactically, the verb forms "oyen" (they hear), the third person plural of the present of "oír"; "oyendo" (hearing), the present participle; and "oído" (heard), the past participle, will not fit correctly into this sentence. There is, however, an idiomatic construction based on **al + infinitive** which means "upon doing something." We find this form in (C).

3. **(B)** After verbs of perception (*oír, ver*), the infinitive is used. Therefore, (A), the preterite, and (C) and (D), the present participles, are incorrect.

4. **(A)** Verbs used as gerunds in Spanish (either as the subject or object of the verb) must be in the infinitive form. (B), the present participle, and (D), the present tense, are incorrect. (C) is incorrect because the infinitive is necessary to maintain parallel structure (infinitive/infinitive).

5. **(A)** The only verbal form that can follow "al" is the infinitive. It means "upon" + "–ing" in English.

6. **(C)** The key to this question is to remember that the infinitive can function as the subject of a sentence, but not the gerund (A) or the past participle (B). (D) "to smoke" is not good for "the body."

7. **(A)** This is another example of the use of the infinitive as the subject of the sentence. Therefore, (B), the present participle, (C), the past participle, and (D), the preterite are incorrect.

8. **(C)** After prepositions in Spanish the infinitive must be used. In the context of this sentence, the translation "without seeing it" makes most sense. "It" refers to *película,* which is feminine. (A) needs the direct object pronoun *la*, (D) has the incorrect direct object pronoun, and (B) is the present indicative, a conjugated verb form.

9. **(C)** The correct verb form after a preposition in Spanish is the infinitive. This would eliminate the present participle (A) and the subjunctive in (D). Choice (B) is a gerund and is not used after a preposition.

10. **(B)** After verbs of perception (ver/oír) the infinitive is used in Spanish. Therefore, the present participle (C), the preterite tense (D), and the noun meaning "departure" in (A) are incorrect.

FORMATION OF THE SUBJUNCTIVE

Present Subjunctive—Regular

	amar to love	*comer* to eat	*vivir* to live
yo	ame	coma	viva
tú	ames	comas	vivas
él/ella/Ud.	ame	coma	viva
nosotros, —as	amemos	comamos	vivamos
vosotros, —as	améis	comáis	viváis
ellos/ellas/Uds.	amen	coman	vivan

Present Subjunctive—Irregular

caber	quepa, quepas, quepa, quepamos, quepáis, quepan
caer	caiga, caigas, caiga, caigamos, caigáis, caigan
dar	dé, des, dé, demos, deis, den
decir	diga, digas, diga, digamos, digáis, digun
estar	esté, estés, esté, estemos, estéis, estén
haber	haya, hayas, haya, hayamos, hayáis, hayan
hacer	haga, hagas, haga, hagamos, hagáis, hagan
ir	vaya, vayas, vaya, vayamos, vayáis, vayan
oír	oiga, oigas, oiga, oigamos, oigáis, oigan
poner	ponga, pongas, ponga, pongamos, pongáis, pongan
saber	sepa, sepas, sepa, sepamos, sepáis, sepan
salir	salga, salgas, salga, salgamos, salgáis, salgan
ser	sea, seas, sea, seamos, seáis, sean
tener	tenga, tengas, tenga, tengamos, tengáis, tengan
traer	traiga, traigas, traiga, traigamos, traigáis, traigan
valer	valga, valgas, valga, valgamos, valgáis, valgan
venir	venga, vengas, venga, vengamos, vengáis, vengan
ver	vea, veas, vea, veamos, veáis, vean

Present Subjunctive—Spelling Changes

—car	atacar	ataque, ataques, ataque, etc.
—gar	entregar	entregue, entregues, entregue, etc.
—zar	rezar	rece, reces, rece, etc.
—ger	coger	coja, cojas, coja, etc.
—gir	dirigir	dirija, dirijas, dirija, etc.
—guir	distinguir	distinga, distingas, distinga, etc.

–guar	averiguar	averigüe, averigües, averigüe, etc.
–uir	huir	huya, huyas, huya, etc.
–quir	delinquir	delinca, delincas, delinca, etc.
–cer	conocer	conozca, conozcas, conozca, etc.
	vencer	venza, venzas, venza, etc.
–cir	conducir	conduzca, conduzcas, conduza, etc.

Present Subjunctive–Stem Changes

If a verb has only one stem change, it will appear in all persons except *nosotros* and *vosotros*. If there are two stem changes given, the second one will appear in the *nosotros/vosotros* forms of the present subjunctive while the first one will appear in all other persons.

(ú) actuar to act	(í) enviar to send	(ue, u) morir to die	(i, i) pedir to request	(ie, i) sentir to feel or regret
actúe	envíe	muera	pida	sienta
actúes	envíes	mueras	pidas	sientas
actúe	envíe	muera	pida	sienta
actuemos	enviemos	muramos	pidamos	sintamos
actuéis	enviéis	muráis	pidáis	sintáis
actúen	envíen	mueran	pidan	sientan

Past (Imperfect) Subjunctive–Regular

To form this tense, remove *–ron* from the end of the third person plural of the preterite and add the following endings:

| –ra, | –ras, | –ra, | ´–ramos, | –rais, | –ran |
| –se, | –ses, | –se, | ´–semos, | –seis, | –sen |

Either set of endings is correct, with the first set being the more widely used.

Past Subjunctive–Irregular

andar	anduviera or anduviese, etc.
caber	cupiera or cupiese, etc.
dar	diera or diese, etc.
decir	dijera or dijese, etc.
estar	estuviera or estuviese, etc.
haber	hubiera or hubiese, etc.
hacer	hiciera or hiciese, etc.

ir	*fuera* or *fuese,* etc.
poder	*pudiera* or *pudiese,* etc.
poner	*pusiera* or *pusiese,* etc.
querer	*quisiera* or *quisiese,* etc.
saber	*supiera* or *supiese,* etc.
ser	*fuera* or *fuese,* etc.
tener	*tuviera* or *tuviese,* etc.
traer	*trajera* or *trajese,* etc.
venir	*viniera* or *viniese,* etc.
–ducir	*condujera* or *condujese,* etc.
–uir	*huyera* or *huyese,* etc.

Past Subjunctive–Verbs with Stem Changes

Because the stem for the past subjunctive comes from the third person plural of the preterite, it will be affected by verbs that have stem changes in the preterite.

dormir (ue, u) to sleep	*sentir* (ie, i) to feel/regret	*pedir* (i, i) to ask for
durmiera	*sintiera*	*pidiera*
durmieras	*sintieras*	*pidieras*
durmiera	*sintiera*	*pidiera*
durmiéramos	*sintiéramos*	*pidiéramos*
durmierais	*sintierais*	*pidierais*
durmieran	*sintieran*	*pidieran*

Past Subjunctive–Verbs Like *Leer*

Because *–er* and *–ir* verbs with double vowels (*leer, oír, creer, caer,* etc.) have a *y* in the third person of the preterite, this *y* will be found in all forms of the past subjunctive.

oír	*oyera, oyeras, oyera, oyéramos, oyerais, oyeran*

COMMANDS: FORMAL AND FAMILIAR

The Formal Command

Formal commands (*Ud.* and *Uds.*) are always expressed by the present subjunctive. Some samples follow.

comer (eat)	*(no) coma Ud.*	*(no) coman Uds.*
volver (return)	*(no) vuelva Ud.*	*(no) vuelvan Uds.*
tener (have)	*(no) tenga Ud.*	*(no) tengan Uds.*
atacar (attack)	*(no) ataque Ud.*	*(no) ataquen Uds.*

The Familiar Command

Unlike the formal commands, which are derived from the same form (the present subjunctive), the familiar commands come from several different verb forms to cover the positive, negative, singular, and plural forms.

1. The singular (*tú*) form of the affirmative command is the same as the third person singular of the present indicative.

leer = lee (tú)	*lavar = lava (tú)*	*vivir = vive (tú)*
read!	wash!	live!

2. The plural (*vosotros*) form of the affirmative command is formed by changing the *–r* ending of the infinitive to a *–d*.

leer = leed	*lavar = lavad*	*vivir = vivid*
read!	wash!	live!

3. The negative forms come from the *tú* and *vosotros* forms of the present subjunctive.

leer = no leas (tú)	*lavar = no laves (tú)*
no leáis (vosotros)	*no lavéis (vosotros)*
don't read!	don't wash!

Familiar Commands–Irregulars

The only irregular familiar commands occur in the affirmative singular. All other forms follow the rules stated above.

	tú	*vosotros*	*tú*	*vosotros*
decir	**di**	decid	no digas	no digáis
hacer	**haz**	haced	no hagas	no hagáis
ir	**ve**	id	no vayas	no vayáis
poner	**pon**	poned	no pongas	no pongáis
salir	**sal**	salid	no salgas	no salgáis
ser	**sé**	sed	no seas	no seáis
tener	**ten**	tened	no tengas	no tengáis
valer	**val**	valed	no valgas	no valgáis
venir	**ven**	venid	no vengas	no vengáis

Commands of Reflexive Verbs

Reflexive verbs require the use of reflexive pronouns. The formal command, singular and plural, uses *–se*. The familiar command uses *te* (singular) and *os* (plural). These pronouns **precede** the **negative command** and are **after** and **attached** to the **positive command**. Any time a pronoun is appended to a command form, an accent mark is required. Without it, the stress automatically moves to the next syllable, thus affecting the pronunciation.

Bañarse:	báñese Ud.	no se bañe Ud.
	báñense Uds.	no se bañen Uds.
	báñate tú	no te bañes tú
	bañaos vosotros*	no os bañéis vosotros

* When *os* is appended to the affirmative plural command, the final *–d* is dropped (**exception**: *idos*). If using an *–ir* verb, an accent is required over the *i* (*divertid* + *os* = *divertíos*) to split the diphthong and allow for the *i* to be pronounced separately.

"Let's" Statements

There are two ways to express this statement:

1. *Vamos a* + infinitive:

Vamos a comer.	Let's eat.
Vamos a sentarnos.	Let's sit down.
Vamos a leérselo.	Let's read it to him.

2. First person plural present subjunctive:

comamos	Let's eat.	(*no comamos*)
*leámoselo**	Let's read it to him.	(*no se lo leamos*)
*sentémonos***	Let's sit down.	(*no nos sentemos*)

Exception: *Vámonos* = Let's go. *No nos vayamos.* = Let's not go. The affirmative is not derived from the subjunctive, but from the indicative.

* Because double *s* does not exist in Spanish, this verb form will eliminate one (*leámoselo*).

** Before adding *nos* to the reflexive verb form, the final –*s* is dropped. An accent mark is needed.

"Have"/ "Let"/ "May" Statements

Que + third person singular/plural present subjunctive

Examples:		
	Have her go.	*Que vaya ella.*
	Let him read it.	*Que lo lea.*
	May they do it well.	*Que lo hagan bien.*
	Have them give it to me.	*Que me lo den.*

Note: Pronouns precede these verb forms because they are the conjugated verb of the noun clause.

Dejar is also used to express **let**, with direct object pronouns.

Déjame ver.	Let me see.
Déjanos salir.	Let us leave.

☞ Drill 5

1. No te _____ en el cuarto de Felipe.

   (A) acueste

   (B) acostéis

   (C) acuesten

   (D) acuestes

2. ¡No _____ Ud., por favor!

   (A) me hable

   (B) hábleme

   (C) me habla

   (D) me hables

3. ¡Que lo _____ Ud. bien!

   (A) pasar   (C) pases

   (B) pase   (D) pasa

4. Hola, mis amigos. ¡ _____ para hablar conmigo!

   (A) Siéntense   (C) Sentados

   (B) Siéntese   (D) Sentaos

5. La madre le dijo a su hijo, –¡ _____ al supermercado!

   (A) vete   (C) no vaya

   (B) váyase   (D) no va

6. Antes de salir mi madre me dijo, –¡ _____ el abrigo, hijo!

   (A) póngase   (C) pónete

   (B) póngate   (D) ponte

7. Hijos, no _____ mientras estoy hablando.

   (A) os reís   (C) os reíais

   (B) os riáis   (D) reíos

8. Juanito, cuando salgas, _____ la luz.

   (A) apaga   (C) apagues

   (B) apague   (D) apagaste

9. _____ aquí para poder ver mejor.

   (A) Nos sentamos   (C) Sentémosnos

   (B) Sentémonos   (D) Sentámonos

10. No _____ con vuestros amigos esta noche.

   (A) os vayáis   (C) os vais

   (B) se vayan   (D) idos

Drill 5—Detailed Explanations of Answers

1. **(D)**   This item tests your knowledge of the various forms of the imperative. The choices given are all command forms. We know that we are searching for the "tú" command, i.e., the second person singular imperative, because of the second person singular reflexive pronoun, "te," which is given in the sentence. Furthermore, we know that we must choose a negative imperative from the list because of the "No" in the sentence. Negative familiar singular commands in Spanish correspond to the second person singular of the present subjunctive, which, for "acostarse" (ue) (to go to bed), is "No te acuestes." Choice (A), "acueste," will not work because it is the command form for the third person singular (the "Usted" command), but we are given the second person singular of the reflexive pronoun in the sentence, "te." Choice (B), "acostéis," is the negative command for the "vosotros" form of the verb. Being a negative command, it is also like the corresponding form of the subjunctive of "acostarse," i.e., the second person plural. "Vosotros" is used only in Spain. In all of Central and South America, the third person plural (the "Ustedes" form) is used in its place. "Acostéis" is an incorrect answer here because the reflexive pronoun "te" is not the second person plural form. For (B) to be correct, we would have to say "No os acostéis... ." (C), "acuesten," is wrong also because the reflexive pronoun for it would have to be "se," the third person plural form.

2. **(A)**   The negative formal singular command (Ud.) is required in this sentence. Object pronouns precede negative commands. Choice (B) is incorrect because the pronoun is after and attached to the positive command. Choice (C) is not in a command form, and (D) is the negative familiar command form.

3. **(B)**   The exclamatory statement ("May it go well for you!") requires the use of the present subjunctive, which in this sample is the same as the formal command for "Ud." Choice (A), an infinitive, (C), the "tú" form of the verb, and (D), the present indicative form, are all incorrect.

4. **(D)**   The familiar plural positive command is required in this statement ("amigos"). This is formed by removing the –d from the infinitive before attaching the reflexive pronoun **os** to the end. Choice (C) is incorrect because the –d has been retained. Choices (A) and (B) are both formal commands.

5. **(A)** Because the mother is speaking to her son, the familiar positive command is required in this sample. The familiar singular positive command of **irse** is irregular. Choice (B) is the formal command, (C) is the present subjunctive, and (D) is the present indicative.

6. **(D)** The mother is again addressing her son in this sentence, which requires the use of the familiar positive singular command of **ponerse** (to put on). This is irregular. Both (A) and (B) are formal command forms but (B) also has the incorrect reflexive pronoun attached. Choice (C) is an incorrect verb form.

7. **(B)** Because the children are being asked **not** to laugh in this sentence, the negative familiar plural command form is required. This form comes from the second person plural of the present subjunctive. Choice (A) is the second person plural of the present indicative. Choice (C) is the second person plural of the conditional tense, and (D) is the familiar plural positive command form.

8. **(A)** Because Juanito is being addressed in the familiar ("salgas"), the familiar positive singular command is required. For regular verbs this comes from the third person singular of the present tense. Choice (B) is the formal command, (C) is the second person singular of the present subjunctive, and (D) is the preterite tense.

9. **(B)** One way to express **let's** in Spanish is by using the "nosotros" form of the present subjunctive. If the verb is reflexive, the pronoun **nos** is attached to the end of this form, after removing the –s. Choice (A) is the present indicative. Choice (C) has retained the –s of the verb, and (D) is not in the present subjunctive.

10. **(A)** Because "vuestros" indicates that the command should be familiar plural and because the sentence is negative, the command form here will come from the "vosotros" form of the present subjunctive. Pronouns precede negative commands. Choice (B) is the third plural of the present subjunctive, (C) is the second plural of the present indicative, and (D) is the familiar plural positive command form.

THE SUBJUNCTIVE–USES

Subjunctive vs. Indicative

The indicative mood tenses express certainty or factual knowledge. The subjunctive mode is used to convey ideas in the realm of all areas other than those of objective fact: concepts that are hypothetical, contrary to fact, those which embody the expression of feelings of the speaker toward a state or action. Because the subjunctive is a **subjoined, subordinate, dependent** verb form, it is logical that it will occur in the **dependent clause** of the sentence. There are four types of clauses that could contain the subjunctive: noun, adjective, adverb, and "if."

The Noun Clause

The noun clause is a group of words that acts as the subject or object of the main clause. The subjunctive will occur in this clause if two conditions are met:

1. a change of subject between two clauses,

2. a specific category of verb is used in the main clause: wishing/wanting, emotion, impersonal expression, doubt/denial, or indirect command

To join the independent clause to the dependent clause, the relative pronoun *que* (that) is required in Spanish. In English we often leave this word out. Note the two possible ways to express the following statement in English.

I hope he's here.   I hope **that** he's here.

Category I–Wishing/Wanting

querer (to want)   *Quiero **que Juan vaya**.*
                                 I want Juan to go.

Others: *desear* (to want), *preferir* (to prefer), *gustar* (to like), etc.

Category II–Emotion

temer (to fear)   *Temo **que Juan vaya**.*
                                 I fear Juan (may, will) go.

Others: *tener miedo de* (to be afraid of), *lamentar* (to regret), *ojalá que* (if only), *sentir* (to regret/feel)

Category III–Impersonal Expression

An impersonal expression is a combination of **to be** with an adjective. The subject is always **it**. In Spanish, **to be** will come from *ser*.

es importante	*Es importante **que Juan vaya**.*
	It's important for Juan to go.

Others: *Ser* + adjective (*necesario, natural, probable, posible, mejor, lástima, triste*, etc.)

Note: Some impersonal expressions will **not** prompt a subjunctive if they imply **no doubt**. See exceptions on the next page. These expressions will require subjunctive only if negative.

Category IV–Doubt/Denial

dudar (to doubt)	*Dudo **que Juan vaya**.*
	I doubt Juan will go/is going.

Others: *negar* (to deny), *suponer* (to suppose), *puede ser* (it may be), *creer* (to believe)*, *pensar* (to think)*, *tal vez/quizás* (perhaps)

* *Creer/pensar* commonly take subjunctive if they are negative or in a question. This is dependent upon the speaker's point of view. If he/she actually believes or thinks what he/she is saying, the indicative will be used.

Category V–Indirect Command

pedir (to ask for)*	*Le pido a **Juan que vaya**.*
	I ask Juan to go.

Others: *decir* (to tell), *sugerir* (to suggest), *exigir* (to demand), *insistir en* (to insist on), *aconsejar* (to advise), *rogar* (to beg)

Note: Several verbs from this category may be used with the infinitive or the subjunctive.

permitir (to permit)	*dejar* (to allow)
hacer (to make)	*aconsejar* (to advise)
impedir (to prevent)	*mandar* (to command)
prohibir (to prohibit)	*recomendar* (to recommend)

*(Te) aconsejo que **vayas**.* or *Te aconsejo ir.*
I advise you to go.

*No (me) permiten que **fume**.* or *No me permiten fumar.*
They do not permit me to smoke.

* Many verbs in this category require the use of the indirect object pronoun in the independent clause used with the second subject: *rogar, pedir, decir, aconsejar*, etc.

Example: *Te ruego que (tú) hables con ella.*
I beg you to speak with her.

Exceptions

The following expressions are used with the **indicative unless** they are **negative**.

occurre que	
sucede que	it happens that
es evidente que	it's evident that
es cierto que	it's certain that
es verdad que	it's true that
es seguro que	it's sure that
es obvio que	it's obvious that
es que	it's that
se sabe que	it's known that
parece que	it seems that
no es dudoso que	it's not doubtful that

Sequence of Tenses

Whether the present or past subjunctive is used in the dependent clause is based on the tense used in the independent or main clause. Sequence primarily means the present subjunctive will follow present tense forms, while past subjunctive will follow past tense forms. Following is a list of tenses with sequence indicated.

Independent Clause (Indicative)		Dependent Clause (Subjunctive)
Present	*espero*	
Present Progressive	*estoy esperando*	*que vaya*
Future	*esperaré*	
Present Perfect	*he esperado*	
Future Perfect	*habré esperado*	*que haya ido*
Command	*espere/espera*	
Preterite	*esperé*	*que fuera*
Imperfect	*esperaba*	

Past Progressive	*estaba esperando*	
Conditional	*esperaría*	***que hubiera ido***
Past Perfect	*había esperado*	***que hubiese ido***
Conditional Perfect	*habría esperado*	

The Adjective Clause

An adjective clause is one that modifies or describes a preceding noun. This noun is called the antecedent and it will determine if the subjunctive will exist in the adjective clause itself. This antecedent must be (1) negative or (2) indefinite for the subjunctive to exist in the adjective clause.

To determine this, one must focus not solely on the antecedent itself but the surrounding words (the verb and/or any articles used with that noun).

Compare these two adjective clauses:

Indicative:	Subjunctive:
Tengo un coche que es nuevo. (antecedent=coche) [exists because he **has** it]	***Busco*** *un coche que sea nuevo.* [does not yet exist]
Busco **el** *libro que tiene la información.* (antecedent=libro) [a specific book exists with the information]	*Busco* **un** *libro que tenga la información.* [no specific book]
Hay **varios** *hombres que van con nosotros* (antecedent=hombres) [these men exist]	*No hay* **ningún** *hombre que vaya con nosotros.* [a negative antecedent]

The Adverbial Clause

An adverbial clause answers the questions when? where? how? why? etc. These clauses are introduced by conjunctions. These conjunctions can be broken down into three separate types:

1. conjunctions **always** followed by the subjunctive

2. the *–quiera* group conjunctions (which are **always** followed by the subjunctive)

3. conjunctions **sometimes** followed by the subjunctive

Always Subjunctive

a fin de que/para que	so that
a menos que/salvo que	unless
con tal que	provided that
antes (de) que	before
en caso de que	in case (that)
sin que	without
a condición de que	on condition that

Examples: *Salió sin que yo lo supiera.*
He left without my knowing it.

Lo haré antes de que lleguen.
I'll do it before they arrive.

The *–quiera* Group

dondequiera que	wherever
cualquier (a) que	whatever
quienquiera que	whoever
quienesquiera que	whoever
cuandoquiera que	whenever
por + adj/adv + *que*	however, no matter how

Examples: *Dondequiera que vayas, serás feliz.*
Wherever you go, you'll be happy.

Por enferma que esté, ella asistirá.
No matter how sick she is, she'll attend.

Sometimes Subjunctive

Adverbial clauses begun with these conjunctions will have subjunctive only if there is speculation or doubt as to whether the action will take place in the future.

aunque	although
cuando	when
después (de) que	after
en cuanto	as soon as
luego que	as soon as
tan pronto como	as soon as
así que	so that
hasta que	until
mientras	while

Subjunctive	Indicative
*Aunque **cueste** mucho, lo quiero.*	*Aunque **costó** mucho, lo compré.*
Although it may cost a lot, I want it.	Although it cost a lot, I bought it.
*Léalo hasta que **llegue**.*	*Lo leí hasta que **llegó**.*
Read it until he arrives.	I read it until he arrived.
*Dijo que lo haría cuando **llegara**.*	*Lo hizo cuando **llegó**.*
He said he would do it when he arrived.	He did it when he arrived.
[hasn't gotten here yet]	

Normally, if the verb in the independent clause is in the future or command form, the subjunctive will be needed in the dependent clause. However, as is noted in the last example, this is not always the case. One must always think in terms of "has this happened yet or not?" and use the subjunctive accordingly.

The "If" Clause

The imperfect and pluperfect subjunctives are used in contrary-to-fact statements, as follows:

If Clause	Result Clause
Si yo estudiara/estudiase más, . . .	*recibiría (recibiera) buenas notas.*
If I studied more, . . .	I would get good grades.
Si yo hubiera/hubiese estudiado más, . . .	*habría (hubiera) recibido buenas notas.*
If I had studied more, . . .	I would have gotten good grades.

Note: The present subjunctive is **never** used in the **if** clause. Instead, the proper sequence (present indicative with future) follows:

Si yo estudio más, . . .	*recibiré buenas notas.*
If I study more, . . .	I will get good grades.

Como Si (as if) Statements

"As if" statements are always followed by the imperfect or the pluperfect subjunctive.

Habla como si la conociera bien.
He speaks as if he knew her well.

Me castigó como si lo hubiera hecho.
He punished me as if I had done it.

The *–ra* Form as Polite Request

The *–ra* forms of the imperfect subjunctive of **querer, poder**, and **deber** are often used instead of the conditional of these verbs to express a polite request or statement.

Quisiera hacerlo.	I would like to do it.
¿Pudieras pasarme la sal?	Could you pass me the salt?
Debieran comprarlos.	They should buy them.

☞ Drill 6

1. Mis padres no deseaban que yo _____ eso.

   (A) hiciera   (C) haría

   (B) hacía   (D) haga

2. Si estuviera aquí, _____ hablar con ella.

   (A) me gustará   (C) trataría de

   (B) podemos   (D) me negué a

3. Te lo dirán cuando te _____.

   (A) ves   (C) visitemos

   (B) lo venden   (D) ven

4. Dijeron que nos enviarían el paquete tan pronto como _____.

   (A) lo recibieron   (C) tengan tiempo

   (B) llegara   (D) sabrán nuestra dirección

5. Me aconsejó que _____.

   (A) no siguiera la ruta de la costa   (C) voy al médico

   (B) duerma más   (D) venga inmediatamente

6.   ¡Ojalá que me _____ un recuerdo de París!

   (A) traen   (C) enviarán

   (B) han comprado   (D) den

7.   María le dio el periódico a Enrique para que él lo _____

   (A) lee   (C) lea

   (B) leyeran   (D) leyera

8.   Si yo fuera al centro, te _____ algo.

   (A) compraría   (C) compre

   (B) compré   (D) compraré

9.   Yo conozco a un señor que _____ español muy bien.

   (A) hable   (C) hablando

   (B) habla   (D) hablara

10. Su madre le dijo que _____ todo o no podría tener postre.

   (A) come   (C) comía

   (B) coma   (D) comiera

11. Lo harán cuando _____.

   (A) llegas   (C) puedan

   (B) entran   (D) tienen tiempo

12. Si _____ dinero, iría a Bolivia.

   (A) tenía   (C) tengo

   (B) tuviera   (D) tuve

13. _____ que tienes razón.

   (A) Creo   (C) Niego

   (B) Dudo   (D) Me alegro de

14. Siento que ellos _____ con Uds. ayer.

    (A) no estuvieron   (C) no estaban

    (B) no estuvieran   (D) no estarán

15. Si yo tuviera tiempo en Roma te _____

    (A) visito   (C) visitaré

    (B) voy a visitar   (D) visitaría

16. No estoy seguro, pero tal vez él _____

    (A) viniera   (C) viene

    (B) vendrá   (D) venga

17. Mi consejero me dijo que no dijera nada hasta que alguien me lo _____.

    (A) pide   (C) ha pedido

    (B) pidiera   (D) va a pedir

18. Se lo expliqué en detalle para que lo _____.

    (A) comprendiera   (C) comprende

    (B) comprenda   (D) comprendió

19. Mi madre dice que está bien que vaya mi hermano, con tal de que se lo _____.

    (A) cuida   (C) cuidaba

    (B) cuidara   (D) cuide

20. Le pedí que _____ temprano para acabar temprano.

    (A) venga   (C) venir

    (B) viniera   (D) venía

21. No quiere que su hijo _____ malas costumbres.

    (A) tenga   (C) tengan

    (B) tiene   (D) tienen

22. No creo que mis amigos me _____ abandonado.

    (A) han   (C) hayan

    (B) habían   (D) hubieran

23. Si él te _____ un beso, ¿cómo reaccionarías?

    (A) daba   (C) diera

    (B) da   (D) dar

24. No vendrías si _____ lo que te espera.

    (A) sabías   (C) sabes

    (B) supieras   (D) supiste

25. Mis padres me compraron un automóvil para que _____ a pasear.

    (A) salgo   (C) salga

    (B) salir   (D) saliera

26. Por bien que _____ Ana, no quiero jugar con ella.

    (A) juega   (C) está jugando

    (B) juegue   (D) jugara

27. Habla con ella como si la _____ bien.

    (A) conoce   (C) conociera

    (B) conozca   (D) conoció

28. Es evidente que los chicos no _____ en sus cuartos.

    (A) están   (C) son

    (B) estén   (D) sean

29. Mi mamá quería que _____ nuestra tarea a tiempo.

    (A) hagamos   (C) hiciéramos

    (B) hacemos   (D) hicimos

30. Si yo hubiera sabido la respuesta, se la _____.

   (A) diría   (C) había dicho

   (B) habría dicho   (D) diga

Drill 6—Detailed Explanations of Answers

1. **(A)** The verb "desear" can express volition, or desire that some-thing happen. With verbs of this type, if there are two different subjects in the two clauses of the sentence, i.e., if someone is bringing his will to bear on someone or something else, then the subjunctive is required. In our sentence the two different subjects are "Mis padres" and "yo." My parents were exerting their will on me. The sentence, however, requires the imper-fect subjunctive, "hiciera," rather than the present subjunctive "haga," because the first verb, "deseaban," is in a past tense, the imperfect. Span-ish normally observes a logical tense sequence in sentences requiring the subjunctive. If the first verb, the one that **causes** the subjunctive (in this case, "deseaban"), is in a past tense or the conditional tense, a past sub-junctive is required (in this case, the imperfect subjunctive). On the other hand, if the verb that causes the subjunctive is in a present tense or the future, a present subjunctive is used. Note that we would not use the subjunctive, but rather the infinitive, if there were not two separate sub-jects involved: "Yo no deseaba decir eso" (I didn't want to say that).

2. **(C)** Sentences with subordinate clauses beginning with "si" (if), which establish an unreal or hypothetical situation, contain a past tense of the subjunctive (imperfect or pluperfect subjunctive). Our statement be-gins with such a clause. In these cases, the other clause (the one which shows what would happen if the "si" clause were true) is in the conditional or conditional perfect tense. Since the "si" clause (the hypothesis) is given here in a simple imperfect subjunctive, rather than the pluperfect subjunc-tive, we also should use the simple conditional tense in the result clause, rather than the conditional perfect. Note that there are times when one might use the future tense in a result clause, but in those cases the verb of the "si" clause is in the simple present or the present perfect. In such instances, the situation is viewed as much less hypothetical and possible of happening. Compare the following examples: "Si estudia, entonces sacará buenas notas" (If he studies . . . and it is possible he will . . . , then he will get good grades); "Si estudiara, entonces sacaría buenas notas" (If he were to study . . . but he doesn't . . . , then he would get good grades.) Only

choice (C) could be used in this sentence because it is the only one which appears in the conditional tense. Choice (A) is in the future, (B) is in the present, and (D) is in the preterite. Remember that "tratar de" + infinitive is an idiom meaning "to try to." The expression "negarse a" + infinitive signifies "to refuse to."

3.   **(C)**   The word "cuando" in our sentence is an adverb which pertains to time. When adverbs of time such as "cuando," "hasta que," "tan pronto como," "así que," "luego que," and "mientras" refer to the future, we are obliged to use the subjunctive following them. Of the four possible choices, the only verb form which is subjunctive is found in (C), "visitemos," the first person plural of the present subjunctive of "visitar" (to visit). In (A), "ves," we find the second person singular of the present indicative of "ver" (to see); (B) gives us the third person plural of the present indicative of "vender" (to sell); in choice (D), we find the third person plural of the present indicative of "ver." Remember that we do not always use the subjunctive after these adverbs of time. If the sentence does not refer to some future time, or if it expresses a customary or habitual situation, the indicative is used: "Siempre los veo cuando **vienen** a nuestro pueblo." (I always see them when they come to our town.) There are even situations in the **past** in which we may refer to some action that was **yet to happen** at some future time. In such instances, a subjunctive is also used following the adverb of time: "Iban a hablarles cuando **llegaran**" (They were going to speak to them whenever they arrived). Note that here we have had to use the imperfect subjunctive of "llegar," rather than the present subjunctive, because we are talking about something that was yet to happen in the past. This sentence implies that they had not yet arrived but were to arrive at some future time. Now, compare the following sentences: "Tratarán de hacerlo cuando tengan tiempo" (They will try to do it whenever they have time); "Dijeron que tratarían de hacerlo cuando tuvieran tiempo" (They said that they would try to do it whenever they had time). In the first example, the verb of the main clause, "tratarán," is future. If the verb of the main clause is future or some present form, then we use a form of present subjunctive. In the second example, the principal verb, "tratarían," is conditional. If the main verb is conditional or a past tense, we use a past form of the subjunctive, in this case, the imperfect subjunctive: "tuvieran."

4.   **(B)**   For a complete explanation of the use of the subjunctive following adverbs of time such as "tan pronto como" (as soon as), see the explanation for question 3. Also, pay particular attention to the example there which illustrates the use of the past subjunctive after these expres-

sions if the main verb is in a past tense, as is the case in our sentence here. Choice (A) does not qualify because it is in the preterite tense of the indicative. Choice (C) is given in the present subjunctive, rather than the imperfect subjunctive. (D) appears in the future tense of the indicative.

5.   **(A)**   The verb "aconsejar" (to advise) embodies an expression of will or desire that someone else do something. It carries an implicit command. After such verbs it is necessary to use a subjunctive form in the dependent clause. Because the main clause of our sentence uses a past tense (preterite) of the verb "aconsejar," we must use a past tense of the subjunctive, the imperfect subjunctive. Choice (B) employs the present subjunctive of the verb; (C) offers us the present indicative; in (D), we once again find a present subjunctive.

6.   **(D)**   The noun "recuerdo" in our sentence means "souvenir." "Ojalá" and "Ojalá que" both mean "Oh, if only . . . " or "I wish or hope that . . . " They are expressions of desire. Unlike many such expressions, they do not require a change of subject to produce a subjunctive in the following verb. In fact, if there is a verb after them, the subjunctive is obligatory. For that reason, choices (A), (B), and (C), are not useful to us. (A) is the third person plural of the present indicative of "traer" (to bring). (B) gives us the third person plural of the present perfect tense of "comprar" (to buy). (C) is the third person plural of the future of "enviar" (to send). Following "Ojalá" and "Ojalá que," if the present or present perfect subjunctive is used, the implication is that the situation is feasible and possible of happening. When we say "¡Ojalá que me den un recuerdo de París!," we mean "I hope that they will give me a souvenir from Paris!" (and it is **possible** that they will). On the other hand, we use a past subjunctive (imperfect or pluperfect) after these two expressions to show that the situation is highly hypothetical, unreal, or impossible: "¡Ojalá que **fuera** millonario!" (I wish I were a millionaire! . . . but I'm not, and probably never will be . . .).

7.   **(D)**   After the expression **para que,** the subjunctive must be used, and this sentence is in the past. The imperfect subjunctive is used after a principle clause containing the preterite, imperfect, or conditional tenses. Choice (D) is the only one in the imperfect subjunctive which is also singular.

8.   **(A)**   In an "if" clause in the past, using the subjunctive, the conditional is the appropriate form to follow.

9. **(B)** A known individual or thing does not require the subjunctive, but an unknown, i.e., an indefinite person or thing, does. In this case, it is known, present tense, and indicative. Therefore, choice (B) is correct.

10. **(D)** The imperfect subjunctive is necessary since the verb of the main clause is in the past and it requires the subjunctive following the rule of a verb of request (or similar meaning) directing an action of an object or person different from the subject.

11. **(C)** In our sentence, the word "cuando" is what we term an adverb of time. We can tell from the verb "harán" that we are talking about the future. Whenever an adverb of time refers to the future, we are required to use a subjunctive form of the verb in the following clause. Generally, if the main verb appears in the future or present tenses, we use the present tense of the subjunctive. Among the verbs which are your possible choices, only "puedan" is a present subjunctive form. All of the other choices appear in the present indicative. Even sentences whose main verb is in a past tense may occasionally refer to some future time, e.g., "Dijeron que lo harían cuando **pudieran**" (They said that they would do it whenever they could). Observe that here we cannot use the present subjunctive. We must, on the other hand, use the imperfect subjunctive because we are referring to the past. When the verb does not refer to a future time or when it indicates a customary action, we use an indicative tense following adverbs of time: "Siempre me llaman cuando pueden" (They always call me when they can). Other common adverbs of time which have the same effect are: "hasta que," "tan pronto como," "mientras que," "así que," "luego que," and "en cuanto."

12. **(B)** Dependent clauses beginning with "si" (if) require the use of the **imperfect subjunctive** if they set up an impossible, hypothetical, or unreal situation. Then, in the other clause, we use the **conditional** tense to show what would happen (what the result would be) if that hypothesis were true. The only imperfect subjunctive form appearing among the choices is (B) "tuviera." (A) "tenía" is the imperfect indicative; (C) "tengo" is the present indicative; (D) "tuve" is the preterite. When we say "Si tuviera dinero, iría a Bolivia," we mean "If I had money (but I don't), I would go to Bolivia." In other words, we are emphasizing the unreality or impossibility of my having enough money. If, on the other hand, we wanted to imply that it is not totally unfeasible that I will have the money, we would say in English, "If I have the money, I will go to Bolivia." Notice that here, in the "if" clause, we have used the **present indicative**, and in the result clause, the **future** tense. This pattern would be observed

also in Spanish: "Si tengo dinero, iré a Bolivia." Suppose we were talking about a situation in the past and we wanted to set up an unfeasible hypothesis or assumption: "If I had had money, I would have gone to Bolivia" ("Si hubiera tenido dinero, habría ido a Bolivia"). Here we have used compound or perfect tenses: in the "si" clause, the **pluperfect subjunctive**; in the result clause, the **conditional perfect**. Remember this caution: we never use a present or a present perfect subjunctive immediately after the word "si."

13. **(A)** How much do you remember about the uses of the subjunctive as opposed to the indicative? A careful scrutiny of the possible choices reveals that (B) "Dudo" (I doubt), (C) "Niego," (I deny), and (D) "Me alegro de" (I am happy) would require a subjunctive following them if we were to use them in the sentence. This sentence does not give the subjunctive form of "tener," "tengas," but rather the indicative, "tienes." Consequently, we must use (A) Creo (I believe), which does not require a subjunctive following it if it is used affirmatively. There are only two possible times when we **may** use the subjunctive after "creer": (1) if "creer" is used negatively, e.g., "No creo que tengas razón" (I don't believe you are right) and (2) if "creer" is used in a question, e.g., "Crees que llueva mañana?" (Do you think it will rain tomorrow?). Even when "creer" is used negatively or interrogatively, the speaker has the **option** of using the indicative, rather than the subjunctive, following "creer" if he wishes to show that he himself feels no doubt about the situation. Earlier, we indicated that the verb "dudar" requires the subjunctive. That is because expressions which cast doubt on the second clause of the sentence bring about a subjunctive in the subordinate verb. The verb "negar" (ie) (to deny) produces a subjunctive in the following clause whenever it denies the validity or truth of the subordinate clause. Expressions of emotion, such as "alegrarse de" (to be happy), bring about a following subjunctive only if there is a change of subject between the two verbs. Otherwise, simply the infinitive is used.

14. **(B)** "Siento" is the first person singular of the present tense of "sentir" (ie, i) (to be sorry). "Sentir" is a verb of emotion. It requires a subjunctive in the second part of the sentence when we have two different subjects. For this reason, (A) "no estuvieron," the preterite of "estar" (to be), (C) "no estaban," the imperfect of "estar," and (D) "no estarán," the future of "estar," are all wrong. (B), however, "no estuvieran," the imperfect subjunctive of "estar," is correct. Notice that although "Siento" is given in the present tense, we must use a past tense of the subjunctive

because the action of the subordinate clause took place in the past. The word "ayer" (yesterday) is our clue.

15. **(D)** In an "if" clause in the present tense, the independent clause is usually in the future and the dependent clause in the present subjunctive. If, however, the "if" clause is in the past, the independent clause is in the conditional. None of the other answers is correct.

16. **(D)** After the expression **tal vez** indicating a future idea, the present subjunctive is used. Choice (A) is past subjunctive. Only choice (D) is correct.

17. **(B)** The use of the subjunctive is required after **hasta que**. In this case, the sentence is in the past, so the imperfect subjunctive is required, even though the idea of the sentence indicates some action in the future.

18. **(A)** After the expression **para que** the subjunctive can be expected. The introductory sentence begins in the preterite, so the imperfect subjunctive should be chosen.

19. **(D)** After the expression **con tal de que** one expects the subjunctive. It should be noticed that this sentence is in the present tense. The only answer in the present subjunctive is (D). The reflexive in this answer is sometimes referred to as the dative of interest, or it could be considered as the indirect object meaning "for her."

20. **(B)** First you have to decide between the subjunctive and the indicative mood (choice (C), an infinitive, is ungrammatical in the context), and once you decide that the correct mood is the subjunctive (because it is governed by a verb—"pedir"—that always requires a subjunctive), then you have to opt between (A) and (B), that is, the present and the past. Since the main verb is in the past, the subjunctive form to follow must be in the same tense.

21. **(A)** You should first eliminate the last two choices as ungrammatical since they are plural and "hijo" is not. Then you must decide between subjunctive (the correct choice because "querer" always requires the subjunctive) and indicative.

22. **(C)** The four choices break down into two indicatives and two subjunctives. You must choose a subjunctive form at this point because

when "creer" is preceded by a negative, it requires the subjunctive mood. Finally, this subjunctive verb must be (like "creo") in the present.

23. **(C)** Three of these choices are ungrammatical, (A), (B), and (D) the first two because there is no tense correlation between "daba" (an imperfect form) or "da" (a present) and "reaccionarías" (a conditional form), and the third one because the infinitive must be conjugated. You should also realize that the structure of the sentence is of the "if/then" type, which always requires a subjunctive in the "if" clause.

24. **(B)** This is also an "if/then" clause (inverted: "then/if"). Consequently, the "if" clause must contain a subjunctive form, the only one available being (B).

25. **(D)** Your task in this question is easy if you know that "para que" always takes a subjunctive, though you still have to decide between (C) and (D). The key to this part of the answer is the main verb ("compraron"), which is in the past; therefore, the subjunctive verb that depends on it must also be in the past.

26. **(B)** This adverbial phrase requires the use of the present subjunctive to follow sequence. Therefore, (A) the present tense, (C) the present progressive, and (D) the past subjunctive are incorrect.

27. **(C)** "Como si" is always followed by the past subjunctive. Therefore, choice (A) the present indicative, (B) the present subjunctive, and (D) the preterite are incorrect.

28. **(A)** Although this sentence begins with an impersonal expression and there is a change in subject (i.e., a second clause follows), the subjunctive is not required in the noun clause because there is no doubt implied. Other expressions of this type are "es verdad," "es cierto," "no es dudoso," and "es obvio que." This will eliminate choices (B) and (D), which are both in the present subjunctive. Choice (C) is incorrect because this sentence points out location for which the verb **estar** is used.

29. **(C)** This sentence requires the use of the subjunctive because it begins with a verb of volition and there is a change in subject (from "mamá" to "we"). Because the verb in the independent clause (quería) is in the imperfect tense, to maintain proper sequencing, the past subjunctive is required in the dependent clause. Choice (A) is present subjunctive.

Choice (B) the present indicative and (D) the preterite are incorrect since this sentence requires the use of the subjunctive.

30. **(B)**   An "if" clause containing a compound verb form (the perfect tense) in the past subjunctive requires the use of a compound tense in the other clause, commonly written in the conditional tense. Choice (A), although it is in the conditional tense, is not compound. Choice (D) is in the present subjunctive and is, therefore, incorrect in this context. Choice (C) is a compound tense but in the pluperfect, not in the conditional perfect tense.

CONJUGATION OF *SER*

Indicative

	Present	Imperfect	Preterite	Future	Condit.
yo	soy	era	fui	seré	sería
tú	eres	eras	fuiste	serás	serías
él/ella/Ud.	es	era	fue	será	sería
nosotros, –as	somos	éramos	fuimos	seremos	seríamos
vosotros, –as	sois	erais	fuisteis	seréis	seríais
ellos/ellas/					
Uds.	son	eran	fueron	serán	serían

Subjunctive

	Present	Imperfect
yo	sea	fuera/fuese
tú	seas	fueras/fueses
él/ella/Ud.	sea	fuera/fuese
nosotros	seamos	fuéramos/fuésemos
vosotros	seáis	fuerais/fueseis
ellos/ellas/Uds.	sean	fueran/fuesen

Imperative

Singular	Plural
sé (tú)	sed (vosotros)
no seas (tú)	no seáis (vosotros)
(no) sea (Ud.)	(no) sean (Uds.)

Participles

Past Participle: *sido*
Present Participle: *siendo*

CONJUGATION OF *ESTAR*

Indicative

	Present	Imperfect	Preterite	Future	Condit.
yo	estoy	estaba	estuve	estaré	estaría
tú	estás	estabas	estuviste	estarás	estarías
él/ella/Ud.	está	estaba	estuvo	estará	estaría
nosotros, –as	estamos	estábamos	estuvimos	estaremos	estaríamos
vosotros, –as	estáis	estabais	estuvisteis	estaréis	estaríais
ellos/ellas/ Uds.	están	estaban	estuvieron	estarán	estarían

Subjunctive

	Present	Imperfect
yo	esté	estuviera/estuviese
tú	estés	estuvieras/estuvieses
él/ella/Ud.	esté	estuviera/estuviese
nosotros, –as	estemos	estuviéramos/ estuviésemos
vosotros, –as	estéis	estuvierais/estuvieseis
ellos/ellas/Uds.	estén	estuvieran/estuviesen

Imperative

	Present	Imperfect
	está (tú)	estad (vosotros)
	no estés (tú)	no estéis (vosotros)
	(no) esté (Ud.)	(no) estén (Uds.)

Participles

Past Participle: *estado*
Present Participle: *estando*

Uses of *Ser*

"To be" followed by a predicate noun (a noun that is the same person as the subject) is always *ser*.

*Él **es** médico.*
He **is** a doctor.

Somos hombres con una misión.
We **are** men on a mission.

To express origin, ownership, or material consistency.

¿Es Ud. de Atlanta?
Are you from Atlanta?

Ese libro es de la biblioteca.
That book **is** the library's.

Esta mesa es de madera.
This table **is** (made) of wood.

Ser is used to mean "to take place."

La fiesta fue ayer.
The party **was** yesterday.

La reunión es mañana.
The meeting **is** tomorrow.

The use of *ser* with an adjective denotes that the speaker considers the quality signified by the adjective an essential or permanent component of the noun.

El agua es clara.
Water **is** clear.

La madera es dura.
Wood **is** hard.

Mi hermano es alto.
My brother **is** tall.

To tell time/dates/seasons:

Son las dos y media.	It is 2:30.
Es verano.	It is summer.
Es el primero de enero.	It is January 1.
Será tarde.	It will be late.

With "impersonal expressions"—these are expressions with adjectives whose subject is "it."

Es posible.	It's possible.
Será imposible.	It will be impossible.
Ha sido necesario.	It has been necessary.

To express religion or occupation:

Soy católica.	I am Catholic.
Son doctores.	They are doctors.

With the adjective *feliz:*

Ella es feliz.	She is "happy go lucky."

To express "passive voice"—when the agent (doer) is expressed:

La información fue leída por el profesor.
The information was read by the teacher.

With personal pronouns:

Soy yo.	It is I.
Es ella.	It is she.

Uses of *Estar*

Estar is used to express location.

El estadio **está** a dos cuadras.
The stadium **is** two blocks away.

*Los pañuelos **están** en el cajón.*
The handkerchiefs **are** in the drawer.

Estar is used with the present participle of other verbs to form the progressive tense.

***Está** lloviendo.*
It **is** raining.

***Están** comprando los boletos.*
They **are** buying the tickets.

Estar is used with adjectives to indicate a change from the norm, a temporary state of the subject, or a subjective reaction.

***Estaba** gordo cuando lo vi.*
He **was** fat when I saw him.

*El postre **está** rico.*
The dessert **is** good.

To express the result of a previous action:

*La tarea **está** hecha.*
The homework **is** done.

La casa está bien construida.
The house **is** well built.

With certain idiomatic expressions:

Mi primo está de médico allí.
My cousin "**acts** as" a doctor there.

Estamos por salir ahora.
We **are** in favor of leaving now.

Estoy por llorar.
I **am** about to cry.

Adjectives that Change Meaning with *Ser* or *Estar*

Mi tío es bueno.	My uncle is **good.**
Mi tío está bueno.	My uncle is **in good health.**
Tú perro es malo.	Your dog is **bad.**
Tu perro está malo.	Your dog is **sick.**
La función es aburrida.	The show is **boring.**
Mi esposa está aburrida.	My wife is **bored.**
Mi hijo es listo.	My son is **smart.**
Mi hijo está listo.	My son is **ready.**
Este edificio es seguro.	This building is **safe.**
El portero está seguro.	The porter is **sure.**
Ese hombre es cerrado.	That man is **narrow-minded**.
La puerta está cerrada.	The door is **closed.**
Su hija es callada.	His daughter is **taciturn**.
La noche está callada.	The night is **silent**.

Use of *Lo* with *Estar/Ser*

In Spanish, when a question with a form of *ser* or *estar* is followed by an adjective, the neuter object pronoun *lo* replaces that adjective in the reply.

¿Estás enfermo?	Are you ill?
Sí, lo estoy.	Yes, I am.
¿Son ricos los García?	Are the Garcías rich?
Sí, lo son.	Yes, they are.

☞ Drill 7

1. ¿De dónde _____ Uds?

    (A) van   (C) son

    (B) se dirigen   (D) están

2. Esos cocos _____ de Cuba, ¿verdad?

    (A) están   (C) son

    (B) estarán   (D) sean

3. La boda _____ en la iglesia.

    (A) estuvo   (C) fue

    (B) fueron   (D) estando

4. Yo _____ dos noches en la selva.

    (A) esté   (C) estuve

    (B) era   (D) fui

5. El padre de Alicia _____ médico.

    (A) está   (C) estaba

    (B) es   (D) estará

6. Tú _____ equivocado cuando dijiste que yo no iría a la fiesta.

    (A) eres   (C) eras

    (B) estás   (D) estabas

7. Los niños han _____ tristes desde que sus padres les pro-
   hibieron ver televisión.

    (A) sido   (C) estado

    (B) sidos   (D) estados

8. El accidente _____ en la esquina, cerca de la tienda.

   (A) estuvo   (C) está

   (B) fue   (D) estaría

9. Los deportistas _____ débiles porque no han comido en tres días.

   (A) son   (C) eran

   (B) están   (D) habían sido

10. _____ posible hacer la tarea.

   (A) Serán   (C) Está

   (B) Ha sido   (D) Estaría

Drill 7—Detailed Explanations of Answers

1. **(C)** The question we most likely want to ask is "Where are you from?" The verb "ser" is used when we are talking about origin; for example, "Soy de los Estados Unidos" (I am from the United States). In our question we are not talking about where these people are, i.e., what their location is. Consequently, "están" (D) would be wrong here. "Estar" does not refer to origin but to location. "Van" (A), and "se dirigen," (B) are normally followed by the preposition "a" (to), because people "go" or "direct themselves" **to** a place, not **from** a place, as "de" would mean.

2. **(C)** The origin of people and things is expressed in the verb **ser**. The subjunctive form is not needed here.

3. **(C)** **Ser** is used for an event or time, and in this case it is singular and in the past.

4. **(C)** To answer correctly, you must understand the differences between the two verbs in Spanish which mean "to be": "ser" and "estar." Only the latter is used to refer to position or location. This immediately eliminates choice (B) "era" (the imperfect of "ser") and (D) "fui" (the preterite of "ser"). (A) "esté" is a form of "estar" but not the right one. It is the first person present of the subjunctive, and there is no reason to use a subjunctive form in this sentence. On the other hand, (C) "estuve" (I was),

the first person preterite of "estar," works fine. We have used the preterite of "estar" rather than the imperfect because we know that the action came to an end. The expression "dos noches" puts a limit on the duration of my stay in the jungle ("selva"). Therefore, "estaba" (the imperfect) should not be used here. This particular use of the preterite of "estar" means the same as "pasé" (I spent).

5. **(B)** The only correct way to translate the verb "to be" when the complement is a noun is by means of "ser" and not "estar."

6. **(D)** The primary choice is between "ser" and "estar." In the expression "to be wrong," only "estar" can be used. In addition, you have to realize that the blank has to be filled with a verb in the past to correlate with "dijiste." This eliminates (B).

7. **(C)** The first thing you should notice here is that a form of "haber" is to be followed by some form of "to be." If you analyze the problem in this way, you'll immediately eliminate (B) and (D), provided you remember that a past participle is invariable in gender and number. Now you are left with the choice between "ser" and "estar," which should go in favor of "estar" because the action (or description "to be sad") began at a certain point and is thus a deviation from the norm (not to be sad).

8. **(B)** If you chose any of the forms of "estar" you might be confusing the sense of location with the notion of occurrence or happening that is translated into Spanish with "ser." To take place ("ser") is not the same as "to be located."

9. **(B)** Now an anomalous element (not eating in three days) has been introduced in the picture of normality described in the previous question, which explains why the right choice is "están" and not any of the other forms of "ser."

10. **(B)** Impersonal expressions (the subject of the verb **to be** is **it** followed by an adjective) require the third person singular of the verb **ser** in Spanish. This would eliminate (C) and (D) since they are both from **estar** and (A) because it is plural.

PRONOUNS

Personal Pronoun Chart

Subject	Prepositional	Direct	Indirect
yo	*mí*	*me*	*me*
tú	*ti*	*te*	*te*
él	*él*	*le**	*le–a él*
ella	*ella*	*la*	*le–a ella*
ello	*ello*	*lo*	*le–a ello*
Ud.	*Ud.*		*le–a Ud.*
	sí		*(se)*
nosotros, –as	*nosotros, –as*	*nos*	*nos*
vosotros, –as	*vosotros, –as*	*os*	*os*
ellos	*ellos*	*los*	*les–a ellos*
ellas	*ellas*	*las*	*les–a ellas*
Uds.	*Uds.*		*les–a Uds.*
	sí		*(se)*

* *Le* is used to translate **him** or **you**. In Spain the direct object pronouns *lo* and *los* are often replaced by *le* and *les* when the pronoun relates to a person or to a thing personified. For the CLEP Spanish exam, one should follow the Latin American usage and avoid this substitution.

Subject Pronouns

These pronouns are usually omitted in Spanish, as the verbal form by itself indicates person and number. (For the sake of clarity, *Ud.* and *Uds.* are usually not omitted.) Naturally, subject pronouns are used when confusion would result otherwise and in order to emphasize a statement. Often the particle *mismo (misma, mismos, mismas)* is used to add emphasis.

Fue a comprar vino.
He went to buy wine.

Ud. fue a comprar vino.
You went to buy wine.

Ud. mismo fue a comprar vino.
You yourself went to buy wine.

Second Person Subject Pronouns

Tú (you, singular) differs from *usted* in terms of familiarity. *Tú* is more intimate; *usted* is more formal. As a rule of thumb, *tú* is used with those people with whom the speaker is on a first-name basis.

In certain parts of Latin America (Argentina, Uruguay, Paraguay, Central America), the form *vos* is often used instead of *tú*.

Vos comes with its own verbal forms: *Vos venís a la hora que querés (Tú vienes a la hora que quieres).* You come at whatever time it pleases you.

Vosotros (you, plural) differs from *ustedes* regionally. In Latin America and in southern Spain, *vosotros* has been replaced by *ustedes*.

Ser Followed by a Subject Pronoun

In Spanish, the subject pronoun follows "to be."

*Soy **yo.***
It is **I**.

*Fue **ella** quien me envió el regalo.*
It was **she** that sent me the present.

OBJECT PRONOUNS

The direct object pronouns answer the question "whom" or "what"; the indirect object pronouns answer the question "to (for) whom" or "to (for) what."

*Ella **me** dió un regalo.*
She gave **me** a present. (**To whom** did she give a present?)

*Nosotros **lo** vimos.*
We saw **him**. (**Whom** did we see?)

Prepositional Complement with Indirect Object Pronoun

The indirect object pronoun can be clarified or emphasized by the addition of a prepositional complement (*a* + prepositional pronoun).

*Yo **le** hablé ayer.*
Yesterday I spoke to **him/her/you**.

*Yo **le** hablé **a ella** ayer.*
Yesterday I spoke to **her**.

Special Uses of the Indirect Object Pronoun

a) **Redundant Indirect Object Pronoun**. An indirect object pronoun is used in Spanish even when the indirect object noun is present in the sentence. The latter, however, must designate a person.

Les dije a **los empleados** que trabajaran más.
I told the employees to work harder.

Common verbs of this type are: *pedir* (to ask for), *preguntar* (to ask), *dar* (to give), *decir* (to tell), *gustar* (to like), and *regalar* (to give).

¡Pídaselo a Jorge!   Ask George for it!

b) **Dative of Interest**. Indirect object pronouns are also used to represent the interested party involved in the action designated by the verb. (In these cases English uses a possessive adjective or pronoun.)

Also, when the action results in some disadvantage or loss to the person directly concerned with the action, the indirect object is used. These are usually expressed with **from + person** in English.

Me robaron la billetera.
They stole my wallet.

Le mataron al perro.
They killed his dog.

Ella siempre le esconde la medicina al paciente.
She always hides the medicine from the patient.

c) **for + person** is often expressed in Spanish by an indirect object rather than by *para + person*, particularly when a service is rendered.

Le lavé la ropa a ella.
I washed the clothes for her.

Ella me cocinó la comida.
She cooked the meal for me.

Juan nos arregló la puerta.
Juan fixed the door for us.

Exceptions: With *ser*–   *Este té es para ti.*
                              This tea is for you.

Where the indirect object is receiving a concrete object, either way is acceptable.

> *Te traje flores.* **or**
> *Traje flores para ti.*

d) **Use the definite article** and indirect object pronoun if the subject of the sentence performs an action on a part of someone else's body.

*Ella **le** lavará la cara a María.*
She will wash Mary's face (for her).

*Julio **le** cortó el pelo a su hijo.*
Julio cut his son's hair (for him).

e) **After *ser* used impersonally**, the indirect object pronoun may be employed to denote the person **to** whom the impersonal expression is applicable.

***Le** será fácil hacerlo.*
It will be easy **for him** to do it.

When Not to Use the Indirect Object Pronoun

In the following two instances, the indirect object pronoun should be avoided and the prepositional phrase used in its place.

a) **After verbs of motion** (*ir, venir, correr,* etc.)

*¡Ven **a mí**, Paco!*	Come to me, Paco!
*El niño corrió **a ellos**.*	The boy ran to them.
*¡No se acerque **a él**!*	Don't approach him!

b) **When the direct object is in the first or second person** (that is when it is **me, te, nos, os**), Spanish uses the prepositional phrase instead of the indirect object pronoun.

*Me presentaron **a él**.*
They presented **me** (D.O.) to him (prepositional phrase).

*Nos mandó **a ellos**.*
He sent **us** (D.O.) to them (prepositional phrase).

Special Uses of the Direct Object Pronoun

a) **Neuter Direct Object Pronoun**. In English the verb "to be" does not require a direct object pronoun, but in some cases both *estar* and *ser* need a **neuter** direct object pronoun to make the sentence grammatical. In these cases *lo* refers back to the whole idea expressed in the previous sentence.

¿Es Ud. médico? Sí, lo soy.
Are you a doctor? Yes, I am.

¿Estáis enfermos? No, no lo estamos.
Are you sick? No, we are not.

The neuter direct object pronoun may also be used with the verb "to know."

¿Sabes que Catalina se casó ayer? Sí, lo sé.
Do you know that Catalina got married yesterday? Yes, I know.

¿Tienes dinero que prestarme? ¡Ya lo creo!
Do you have money to lend me? You bet!

b) ***Haber* with Direct Object Pronoun**. The verb *haber* sometimes requires the use of a direct object pronoun unknown in English. Note that the direct object pronoun in the following example is no longer neuter.

¿Hay chicas en la fiesta? Sí, las hay.
Are there girls at the party? Yes, there are.

c) ***Todo* with Direct Object Pronoun**. A direct object pronoun is required before the verb when the object of the verb is *todo*. Note that the object pronoun agrees in number and gender with *todo*.

Lo he visto todo.
I have seen everything.

Las aprendí todas.
I learned them all.

d) **Verbs that contain prepositions in their meaning** (*esperar*–to wait **for**, *mirar*–to look **at**, *buscar*–to look **for**, *escuchar*–to listen **to**, etc.) will use the direct object pronouns.

La miré.
I looked at her.

Los buscaré para siempre.
I'll look for them always.

e) **Verbs used with D.O. + infinitive** = *dejar* (to let), *hacer* (to make), *ver* (to see), and *oír* (to hear).

*No **lo** dejen jugar.*
Don't let him play.

***Lo** hizo recitar.*
He made him recite.

***La** vi entrar.*
I saw her enter.

f) **Redundant direct object pronouns** are needed as follows:

1. With the noun when the object is a person or proper name.

   *Conociéndo**la** a Eloisa* . . .
   Knowing Eloisa . . .

   *Ojalá que **lo** cojan al ladrón.*
   I hope they catch the thief.

2. When the object precedes rather than follows the verb.

   La salida (D.O.) ***la** encontrará a su derecha.*
   The exit, you'll find it to your right.

Position of Object Pronouns in the Sentence

Unlike English, object pronouns in Spanish precede the conjugated verb (see examples above). However, they are attached at the end of the verb when the verbal form is an affirmative command, an infinitive, or a present participle.

*Ud. **le** escribe.* You write **to him.**	conjugated—present tense
*¡Escríba**le**! (or) ¡Escríb**ele**!* Write **to him!** (or her)	positive command
*Uds. **la** perdonaron.* You forgave **her.**	conjugated—preterite tense
*Hubo que perdonar**la**.* It was necessary to forgive **her.**	infinitive
***Los** dejó sobre la mesa.* He left **them** on the table.	conjugated—preterite tense
*Salió dejándo**los** sobre la mesa.* He went out leaving **them** on the table.	present participle

Note: When the infinitive or the present participle is subordinated to an auxiliary verb such as *querer, ir, poder,* or *estar,* the direct object pronoun can go before these verbs or after, and attached to the infinitive or present participle:

I'm going to see **him.**	*Voy a ver**lo.***
I'm going to see **him.**	***Lo** voy a ver.*
I'm looking at **her.**	***La** estoy mirando.*
I'm looking at **her.**	*Estoy mirán**dola.***

Syntactic Order of Object Pronouns

When a verb has two object pronouns, the indirect object pronoun precedes the direct object pronoun.

Envían una carta.	They send a letter.
***Nos** envían una carta.*	They send a letter **to us.**
***Nos la** envían.*	They send **it to us.**
*¡Envíen**nosla!***	Send **it to us!**
*¡No **nos la** envíen!*	Don't send **it to us!**

But when the two object pronouns in the sentence are third person pronouns, the **indirect** object pronoun (*le* or *les*) is replaced by *se.*

Escribes una carta.	You write a letter.
***Les** escribes una carta.*	You write a letter **to them.**
***Se la** escribes.*	You write **it to them.**
*¡Escríbe**sela!***	Write **it to them!**

Prepositional Pronouns

Prepositions are words or phrases that relate words to one another. They may be followed by nouns, pronouns, or verbs (in the infinitive form in Spanish).

Here is a basic list of prepositions:

a	to, at	*excepto**	except
bajo	under	*hacia*	toward
como*	like	*hasta*	until, as far as, to
con**	with	*menos**	except
contra	against	*para*	for
de	from, of	*por*	for
desde	from, since	*salvo**	except
durante	during	*según**	according to
en	in, at, on	*sin*	without
entre*	between, among	*sobre*	on, upon, over, above

*These prepositions are used with **subject** pronouns, not the prepositional group.

> *según él y yo*   according to him and me

**With this preposition the prepositional pronouns *mí, ti*, and *sí* combine to form *conmigo, contigo, consigo*. These combinations are invariable; there are no plural or feminine forms.

Here is a basic list of compound prepositions:

además de	besides	*encima de*	on top of
alrededor de	around	*en cuanto a*	in regard to
antes de	before	*enfrente de*	in front of
a pesar de	in spite of	*en lugar de*	instead of
cerca de	near	*en vez de*	instead of
debajo de	under	*frente a*	in front of
delante de	in front of	*fuera de*	outside of
dentro de	within	*lejos de*	far from
después de	after (time)	*para con**	toward
detrás de	behind	*por + inf*	because of

*To show an attitude toward, as in "*Es muy cariñoso (para) con su mujer.*"

Use of *Sí, Consigo*

Sí is a special prepositional form of the pronoun *se*. It is often combined with a form of *mismo (–a, –os, –as)* to express "self." Note the difference between these two examples.

> *Ella no se refiere a sí misma.*
> She is not referring to herself.

> vs.

> *Ella no se refiere a ella.*
> She is not referring to her (someone else).

> *Están disgustados consigo mismos.*
> They are disgusted with themselves.

> vs.

> *Están disgustados con ellos.*
> They are disgusted with them (others).

Use of *Ello*

Ello means **it** when referring to situations or statements, but not to nouns.

Todo fue horrible; no prefiero hablar de ello.
It was all horrible; I prefer not to talk about it.

Para vs. *Por*

In general, *por* expresses the ideas contained in "for the sake of," "through," "exchange"; whereas *para* expresses destination, purpose, end, intention.

a) *Por* means "through"; *para* refers to destination.

*Iba **por** el parque.*	I was walking **through** the park.
*Iba **para** el parque.*	I was **on** my **way to** the park.

b) *Por* refers to motive; *para* to purpose or end.

*Lo hizo **por** mí.*
He did it **for** me (for my sake, on my behalf).

*El artesano hizo una vasija **para** mí.*
The artisan made a vase **for** me.

c) *Por* expresses the idea of exchange.

*Lo cambié **por** una camisa.*   I exchanged it **for** a shirt.

d) *Por* denotes a span of time; *para* designates an endpoint in time.

*Los exiliados caminaron **por** tres días y tres noches.*
The exiles walked **for** (during, for the space of) three days and three nights.

*El traje estará listo **para** el lunes.*
The suit will be ready by Monday.

e) *Para* translates "in order to."

*Fui a su casa **para** hablar con él.*
I went to his house **in order to** speak to him.

f) *Por* and *para* have set meanings in certain idiomatic constructions.

por *ejemplo*	**for** example
por lo menos	at least
para *siempre*	**for**ever
No es **para** *tanto.*	It's not that serious.

g) Other expressions using *por*.

por ahora	for now
por avión	by plane
por consiguiente	consequently
por desgracia	unfortunately
por ejemplo	for example
por encima	on top of
por escrito	in writing
por eso	therefore
por fin	finally
por lo común	generally
por lo contrario	on the contrary
por lo general	generally
por regla general	as a general rule
por lo tanto	consequently
por lo visto	apparently
por otra parte	on the other hand
por poco	almost
por si acaso	in case
por supuesto	of course
por teléfono	by phone
por todas partes	everywhere

Idioms with *A, De, En, Sin*

a) Idioms with *a*

a caballo	on horseback
a casa/en casa	at home
a causa de	because of
a eso de	at about (with time)
a fines de	at the end of
a fondo	thoroughly
a fuerza de	by dint of
a la derecha	to the right
a la izquierda	to the left

a la orden	at your service
a la vez	at the same time
a lo largo (de)	in the long run
a lo lejos	in the distance
a lo menos (al menos)	at least
a mano	by hand
a mas tardar	at the latest
a mediados (de)	in the middle
a menudo	often
a mi parecer	in my opinion
a pie	on foot
a pierna suelta	without a care
a principios de	at the beginning of
a saltos	by leaps and bounds
a solas	alone
a tiempo	on time
a través de	across
a veces	at times
a la española (francesa, etc.)	in the Spanish/French way
a la larga	in the long run
a la semana	per week
al aire libre	outside
al amanecer	at dawn
al anochecer	at nightfall
al cabo	finally
al contrario	on the contrary
al día	up to date
al fin	finally
al lado de	next to
al parecer	apparently
al por mayor	wholesale
al por menor	retail
al principio	at first

b) Idioms with *de*

de antemano	ahead of time
de arriba	upstairs
de balde	freely
de broma	jokingly
de buena gana	willingly
de cuando (vez) en cuando	from time to time

de día (noche)	by day, at night
de día en día	from day to day
de esta (esa) manera	in this (that) way
de este (ese) modo	in this (that) way
de hoy (ahora) en adelante	from today (now) on
de mala gana	unwillingly
de mal humor	in a bad mood
de manera que/de modo que	so that
de memoria	by heart
de moda	in style
de nada	you're welcome
de ninguna manera/de ningún modo	by no means
de nuevo	again
de otro modo	otherwise
(abrir) de par en par	(to open) wide
de pie	standing
de prisa	in a hurry
de pronto/de repente	suddenly
de rodillas	kneeling
de todos modos	anyway
de uno en uno	one by one
de veras	really

c) Idioms with *en*

en bicicleta	by bike
en broma	jokingly
en cambio	on the other hand
en caso de	in case of
en contra de	against
en cuanto	as soon as
en cuanto a	as for, in regard to
en efecto	in effect
en este momento	at this time
en lugar (vez) de	instead of
en marcha	under way, on the way
en medio de	in the middle of
en ninguna parte	nowhere
en punto	sharp (telling time)
en seguida	at once
en suma	in short, in a word

en todas partes	everywhere
en vano	in vain
en voz alta (baja)	in a loud (low) voice

d) Idioms with *sin*

sin aliento	out of breath
sin cuento	endless
sin cuidado	carelessly
sin duda	without a doubt
sin ejemplo	unparalleled
sin embargo	nevertheless
sin falta	without fail
sin fondo	bottomless
sin novedad	same as usual

Verbs with Prepositions

a) Verbs with *con*

amenazar	to threaten to
casarse	to get married to
contar (ue)	to rely on
cumplir	to keep (one's word)
encontrarse (ue)	to run into by chance
enojarse	to get angry with
estar de acuerdo	to agree with
meterse	to pick a quarrel with
quedarse	to keep
soñar (ue)	to dream about
tropezar (ie)	to meet by chance with

b) Verbs with *en*

apoyarse	to lean on
confiar (í)	to trust in
consentir (ie, i)	to consent to
consistir	to consist of
convenir	to agree to/on
convertirse (ie, i)	to become, change into
empeñarse	to insist on
especializarse	to major in
fijarse en	to notice, stare at
influir	to influence

insistir	to insist on
meterse	to get involved in
pensar (ie)	to think about
reparar	to notice
quedar	to agree to
tardar	to delay in

c) Verbs with *de*

acabar de + inf	*Acabo de comer.*	I just ate.
	Acababa de comer.	I'd just eaten.
	Acabé de comer.	I finished eating.

acordarse (ue)	to remember
alegrarse	to be glad
alejarse	to go away from
apoderarse	to take possession of
aprovecharse	to take advantage of
arrepentirse (ie, i)	to repent
avergonzarse (ue)*	to be ashamed
burlarse	to make fun of
carecer	to lack
constar	to consist of
cuidar	to take care of
darse cuenta	to realize
dejar	to stop (doing something)
depender	to depend on
despedirse (i, i)	to say good-bye to
disfrutar	to enjoy
enamorarse	to fall in love with
encargarse	to take charge of
enterarse	to find out about
fiarse (í)	to trust
gozar	to enjoy
olvidarse	to forget about
oír hablar	to hear about
pensar (ie)	to think about
preocuparse	to be worried about
quejarse	to complain about
reírse (í, i)**	to laugh at
servir (i, i)	to serve as
servirse (i, i)	to make use of
tratar	to try to + inf.
tratarse	to be a question of

*This verb will have a dieresis mark over the *ü* in the present indicative and subjunctive, in all forms except *nosotros* and *vosotros*: *me avergüenzo,* but *nos avergonzamos*

**This verb is conjugated as follows:

Present Indicative	Present Subjunctive	Preterite	Imperfect Subjunctive
me río	me ría	me reí	me riera/se
te ríes	te rías	te reíste	te rieras/ses
se ríe	se ría	se rió	se riera/se
nos reímos	nos riamos	nos reímos	nos riéramos/semos
os reís	os riáis	os reísteis	os rierais/seis
se ríen	se rían	se rieron	se rieran/sen

Present Participle: *riendo*

Past Participle: *reído*

Formal Commands: *ríase, no se ría   ríanse, no se rían*

Familiar Commands: *ríete, no te rías reíos, no os riáis*

d) Verbs with *por*

acabar	to end up by
dar	to consider, to regard as
esforzarse (ue)	to make an effort
interesarse	to be interested in
preguntar + person	to ask for (a person)
tomar	to take (someone) for

e) Verbs with *a*

Verbs of beginning, learning, and motion are followed by an *a* in Spanish.

Beginning	Learning	
comenzar (ie) a	*aprender a*	to learn
echarse a	*enseñar a*	to teach
empezar (ie) a		
ponerse a		
principiar a		

Motion

acercarse a	to approach
apresurarser a	to hurry to
dirigirse a	to go toward
ir a	to go to
regresar a	to return to
salir a	to leave to
subir a	to go up
venir a	to come to
volver a (ue)	to return to

Other verbs followed by *a*:

acertar (ie) a	to happen to
acostumbrarse a	to become used to
alcanzar a	to succeed in (doing something)
asistir a	to attend
asomarse a	to appear at
aspirar a	to aspire to
atreverse a	to dare to
ayudar a	to help
condenar a	to condemn to
convidar a	to invite to
cuidar a	to take care of (person)
decidirse a	to decide to
dedicarse a	to devote oneself to
detenerse a	to pause to
disponerse a	to get ready to
exponerse a	to run the risk of
invitar a	to invite to
jugar (ue) a	to play (game)
negarse (ie) a	to refuse to
obligar a	to obligate to
oler (ue) a*	to smell like
parecerse a	to resemble
querer (ie) a	to love
resignarse a	to resign oneself to
saber a	to taste like
ser aficionado, –a a	to be fond (a fan) of
someter a	to submit to
sonar a	to sound like
volver (ue) a + verb	to (do something) again

*This verb in the present indicative and subjunctive (except for *nosotros* and *vosotros*) will begin with "h." *El huele a ajo.* He smells like garlic.

Conjunctions

Conjunctions are words or phrases that connect clauses to one another. The following is a basic list of conjunctions:

o (u)	or
y (e)	and
pero, mas, sino que	but
ni	nor, neither
que	that
si	if, whether

Uses of the Basic Conjunctions

a) *O* changes to *u* in front of words beginning with *o* or *ho:*

   *No sé si lo dijo Roberto **u** Horacio.*
   I don't know whether Roberto **or** Horacio said it.

b) *Y* changes to *e* in front of words beginning with *i* or *hi:*

   *Padre **e** hijo viajaban juntos.*
   Father **and** son were traveling together.

   Note: *Y* does not change in front of *y* or *hie:*

*fuego **y** hielo*	fire **and** ice.
*Tú **y** yo.*	You **and** I.

Pero vs. *Sino*

Pero, mas, and *sino* mean "but." (*Mas* with an accent mark, however, is an adverb meaning "more.") *Pero* and *mas* are interchangeable, but *pero* and *sino* have different uses. *Sino* (or *sino que*) has the sense of "rather" or "on the contrary." For *sino* or *sino que* to be used, the first part of the sentence must be negative.

No dije roca **sino** foca.
I didn't say "rock" **but** "seal."

*No vino para quedarse **sino que** vino y se fue.**
She didn't come to stay **but** came and left.

*Mi abuelo ya murió **pero** me dejó un buen recuerdo.*
My grandfather already died **but** he left me good memories.

*When the contrast is between clauses with different verb forms, *que* is introduced.

Correlative Conjunctions

Conjunctions such as *ni...ni* (see above) are not uncommon in Spanish. Other pairs are:

o . . . o	either . . . or
ya . . . ya	whether . . . or, sometimes . . . sometimes
no sólo . . . sino también	not only . . . but also

Decídete. O te vas o haces lo que te digo.
Make up your mind. **Either** you leave **or** you do as I say.

Ella no sólo gana el dinero sino que también lo gasta.
She not only earns the money but also spends it.

Conjunctive Phrases

Some conjunctions may require the use of the subjunctive. (See subjunctive–the adverbial clause.) The others follow:

apenas . . . cuando	hardly . . . when
a pesar de que	in spite of
conque	so then, and so, then
desde que	since
empero	however
entretanto que	meanwhile
más bien que	rather than
mientras tanto	meanwhile
no bien . . . cuando	no sooner . . . than
no obstante	notwithstanding

☞ Drill 8

1. Mi viejo amigo Fernando trabaja _____ la Compañía Equis.

    (A) por   (C) cerca

    (B) a   (D) para

2. Miguelín _____ trajo café de Colombia.

   (A) ti   (C) mí

   (B) nos   (D) ella

3. _____ a él, no a ella.

   (A) Le parecen   (C) Se negaron

   (B) Se lo enseñaron   (D) Los vieron

4. Ayer compré unas sillas nuevas; son muy elegantes y juegan bien con los otros muebles. Son nuevecitas y no quiero que la gente se siente en _____.

   (A) las   (C) les

   (B) ellas   (D) ella

5. María me dijo un secreto. _____ dijo el otro día.

   (A) Me lo   (C) Me los

   (B) Lo me   (D) No me lo

6. Cuando entramos en el dormitorio, nos dimos cuenta de que los ladrones sólo habían robado nuestras corbatas nuevas. _____ llevaron toditas.

   (A) Las nos   (C) Se las

   (B) Nos la   (D) Me la

7. Invité a Carmela a que fuera _____.

   (A) conmigo   (C) con yo

   (B) con mi   (D) de aquí

8. Siempre al comer me gusta el pan con mucha mantequilla. A la mesa tengo que decirles a los otros que _____.

   (A) me pasen   (C) me la pasen

   (B) pásenmela   (D) se la pasen

9. —Mamá, prepáreme la comida. Ella me dice, _____.

    (A) "Te lo estoy preparando."

    (B) "Estoy preparándotela."

    (C) "La te preparo."

    (D) "Prepárotela."

10. Como era natural, el perro salió _____ la puerta.

    (A) para   (C) a

    (B) por   (D) de

11. Raúl no entendía el subjuntivo; el profesor _____.

    (A) se lo explicó   (C) lo explica

    (B) se los explica (D) los explicó

12. Nuestros enemigos están trabajando _____.

    (A) con nos   (C) contra nosotros

    (B) contra nos   (D) connos

13. La silla estaba _____ la mesa.

    (A) antes de   (C) en cuanto a

    (B) detrás de   (D) después de

14. Mi novia quería casarse conmigo pero nunca _____ dijo.

    (A) se le   (C) me lo

    (B) se lo   (D) lo me

15. Al presidente _____ trataron de asesinar hace varios años.

    (A) se   (C) ello

    (B) lo   (D) les

16. Carmen es muy bella. Ayer _____ vi.

    (A) la   (C) les

    (B) lo   (D) se

17. Me pidieron que _____ entregara el informe directamente al jefe.

    (A) lo

    (B) le

    (C) se

    (D) la

18. El fugitivo ha regresado; yo mismo _____ vi.

    (A) lo

    (B) te

    (C) les

    (D) se

19. Él _____ dio un beso al despedirse.

    (A) lo

    (B) la

    (C) le

    (D) se

20. Este político sabe mucho _____ la poca educación que tiene.

    (A) a causa de

    (B) para

    (C) por

    (D) porque

21. Todos mis amigos van al mercado menos _____.

    (A) mí

    (B) mi

    (C) conmigo

    (D) yo

22. Ella no es alta _____ baja.

    (A) pero

    (B) sino

    (C) también

    (D) sino que

23. Yo no conozco al niño _____ me gusta su coche nuevo.

    (A) pero

    (B) sino

    (C) pero que

    (D) sino que

24. Ella siempre _____ esconde su dinero a mi madre y a mí.

    (A) nos

    (B) le

    (C) les

    (D) los

25. No puedo ver a mis amigas; tengo que _____.

    (A) buscarles   (C) buscarlas

    (B) las buscar   (D) las busco

26. Fue horrible; prefiero no pensar en _____.

    (A) lo   (C) ella

    (B) él   (D) ello

27. Esta taza es _____ el café. ¡Démela, por favor!

    (A) por   (C) en

    (B) para   (D) con

28. La semana pasada me quedé en casa _____ tres días.

    (A) por   (C) en

    (B) para   (D) de

29. ¿Cuánto dinero me dará Ud. _____ mi trabajo?

    (A) por   (C) de

    (B) en   (D) para

30. _____ el viernes tenemos esta lección.

    (A) En   (C) Para

    (B) Por   (D) De

Drill 8—Detailed Explanations of Answers

1. **(D)** To work **for**, in the sense of "to be employed by," requires the use of "para" rather than "por." For this reason, (A) is wrong, but (D) is right. Thinking that you wanted to say "at," you might have mistakenly chosen answer (B), but the word "a" normally means "at" only when it follows verbs of motion: "Tiró la pelota a la pared" (He threw the ball at the wall). When motion is not involved, we use the preposition "en" to mean "at": "Mi madre está en el mercado" (My mother is at the market). Choice (C) is wrong because "near to" is "cerca **de**" and not simply "cerca."

2. **(B)** In the sentence, the verb "trajo" is the third person preterite of "traer" (to bring). We know that Miguelín brought someone coffee, i.e., Miguelín brought coffee **to** someone. The indirect object pronouns, which mean "to" or "for," are "me" (to or for me), "te" (to or for you, familiar singular), "le" (to or for him, her, you, polite singular), "nos" (to or for us), "os" (to or for you, familiar plural), and "les" (to or for them, you, polite plural). In the list of possible answers, we encounter only one pronoun from this list, "nos." In (A), we see the second person singular familiar form of the prepositional pronoun, i.e., a pronoun which is used following a preposition. Since there is no preposition this choice is incorrect.

3. **(B)** Choice (A) is incorrect because "parecerse a" (to resemble) requires a reflexive pronoun, but we are given the third person singular indirect object pronoun. In (C), we find the reflexive form of "negar," which is used in the idiomatic expression "negarse a" + infinitive (to refuse to). The "a" in our sentence, however, is not followed by an infinitive, but rather by a prepositional pronoun, "él." In (D), we have used the third person plural masculine form of the direct object pronoun. Since we are referring to "él" (him), for this to be correct, we would have to use the masculine singular form of that pronoun, "lo." (B) is correct. It says, "Se lo enseñaron" (They showed or taught it to him). Observe the two object pronouns at the beginning of this answer. Remember that if we have two third person object pronouns (the first indirect, the second direct), the first of these automatically changes to "se." In our sentence, then, the "Se" would actually stand for the word "le." English speakers might question why the indirect object pronoun appears here since later in the sentence we find the prepositional phrase "a él," which means "to him." Nevertheless, the redundant use of the indirect object pronoun is typical of Spanish style, even though there may be a prepositional phrase later in the sentence which explicitly states the same idea.

4. **(B)** After a preposition, the object pronoun is expressed by the subject pronoun with the exception of the first and second persons singular. In this case, **ellas** is plural and would be the only correct answer because it refers to "chairs."

5. **(A)** The indirect object pronoun always precedes the direct. Both precede the verb unless this is in the infinitive. **Me lo** is the only correct answer because **lo** refers to **secreto**. Choice (D), although grammatically correct, does not follow the train of information given in the first sentence.

6. **(C)**   The passive voice in Spanish can be translated by the reflexive **se**, and choice (C) is the only possible one because **las** refers to **corbatas**. (A) has the plural **las**, but the indirect object does not precede the direct.

7. **(A)**   The first and second persons singular with the preposition **con** are always **conmigo** and **contigo**. Occasionally **consigo** is used, meaning **con él, con ella,** or **con usted**. The verb **invitar** is one of the verbs which, when followed by a change in subject, requires the subjunctive, and in this case, it is in the past. **Fuera** is the imperfect subjunctive form of **ir**.

8. **(C)**   The indirect object pronoun always precedes the direct. In this case, the subjunctive is required because of the verb **decir**, as a request with a change of subject. The **la** refers to **mantequilla**. (A), (B), and (C) have **me**, but only (C) includes both the indirect and the direct objects in their proper position.

9. **(B)**   The use of the auxiliary **estar** is correct with the present participle. The indirect and direct objects are joined in that order following the present participle. **Te** is used because the familiar form is appropriate, and the **la** refers to **comida**.

10. **(B)**   **Por** is correct. It is the correct word for "through" in this context.

11. **(A)**   The indirect object pronoun **le** is changed to **se** when used in conjunction with a direct object pronoun. **Lo**, in this sentence, refers to the subjunctive in the sentence. Choice (C) is a remote possibility, but is not totally correct grammatically.

12. **(C)**   After a preposition, the subject pronoun should be used except for the first and second persons singular. Our enemies are supposedly working "against us," so choice (C) is the only correct answer.

13. **(B)**   The preposition "antes de," in (A), means "before." It refers to time, not location. The sentence is talking about the position of the "chair" ("silla"). If we meant "before" in the sense of "in front of," we would have to use the preposition "delante de." The contrary of "delante de" is "detrás de" (behind, in back of), which fits well in our sentence. In (D), "después de" (after), we have another preposition which refers to time, not location. In (C) "en cuanto a" means "about" in the sense of "concerning."

14. **(C)**   Neither of the first two choices can be the correct answer because in both "se" refers to a third person not to be found in the question. Choice (D) has the right object pronouns but in the wrong order. Choice (C) is the right answer because it contains the appropriate indirect object pronoun ("she said **to me**) and direct object pronoun ("she said **it** to me) in the correct sequence.

15. **(B)**   The correct answer is the only direct object pronoun available. This is a peculiar but common use of the pronoun, which wouldn't be necessary if the sentence were in the normal syntactic order, namely, with the subject in front (an implicit "ellos") and the direct object ("presidente") in back. When the usual order is inverted, then a redundant object pronoun must be introduced.

16. **(A)**   The question calls for a direct object pronoun. Of the two available, you need to choose the feminine form to go with "Carmen."

17. **(B)**   This question calls for the indirect object pronoun, which you have to identify (there is only one) from the choices offered. The reason for this type of pronoun is that Spanish tends to reinforce the indirect object ("jefe") when it refers to a person.

18. **(A)**   Here you need a direct object pronoun that refers to "el fugitivo" and the only possibility among the four choices is "lo."

19. **(C)**   The direct object in this sentence is "un beso" and since it is present in the phrase there is no need for a direct object pronoun (such as "lo" or "la"). What the sentence does need is an indirect object pronoun referring to the implicit person (or pet or whatever) in the statement.

20. **(B)**   "Para" is used whenever the idea of "considering" is implied.

21. **(D)**   After certain prepositions (menos, excepto, salvo, entre, como, and según), subject pronouns are used in Spanish. Therefore, choice (A), which is prepositional, is incorrect. Choice (B) means "my" and choice (C) means "with me."

22. **(B)**   "Sino" has the sense of "rather" or "on the contrary" and is used as the conjunction in a negative sentence where the second part directly contradicts the first. It is important to note that direct contradictions must be between equal parts of speech, in this case, between the adjectives "alta" and "baja." Choice (A) is incorrect because it cannot be

used where a direct contradiction is implied. Choice (C) "also" makes no sense in this context. Choice (D) is used when the direct contradiction is between two conjugated verbs (i.e., Ella no quiere sentarse sino que quiere levantarse.)

23. **(A)**   Even though the first part of this sentence is negative, the second part is not a direct contradiction of the first. Therefore, choice (B) and (D) are incorrect. Choice (C) "pero que" (but that) makes no sense.

24. **(A)**   When the action results in some disadvantage or loss ("hides") to the person directly concerned with the action, the indirect object pronoun is used. In English these statements are commonly expressed with **from + person**. Choice (A) is correct because the indirect object must correlate with the phrase "a mi madre y a mí," which is equivalent to **us**. Choices (B) "to him," (C) "to them," and (D) "to you" are also indirect object pronouns but do not correlate with the previously mentioned phrase.

25. **(C)**   Verbs which include a preposition in their meaning (buscar–to look for, esperar–to wait for, mirar–to look at) are used with direct object pronouns. Choice (A) is incorrect because it has an indirect object pronoun. Choice (C) has the correct direct object pronoun but it is incorrectly placed. Choice (D) is incorrect because the conjugated verb "busco" cannot follow "tengo que," which requires the use of the infinitive.

26. **(D)**   The neuter pronoun "ello" (it) is used to refer to entire happenings, events, or occurrences previously alluded to. Choice (A) is a direct object pronoun and cannot be used after a preposition. Choices (B) "he/it (m)" and (C) "she/it (f)" are incorrect since there is no reference to anything specific that is either masculine or feminine in gender.

27. **(B)**   To indicate what something is intended for, use **para**. The intended use of the cup is for coffee.

28. **(A)**   **Por** is used to express a length of time. In this example, the length of time is three days.

29. **(A)**   **Por** is used when "in exchange for" is intended. In this sample it is money in exchange for work.

30. **(C)**   **Para** is used to express some point in future time. In this sample the future time indicated is Friday.

GUSTAR

Gustar and verbs like it follow a certain pattern that is unlike English. These verbs are commonly used in the third person singular and plural in conjunction with the indirect object pronoun group.

Gustar's Pattern

Because *gustar* means "to be pleasing to," its translation into Spanish from the English "to like" will require setting the verb up according to the following pattern:

I like cars. = Cars **are pleasing** to me.
= *Me **gustan** los coches.*

In the example given, after rearranging the sentence to fit the Spanish pattern, the indirect object surfaces (to me). In addition, one can see that the new subject (cars) will require using the verb in the third person plural. The following chart shows the indirect object pronoun group with **all** six persons "explained" with the prepositional phrase.

me	– a mí	nos	– a nosotros
te	– a ti	vos	– a vosotros
le	– a él	les	– a ellos
le	– a ella	les	– a ellas
le	– a Ud.	les	– a Uds.

This additional prepositional phrase that can accompany each of the indirect object pronouns can be used to:

1. further emphasize the indirect pronoun itself.

   *A **mí** me gusta la música clásica.*
   I **really** like classical music.

2. further clarify the meaning of le/les.

   *A **ella** le gustaban las películas de horror.*
   She liked horror movies.

3. provide a place to put names/nouns/proper nouns.

   *A **Juan** le gustará ir al cine conmigo.*
   Juan will like to go to the movies with me.

   *A **los chicos** les gustan los coches.*
   Boys like cars.

"*Gustar*" Types

Verbs that follow the "*gustar* pattern":

agradar	to be pleasing	*Nos agrada ir.* It pleases us to go.
bastar	to be enough	*Me basta un traje.* One suit is enough for me.
doler (ue)	to be painful	*Me duele la cabeza.* My head aches.
parecer	to seem	*A él le parece imposible.* It seems impossible to him.
placer	to be pleasing	*Nos place verte.* It pleases us to see you.
quedar	to have left	*Me quedó un buen libro.* I had one good book left.
sobrar	to be left over	*Les sobran tres dólares.* They have $3.00 left over.
tocar	to be one's turn	*A María le toca.* It's Mary's turn.

"To Need"

"To need" can be expressed three ways: *faltar, hacer falta,* and *necesitar.*

I need a car.	*Me falta un coche.* *Me hace falta un coche.* *Necesito un coche.*
I needed a car.	*Me faltó/faltaba un coche.* *Me hizo/hacía falta un coche.* *Necesité/Necesitaba un coche.*

Note: The verb "*faltar/hacer falta*" is commonly used in the present, preterite, and imperfect tenses. If one needs to express "need" in other tenses, use *necesitar.*

☞ **Drill 9**

1. A Roberto _____ gusta ir a la playa todos los días durante el verano.

   (A) se
   (B) os
   (C) le
   (D) te

2. _____ chico le gusta jugar al tenis.

   (A) El
   (B) Al
   (C) A
   (D) nothing needed

3. A Rob y a mí _____ el helado.

   (A) les gusta
   (B) les gustan
   (C) nos gusta
   (D) nos gustan

4. Me encanta _____ dinero.

   (A) gastar
   (B) gastando
   (C) gastaré
   (D) pasar

5. _____ falta dos dólares.

   (A) Me hace
   (B) Me hacen
   (C) Me haces
   (D) Me hago

6. ¿A quiénes _____ toca?

   (A) lo
   (B) le
   (C) les
   (D) los

7. A mis amigos _____ el chocolate.

   (A) les gustó
   (B) les gustaron
   (C) le gustó
   (D) nos gustó

8. _____ nos encantó la cuidad.

    (A) A María   (C) A vosotros

    (B) A las mujeres   (D) A los niños y a mí

9. A José _____ dos cursos difíciles.

    (A) le bastará   (C) se bastarán

    (B) le bastarán   (D) bastarán

10. A Juan no le importaba _____.

    (A) los coches   (C) estudiando

    (B) ir al cine   (D) a trabajar

Drill 9—Detailed Explanations of Answers

1. **(C)** Normally, with the verb "gustar" and similar verbs, we use indirect object pronouns (me, te, le, nos, os, les). Although we usually translate "gustar" to mean "to like," we should remember that it literally means "to be pleasing **to**." This explains the use of "A" before "Roberto" in the sentence. It is pleasing "**to** Roberto." The indirect object pronoun can mean "to" or "for." It is for this reason that the indirect object pronoun is required here. Because "Roberto" is a singular noun, we must then use the third person singular indirect object pronoun "le."

2. **(B)** "Gustar" type verbs use indirect object pronouns, which can be further clarified by using prepositional phrases. These phrases begin with "a" and normally precede the indirect object pronoun that they go with. Choice (A) is incorrect because the preposition "a" is required. Choice (C) is missing the article "el" which is needed before the noun "chico."

3. **(C)** The "a" phrase contains the hint as to which indirect object pronoun to select. By including "me" with "Rob" the corresponding pronoun is "we" (nos). The verb is singular because the noun "helado" is singular. Choices (A) and (B) have the incorrect object pronoun. Choice (D) has the incorrect form of "gustar."

4. **(A)** If a verb follows any verb used like "gustar," it must be in the gerund form (infinitive) since it is acting as the actual subject of the

statement. Choices (B) the present participle and (C) the future tense are both in the incorrect form. Choice (D), although it is an infinitive, is incorrect because this verb means to spend "time" not "money."

5. **(B)** The main verb in this expression (hacer), which means "to need" must match the item(s) needed. In this case two dollars are needed, which is plural. Answer (A) is singular and will not match the subject. Answer (C) the "tú" form of the verb and answer (D) the "yo" form of the verb **hacer** are not acceptable forms of this verb when used in this manner. It must either be third singular or third plural.

6. **(C)** This "gustar" type means "to be one's turn." The prepositional phrase ("a quiénes) contains the hint as to which indirect object pronoun to select. Choices (A) and (D) are direct object pronouns and are not used with "gustar" types. Choice (B) is singular and will not match "a quiénes."

7. **(A)** Because the noun "chocolate" is singular, a singular form of **gustar** is required. The prepositional phrase "A mis amigos" corresponds to the indirect object pronoun "les," Choice (B) is incorrect because the verb is plural. Choices (C) and (D) have the incorrect I.O. pronouns.

8. **(D)** Because the indirect object pronoun "nos" has been used in this sentence, the corresponding prepositional phrase must match it. "A María" (A) would require "le," "A las mujeres" (B) would require "les," and "A vosotros" (C) would require using "os."

9. **(B)** The verb must be plural to match "dos cursos difíciles," and the indirect object pronoun must correspond to the prepositional phrase "A José." Choice (A) has the incorrect verb form. Choice (C) has a reflexive pronoun, and (D) is missing the indirect object pronoun entirely.

10. **(B)** After the verb "importaba" either an infinitive or a singular noun may be used. Choice (A) has a plural noun, and (C) is the present participle of "estudiar." Choice (D) has an additional "a" before the infinitive, which is unnecessary.

DEMONSTRATIVES: ADJECTIVES/PRONOUNS

These two groups share identical forms except that the accent mark is used over the pronouns.

Adjective		Pronoun	
this	*este, esta*	this one	*éste, ésta*
that	*ese, esa*	that one	*ése, ésa*
that*	*aquel, aquella*	that one*	*aquél, aquélla*
these	*estos, estas*	these	*éstos, éstas*
those	*esos, esas*	those	*ésos, ésas*
those*	*aquellos, aquellas*	those*	*aquéllos, aquéllas*

*These demonstratives are used to indicate greater distance from the speaker as well as distance in time. *Ése* (etc.) refers to something near the listener but removed from the speaker, whereas *aquél* (etc.) refers to something far from **both** the speaker and listener.

En aquella época . . .	At that time . . .
Aquellas montañas . . .	Those mountains . . .

Note: The definite article (*el, la, los, las*) followed by *de* or *que* is often translated as a pronoun.

*mi corbata y **la de** mi hermano*
my tie and **that of** my brother

*Este libro y **el que** tiene Juan son interesantes.*
This book and **the one that** Juan has are interesting.

NEUTER FORMS

The neuter forms (*eso, esto, aquello*) are used when the gender is not determined or when referring to vague or general ideas. These words do not vary in gender or number.

¿Qué es esto?
What is this?

Estoy enfermo y esto me enoja.
I'm ill and this makes me angry.

Former and Latter

The pronoun *éste* (*–a, –os, –as*) is used to translate **the latter** (the latest or most recently mentioned), while *aquél* (*–la, –los, –las*) expresses **the former** (the most remotely mentioned).

Juana and Pablo are siblings; the former is a doctor, the latter is a dentist.

Juana y Pablo son hermanos; éste es dentista, aquélla es doctora.

Note: In English we say "the former and the latter," but in Spanish this order is reversed.

☞ Drill 10

1. Querida, ¿no crees que _____ anillo es tan lindo como los otros?

   (A) esto
   (C) este

   (B) aquello
   (D) esa

2. Mis nietos me regalaron _____ televisor.

   (A) eso
   (C) aquel

   (B) esto
   (D) esté

3. Muéstreme otro apartamento, no me gusta _____.

   (A) esto
   (C) esté

   (B) este
   (D) éste

4. _____ problemas son fáciles de resolver.

   (A) Estos
   (C) Estas

   (B) Estes
   (D) Esas

5. Llegó tarde y _____ me hace enojar.

   (A) eso
   (C) esta

   (B) ésta
   (D) aquel

6. ¿Qué es _____ ?

    (A) éste   (C) ésto

    (B) esto   (D) ésta

7. Estas camisas y _____ a lo lejos son caras.

    (A) ésos   (C) aquellas

    (B) aquéllas   (D) ésas

8. Rolando y Antonia son hermanos; ésta es alta y _____ es inteligente.

    (A) este   (C) aquél

    (B) aquel   (D) ése

9. Me gustan _____ guantes porque son de cuero.

    (A) cstos   (C) estas

    (B) éstos   (D) éstas

10. Mi corbata y _____ Juan son de seda.

    (A) ella de   (C) éste de

    (B) ésa de   (D) la de

Drill 10—Detailed Explanations of Answers

1.   **(C)**   The masculine demonstrative adjective "este" means "this" and should be used to modify a masculine singular noun, just as is required by the sentence. "Esto" (this) in (A) and "aquello" (that) in (B) are pronouns, not adjectives, and they are neuter, i.e., they are neither masculine or feminine. The neuter pronouns "esto," "eso" (that), and "aquello" (that) are used to refer to ideas or concepts (not specific nouns), for example "Llueve mucho aquí. **Eso** no me gusta." Here the word "eso" does not refer to any particular word, nor does it modify anything. Rather, as a pronoun, it stands for or takes the place of the whole idea which was previously expressed, "Llueve mucho aquí." "Esa" in (D) is clearly wrong

because we cannot use a feminine form of the adjective to modify a masculine noun.

2. **(C)**   The verb "regalar" means "to give a gift." A "televisor" is a "television set." Choice (D) is inappropriate because it is a form of the present tense of the subjunctive "estar." The syntax of the sentence does not require a verb in the blank. All of the remaining choices are demonstratives, but only one, "aquel" (that), may function as an adjective, which is what we need in the blank in order to modify the word "televisor." (A) "eso" (that) and (B) "esto" (this) are not adjectives, but rather **neuter demonstrative** pronouns. Because they are neuter (neither masculine nor feminine), they cannot be used to refer to any specific noun. Instead, they are used to refer to whole concepts or ideas which have previously been mentioned: "Hace mucho calor en esta región y **esto** no me gusta" (It's very hot in this region, and I don't like this). The word "esto" in this sentence refers to no specific noun, but rather to the whole idea previously stated, "Hace mucho calor en esta región . . . "

3. **(D)**   The demonstrative adjective form for "this" is converted into a pronoun by using the orthographic accent. (A) "Esto" is considered neuter, since it does not refer to a masculine or feminine noun. Choice (B) is the correct form for the masculine, but it needs the accent. Choice (C) is the correct form for the imperative. Only choice (D) is the proper form.

4. **(A)**   "Problema" is masculine, which eliminates (C) and (D). The plural form of "este" (B) is "estos."

5. **(A)**   When referring to an entire event, happening, or occurrence, the neuter form "eso" is used. Choice (B) is the feminine singular demonstrative pronoun meaning "this one." Choice (C) is the feminine singular demonstrative adjective meaning "this." Choice (D) is the masculine singular demonstrative adjective meaning "that" (in the distance).

6. **(B)**   The neuter demonstrative is used when one doesn't know the gender of the item asked about. Choice (A) is the masculine singular demonstrative meaning "this one." Choice (C) is incorrect because the neuter forms do not require accent marks. Choice (D) is the feminine singular demonstrative pronoun meaning "this one."

7. **(B)**   Because this demonstrative is replacing "camisas," it is being used as a pronoun and must, therefore, have the accent mark to differentiate it from the adjective. Also, "a lo lejos" (in the distance) requires some

form of "aquél." Although (A) and (D) are pronouns, neither one is used for distance and (A) is the wrong gender. (C) is the demonstrative adjective meaning "that" and must precede a noun, *not* replace it.

8. **(C)** "Latter" (a form of "éste") and "former" (a form of "aquél") are expressed using the demonstrative pronouns. Whereas we say "the former . . . the latter," in Spanish this is reversed. In this sentence the former, Rolando, is being referred to by the statement " . . . es inteligente." Therefore, the masculine singular form "aquél" is needed to express "former." Choices (A) and (B) are incorrect because they are demonstrative adjectives. Choice (D) means "that one" and is not used to express "former or latter" in Spanish.

9. **(A)** "Guantes" (gloves) is the masculine noun requiring the demonstrative adjective. Choice (C) is incorrect because it is feminine. Choices (B) and (D) are demonstrative pronouns and cannot be used to modify nouns.

10. **(D)** Before the preposition **de**, the demonstrative is replaced by the definite article which will have the same gender as the noun referred to, in this case "corbata." Choices (B) and (C) are still in the demonstrative forms. Choice (C) also has the incorrect gender. Choice (A) makes no sense when translated ("she of").

RELATIVE PRONOUNS

Relative pronouns come in both a long and short form, as follows:

$$
\left.\begin{array}{l} que \\ quien \\ quienes \end{array}\right\} \text{who, that, which, and whom} \left\{\begin{array}{l} el\ que/el\ cual \\ la\ que/la\ cual \\ los\ que/los\ cuales \\ las\ que/las\ cuales \end{array}\right.
$$

El hombre **que** vi es médico.
The man that I saw is a doctor.

La mujer con **quien** hablé es mi hermana.
The woman with whom I spoke is my sister.

Las chicas con **quienes** ando son estudiantes.
The girls with whom I walk are students.

Note: When referring to people, after a preposition only *quien* or *quienes* may be used.

La madre de Juan, **la que/la cual** está allí, llegó tarde.
John's mom, who is there, arrived late.

La madre de Juan, **que/quien** es médico, llegó.
Juan's mom, who is a doctor, arrived.

Aquí está la mesa, sobre **la que/la cual** está la caja.
Here's the table upon which is the box.

Note: The difference between **el que/el cual** is one of formality, **el cual** being more formal and less idiomatic than **el que**.

Use of the Long Forms

With reference to the samples above, the long form of the relative pronoun is preferred when:

1. introducing a parenthetical clause whose antecedent is ambiguous; the long form always refers to the antecedent farthest away from that clause.

   Note: When referring to the closest of the double antecedent, use the shorter form.

2. using a long preposition followed by a relative pronoun.

   Note: **por, sin,** and **para** must be included since putting **que** after these words will result in a change in meaning.

por qué = why   *por la que* = through which
sin que = without + subj.   *sin la que* = without which
para que = so that + subj.   *para la que* = for which

The Neuter Pronouns

1. *lo que*   that which, what
   Lo que dijo es verdad.   What you said is true.

2. *lo que/lo cual*
   "which" when referring to an entire idea, event, etc.

   *Todos los estudiantes salieron bien, **lo que/lo cual** le gustó a la maestra.*
   Everyone passed, which the teacher liked.

Note: *Lo que/lo cual* are only interchangeable when used as in (2) above. *Que* standing alone cannot be used.

Idiomatic Uses of the Pronouns

el que/quien   he who
la que/quien   she who
los que/quienes   those who
las que/quienes   those who (f)

Note: There are **no** accent marks. *Quien* is most commonly used in proverbs.

Whose = *Cuyo* vs. *De Quién*

Cuyo (*–a, –os, –as*) acts as an adjective and will agree with the noun following it.

El hombre cuya hija acaba de graduarse . . .
The man whose daughter has just graduated . . .

Note: When referring to parts of the body, use *a quien* instead of *cuyo.*

La niña, a quien la madre lavó las manos, es bonita.
The girl, whose hands her mother washed, is pretty.

De quién/de quienes is an interrogative and is followed by a verb.

¿De quién es este libro?   Whose is this book?
No sé de quien es.   I don't know whose it is.

☞ Drill 11

1. Los señores de _____ te hablo son extranjeros aquí.

   (A) que

   (B) cuales

   (C) cuyos

   (D) quienes

2. Marta, _____ hijo es ingeniero, vive en Buenos Aires.

   (A) quien

   (B) cuya

   (C) de quien

   (D) cuyo

3. _____ que no puedo entender es por qué se fue sin decir adiós.

   (A) Lo

   (B) Ello

   (C) El

   (D) Esto

4. ¿Conoces a los hombres con _____ el jefe acaba de hablar?

   (A) quien

   (B) quienes

   (C) las cuales

   (D) que

5. _____ estudia, aprende.

   (A) Quienes

   (B) Lo que

   (C) El que

   (D) Él que

6. La chica, _____ la madre cortó el pelo, es mi amiga.

   (A) a que

   (B) a quien

   (C) de quién

   (D) cuya

7. El padre de Anita, _____ es profesora, acaba de morir.

   (A) quien

   (B) la cual

   (C) el cual

   (D) a quien

8. La puerta, por _____ entró la reina, es del siglo IX.

    (A) quien   (C) qué

    (B) cual   (D) la cual

9. Mi hija Anita juega bien al tenis, _____ es bueno.

    (A) que   (C) cual

    (B) lo cual   (D) quien

10. En este edificio hay una gran ventana, _____ se ve las montañas.

    (A) por la cual   (C) por que

    (B) por cual   (D) por el que

Drill 11—Detailed Explanations of Answers

1. **(D)**   We need a relative pronoun to complete the sentence correctly. A relative pronoun is one that relates back to a specific noun, pronoun, or idea stated earlier in the sentence (in this case, "señores"). The most common relative pronoun for both people and things is "que," but **following a preposition** (in this case, "de"), if we are referring to people, we may **not** use "que." On the contrary, we use "quien" (if we are referring back to a singular noun) or "quienes" (if we are referring back to a plural noun, as is the case in our sentence). The longer forms of the relative pronoun, "los que" and "los cuales," may also be used in this same situation, but are perhaps less frequent. Note that these must agree in number and gender with the noun to which they refer. Choices (A) and (B) could be correct only if we placed "los" in front of them.

2. **(D)**   In our sentence, the word "ingeniero" means "engineer." "Cuyo" is a relative adjective which means "whose." By "relative" we mean a word which relates back to a noun which is previously mentioned in the sentence. In this instance, "cuyo" relates back to "Marta." It is she whose son is an engineer. Since "cuyo" is an adjective, it must agree in number and gender with the noun which follows it. In this case, then, "cuyo" agrees with "hijo," not with "Marta," and must be masculine singular. "Cuyo" and its other forms ("cuya," "cuyos," and "cuyas") are not used as interrogatives, i.e., to ask questions. If we want to ask "Whose is

this book?", we would have to inquire "¿De quién es este libro?" Choice (A) "quien" is incorrect, for it is not the masculine form and cannot modify "hijo." (C) "de quién" will not fit because it cannot be followed immediately by a noun. It means "of whom."

3. **(A)** For this answer you need to remember that "que" is preceded by "lo" (a particle that never varies regardless of the context) when the construction can be translated as "that which."

4. **(B)** After a preposition when referring to a person or persons, a form of "quien" or "quienes" is needed. Because the antecedent (hombres) is plural, choice (B) is correct. Choice (C) could have qualified if it were masculine and choice (D) cannot refer to people.

5. **(C)** Although this sentence translates as "he who studies, learns," the relative pronoun without the accent is the correct answer. Choice (A) does not qualify because it is plural. Choice (B) means "that which" and choice (D) has an accent and is, therefore, incorrect.

6. **(B)** When referring to parts of the body, use **a quien** instead of a form of **cuyo**, which eliminates choice (D). Choice (C) is incorrect because it means "whose," as an interrogative and would be followed by a verb. Choice (A) means "to which" and makes no sense in this sentence. Also, after a preposition, when referring to people, use "quien" or "quienes."

7. **(A)** When referring to the last person mentioned in the double antecedent, a form of "quien" is used. Because it is stated that this person is a "profesora," we know the clause refers to Anita. Choice (C) would be correct if referring to the "padre." Choice (B) is the long form and would need to refer to "padre" which is the wrong gender, and choice (D) means "whom" or "to whom" which is not grammatically correct.

8. **(D)** The longer forms of the relative pronouns follow long prepositions or, as in this case, ones that would change meaning if used with the short form. In this case the translation "through which" cannot be stated using choice (C) "por qué" since that would mean "why." Choice (A) refers to people and choice (B) requires a definite article (in this case **la**) to be correct.

9. **(B)** The neuter form **lo cual** is correct since the second part of the sentence ("which is good") refers to the entire event or occurrence (the

fact that Anita plays tennis well) stated in the first part of this sentence. Choices (A) and (C) would each need "lo" to be correct. Choice (D) would refer to people.

10. **(A)** Choices (A) and (D) each mean "through which," however, because the antecedent is feminine (ventana), choice (A) is correct. Choice (B) would need the definite article "la" to be correct. Choice (C) is confusing since it could be "why" if it had an accent.

AFFIRMATIVES AND NEGATIVES

The Affirmative and Negative Words

no	no	*sí*	yes
nadie	nobody, no one	*alguien*	someone
nada	nothing	*algo*	something
tampoco	neither	*también*	also
sin	without	*con*	with
ni . . . ni	neither . . . nor	*o . . . o*	either . . . or
jamás	never, not ever	*siempre*	always
nunca	never, not ever		
ninguno	none	*alguno*	some, any

Negative Expressions

ni (yo, Juan, ella) tampoco	nor (I, Juan, she) either
ni siquiera	not even
ya no	no longer
todavía no	not yet
sin novedad	nothing new
no . . . más que	only
no . . . más de	no more than
ahora no	not now
más que	more than
mejor que	better than
peor que	worse than
antes de	before
de ningún modo	by no means
de ninguna manera	by no means
apenas	hardly
no sólo . . . sino también	not only . . . but also

The Rules for Usage

Unlike English, statements with double (or more) negatives are correct. A negative sentence in Spanish, whether it has only one negative word or many, **must have** one negative **before** the verb. If there is more than **one** negative, the Spanish sentence may be written two ways.

*No tengo **nada**.*	***Nada** tengo.*
*No veo a **nadie**.**	*A **nadie** veo.*
*No como **ni** pan **ni** queso.*	***Ni** pan **ni** queso como.*

Sentences with multiple negatives are common.

No dije nunca nada a nadie.
I **never** said **anything to anyone**.

If a personal *a* is required, it must accompany the negative.

Use of *Ninguno*

The plural forms of *ninguno, –a –os, –as* are no longer used. This word may be used with the noun or to replace the noun. *Ninguno, –a* and *Alguno, –a, –os, –as* have shortened forms before masculine, singular nouns: *ningún, algún.*

Ningún libro . . . no tengo ninguno
No book . . . I don't have any.

Ninguna pluma . . . no hay ninguna aquí
No pen . . . there isn't any here.

Ninguno de ellos salió.
None of them left.

Ninguna de ellas irá.
None of them will go.

¿Tiene amigos Juan?
Does Juan have friends?

No tiene ninguno.
He hasn't any.

Use of *Alguno*

When *alguno, –a* follows a noun in Spanish, it makes the negative more emphatic (= at all). This happens with singular nouns only.

Juan no tiene ninguna novia.
Juan doesn't have **any** girlfriend.

Juan no tiene novia alguna.
Juan doesn't have a girlfriend **at all**.

Uses of *Jamás* and *Nunca*

The English **"never"** is normally expressed by *nunca* and **"never again"** by *nunca más*. In modern Spanish, *jamás* is a learned form mainly in literature. In spoken Spanish it is used to give great emphasis to **never**. In that case it means **absolutely never**.

No volvió jamás a ver a su novia.
He never again saw his girlfriend.

Jamás lo sabrás.
You'll absolutely never know it.

¡Nunca jamás!
Never again!

Jamás also means **ever** in a question expecting a negative answer.

¿Ha visto Ud. jamás nada que iguale a esto? ¡Nunca!
Have you **ever** seen anything to equal this? **Never**!

Nada as Intensifier

Nada may be used adverbially with the meaning "not at all."

Manuel no trabaja nada.
Manuel does absolutely no work.

No hemos dormido nada.
We haven't slept a wink.

No ha sido nada cómodo el cuarto.
The room wasn't comfortable at all.

Algo to Mean "Somewhat"

Algo may be placed before an adjective to express the meaning "somewhat."

Este curso es algo fácil.
This course is somewhat easy.

Estamos algo inquietos.
We are somewhat worried.

Note: *¿Sabes una cosa?*
Do you know something?

¿Sabes algo?
Do you know anything?

Pero vs. *Sino/Sino Que*

Pero, sino, and *sino que* all mean **but**. However, *sino* and *sino que* are used:

(a) when the first clause is negative **and**

(b) the second clause contradicts the first—this contrast must be between two equivalent parts of speech (noun–noun, adjective–adjective, infinitive–infinitive). *Sino que* connects the same way, but must be followed by a **conjugated** verb.

*No habla español, **sino** inglés.*	noun–noun
He doesn't speak Spanish, but English.	

*No le gusta el blanco, **sino** el azul.*	adjective–adjective
He doesn't like white, but blue.	

*No quiere estudiar, **sino** jugar.*	infinitive–infinitive
He doesn't want to study, but to play.	

*No cerró la puerta, **sino que** la dejó abierta.*	conjugated verb–
He didn't leave the door open, but left it closed.	conjugated verb

But: *No habla bien, **pero** me gusta su traje.*
   He doesn't speak well, but I like his suit.

Note: *Pero* = "but nevertheless"
    Sino = "but on the contrary"

☞ Drill 12

1. Viene a vernos _____.

   (A) nunca   (C) nadie

   (B) alguien   (D) jamás

2. No me dijo _____ sobre el asunto.

   (A) nadie   (C) algo

   (B) nada   (D) ninguno

3. ¿Tienes algunos amigos íntimos? No, no tengo _____.

   (A) ningunos   (C) ningún

   (B) nadie   (D) ninguno

4. _____ día voy a hacerme médico.

(A) Alguna   (C) Ninguno

(B) Algún   (D) Alguno

5. Nunca hace nada por nadie. No tiene _____.

(A) amigo alguno   (C) algún amigo

(B) ningunos amigos   (D) amigos algunos

6. Él juega mejor que _____.

(A) algo   (C) alguien

(B) ninguno   (D) nadie

7. Nadie va con ellos, ni con Juan _____.

(A) ni   (C) nadie

(B) tampoco   (D) también

8. _____ de las camisas me queda bien.

(A) Nada   (C) Ningún

(B) Ninguna   (D) Ningunas

9. _____ veo en el estadio.

(A) Nadie   (C) A nada

(B) Ningún   (D) A nadie

10. Sin decirme _____, se fue para siempre.

(A) algo   (C) nada

(B) alguna cosa   (D) ninguno

Drill 12—Detailed Explanations of Answers

1. **(B)** Choices (A), (C), and (D) are all negatives. None of them can be used in the blank because, if a negative word such as "nunca" (never),

"nadie" (no one), "ninguno" (none, not any, no one), or "jamás" (never) come after the verb, then there must be a "no" in front of the verb. In other words, we must use a double negative. This does not happen in this sentence. Of the four choices, only the indefinite "alguien" (someone) is acceptable.

2. **(B)** In Spanish the double negative is required when "no" is at the beginning of the sentence, which eliminates (C) because "algo" is a positive particle. Choice (A) is not appropriate because "nadie" refers to persons, and (D) is equally inappropriate because there is no specific antecedent in the question to which "ninguno" could refer.

3. **(D)** "Ninguno" is used exclusively in the singular forms either to modify or refer to previously mentioned nouns. Choice (A) is incorrect because it is plural. Choice (B) means "nobody" and cannot be used to replace the noun "amigos." Choice (C) is apocopated, which is not necessary since it does not precede a masculine noun.

4. **(B)** Both "alguno" and "ninguno" have apocopated forms (drop the –o) before masculine singular nouns. "Día" is a masculine singular noun, which makes (A) incorrect because it is feminine. Choices (C) and (D) would need to be apocopated to be used correctly before "día."

5. **(A)** When a form of "alguno" is used **after** the noun, it makes the statement more negative and is commonly translated with "at all." Because it is being used like "ninguno" in this type of statement, it will only be correct in the singular forms. Because both (B) and (D) are plural, neither is correct. Although (C) is singular, because "algún" precedes the noun, it no longer is a negative and would only be correct in this statement written as "ningún."

6. **(D)** Comparative expressions like "mejor que" (better than), "peor que" (worse than), and "más que" (more than), for example, are negative. Therefore, (A) and (C), which are both affirmative, cannot follow this expression. Choice (B), although negative, is incorrect since there is no noun to which it refers.

7. **(B)** The expression "ni . . . tampoco" (nor . . . either) is used in statements such as this one. "Tampoco" is the negative form of "también" (also). Choice (A) is incorrect because "ni" must be followed by something, a noun, pronoun, verb, etc., in order to be used. It cannot stand alone. Choice (C), which means "no one" or "nobody," makes no sense in

this statement. "También" (also) is affirmative and cannot be used after the negative "ni."

8. **(B)**   Forms of "ninguno" are used only in the singular and modify or refer to nouns. In this statement, this word refers to "camisas," which is feminine. "Ninguna" in this sample is also the subject of "queda." Choice (D) is incorrect because it is plural. Answer (C) is incorrect because it is apocopated and this can only occur before a masculine singular noun. "Nada" (A) cannot be used to modify or refer to nouns.

9. **(D)**   Because "nadie" is the direct object of the verb "veo" in this example and also refers to a person, the personal "a" is required before it whether it precedes or follows the verb. Choice (A) needs a personal "a." Choice (B) can only be used before masculine singular nouns. Choice (C) means "to nothing" and makes no sense in this context.

10. **(C)**   "Sin" is a preposition that is considered negative. Choices (A) and (B) are both affirmative forms. Choice (D) must have a noun either to modify or to refer to.

INTERROGATIVES

Interrogative Words

qué	what, which, what a + noun
quién, quienes	who, which one(s)
cuál, cuáles	which, what, which one(s)
cuánto, –a, –os, –as	how much, how many
cuándo	when
dónde	where
adónde	(to) where
por qué	why (answer uses *porque*)
para qué	why (answer uses *para*)
cómo	how
a quién, a quiénes	whom
de quién, de quiénes	whose

Note: **All** interrogatives have accent marks.

Common Interrogatory Expressions

¿De qué trata?

¿Por qué debería uno...?

¿Dónde tiene lugar?

¿Cuál es el problema?

¿Qué le pasó a...?

¿Cuánto cuesta?

¿Cómo se caracteriza mejor?

¿Qué tiene que hacer...?

¿A qué se debe...?

¿Para qué... (verb)?

¿Qué opina?

¿Qué puede afectar...?

¿En qué consiste...?

¿De qué... (verb)

¿A qué se refiere esta conversación?

¿Qué tipos...?

¿Qué podrán hacer...?

¿Qué hará...?

Uses of *Qué*

a) To ask a definition:

¿Qué es el amor?
What is love?

b) To ask about things not yet mentioned (choice involved):

¿Qué prefieres, manzanas o peras?
Which ones do you prefer, apples or pears?

c) To express **what a**!:

¡Qué día (tan/más) hermoso!
What a beautiful day!

d) To precede a noun:

¿Qué clases te gustan?
What/which classes do you like?

Uses of *Cuál/Cuáles*

a) Followed by *de* = which one(s) of several:

¿Cuál de los libros es más necesario?
Which of the books is most necessary?

b) Refers to a definite object already mentioned (choice involved):

Hay dos vestidos, ¿cuál prefieres?
There are two dresses, **which** do you prefer?

c) Followed by *ser* when there are a number of possibilities:

¿Cuál es la fecha?
What is the date?

¿Cuál es la capital?
What is the capital?

Por Qué, Para Qué, and *Porque*

Por qué and *para qué* both mean *why*. The former is used if the expected answer will begin with *porque* (because). The latter starts a question where the expected answer will begin with *para* (in order to).

¿Por qué vas al cine?
Why do you go to the movies?

Porque *me gusta la película.*
Because I like the film.

*¿**Para qué** vas al cine?*
Why do you go to the movies?

Para ver a mi actor favorito.
In order to see my favorite actor.

Dónde/Adónde vs. Donde

a) ***Adónde*** is used with verbs of motion.

*¿**Adónde** vas?*

b) ***Donde*** (without the accent) requires a noun to refer to.

*La casa **donde** vivo es vieja.*

c) ***Dónde*** (with accent) is the interrogative.

*¿**Dónde** está la casa?*

Note: There are other combinations with ***dónde*** . . . ***de dónde***, ***por dónde***, etc.

Cuándo vs. Cuando

a) ***Cuando*** (without accent) can be replaced by **as** and not change the meaning drastically.

*Te lo diré **cuando** venga Julio.*
I'll tell you **when/as** Julio arrives.

b) ***Cuándo*** (with accent) is the interrogative.

*¿**Cuándo** vas a salir?*

Quién/Quiénes

a) With prepositions to refer to people:

*¿**Con quién** hablas?*
With whom do you speak?

b) With **de** to express **whose**:

*¿**De quién** es el carro?*
Whose is the car?
(Whose car is it?)

Note: The word order must be changed to express the Spanish sentence correctly: **Of whom** is the car?

A Quién/A Quiénes

Whom is often misused in English. It is used as the object of the verb. **Who,** on the other hand, can only be the subject of the verb. Note the differences below.

Who is the subject of "is."

Who is going with me?　　　　*¿Quién va conmigo?*

Whom is the object of "see"; the subject is **you**.

Whom do you see?　　　　*¿A quién ves?*

In Spanish, the **whom** statements are actually a combination of the **personal "a"** and the words *quién/quienes*. In some sentences, the *"a"* may act as an actual preposition and have a translation.

¿A quién escribiste?
To whom did you write?

¿A quiénes enviaron el paquete?
To whom did they send the package?

☞ Drill 13

1. ¿ _____ es tu número de teléfono?

    (A) Qué　　　　　　　　(C) Que

    (B) Cual　　　　　　　　(D) Cuál

2. ¿ _____ día es hoy?

    (A) Cuál　　　　　　　　(C) Cómo

    (B) Qué　　　　　　　　(D) A cuál

3. ¿ _____ de los libros es mejor?

    (A) Cuáles　　　　　　　(C) Qué

    (B) Cuál　　　　　　　　(D) Quiénes

4. Mamá, ¿ _____ sirven los anteojos?

    (A) porque   (C) para qué

    (B) por qué   (D) para

5. ¿ _____ vestidos quieres comprar?

    (A) Cuál   (C) Cuáles

    (B) Qué   (D) Cómo

6. El pueblo _____ vivo es viejo.

    (A) donde   (C) a donde

    (B) dónde   (D) que

7. No sé _____ es ese carro.

    (A) quién   (C) que

    (B) de quien   (D) de quićn

8. ¡ _____ día más hermoso!

    (A) Qué un   (C) Qué

    (B) Cuál   (D) Qué una

9. ¿ _____ es la astronomía?

    (A) Qué   (C) Quién

    (B) Cuál   (D) A quién

10. ¿ _____ son los meses del año?

    (A) Cuál   (C) Qué

    (B) Cuáles   (D) De quién

Drill 13—Detailed Explanations of Answers

1. **(D)** From the question marks in our sentence we can tell that we need an interrogative pronoun, a pronoun which asks a question, in the

blank. There are only two of these given in the list of possible answers: (A) "Qué" and (D) "Cuál." How do we know that these two are interrogative pronouns? Because this type of pronoun always bears an accent mark. The word "Que," in (C), is a relative pronoun, one that relates back to a previous noun in a sentence: "Los turistas **que** hablan francés . . . " Here the "que" refers back to "turistas." In (B), the word "Cual" is part of another relative pronoun, "el cual," "la cual," "lo cual," which is designed to show gender and is used for the sake of clarity when we have previously been talking about two nouns: "La madre de José, la cual tiene dos hermanos, viaja por España." If we did not use this longer, feminine form ("la cual"), i.e., if we were to say instead "que" or "quien," we would be referring to the noun immediately preceding the relative pronoun ("José"). But since we want to show that it is José's mother, and not José, who has two brothers, then we must use this longer pronoun or its alternate form, "la que." In English, we say "What is your telephone number?" In Spanish, the interrogative word "qué" asks for a definition. If we ask "¿Qué es la física?" we are asking for a definition of what physics is. In our sentence, we do not want to ask for a definition of what one's telephone number is, which is what (A) "Qué" would imply. Instead, we must ask, "Which one" ("Cuál"), out of all the possible numbers in the directory, is your phone number. In other words, "cuál" asks for a choice or selection from a number of possibilities.

2.   **(B)**   Before a noun, "qué" means "what/which." Choice (A) is not correct because it cannot modify a noun. Choice (C) means "how" and (D) means "to which."

3.   **(B)**   "Cuál" is used with a form of **ser** to mean "which." It is also the subject of the verb, which is singular. Choice (A) is incorrect because it is plural. Choice (D) means "who" and choice (C), which can also mean "what/which," cannot be used before a "de" phrase where there is an indication of choice.

4.   **(C)**   "Para qué" is used when the question intimates "for what purpose/use." Choice (A) "because" and (D) "in order to" are not interrogatives and make no sense. Choice (B) means "why" and does not fit within the intended meaning of this question.

5.   **(B)**   "Qué" is used before a noun to mean "what/which". Therefore, choices (A) and (C) are incorrect since neither can precede a noun. Choice (D) means "how."

6. **(A)** "Donde" without an accent requires a noun to refer to, in this case "pueblo." Because an indirect question is not being asked, choice (B) is incorrect since all interrogatives have accent marks. Choice (C) is used in questions with verbs of motion (i.e., Where are you going?). Choice (D) is the relative pronoun meaning "that."

7. **(D)** Because an indirect question is being asked, the accented form of "whose" is required. This would make choice (B) incorrect. Choice (A) means "who" and choice (C) is a relative pronoun meaning "that."

8. **(C)** Because "¡qué!" in this context means "What a!" and the indefinite article (a) is included in its translation, choices (A) and (D) would be incorrect. Choice (B) is never used to mean "What a!" and again a form of "cuál" is not correct before a noun.

9. **(A)** "Qué" is used before a form of **ser** when asking for a definition, as in this example. Choices (C) "who" and (D) "whom" make no sense. "Cual" precedes a form of **ser** when there are a number of possibilities, which makes choice (B) incorrect.

10. **(B)** A form of "cuál" will precede a form of **ser** when a number of possibilities are given to choose from (i.e., months). Because it is the subject of the verb and because the verb is plural, choice (A) is incorrect. Answer (D) means "whose" and makes no sense in this context. Choice (C) can only be used before a form of **ser** when asking a definition.

THE PERSONAL *A*

Normally the preposition *a* means **to** or **at** in Spanish. There are instances when this preposition will appear in the sentence with **no** apparent translation into English. In this case, this preposition is called the personal *"a."* This *a* will appear in the Spanish sentence if the **direct object** of the verb:

a) refers to a person in some way:

No veo a Juan/a su amigo/al ejército/a nadie.
I don't see Juan/his friend/the army/anyone.

b) refers to a domestic animal:

Juan ama mucho a su perro, Spot.
Juan loves his dog, Spot.

c) refers to a specific geographical location (if they do **not** have an article):

Visito a España/a Barcelona/a México.
I visit Spain/Barcelona/Mexico.

But: Visito **el** Perú.

Omission of the Personal *A*

a) After the verb *tener*, unless it means "keep/hold":

Tengo dos hermanos.	I have two brothers.
But:	*Tengo al culpable en la cárcel.* I have the guilty one in jail.

b) Before an indefinite personal direct object (usually modified by a numeral or an indefinite article):

Vi tres hombres en el bosque.
I saw three men in the forest.

Oí un ladrón dentro del banco.
I heard a thief inside the bank.

c) When the personal *"a"* would be in close proximity to another *a* (such as one meaning "to," "at," "toward" or the *a* preceding an indirect object):

Presenté mi esposo a mis amigos.
I introduced my husband to my friends.

POSSESSIVES: ADJECTIVES/PRONOUNS

The possessive adjectives:

my	*mi, mis*	our	*nuestro, –a, –os, –as*
your	*tu, tus*	your	*vuestro, –a, –os, –as*
his/her/your	*su, sus*	their/your	*su, sus*

The possessive adjectives precede the noun they modify and match it as closely as possible in gender and number.

mi casa, mis casas	my house, my houses
nuestra pluma, nuestras plumas	our pen, our pens

Because the third person adjective has several possible translations, the following may be done for clarification:

su casa =	his house	*la casa de él*
	her house	*la casa de ella*
	your house (s)	*la casa de Ud.*
	their house (f)	*la casa de ellas*
	their house (m)	*la casa de ellos*
	your house (pl)	*la casa de Uds.*

The Possessive Pronouns

The pronoun group is used **to replace** the noun already stated and, therefore, takes on the properties of that noun. This includes retention of the definite article. Also note the difference in translation.

mine	*el mío, la mía*
	los míos, las mías
yours	*el tuyo, la tuya*
	los tuyos, las tuyas
his/hers/yours	*el suyo, la suya*
	los suyos, las suyas
ours	*el nuestro, la nuestra*
	los nuestros, las nuestras
yours	*el vuestro, la vuestra*
	los vuestros, las vuestras
theirs/yours	*el suyo, la suya*
	los suyos, las suyas

Again, because the third person pronouns have several possible meanings, clarification with the prepositional phrase is also possible. With the pronouns, however, the definite article must be retained.

mi coche y el suyo	my car and his	*y el de él*
	my car and hers	*y el de ella*
	my car and yours	*y el de Ud.*
	my car and theirs (f)	*y el de ellas*
	my car and theirs (m)	*y el de ellos*
	my car and yours	*y el de Uds.*

Uses of the Pronouns

The possessive pronouns are used primarily in three areas:

a) As the replacement for the noun:

| my house and **ours** | *mi casa y **la nuestra*** |

b) As an "adjective" with nouns, as follows:

| several friends of **mine** | *unos amigos **míos*** |
| Note: | "of" is **not** expressed. |

c) As the possessive used after *ser*:

| *¿Este vestido?* | This dress? |
| *Es **tuyo**.* | It is **yours**. |

| *¿Estos carros?* | These cars? |
| *Son **nuestros**.* | They are **ours**. |

Note: The definite article is normally omitted after *ser*.

Possessives with Clothing/Body Parts

Normally, with parts of the body and clothing, the possessive adjective is replaced by the definite article. However, in the following instances, the possessive is correct.

a) With body parts:

1. When ambiguity would result without it.

2. When the body part is modified.

   Ella levantó sus grandes ojos azules.

3. When the body part is the subject.

   Tus manos tienen callos.

b) With clothing:

 1. When the article worn is the subject.

 Su camisa está allí.

 2. When the article is **not** being worn by the subject.

 *Encontré **mis** calcetines allí.*

☞ **Drill 14**

1. Ayer vimos _____ señorita Corrales.

 (A) a la   (C) a

 (B) la   (D) la a

2. Mi hermana es más alta que _____.

 (A) la suya   (C) su

 (B) el suyo   (D) mía

3. ¿Conoce Ud. _____ padres?

 (A) mi   (C) a mis

 (B) mis   (D) míos

4. Su amigo es más inteligente que _____.

 (A) la nuestra   (C) los míos

 (B) el nuestro   (D) el mío

5. Los hombres se pusieron _____ antes de salir.

 (A) el sombrero   (C) su sombrero

 (B) sus sombreros (D) sombreros

6. Se quitaron _____ al entrar en la casa.

 (A) sus abrigos   (C) sus guantes

 (B) su abrigo   (D) el abrigo

7. ¿De quién es este lápiz? –Es _____.

    (A) mío   (C) de mi

    (B) el mío   (D) de mí

8. Mis hermanas y _____ Isabel son bellas.

    (A) las que   (C) las

    (B) las de   (D) aquellas

9. Tu casa es más grande que _____.

    (A) el mío   (C) mío

    (B) mi   (D) la mía

10. Sus pirámides y _____ vienen de épocas distintas.

    (A) los nuestros   (C) las nuestras

    (B) nuestros   (D) nuestras

11. Tengo _____ padre en el hospital.

    (A) mi   (C) a mi

    (B) a mí   (D) el

Drill 14—Detailed Explanations of Answers

1. **(A)** The personal "*a*" must be used when speaking about a person, and the article should accompany a title when not in direct address. The answer (A) is the only one fulfilling these requirements.

2. **(A)** The long form of the possessive is used when the noun is replaced. Because the possessive is now being used as a pronoun, it will take on the properties of the noun it has replaced, including the definite article. The noun in this example is "hermana." Choice (B) is incorrect because it is the wrong gender. Choice (C) is a possessive adjective and must be used with a noun. Choice (D) is the possessive pronoun but needs an article.

3.   **(C)**   The possessive adjective is required to match the noun "padres." Also, because "padres" is the direct object of the verb and refers to a person, the personal *a* is also required. Choice (A) needs to be plural and have a personal *a*. Choice (B) needs the personal *a* and choice (D) is the possessive pronoun, which cannot precede the noun.

4.   **(B)**   All choices are possessive pronouns but only (B) is the correct gender for "amigo."

5.   **(A)**   With parts of the body and clothing in Spanish, the possessive is replaced by the definite article. The ownership is established by the reflexive pronoun. In addition, in Spanish, each person wears only **one** hat at a time and even if the subject is plural, the article of clothing remains singular. Answer (C) has the possessive and is incorrect. Choice (B) is plural and has the possessive, and choice (D) needs to be singular with a definite article to be correct.

6.   **(D)**   For the same reason given in number 5 above, each person wears only one coat and the possessive must be replaced by the definite article. Choice (A), therefore, is incorrect because it is plural and has retained the possessive. Choice (B) needs to replace the possessive with the article "el." Choice (C) would be correct if "sus" were replaced with "los" since gloves are worn in pairs.

7.   **(A)**   The long form of the possessive is used to replace a noun previously referred to. In this example, the noun is "lápiz." Normally, the long form has a definite article. However, after **ser** the article is omitted. Choice (B) is incorrect because it has the article. Choice (C) means "of my", and choice (D) is incorrect because in spoken Spanish "of me" is not used in this manner. Forms of "mío" are used instead.

8.   **(B)**   To eliminate **'s** in Spanish, an **of** phrase is used. When replacing a possessive such as this one (Isabel's) wherein there is a name to deal with, the definite article is retained followed by **de**. Because the noun here is "hermanas," the feminine plural article is needed. Neither (C) nor (D) make sense when placed directly before Anita. Choice (A) can be translated "those that or those who" but neither make sense in front of Anita.

9.   **(D)**   The long form of the possessive with the definite article is needed to replace the noun previously mentioned ("casa"). Choice (A) is the wrong gender. Choice (B) is the possessive adjective which means "my" and must precede a noun, and choice (C) needs to be feminine with an article to be correct.

10. **(C)** Again, the long form of the possessive with the definite article is needed to replace the noun previously mentioned ("pirámides") which is feminine plural. Choice (A) is the wrong gender. Choice (B) is the wrong gender and needs an article, and choice (D) needs a definite article to be correct.

11. **(C)** The personal "a" is used after **tener** when it means "keep or hold" as it does in this sample. Also, the possessive adjective "mi" has no accent. Choice (A) needs a personal "a." In choice (B) the accented "mí" means me and is prepositional, not possessive. Choice (D) needs a personal "a."

THE PASSIVE VOICE

The passive voice is the "mirror image" of the active voice. In passive voice statements, the subject receives the action of the verb instead of actually doing it.

Active: I built the house.
                 Construí la casa.

Passive: The house was built by me.
                 La casa fue construida por mí.

The combination of *ser* with the **past participle** of the transitive verb constitutes the "true passive" in Spanish. The past participle is used as an adjective and must agree with the subject in number and gender. The formula follows:

ser + **past participle** + *por* + **agent** (doer)

Whenever the agent is expressed, this formula is used.

Agent Expressed by *De*

By is normally translated by *por*. If, however, the past participle expresses feelings or emotion, **by** is translated by *de*.

Juana es amada (respetada, odiada, admirada) de todos.
Juana is loved (respected, hated, admired) by all.

Reflexive Substitute for the Passive Voice

Commonly, when the agent is **not** expressed and the subject is a thing, the passive "Spanish" statement will be written using the third person singular or plural of the verb with the pronoun *se*.

Aquí se habla español.   Spanish is spoken here.
Se vendieron guantes allí.   Gloves were sold there.

Note: The subject follows the verb.

Third Person Plural Active Equivalent for Passive Voice

The best way to avoid using a passive construction is to convert the passive statement to an active one by using the subject **they**.

The house was sold.   =   They sold the house.
Se vendió la casa.   =   *Vendieron la casa.*

No Agent Expressed, Person Acted Upon

In sentences where the agent is indefinite (not mentioned or implied) and a person is acted upon, the indefinite *se* is coupled with the **third singular** of the verb.

The man was killed.
Se mató al hombre.

He was killed.
Se le mató.

The girls will be punished.
Se castigará a las chicas.

They will be punished.
Se las castigará.

Note: The person acted upon is the direct object of the Spanish sentence. Therefore, direct object pronouns are used to replace it, with one expection—*les* is used instead of *los* for the masculine plural.

The men will be killed.
Se matará a los hombres.

They will be killed.
Se les matará.

Idiomatic Expressions with *Se*

Se plus the third person singular of the verb will render "impersonal" subject statements. In English we say **people**, **one**, **they**, **you**, and the like. This type of statement may also be translated as a passive construction.

se dice = it is said
[dicen] people say
they say
one says
you say

se cree = it is believed
[creen] people believe
they believe
one believes
you believe

This may also be rendered with the third person plural of the verb.

The Apparent Passive: *Estar* Plus the Past Participle

The true passive in Spanish is formed with *ser* and a past participle. Constructions formed with *estar* and a past participle are different. Instead of expressing an action carried out by an explicit or implicit agent, the apparent passive denotes a state or a condition resulting from a previous action. The past participle becomes an adjective. Compare the following examples:

Apparent Passive

La puerta está abierta.
The door **is** open. (The action of opening it happened earlier.)

True Passive

> *La puerta es abierta (por el niño).*
> The door **is opened** (by the boy). (We see the action happening now.)

Apparent Passive

> *La pieza estaba reservada.*
> The room **was** reserved. (Someone reserved it earlier.)

True Passive

> *La pieza había sido reservada (por el turista).*
> The room had **been reserved** (by the tourist).

☞ Drill 15

1. _____ la mujer.

   (A) Asesinaron a   (C) Asesinamos

   (B) Se asesinaron a   (D) Fue asesinado

2. La universidad _____ por el presidente Juárez.

   (A) fundó   (C) fue establecida

   (B) estaba fundado   (D) se estableció

3. El asesino fue _____ por el policía.

   (A) muerto   (C) morido

   (B) matado   (D) muriendo

4. La ventana _____ abierta por el viento.

   (A) sido   (C) estaba

   (B) estuvo   (D) fue

5. La señora García es respetada _____ todos los alumnos.

   (A) de   (C) a

   (B) por   (D) con

6. _____ que va a mejorar la economía.

   (A) Se dicen   (C) Se dice

   (B) Es dicho   (D) Está dicho

7. Aquí _____ español e inglés.

   (A) es hablado   (C) son hablados

   (B) se habla   (D) se hablan

8. ¿Los traidores? _____ matará mañana.

   (A) Se les   (C) Se

   (B) Se los   (D) Los

9. Al entrar, vi que las ventanas _____ abiertas.

   (A) fueron   (C) han sido

   (B) estaban   (D) han estado

10. Esas casas fueron _____ por un arquitecto famoso.

    (A) construida   (C) construidos

    (B) construido   (D) construidas

Drill 15—Detailed Explanations of Answers

1. **(A)** When a person is acted upon in a passive voice sentence, the statement may be expressed three ways: by using true passive ("ser" + past participle) which matches the noun (thus eliminating answer choice (D)), by using an active voice statement requiring the personal *a* (thus eliminating choice (C)), or by using the third singular of the verb preceded by the reflexive **se** followed by the personal *a* (thus eliminating choice (B)). (A) is correct in the active voice with the personal *a*.

2. **(C)** Choice (A) "fundó" means "founded," but it will not function in the sentence because the "university" ("universidad") did not found anything. On the contrary, it was founded "**by** President Juárez." This gets us into what is called the passive voice. In a passive sentence, the subject

is acted upon by someone or something. In our sentence, the subject, "universidad," is acted upon by "el presidente Juárez." To form the passive voice in Spanish, we follow this pattern: the proper tense and form of the verb "ser" + past participle. Look at the correct answer: "fue establecida." You will see that we have followed this pattern. One other thing you will notice is that in the passive voice, the past participle always agrees in number and gender with the subject. In our sentence, "establecida" is feminine singular to agree with "universidad." Observe also that the verb "fue" is third person singular since the subject, "universidad," is a singular noun. The passive voice must always be used when the subject is acted upon and the doer of the action is expressed by a "por" phrase ("por el presidente Juárez"). (B) "estaba fundado" is incorrect because (1) we have not used the verb "ser," but rather "estar" (therefore, we are not indicating an action; we are merely describing a state), and (2) the past participle does not agree with the subject "universidad." Now look at (D), "se estableció." Sometimes the reflexive form of the verb can be used as a substitute for the true passive voice, but never when we have a "por" phrase which indicates who did the action, as is the case in our sentence.

3.   **(A)**   The last two choices are ungrammatical. In order to identify the correct answer, you have to know that the past participle of the verb "matar" is "muerto" when the sentence refers to people.

4.   **(D)**   To get the right answer you must recognize that this construction is in the passive voice, which means that it's always formed with the appropriate form of "ser"—but not with the past participle (as in choice (A)) because this particular form needs the support of "haber."

5.   **(A)**   In a passive voice statement, **by** is usually translated by **por**. If the past participle expresses feeling or emotion, rather than action, **by** is translated by **de**. Therefore, choice (B) is incorrect. Because **de** is the only choice to complete this passive statement, (C) and (D) are both incorrect.

6.   **(C)**   The pronoun **se** used with the third person singular of the verb expresses an indefinite subject. This can be translated a number of ways: it is said, people say, they say, one says, etc. Choice (A) is incorrect because the verb is plural. Both (B) and (D) appear to have the literal translation needed but this type of statement is done with **se** + third person singular of the verb.

7.   **(D)**   If the agent (doer) is not mentioned and the subject of the statement is a thing, the reflexive construction is used for the passive. The verb will, in these cases, match the noun. In this case the actual subject ("español e inglés") is plural. Choices (A) and (C) are written in the true passive formula (**ser** + past participle) but cannot be used when the subject is a thing. Choice (B) is incorrect because the verb is singular.

8.   **(A)**   The indefinite **se** is used when the agent (doer) is indefinite (not mentioned or implied) and a person is being acted upon. In this case, the verb is always third person singular and the person acted upon becomes the direct object. "Los," however, is the only direct object pronoun not used and is replaced by "les." Therefore, choice (B) is incorrect because "los" has been used. Choice (C) needs the pronoun "les" and choice (D) is simply the direct object pronoun by itself.

9.   **(B)**   When there is a focus on the "resultant state of a previous action" and **not** on the action itself, a form of **estar** will precede the past participle. The past participle will still be used as an adjective. Therefore, choices (A) and (C) are incorrect because **ser** has been used. Choice (D) when translated (Upon entering, I saw that the windows have been opened.) is incorrect usage of the perfect tense.

10. **(D)**   The focus is on the past participle and its function as an adjective in the passive voice statement. It must agree in this sample with "casas." All other answers use incorrect gender or number.

MEASURES OF TIME

The word *tiempo* in Spanish designates both "time" and "weather," as in the following examples:

*Ha pasado tanto **tiempo** desde que nos vimos.*
So much **time** has passed since we saw each other.

*¿Cómo está el **tiempo** hoy?*
How is the **weather** today?

The following are some of the expressions Spanish uses to measure or divide time.

Seasons of the Year

las estaciones – the seasons
el verano – summer
el invierno – winter

el otoño – fall
la primavera – spring

Months of the Year

el mes – the month
enero – January
marzo – March
mayo – May
julio – July
septiembre – September
noviembre – November

febrero – February
abril – April
junio – June
agosto – August
octubre – October
diciembre – December

Note: In Spanish, the names of the months are not capitalized.

Days of the Week

el día – the day
el lunes – Monday
el miércoles – Wednesday
el viernes – Friday
el domingo – Sunday

la semana – the week
el martes – Tuesday
el jueves – Thursday
el sábado – Saturday

Note: The days of the week (which are not capitalized in Spanish) are preceded by the definite article except after a form of *ser*:

el lunes – Monday; on Monday   *los lunes* – Mondays; on Mondays
Es lunes. – It is Monday.

Other Expressions of Time

hoy – today
mañana – tomorrow*
anteanoche – the night before last
pasado mañana – the day after tomorrow
la madrugada – dawn
el mediodía – noon
la noche – night (time)
tarde – late

ayer – yesterday
anoche – last night
anteayer – the day before yesterday
el día siguiente – the following day
la mañana – the morning*
la tarde – afternoon
la medianoche – midnight
pronto – soon

*Be sure to distinguish between *mañana* (tomorrow) and *la mañana* (the morning).

TELLING TIME

When telling the time of day, the word "time" is rendered as *hora*.

*¿Qué **hora** es?*   What **time** is it?

When telling the hours of the day, Spanish uses the feminine definite article before the time expression.

*Es **la** una.*   It's one o'clock.
*Son **las** dos.*   It's two o'clock.

Note: To specify A.M., Spanish uses *de la mañana* or *de la madrugada*. (The hours after midnight but before dawn). P.M. is expressed with either *de la tarde* or *de la noche.*

*Son las tres **de la mañana.***   It's three A.M.
*Son las cinco **de la tarde.***   It's five P.M.

To render the half-hour, Spanish uses *media*. To render the quarter-hour, *cuarto* or *quince* are used.

*Son las diez y **cuarto**. Son las diez y **quince**.*
It's a **quarter** past ten. It's ten **fifteen.**

*Son las diez y **media.***
It's **10:30**. It's **half past** ten.

*Son las once menos **cuarto**. Son las once menos **quince**.*
It's a **quarter** of eleven.

Falta un **cuarto** (Faltan **quince**) para las once.*
It's a **quarter** of eleven.

*Faltar means "to be wanting, lacking."

Note: *y* is used through the half-hour and *menos* is used after the half-hour.

Portions of time other than the half- or quarter-hour are expressed thus:

Son las seis y diez.	It's 6:10.
Son las seis y veinte.	It's 6:20.

Son las siete menos veinte. (Faltan veinte para las siete.)
It's 6:40. (It's twenty of seven.)

At plus the hour is expressed with *a + la/las*.

A la una/A las dos salí.	At one/at two I left.

To tell time in the past, use the imperfect tense.

Era la una/Eran las dos.	It was 1:00/2:00.

To express "a little after" the hour, use *y pico*.

Llegó a las cinco y pico.	He arrived a little after 5:00.

To express "at about," use *a eso de* + the hour.

Salió a eso de las seis.	He left about 6:00.

When **no** exact hour is indicated, "in the morning/afternoon/evening" is expressed with *por la mañana, por la tarde, por la noche*.

If using the 24-hour clock, the following applies:

1:00 p.m.	*trece horas*
2:00 p.m.	*catorce horas*
8:00 p.m.	*veinte horas*
15:30 (3:30 p.m.)	*quince horas treinta*
20:42 (8:42 p.m.)	*veinte horas cuarenta y dos*
9:10 (9:10 a.m.)	*nueve horas diez*

Note: *Cuarto, media*, and *y* are not used.

HACER WITH EXPRESSIONS OF TIME

With expressions of time, *hacer* is an impersonal verb. Only the third person singular is used.

Hace (Tiempo) Que + Present Indicative of Main Verb

This formula shows that the action is still going on in the present. Note that Spanish uses the simple present where English uses the present perfect.

Hace una semana que el prisionero no come.
The prisoner has not eaten for a week.

Hace muchos días que llueve.
It has been raining for many days.

Note: By turning the sentence around, the conjunction *que* can be suppressed. (In negative sentences, it is possible to use a compound tense.)

El prisionero no come hace una semana.
(El prisionero no ha comido hace una semana.)
The prisoner has not eaten for a week.

Llueve hace muchos días.
It has been raining for many days.

Hace (Tiempo) Que + Preterite of Main Verb

This formula designates the sense of time expressed by the English particle "ago."

Hace tres días que la vi. (La vi hace tres días.)
I saw her three days ago.

Hace años que nos dejaron. (Nos dejaron hace años.)
They left us years ago.

Hacía (Tiempo) Que + Imperfect of Main Verb

This formula shows that the action was still going on in the past.

Hacía tres días que llovía. (Llovía hacía tres días.)
It had been raining for three days.

Hacía tiempo que te esperaba. (Te esperaba hacía tiempo.)
I had been waiting for you for a while.

AGE

Cumplir años and *tener años* are the expressions most commonly used to indicate age:

Mi padre tiene cuarenta y dos años.
My father is 42 (years of age).

Hoy es mi cumpleaños. Cumplo ocho.
Today is my birthday. I turn eight.

To express "at the age of 40 (or any number)," one says "*a los cuarenta años.*"

WEATHER EXPRESSIONS

In English these weather expressions are formed with the verb "to be"; in Spanish they are formed with the verb *hacer* used impersonally.

Hace calor.	It **is** hot.
Hizo frío.	It **was** cold.
Hará buen tiempo.	The weather **will be** good.
Hace sol.	It **is** sunny.
Hacía viento.	It **was** windy.
¿Qué tiempo hace?	What's the weather like?
Hace mal tiempo.	The weather **is** bad.

With *Tener*

When the sentence is personal, Spanish uses *tener* where English uses "to be."

Tengo calor.	I **am** hot.
Teníamos frío.	We **were** cold.

With *Haber* Used Impersonally

Notice that the third person singular of the present indicative changes from *ha* to *hay* when *haber* is impersonal.

Hay neblina.	It **is** misty (foggy).
Hubo humedad.	It **was** damp.
Habrá tempestad.	It **will be** stormy.

With *Nevar* and *Llover*

"To snow" and "to rain" are rendered by the impersonal verbs *nevar* and *llover,* respectively:

Ayer nevó.	**It snowed** yesterday.
Mañana lloverá.	Tomorrow **it will rain.**

CARDINAL AND ORDINAL FORMS OF NUMERALS

The cardinal and ordinal forms of numbers in Spanish are as follows:

Cardinal Numbers

1	uno/a	11	once
2	dos	12	doce
3	tres	13	trece
4	cuatro	14	catorce
5	cinco	15	quince
6	seis	16	diez y seis
7	siete	17	diez y siete
8	ocho	18	diez y ocho
9	nueve	19	diez y nueve
10	diez	20	veinte

21	veinte y uno, –a	300	trescientos, –as
22	veinte y dos	400	cuatrocientos, –as
30	treinta	500	quinientos, –as
40	cuarenta	600	seiscientos, –as
50	cincuenta	700	setecientos, –as
60	sesenta	800	ochocientos, –as
70	setenta	900	novecientos, –as
80	ochenta	1,000	mil
90	noventa	1,100	mil cien(to)/a
100	cien(to)/a	2,000	dos mil
101	ciento uno, –a	1,000,000	un millón (de)
200	doscientos, –as	2,000,000	dos millones (de)

Note: The cardinal numbers from 16 to 29 may be written together: *dieciséis, diecisiete, dieciocho, diecinueve, veintiuno, veintinueve.* Beyond 30, cardinal numbers are written: *treinta y uno, treinta y dos,* etc.

Ordinal Numbers

First	primero	Sixth	sexto
Second	segundo	Seventh	séptimo
Third	tercero	Eighth	octavo
Fourth	cuarto	Ninth	noveno (nono)
Fifth	quinto	Tenth	décimo

a) Ordinal numbers are variable in gender and number:

*Eres la **cuarta** persona que me pregunta lo mismo.*
You are the **fourth** person to ask me the same thing.

*Los **primeros** en irse fueron los últimos en llegar.*
The **first** to leave were the last to arrive.

b) *Primero* and *tercero* drop their final *"o"* in front of masculine singular nouns:

*el **tercer** ojo*   the **third** eye

c) Ordinal numbers precede the noun except when referring to kings, dukes, popes, or some other kind of succession:

*Juan Carlos **Primero** es el rey de España.*
Juan Carlos I is the king of Spain.

*Juan Pablo **Segundo** es el Papa.*
John Paul II is the pope.

d) Usage dictates that after *décimo* no more ordinal numbers are used; they are replaced by cardinal numbers situated after the noun:

*La **décima** carrera fue más emocionante que la (carrera) **once**.*
The **tenth** race was more exciting than the **eleventh** (race).

*España no tuvo un rey llamado Pedro **Quince**.*
Spain did not have a king named Pedro the Fifteenth.

Un, Una, or Uno

Un and *una* (like the indefinite articles they resemble) are used according to the gender of the noun they precede. *Uno* is used alone (i.e., not before a noun).

un *libro,* **una** *mujer, veinte y* **uno**

Note: **un** will precede a noun that begins with a stressed *a–* or *ha–* for pronunciation.

el águila *=* **un** águila   *el* hacha *=* **un** hacha
the eagle = an eagle   the hatchet = a hatchet

Ciento vs. Cien

a) *Ciento* will apocopate to *cien* before any noun or a number larger than itself (i.e., *mil, millones*).

cien casas	*cien soldados*	*cien mil*	*cien millones*
100 houses	100 soldiers	100,000	100 million

But: *ciento once, ciento veinte y tres, ciento sesenta*

Note: After 100, an **y** is not placed between it and the next number.

b) **Ciento** and **mil,** when used as collective nouns, may be plural.

muchos miles de dólares	*cientos (centenares) de leguas*
many thousands of dollars	hundreds of leagues

Note: *Centenar* is preferred to *ciento* as a collective noun.

c) The multiples of 100 (200–900) have both masculine and feminine forms.

doscientas una mujeres	*quinientos un hombres*
201 women	501 men

d) Although **ciento** should be used when the number stands alone, in everyday speech it is apocopated as follows:

Hemos comprado cien.	*Yo vivo en el cien.*
We have bought 100.	I live in number 100.

Expressing Millions

Millón is considered a noun and therefore takes the indefinite article and is followed by the preposition *de:*

un millón de dólares	*doscientos millones de aves*
one million dollars	200 million birds

DATES

Contrary to English usage, **cardinal** numbers are used to indicate dates **except in the case of the first of the month:**

el **primero** de mayo	the first of May
el **dos** de mayo	the second of May
el **tres** de mayo	the third of May
el **diez** de mayo	the tenth of May
el **treinta** de mayo	the thirtieth of May

The year may be added to these dates by inserting the preposition *de:*

*el tres de octubre **de** 1951*   October 3, 1951
*el veinte de abril **de** este año*   April 20 of this year

In dating letters the definite article is omitted.
It's common to replace *de este año* by *del corriente* (of the current year):

el veintiocho de febrero del corriente.
February 28 of this year.

"What day is today?" may be rendered literally as *¿Qué día es hoy?* or idiomatically as *¿A cómo estamos (hoy)?* The latter expression implies a date as an answer, not just the day of the week:

¿A cómo estamos? Estamos a trece de junio.
What's the date? It is June 13.

¿Qué día es hoy? Hoy es lunes.
What day is today? Today is Monday.

ARITHMETIC SIGNS

+   *más*
−   *menos*
×   *por*
÷   *dividido por*

$2 + 2$ is dos **más** dos
$10 ÷ 5$ is *diez **dividido por** cinco*
$3 × 3$ is *tres **por** tres*

COLLECTIVE NUMERALS

un par	a pair
una decena	ten
una docena	a dozen
una quincena	fifteen, two weeks
una veintena	twenty
una centena (un centenar)	hundred
un millar	thousand

*Pagan cada **quincena**.*
They pay every two weeks.

*El libro tiene una **centena** de poemas.*
The book has **one hundred** poems.

*Un **millar** de personas*
A **thousand** people

Note: *Quincenal* is an adjective made from *quincena*. Other similar numerical adjectives are *semanal* (weekly), *mensual* (monthly), *semestral* (half-yearly), and *anual* (yearly).

*Una publicación **quincenal***
A **biweekly** publication

*Una revista **semestral***
A **half-yearly** magazine

FRACTIONS

1/2	*un medio*	1/3	*un tercio*
1/4	*un cuarto*	1/5	*un quinto*
1/6	*un sexto*	1/7	*un séptimo*
1/8	*un octavo*	1/9	*un noveno*
1/10	*un décimo*		

Two-thirds is either *dos tercios* or *las dos terceras partes*; three-fourths is either *tres cuartos* or *las tres cuartas partes*.

Un medio is only used in arithmetical calculations; the adjective meaning "half" is *medio/a;* the noun meaning "half" is *la mitad:*

*Trabajamos sólo **medio** día hoy.*
Today we only worked **half** a day.

***La mitad** del electorado no votó.*
Half of the electorate did not vote.

☞ Drill 16

1. ¿Cuánto tiempo _____ que esperaban el tren?

    (A) hace   (C) hacían

    (B) hizo   (D) hacía

2. _____ tres horas que regresó de su viaje.

    (A) Hacen   (C) Hace

    (B) Ha   (D) Desde

3. Mis botas están sucias porque _____ lodo afuera.

   (A) hay   (C) es

   (B) hace   (D) está

4. No puedo conducir bien porque _____ neblina.

   (A) está   (C) hace

   (B) es   (D) hay

5. Había (231) _____ mujeres en el estadio.

   (A) doscientos treinta y uno   (C) doscientas treinta y una

   (B) doscientas treinta y uno   (D) doscientas treinta y unas

6. Ganó (100 million) _____ dólares en la lotería.

   (A) cien millón de   (C) ciento millones de

   (B) ciento millón de   (D) cien millones de

7. (The first) _____ de mayo es mi cumpleaños.

   (A) El primero   (C) El uno

   (B) El primer   (D) Primero

8. Había (hundreds) _____ de pájaros en San Juan Capistrano.

   (A) cien   (C) centenares

   (B) cientos   (D) un cien

9. Juan llegó un poco después de las cinco, o sea, _____.

   (A) a las cinco en punto   (C) a las cinco y pico

   (B) a eso de las cinco   (D) hace las cinco

10. Durante el invierno mi mamá siempre _____.

    (A) está fría   (C) hace frío

    (B) tiene frío   (D) es fría

Drill 16—Detailed Explanations of Answers

1. **(D)**   In time expressions involving the verb "hacer," the form of this verb will be third person singular. To balance with "esperaban" in the other part of sentence, "hacer" will be expressed in the imperfect tense also. This renders the translation "had been + ing." Therefore, (A) the present tense and (B) the preterite are incorrect. (C) is incorrect because it is plural.

2. **(C)**   The formula for this kind of expression is *hace* (never in the plural) + **time** + *que* + **preterite** (or **preterite** + *hace* + **time**). In English, this formula translates the particle "ago."

3. **(A)**   Weather conditions used with *haber* are "lodo" (muddy), "neblina" (foggy), "polvo" (dusty), "luna" (moonlight), and "nieve" (snow). A good way to remember is that these conditions are visible, whereas hot and cold are not. Forms of "estar/ser" (to be) are never used to express weather.

4. **(D)**   See the explanation given in number 3 above.

5. **(C)**   Because "doscientos" and "uno" have gender and can be feminine, and because they precede a feminine plural noun in this sample, each must also be feminine. It should be noted that "uno" cannot be plural and still mean "one."

6. **(D)**   "Ciento" apocopates to "cien" before nouns or numbers larger than itself. "Millón" also has a plural form. It will remain "millón" when accompanied by "un." Whenever a noun follows this number, **de** is needed.

7. **(A)**   The first of the month is expressed with the ordinal number "primero." All other days of the month use cardinal numbers. "Primero" apocopates to "primer" before a masculine singular noun. In this case it precedes **de** (a preposition) and apocopation is not needed.

8. **(C)**   Forms of "centenar" are preferred to forms of "ciento" when used as collective nouns.

9. **(C)**   To express "a little after the hour," use **y pico**. "En punto" means "exactly," "A eso de" means "at about," with the hour.

10. **(B)** To express warm or cold personally, **tener** is used. Because "frío" and "calor" are nouns, they do not change in gender to match the subject. "Hace frío" expresses the weather condition itself. Forms of **estar** with "frío/caliente" refer to the warmth or coolness of things (such as soup, tea, coffee, etc.)

VOCABULARY/IDIOMS

Idioms with *Dar*

dar a	to face, to look out upon
dar con	to come upon, to find
dar cuerda (a)	to wind
dar de beber (comer) a	to give a drink to, to feed
dar en	to strike against, to hit
dar gritos (voces)	to shout
dar la bienvenida	to welcome
dar la hora	to strike the hour
darse la mano	to shake hands
dar las gracias (a)	to thank
dar por + past part.	to consider
darse por + past part.	to consider oneself
dar recuerdos (a)	to give regards to
darse cuenta de	to realize
dar prisa	to hurry
dar un abrazo	to embrace
dar un paseo	to take a walk
dar un paseo en coche	to take a ride
dar una vuelta	to take a stroll
dar unas palmadas	to clap one's hands

Idioms with *Haber*

hay	there is, are
había	there was, were
hubo	there was, were (took place)
habrá	there will be
habría	there would be
ha habido	there has been
había habido	there had been
haya	there may be
hubiera	there might be
va a haber	there is going to be
iba a haber	there was going to be
tiene que haber	there has to be
puede haber	there can be
debe haber	there should be
haber de + infinitive	to be (supposed) to
haber sol	to be sunny

haber (mucho) polvo	to be (very) dusty
haber (mucho) lodo	to be (very) muddy
haber (mucha) neblina	to be (very) cloudy, foggy
hay luna	there is moonlight
hay que + infinitive	one must, it is necessary
hay + noun + *que* + inf.	there is/are + noun + inf.

Idioms with *Hacer*

hace poco	a little while ago
hacer buen (mal) tiempo	to be good (bad) weather
hacer (mucho) frío (calor)	to be (very) cold (hot)
hacer (mucho) viento	to be (very) windy
hacer caso de (a)	to pay attention to, to heed
hacer de	to act as, to work as
hacer falta	to be lacking
hacerle falta	to need
hacer el favor de	please + infinitive
hacer el papel de	to play the role of
hacer pedazos	to tear (to shreds)
hacer una broma	to play a joke
hacer una maleta	to pack a suitcase
hacer una pregunta	to ask a question
hacer una visita	to pay a visit
hacer un viaje	to take (make) a trip
hacerse	to become (through effort)
hacerse tarde	to become (grow) late
hacer daño (a)	to harm, to damage
hacerse daño	to hurt oneself

Idioms with *Tener*

tener (mucho) calor (frío)	to be (very) warm (cold)
tener cuidado	to be careful
tener dolor de cabeza (*de estómago,* etc.)	to have a headache, (stomachache, etc.)
tener éxito	to be successful
tener ganas de	to feel like doing something
tener gusto en	to be glad to
tener (mucha) hambre (sed)	to be (very) hungry (thirsty)
tener la bondad de	please + infinitive
tener la culpa (de)	to be to blame (for)
tener lugar	to take place

tener miedo de	to be afraid of
tener por + adj.	to consider
tener prisa	to be in a hurry
tener que	to have to, must
tener que ver con	to have to do with
tener razón (no tener razón)	to be right (wrong)
tener (mucho) sueño	to be (very) sleepy
tener (mucha) suerte	to be (very) lucky
tener vergüenza (de)	to be ashamed (of)

Miscellaneous Verbal Idioms

dejar caer	to drop
echar al correo	to mail
echar de menos	to miss (people)
echar la culpa (a)	to blame
encogerse de hombros	to shrug one's shoulders
estar a las anchas	to be comfortable
estar a punto de + inf.	to be about to
estar conforme (con)	to be in agreement (with)
estar de acuerdo (con)	to agree (with)
estar de pie	to be standing
estar de vuelta	to be back
estar para + inf.	to be about to
guardar cama	to stay in bed
llegar a ser	to become (through effort)
llevar a cabo	to carry out (plans, etc.)
pensar + inf.	to intend
perder cuidado	not to worry
perder de vista	to lose sight of
ponerse + adj.	to become (involuntarily)
ponerse de acuerdo	to come to an agreement
querer decir	to mean
(saber) de memoria	(to know) by heart
tocarle a uno	to be one's turn (uses I.O.)
valer la pena	to be worthwhile
volver en sí	to regain consciousness

Words with the Same English Translation

The following pairs of words cause problems because they share the same translation in English but are not interchangeable in Spanish.

To Know

a) *Conocer* is to know the sense of "being acquainted with" a person, place, or thing.

¿Conoce Ud. a Maria?	Do you know Mary?
¿Conoces bien España?	Do you know Spain well?
¿Conoce Ud. esta novela?	Do you know this novel?

Note: In the preterite, *conocer* means **met** for the first time.

La conocí ayer.	I met her yesterday.

b) *Saber* means to know a fact, know something thoroughly, or to know how (with infinitive).

¿Sabe Ud. la dirección?	Do you know the address?
¿Sabes la lección?	Do you know the lesson?
¿Sabes nadar?	Do you know how to swim?

Note: In the preterite, *saber* means **found out**.

Supiste la verdad.	You found out the truth.

To Leave

a) *Dejar* is used when you leave someone or something behind.

Dejé a María en el cine.	I left Mary at the movies.
Dejó sus libros en casa.	He left his books at home.

b) *Salir* is used in the sense of physically departing.

Salió del cuarto.	He left the room.

To Spend

Gastar refers to spending money. *Pasar* refers to spending time.

Me gusta gastar dinero.	I like to spend money.
Pasé mucho tiempo allí.	I spent a lot of time there.

To Play

Jugar refers to playing a game; *tocar* to playing an instrument.

Juego bien al tenis.	I play tennis well.
Juana toca el piano.	Juana plays the piano.

Note: **Tocar** has other uses as well:

Le toca a Juan.	It's Juan's turn.
Toqué la flor.	I touched the flower.
Alguien tocó a la puerta.	Someone knocked.

To Take

a) *Llevar* means to take in the sense of carry or transport from place to place or to take someone somewhere. It also means to wear.

José llevó la mesa a la sala.	Joe took the table to the living room.
Llevé a María al cine.	I took Mary to the movies.
¿Por qué no llevas camisa?	Why aren't you wearing a shirt?

b) *Tomar* means to grab, catch, take transportation, or take medication.

Ella tomó el libro y comenzó a leerlo.
She took the book and began to read it.

Tomé el tren hoy.
I took the train today.

¡Toma esta aspirina!
Take this aspirin!

To Ask

a) *Pedir* means to request or to ask for something. (If there is a change in subject, it will require the use of the subjunctive.)

Pedí el menú al entrar.	Upon entering I asked for the menu.
Le pido a Juan que vaya.	I ask Juan to go.

b) *Preguntar* means to inquire or ask a question.

Ella le preguntó adonde fue.	She asked him where he went.

To Return

Volver means to come back; *devolver* to give back.

Volví (Regresé) tarde.	I came back late.
Devolví el libro.	I returned the book.

To Realize

Realizar means to "make real" one's dreams, ambitions, or desires. *Darse cuenta de* means to "take note."

Juan realizó su sueño de ser doctor.
Juan realized his dream to be a doctor.

Me di cuenta de que no tenía mis apuntes.
I realized that I didn't have my notes.

To Become

a) *Llegar a ser* + noun/adj. means to become something through natural developments of time/circumstance.

   Llegó a ser capitán/poderoso.
   He became a captain/powerful.

b) *Hacerse* + noun/adj. means to become something through personal will or effort.

   Se hizo abogado/indispensable.
   He became a lawyer/indispensable.

c) *Ponerse* + adj. indicates a sudden change of emotional state or change in physical appearance.

   Ella se puso triste/gorda.
   She became sad/fat.

d) *Convertirse* + noun often indicates a somewhat unexpected change (not a profession).

   Hitler se convirtió en un verdadero tirano.
   Hitler became a real tyrant.

e) *Volverse* + adj. indicates a sudden or gradual change of personality. [Only adjectives that can be used with **both** *ser* and *estar* may follow *volverse*.]

Ella se volvió loca/alegre/sarcástica.
She became mad/happy/sarcastic.

To Enjoy

a) *Gustar, gozar de, disfrutar de* = to get pleasure from.

Me gusta viajar.
Gozo de viajar/Gozo viajando. } I like (enjoy) traveling.
Disfruto de viajar/Disfruto viajando.

b) *Divertirse* (ie, i) = have a good time, enjoy oneself.

Nos divertimos mucho aquí.   We enjoy ourselves a lot here.

To Save

a) *Salvar* means to rescue from destruction.

Ellos le salvaron la vida a ella.
They saved her life.

b) *Guardar* means to keep or put aside.

Voy a guardar mis cuentas.
I am going to keep my bills.

c) *Ahorrar* means **not** to spend or waste.

Vamos a ahorrar agua/dinero.
We are going to save water/money.

d) *Conservar* means to preserve, maintain.

Los indios conservan sus tradiciones.
The Indians preserve their traditions.

To Miss

a) *Extrañar* or *echar de menos* are used when miss = feel the absence of.

¡Cuánto lo extraño/echo de menos!
How much I miss you!

b) *Perder* means to miss an opportunity, deadline, or transportation.

Perdí el autobús/la última parte de la película.
I missed the bus/the last part of the movie.

c) *Faltar a* means to miss an appointment or fail to attend (as in a class, etc.).

Yo perdí la clase ayer. / Yo falté a la clase ayer.
I missed class yesterday.

To Move

a) *Mudarse* or *trasladarse* means to move from place to place (city to city, office to office, etc.)

Cuando era joven, me mudaba mucho.
When I was young, I moved a lot.

La compañía le trasladó a Nueva York.
The company transferred him to New York.

b) *Mover* means to physically move something.

Voy a mover el sofá cerca de la ventana.
I'm going to move the sofa near the window.

To Work

a) *Trabajar* means to work, labor, or toil.

Juan trabaja cada día en la oficina.
Juan works everyday in the office.

b) *Funcionar* means to work, operate, or function.

El coche/tocadiscos no funciona.
The car/record player doesn't work.

To Keep

a) *Quedarse con* means to keep something in one's possession.

Me quedo con la tarea hasta mañana.
I'll keep the homework until tomorrow.

b) *Guardar* means to hold or put away for safekeeping.

Voy a guardar mi dinero en la caja fuerte.
I'm going to keep my money in the safe.

False Cognates

A cognate is a word whose origin is the same as another word in other languages. Often the spelling is identical and the meanings are similar. The false cognates, however, cause the most problems, particularly in the reading comprehension passages.

actual	of the present time
antiguo, –a	former, old, ancient
la apología	eulogy, defense
la arena	sand
asistir a	to attend
atender	to take care of
el auditorio	audience
bizarro, –a	brave, generous
el campo	field, country(side)
el cargo	duty, burden, responsibility
la carta	letter
el colegio	(high) school
el collar	necklace
la complexión	temperament
la conferencia	lecture
la confidencia	secret, trust
constipado, –a	sick with a cold
la consulta	conference
la chanza	joke, fun
la decepción	disappointment
el delito	crime
la desgracia	misfortune
el desmayo	fainting
embarazada	pregnant
el éxito	success
la fábrica	factory
la firma	signature
el idioma	language
ignorar	to be unaware
intoxicar	to poison
largo, –a	long
la lectura	reading
la librería	book store
la maleta	suitcase
el mantel	tablecloth
mayor	older, greater
molestar	to bother

el oficio	trade, occupation
la pala	shovel
el partido	game (sports)
pinchar	to puncture
pretender	to attempt
recordar	to remember
ropa	clothing
sano, —a	healthy
sensible	sensitive
soportar	to tolerate
el suceso	event, happening

☞ Drill 17

1. El tiempo ya había pasado, pero él no _____.

   (A) los realizaba   (C) daba cuenta

   (B) lo realizó   (D) se daba cuenta

2. Me gusta juntar dinero para las necesidades del futuro, por eso tengo una cuenta de _____.

   (A) ahorros   (C) guarda

   (B) salvos   (D) salvar

3. Ramón no _____ a los padres de su novia.

   (A) muerde   (C) conoce

   (B) toca   (D) sabe

4. Ramón no _____ que los padres de su novia son inmigrantes.

   (A) conoce   (C) responde

   (B) sabe   (D) pregunta

5. Quiso abrir la puerta del auto pero en ese momento _____ de que había perdido la llave.

   (A) realizó   (C) se encerró

   (B) se repuso   (D) se dio cuenta

6. En el estadio _____ muchos espectadores ayer.

    (A) tenían   (C) hay

    (B) habían   (D) había

7. La mujer _____ su bolsa en su coche.

    (A) dejó   (C) salió

    (B) partió   (D) se quitó

8. Elena _____ los apuntes al profesor.

    (A) preguntó   (C) pidió

    (B) preguntó para   (D) pidió por

9. Juan _____ la silla de la sala a la cocina.

    (A) llevó   (C) tomó

    (B) levantó   (D) arrancó

10. Cuando vi el huracán, _____ pálida.

    (A) llegué a ser   (C) me hice

    (B) volví   (D) me puse

11. Yo sé jugar al golf y mi mejor amigo sabe _____ piano.

    (A) jugar el   (C) tocar el

    (B) jugar al   (D) tocar al

12. Este alumno no _____ estudiar bien.

    (A) conoce   (C) sabe de

    (B) sabe a   (D) sabe

13. Basta que los turistas _____ la ciudad antes de salir.

    (A) conozcan   (C) saben

    (B) sepan   (D) conocen

14. Los estudiantes _____ a la profesora cómo estaba.

    (A) pidieron   (C) preguntaron

    (B) pusieron   (D) pudieron

15. La señora Gómez _____ el cheque y se fue al banco.

    (A) vendió   (C) llevó

    (B) compró   (D) tomó

16. Mi hermano quiere _____ doctor.

    (A) llegar a ser   (C) ponerse

    (B) volverse   (D) convertirse en

17. No me encanta _____ mucho tiempo en la cárcel.

    (A) gastar   (C) pasar

    (B) gastando   (D) pasando

18. Mis amigas han _____ traer los refrescos.

    (A) de   (C) por

    (B) a   (D) nothing needed

19. Nuestro cuarto da _____ patio.

    (A) por el   (C) al

    (B) para el   (D) en el

20. Juan y María hablan de ganar el premio gordo y esperan tener _____.

    (A) lugar   (C) hambre

    (B) el tiempo   (D) éxito

21. Ese actor sabe _____ de Sancho Panza bien.

    (A) hacer caso   (C) hacer el papel

    (B) hacer falta   (D) hacer un viaje

22. Tengo que _____ los libros a la biblioteca hoy.

    (A) regresar   (C) devolver

    (B) dejar   (D) volver

23. Yo quiero que los chicos _____ en la playa.

    (A) se diviertan   (C) gozan

    (B) gocen   (D) se divierten

24. Cuando me levanto tarde, siempre _____ el autobús.

    (A) falto a   (C) echo de menos

    (B) pierdo   (D) extraño

25. _____ de Los Ángeles hace cinco años.

    (A) Moví   (C) Me mudé

    (B) Movía   (D) Me mudaría

26. Por ser tan viejo mi coche rehusa _____.

    (A) trabajar   (C) empezar

    (B) tejer   (D) funcionar

27. La profesora me dijo, –¡ _____ la tarea para mañana!

    (A) quédese con   (C) salve

    (B) guarde   (D) gaste

28. Murió sin _____ su sueño de ser doctor famoso.

    (A) darse cuenta de   (C) saber

    (B) realizar   (D) ponerse

29. _____ mucha tarea _____ hacer esta noche.

    (A) Hay . . . para   (C) Hay . . . que

    (B) Hay . . . (nothing needed) (D) Hay . . . por

30. Tiene que _____ una razón por sus acciones.

    (A) haber   (C) ser

    (B) estar   (D) pensar

Drill 17—Detailed Explanations of Answers

1. **(D)** **Darse cuenta** must be used here for "to realize." **Realizar** means "to realize" in the sense of gaining or resulting in. (C) would be correct if it were reflexive.

2. **(A)** A "savings account" (**ahorros**) is the only correct answer. None of the other answers indicates this. **Salvar** is "to save," but in the sense of rescuing, not in the banking sense, and **guardar** might mean "to save," but only in the sense "to keep from harm" or "to keep back."

3. **(C)** The correct answer comes down to a choice between "conoce" and "sabe," both modalities of "to know." (The first two choices don't make much sense.)

4. **(B)** Again, an exercise to distinguish between "saber" and "conocer" (and again, the last two choices don't fit semantically or grammatically). When it's a matter of knowing information (as in this case), the correct choice is "saber."

5. **(D)** Choices (B) and (C) simply make no sense in the context. You may think that (A) is the obvious choice since it sounds like it means "realized." It does, but not in the sense demanded by the question, which can only be rendered by (D). ("Realizar" means "to realize" a project or a plan, to make something real.)

6. **(D)** Choice (B) is incorrect because the verb "haber" is impersonal when it translates "there is," "there are," etc. (i.e., when not used in an auxiliary capacity). Choice (C) contradicts the adverb of time in the question ("ayer"), and choice (A) could only be the product of confusion between the meaning and use of "haber" and "tener."

7. **(A)**   "Dejar" means to leave something behind. "Salir" means to physically leave a place. "Partir" means to depart, and "quitarse" means to remove (as in clothing).

8. **(C)**   "Pedir" means to ask for something or to request, while "preguntar" means to inquire or ask a question. Neither needs "por" nor "para" in this sample.

9. **(A)**   "Llevar" means to carry or transport from one place to another or to take someone somewhere. "Tomar" means to take, in the sense of grab or catch. "Levantar" means to lift and "arrancar" means to start, as in an engine.

10. **(D)**   "Ponerse" is used with adjectives to indicate a sudden change of emotional state or physical appearance. "Llegar a ser" is used with adjectives/nouns and means to become something through natural developments of time/circumstance. "Hacerse" also used with adjectives/nouns means to become something through effort. "Volverse" is used with adjectives to indicate a sudden or gradual change of personality.

11. **(C)**   "Jugar a" is used in connection with sports. "Tocar" is used in connection with instruments.

12. **(D)**   "Conocer" means to know or be acquainted with people, places, or things. "Saber" is to know facts or know "how" to do something (when followed by an infinitive).

13. **(A)**   The difference between "saber" and "conocer" is given in number 12. One also needs to recognize that the subjunctive is required in this sample. The sentence begins with an impersonal expression ("it is enough") and there is a change in subject.

14. **(C)**   "Preguntar" is used to inquire or ask a question. "Pusieron" from "poner" means "they put" and "pudieron" from "poder" means "they were able/managed." (A) pidieron means "to ask for" and "to order."

15. **(D)**   "Tomar" means to take in the sense of grab or catch. In this sample Mrs. Gomez is "grabbing" the check to take it to the bank. "Vendió" from "vender" means "she sold," and "compró" from "comprar" means "she bought."

16. **(A)** To become something through the natural development of time/circumstance is "llegar a ser." "Ponerse" and "volverse" must be followed by adjectives. "Convertirse en" is used with nouns but indicates a somewhat unexpected change (not a profession).

17. **(C)** To spend **time** is "pasar." "Gastar" means to spend money. Because this verb is the subject of "me encanta," it is a gerund and must be in the infinitive form in Spanish. In Spanish a present participle may not be treated as a noun.

18. **(A)** The idiom "haber de" means to be (supposed) to. Neither "a" nor "por" is used with this verb. "Han" cannot be used alone.

19. **(C)** "Dar a" means to face. "Dar en" means to hit or strike against, which makes no sense in this sentence.

20. **(D)** "Tener éxito" means to be successful. "Tener lugar" means to take place. "Tener el tiempo" means to have the time, and "tener hambre" means to be hungry.

21. **(C)** "Hacer el papel de" means to play a part or role. "Hacer caso de" means to notice. "Hacer falta" means to need and is used like *gustar*. "Hacer un viaje" means to take a trip.

22. **(C)** To return objects/things, one uses the verb "devolver." Both "regresar" and "volver" are intransitive verbs (cannot take direct objects) and are used to indicate a physical return. "Dejar" means to allow/let.

23. **(A)** "Divertirse" means to enjoy oneself. "Gozar" followed by a present participle or "gozar de" followed by a noun means to get pleasure from. Also, one needs the subjunctive here since there is a verb of volition and a change in subject.

24. **(B)** "Perder" means to miss a deadline or transportation. "Echar de menos" and "extrañar" mean to feel the absence of (as in people). "Faltar a" means to miss an appointment or a class, for example.

25. **(C)** To move from place to place is "mudarse." "Mover" is to move objects. The preterite is needed here since this is an "hace" statement meaning **ago**.

26. **(D)** "Funcionar" means to work/operate/function (as in things). "Trabajar" is for people. "Tejer" means to weave, and "empezar" means to begin or start. To start a car, however, is "arrancar."

27. **(A)** "Quedarse con" means to keep in one's possession. "Guardar" means to put away for safe keeping (as in money or jewelry). "Salvar" means to save lives and "gastar" means to spend money.

28. **(B)** "Realizar" means to realize one's dreams, hopes, or ambitions. "Darse cuenta de" means to take note. "Saber" is to know facts or how to do something and "ponerse" means to become something unexpectedly (as in pale, sick, angry, etc.).

29. **(C)** These are the missing parts of the idiom "*hay* + noun + *que* + infinitive" which is translated: There is a lot of homework to do tonight.

30. **(A)** Through translation, "haber" is the logical choice: There has to be a reason for his actions.

In addition to vocabulary, spelling, and grammar, Part C of the Reading portion of the CLEP Spanish Test provides students with an "original document." Students will be asked to read the short passage and answer two to three questions based on what they have read. A sample document and two practice questions follow.

INSTRUCCIONES PARA INDIVIDUOS QUE DESEAN REGISTRARSE PARA VOTAR.

- Usted tiene derecho de registrarse para votar sí;
  - – Usted es un ciudadano de los Estados Unidos.
  - – Usted tendrá 18 años de edad o más para el tiempo de la próxima elección.
  - – Usted tiene que haber vivido en New Jersey y en su condado por lo menos 30 días antes de las próximas elecciones.
- Formularios de registración para el votante debe ser completado en tinta oscura y en letra clara de imprenta (excepción las firmas).
- Si usted necesita alguna asistencia en completar el formulario, incluyendo la necesidad de un testigo, requiera ayuda en esta oficina.
- Usted no será considerado un votante certificado válido hasta que su formulario sea recibido y aprobado por el Comisionado Certificado del Condado. El Comisionado lo notificará por correo si aceptaron o rechazaron su formulario.
- Para usted poder votar en cualquier elección, usted debe registrarse para el 29 día antes de la elección.
- Si usted tiene alguna pregunta en respecto a su registración por correo, usted debe comunicarse con el Comisionado Certificado del Condado. Las direcciones y teléfonos de los Comisionados Certificados del Condado están listados en la parte inversa de este formulario.
- Usted no podrá registrarse para votar si usted tiene alguna de las siguientes descalificaciones establecidas;
  - – Un tribunal de jurisdicción competente lo ha determinado a usted ser "demente" o un "idiota".
  - – Usted está o será condenado de haber violado el Título 19, Leyes de Elección, por el cual, privarse de derechos civiles es parte del castigo a menos perdonar o devolver por ley al derecho de sufragio.
  - – Usted está sirviendo una sentencia o en libertad condicional o en un período de prueba como resultado de una condena por una ofensa encausable bajo las leyes de ésta u otro estado o de los Estados Unidos.

1. ¿Qué no se permite cuando uno se registra para votar?

    (A) tener menos de 18 años antes de registrarse

    (B) completar el formulario con bolígrafo

    (C) completar el formulario con la ayuda de otro

    (D) firmar el formulario sin testigo certificado

2. No se puede registrar si

    (A) ha sido condenado por la corte

    (B) ha estado en su condado

    (C) un psiquiatra ha determinado que Ud. es demente

    (D) ha cometido un delito o crímen

ANSWERS TO PRACTICE QUESTIONS

1. **(D)**   The correct answer is (D). It is not permitted to sign a voter registration form without the presence of a witness who is registered to vote in the state. (A) is incorrect since you may be younger than 18 years of age at the time of registration as long as you will be 18 years of age at the time of the next election. The form should be completed with an ink pen only, and if needed, the assistance of another person. Therefore, (C) and (B) are incorrect.

2. **(A)**   The correct answer is (A). You may not register to vote if you have been convicted of an offense. (D) is incorrect since you may have committed a crime without conviction, in which case you would not lose your right to vote. (B) simply means that you have been in your county. The determination of "demented" is made by a court of law, not a psychiatrist (C).

▼

CHAPTER 3

ENGLISH TO SPANISH DICTIONARY

Chapter 3

ENGLISH TO SPANISH DICTIONARY

Use the English to Spanish dictionary that appears on the following pages to prepare for the exam. A strong vocabulary will increase your potential for a high score.

After the English to Spanish dictionary, is a Spanish to English version. Use this one to learn the meanings of Spanish words that you were unfamiliar with from the questions or passages.

action – *n.* – *la acción*

actor – *n.* – *el actor*

actress – *n.* – *la actriz*

after – *prep.* – *después de*

airline – *n.* – *la aerolinea*

airplane – *n.* – *el avión*

alley – *n.* – *el callejón*

almost – *adv.* – *casi*

always – *adv.* – *siempre*

ancient – *adj.* – *antiguo*

angry (to get) – *v.* – *enfadarse* (*enojarse, molestarse*)

ankle – *n.* – *el tobillo*

announcer – *n.* – *el (la) locutor (a)*

apple – *n.* – *la manzana*

arm – *n.* – *el brazo*

aroma – *n.* – *el aroma*

arrive – *v.* – *llegar*

artist – *n.* – *el artista / la artista*

athletic – *adj.* – *atlético*

attempt – *v.* – *intentar*

attend – *v.* – *asistir a*

audience – *n.* – *el público*

aunt – *n.* – *la tía*

autumn – *n.* – *el otoño*

avenue – *n.* – *la avenida*

back – *n.* – *la espalda*

bacon – *n.* – *el tocino*

bad – *adj.* – *malo, mal*

banana, plantain – *n.* – *el plátano*
(*la banana*)

bathroom – *n.* – *el baño*

bathtub – *n.* – *la tina / la bañera*

beach – *n.* – *la playa*

beard – *n.* – *la barba*

beautiful – *adj.* – *bello*

bed – *n.* – *la cama*

bedroom – *n.* – *el dormitorio*
(*alcoba*)

beer – *n.* – *la cerveza*

before – *prep.* – *antes de*

begin – *v.* – *empezar*

believe – *v.* – *creer*

better – *adj.* – *mejor*

big – *adj.* – *grande*

bird – *n.* – *el pájaro*

birth – *n.* – *el nacimiento*

birthday – *n.* – *el cumpleaños*

black – *adj.* – *negro*

blind – *adj.* – *ciego*

blue – *adj.* – *azul*

boar – *n.* – *el jabalí*

boat – *n.* – *el bote, la barca*

book – *n.* – *el libro*

bookstore – *n.* – *la librería*

boring – *adj.* – *aburrido*

born (to be) – *v.* – *nacer*

boss – *n.* – *el jefe*

bother – *v.* – *molestar*

box – *n.* – *la caja*

boy – *n.* – *el niño*

bread – *n.* – *el pan*

bring – *v.* – *traer*

bronchitis – *n.* – *la bronquitis*

brother – *n.* – *el hermano*

brown – *adj.* – *marrón, pardo*

brush – *v.* – *cepillarse*

building – *n.* – *el edificio*

bull – *n.* – *el toro*

bus – *n.* – *el ómnibus* (*autobús;*
microbús; la guagua)

business – *n.* – *el negocio*

businessman – *n.* – *el hombre de*
negocios

butter – *n.* – *la mantequilla*

buy – *v.* – *comprar*

cake – *n.* – *la torta (la tarta)*

car – *n.* – *el auto, automóvil, coche,*
carro

carry – *v.* – *llevar*

cat – *n.* – *el gato*

cathedral – *n.* – *la catedral*

chair – *n.* – *la silla*

change – *v.* – *cambiar*

cheese – *n.* – *el queso*

chemist – *n.* – *el químico*

chemistry – *n.* – *la química*

chest – *n.* – *el pecho*

chicken – *n.* – *el pollo*

Christmas – *n.* – *la Navidad / las Navidades*

city – *n.* – *la ciudad*

clean – *adj.* – *limpio*

climate – *n.* – *el clima*

clothing – *n.* – *la ropa*

coat – *n.* – *la chaqueta, el saco, el abrigo*

coffee – *n.* – *el café*

coffin – *n.* – *el ataúd*

cold – *adj.* – *frío*

colleague – *n.* – *el colega*

comb – *n.* – *la peinilla (el peine)*

comb (one's hair) – *v.* – *peinarse*

comet – *n.* – *el cometa*

computer – *n.* – *el ordenador (la computadora)*

conference – *n.* – *la conferencia / el congreso*

corn – *n.* – *el choclo (maíz)*

couch – *n.* – *el sillón*

courageous – *adj.* – *valiente*

course – *n.* – *el curso*

courteous – *adj.* – *cortés*

cow – *n.* – *la vaca*

crime – *n.* – *el delito, el crimen*

crisis – *n.* – *la crisis*

crowd – *n.* – *la muchedumbre*

cup – *n.* – *la taza*

cure – *n.* – *la cura*

daughter – *n.* – *la hija*

daughter-in-law – *n.* – *la nuera*

day – *n.* – *el día*

death – *n.* – *la muerte*

deer – *n.* – *el ciervo (venado)*

departure – *n.* – *la salida*

desk – *n.* – *el escritorio*

dessert – *n.* – *el postre*

die – *v.* – *morir*

difficult – *adj.* – *difícil*

dining room – *n.* – *el comedor*

diploma – *n.* – *el diploma*

dirty – *adj.* – *sucio*

disappointment – *n.* – *la decepción*

doctor – *n.* – *el doctor / la doctora*

dog – *n.* – *el perro*

door – *n.* – *la puerta*

down (to go) – *v.* – *bajar*

downtown – *n.* – *el centro*

drama – *n.* – *el drama*

drawing – *n.* – *el dibujo*

dream – *n.* – *el sueño*

dream – *v.* – *soñar*

dress (oneself) – *v.* – *vestirse*

dresser – *n.* – *la cómoda (el tocador)*

drink – *v.* – *beber (tomar)*

drive – *v.* – *manejar (conducir, guiar)*

drunk (to get) – *v.* – *emborracharse*

eagle – *n.* – *el águila*

ear – *n.* – *la oreja*

early – *adv.* – *temprano*

easy – *adj.* – *fácil*

eat – *v.* – *comer*

elbow – *n.* – *el codo*

elevator – *n.* – *el ascensor*

engineer – *n.* – *el ingeniero*

enough – *adv.* – *bastante*

enter – *v.* – *entrar*

entrance, lobby – *n.* – *la entrada*

envelope – *n.* – *el sobre*

eulogy – *n.* – *el elogio*

event – *n.* – *el suceso*

expensive – *adj.* – *caro*

eyeglasses – *n.* – *los anteojos, las gafas, los espejuelos*

eyelashes – *n.* – *las pestañas*

eyelids – *n.* – *los párpados*

eye – *n.* – *el ojo*

face – *n.* – *la cara*

factory – *n.* – *la fábrica*

fainting – *n.* – *el desmayo*

fall (down) – *v.* – *caer(se)*

family – *n.* – *la familia*

fantastic – *adj.* – *fantástico*

far – *adj.* – *lejos*

farm – *n.* – *la granja*

farmer – *n.* – *el agricultor*

fat – *adj.* – *gordo/a*

father – *n.* – *el padre*

fear – *n.* – *el miedo*

female – *n.* – *la hembra*

field – *n.* – *el campo*

film – *n.* – *la película*

film director ("auteur") or producer – *n.* – *el cineasta*

fingernails – *n.* – *las uñas*

fingers – *n.* – *los dedos*

fire – *n.* – *el fuego*

fireplace; chimney – *n.* – *la chimenea*

fish – *n.* – *el pescado, pez*

fishing – *v.* – *pescar*

flight – *n.* – *el vuelo*

floppy disk – *n.* – *el disco flexible*

fly – *v.* – *volar*

forehead – *n.* – *la frente*

forget – *v.* – *olvidar*

fragile – *adj.* – *frágil*

funny – *adj.* – *divertido*

game – *n.* – *el partido*

garden – *n.* – *el jardín*

glass – *n.* – *el vaso*

goat – *n.* – *la cabra*

God – *n.* – *Dios*

gold – *n.* – *el oro*

good – *adj.* – *bueno*

good-bye – *adiós, hasta luego*

granddaughter – *n.* – *la nieta*

grandfather – *n.* – *el abuelo*

grandmother – *n.* – *la abuela*

grandson – *n.* – *el nieto*

grapes – *n.* – *las uvas*

grass (tended, not wild) – *n.* – *la hierba*

great-grandfather – *n.* – *el bisabuelo*

great-grandmother – *n.* – *la bisabuela*

green – *adj.* – *verde*

greet – *v.* – *saludar*

grow (get) tired – *v.* – *cansarse*

grow – *v.* – *crecer, cultivar*

guide (book) – *n.* – *la guía*

guide (person) – *n.* – *el guía*

hair – *n.* – *el cabello (pelo)*

ham – *n.* – *el jamón*

hand – *n.* – *la mano*

handsome – *adj.* – *guapo*

happy – *adj.* – *feliz, contento*

hard – *adj.* – *duro, difícil*

hard disk – *n.* – *el disco duro*

hatchet – *n.* – *el hacha*

hate – *v.* – *odiar*

head – *n.* – *la cabeza*

health – *n.* – *la salud*

healthy – *adj.* – *sano (a)*

hear – *v.* – *oír, escuchar*

heel – *n.* – *el talón*

hen – *n.* – *la gallina*

hips – *n.* – *las caderas*

hope – *n.* – *la esperanza*

horse – *n.* – *el caballo*

house (big) – *n.* – *la casona*

house – *n.* – *la casa*

hunger – *n.* – *el hambre*

husband – *n.* – *el marido, esposo*

image – *n.* – *la imagen*

intelligent – *adj.* – *inteligente*

interesting – *adj.* – *interesante*

internal – *adj.* – *interior*

intersection – *n.* – *la bocacalle*

iron – *n.* – *el hierro*

joke – *n.* – *la chanza, el chiste*

journalist – *n.* – *el periodista*

joy – *n.* – *la alegría*

judge – *n.* – *el juez*

keep – *v.* – *mantener*

keyboard – *n.* – *el teclado*

king – *n.* – *el rey*

kitchen – *n.* – *la cocina*

kite – *n.* – *la cometa*

knee – *n.* – *la rodilla*

know – *v.* – *saber (conocer)*

lamp – *n.* – *la lámpara*

language – *n.* – *el idioma*

last night – *adv.* – *anoche*

late – *adv.* – *tarde*

later – *adv.* – *luego*

lawyer – *n.* – *el abogado*

learn – *v.* – *aprender*

leave – *v.* – *irse, partir*

lecture – *n.* – *la conferencia*

less – *adv.* – *menos*

letter – *n.* – *la carta*

lettuce – *n.* – *la lechuga*

light – *n.* – *la luz*

like – *v.* – *gustar*

lip – *n.* – *el labio*

listen to – *v.* – *escuchar*

living room – *n.* – *la sala*

long – *adj.* – *largo*

look at – *v.* – *mirar*

lose – *v.* – *perder*

love – *n.* – *el amor*

luck – *n.* – *la suerte*

luggage – *n.* – *el equipaje*

lunch – *n.* – *el almuerzo*

machine – *n.* – *la máquina*

magazine – *n.* – *la revista*

mail – *n.* – *el correo*

mailman – *n.* – *el cartero*

make (do) – *v.* – *hacer*

male – *n.* – *el macho*

man (big) – *n.* – *el hombrón*

map – *n.* – *el mapa*

market – *n.* – *el mercado*

marvelous – *adj.* – *maravillosa/o*

mean – *adj.* – *soez*

meat – *n.* – *la carne*

mechanic – *n.* – *el mecánico*

microwave oven – *n.* – *el microondas*

milk – *n.* – *la leche*

mirror – *n.* – *el espejo*

misfortune – *n.* – *la desgracia*

money – *n.* – *el dinero*

moon – *n.* – *la luna*

more – *adv.* – *más*

morning – *n.* – *la mañana*

mother – *n.* – *la madre*

motorcycle – *n.* – *la moto*

mountain – *n.* – *la montaña*

mountain climbing – *n.* – *el alpinismo*

mouse – *n.* – *el ratón*

mouth – *n.* – *la boca*

move – *v.* – *mover(se)*, *mudarse*

moviehouse – *n.* – *el cine*

muscles – *n.* – *los músculos*

nail – *n.* – *el clavo*

name – *n.* – *el nombre*

near – *adj.* – *cerca*

neck – *n.* – *el cuello*

necklace – *n.* – *el collar*

need – *v.* – *necesitar*

neighbor – *n.* – *el vecino*

neighborhood – *n.* – *el vecindario*

nephew – *n.* – *el sobrino*

never – *adv.* – *nunca*

newspaper – *n.* – *el periódico*, *diario*

niece – *n.* – *la sobrina*

night – *n.* – *la noche*

night table – *n.* – *el velador*

nightmare – *n.* – *la pesadilla*

noise – *n.* – *el ruido*

nose – *n.* – *la nariz*

notes – *n.* – *los apuntes*

nothing – *nada*

nurse – *n.* – *la enfermera*

occupation – *n.* – *el oficio*

old – *adj.* – *viejo*, *antiguo*

older – *adj.* – *mayor*

olive – *n.* – *la aceituna*

order (as in public order) – *n.* – *el orden*

order (to do something) – *n.* – *la orden*

order, ask – *v.* – *pedir*

out (to go) – *v.* – *salir*

outer – *adj.* – *exterior*

oven; furnace – *n.* – *el horno*

owe – *v.* – *deber*

painting – *n.* – *el cuadro*

pants – *n.* – *los pantalones*

paper – *n.* – *el papel*

parachuting – *n.* – *el paracaidismo*

park – *v.* – *estacionarse*

parking lot – *n.* – *la plaza de estacionamiento*

passenger – *n.* – *el (la) pasajero (a)*

passport – *n.* – *el pasaporte*

pay – *v.* – *pagar*

peach – *n.* – *el durazno*

pear – *n.* – *la pera*

pencil – *n.* – *el lápiz*

people – *n.* – *la gente*

photo – *n.* – *la foto*

physician – *n.* – *el médico, la doctor (a)*

physicist – *n.* – *el físico*

pig – *n.* – *el cerdo* (*el chancho, el puerco, el marrano*)

pink – *adj.* – *rosa* (*rosado*)

play – *v.* – *jugar*

player – *n.* – *el (la) jugador (a)*

poem – *n.* – *el poema*

poet – *n.* – *el poeta*

poison (to) – *v.* – *intoxicar, envenenar*

police – *n.* – *la policía*

politician – *n.* – *el político*

Pope – *n.* – *el Papa*

potato – *n.* – *la papa* (*las patatas*)

prefer – *v.* – *preferir*

pregnant – *adj.* – *embarazada*

prepare – *v.* – *preparar*

presence – *n.* – *la presencia*

pretty – *adj.* – *bonito*

price – *n.* – *el precio*

prick, wound – *v.* – *pinchar*

priest – *n.* – *el cura*

printer – *n.* – *la impresora*

problem – *n.* – *el problema*

prophet – *n.* – *el profeta*

purple – *adj.* – *morado* (*violeta*)

pyramid – *n.* – *la pirámide*

queen – *n.* – *la reina*

quiet – *adj.* – *callado*

rabbit – *n.* – *el conejo*

radio – *n.* – *el radio*

read – *v.* – *leer*

reading – *n.* – *la lectura*

reason – *n.* – *la razón*

record player – *n.* – *el tocadiscos*

red – *adj.* – *rojo, colorado*

referee – *n.* – *el árbitro*

refrigerator – *n.* – *el refrigerador, (la) heladera* (*nevera*)

remember – *v.* – *recordar*

rent – *v.* – *alquilar*

responsibility – *n.* – *la responsabilidad*

rest – *v.* – *descansar*

return – *v.* – *regresar* (*volver*)

rice – *n.* – *el arroz*

rich – *adj.* – *rico*

ring – *n.* – *el anillo*

river – *n.* – *el río*

roof; ceiling – *n.* – *el techo*

rooster – *n.* – *el gallo*

run – *v.* – *correr*

sad – *adj.* – *triste*

salad – *n.* – *la ensalada*

salesman – *n.* – *el vendedor*

sand – *n.* – *la arena*

say (tell) – *v.* – *decir*

school (high) – *n.* – *el colegio*

school – *n.* – *la escuela*

sea – *n.* – *el mar*

secret – *n.* – *la confidencia (el secreto)*

see – *v.* – *ver*

sell – *v.* – *vender*

send – *v.* – *enviar, mandar*

sensitive – *adj.* – *sensible*

sentence – *n.* – *la frase*

series – *n.* – *la serie*

shark – *n.* – *el tiburón*

shave – *v.* – *afeitar(se)*

sheep – *n.* – *la oveja*

sheets – *n.* – *las sábanas*

shirt – *n.* – *la camisa*

shoe – *n.* – *el zapato*

shopping – *v.* – *ir de compras*

short – *adj.* – *corto, bajo*

shoulders – *n.* – *los hombros*

shovel – *n.* – *la pala*

shower – *n.* – *la ducha*

sick (person) – *n.* – *el enfermo (a)*

sidewalk – *n.* – *la acera (vereda)*

signature – *n.* – *la firma*

silent (to be) – *v.* – *callar*

silver – *n.* – *la plata*

singer – *n.* – *el cantante*

sink – *n.* – *el lavamanos*

sister – *n.* – *la hermana*

sit down – *v.* – *sentarse*

sleep – *v.* – *dormir*

small – *adj.* – *chico, pequeño*

smile – *n.* – *la sonrisa*

smoke – *n.* – *el humo*

smoke – *v.* – *fumar*

snack – *n.* – *la merienda*

snorkel – *v.* – *bucear*

soccer – *n.* – *el fútbol*

society – *n.* – *la sociedad*

sock – *n.* – *el calcetín, la media*

sofa – *n.* – *el sofá*

soldier – *n.* – *el soldado*

some – *adj.* – *poco*

someone – *n.* – *alguien*

something – *n.* – *algo*

sometimes – *adv.* – *a veces*

son – *n.* – *el hijo*

son-in-law – *n.* – *el yerno*

spinach – *n.* – *la espinaca*

sport – *n.* – *el deporte*

square – *n.* – *la plaza*

squirrel – *n.* – *la ardilla*

stairs – *n.* – *las escaleras*

stand – *v.* – *pararse, ponerse de pie, levantarse*

star – *n.* – *la estrella*

still – *adv.* – *todavía*

stop – *v.* – *detenerse (pararse)*

store – *n.* – *la tienda*

store clerk – *n.* – *el (la) dependiente*

strawberry – *n.* – *la fresa*

street – *n.* – *la calle*

strong – *adj.* – *fuerte*

student – *n.* – *el (la) estudiante*

subway – *n.* – *el subterráneo (metro)*

success – *n.* – *el éxito*

sugar – *n.* – *el azúcar*

suitcase – *n.* – *la maleta*

sun – *n.* – *el sol*

superior – *adj.* – *superior*

surgeon – *n.* – *el cirujano*

sweetheart – *n.* – *el amorcito*

swim – *v.* – *nadar*

switch (light) – *n.* – *el conmutador*

system – *n.* – *el sistema*

table – *n.* – *la mesa*

tablecloth – *n.* – *el mantel*

tailor – *n.* – *el sastre*

talk – *v.* – *hablar (conversar)*

tap – *n.* – *el grifo (la llave)*

tape recorder – *n.* – *la grabadora*

teacher – *n.* – *el profesor (la profesora)*

team – *n.* – *el equipo*

technician – *n.* – *el técnico*

television – *n.* – *la televisión*

temperament – *n.* – *el temperamento*

Thanksgiving – *n.* – *el Día de Acción de Gracias*

theme – *n.* – *el tema*

then – *adv.* – *entonces*

thighs – *n.* – *los muslos*

thin – *adj.* – *flaco*

think – *v.* – *pensar*

thirst – *n.* – *la sed*

thus – *adv.* – *así*

time – *n.* – *la vez*

tip – *n.* – *la propina*

tired – *adj.* – *cansado*

tolerate – *v.* – *soportar*

tongue – *n.* – *la lengua*

too much – *adv.* – *demasiado*

tooth – *n.* – *los dientes*

towel – *n.* – *la toalla*

tower – *n.* – *la torre*

train – *n.* – *el tren*

travel – *v.* – *viajar*

trolley – *n.* – *el tranvía*

turf – *n.* – *el césped*

turkey – *n.* – *el pavo*

turtle – *n.* – *la tortuga*

typist – *n.* – *el mecanógrafo / la mechanógrafa*

unaware (to be) – *v.* – *ignorar*

uncle – *n.* – *el tío*

up (to get) – *v.* – *levantarse (pararse)*

up (to go) – *v.* – *subir*

vacation – *n.* – *las vacaciones*

vase – *n.* – *el florero, el jarrón*

vegetables – *n.* – *las verduras (las legumbres)*

vulgar – *adj.* – *vulgar*

waist – *n.* – *la cintura*

wait – *v.* – *esperar, aguardar*

walk – *v.* – *caminar (andar)*

want – *v.* – *querer*

watch – *n.* – *el reloj*

watch – *v.* – *observar, vigilar*

water – *n.* – *el agua*

watermelon – *n.* – *la sandía*

waves – *n.* – *las olas*

weak – *adj.* – *débil*

wedding – *n.* – *las bodas, el casamiento*

well – *adj.* – *bien*

whale – *n.* – *la ballena*

white – *adj.* – *blanco*

wife – *n.* – *la esposa, la señora, la mujer*

win – *v.* – *ganar*

wind – *n.* – *el viento*

window – *n.* – *la ventana*

wine – *n.* – *el vino*

wood – *n.* – *la madera*

work – *v.* – *trabajar*

worse – *adj.* – *peor*

wrist – *n.* – *la muñeca*

write – *v.* – *escribir*

writer – *n.* – *el (la) escritor (a)*

yard – *n.* – *el patio*

yellow – *adj.* – *amarillo*

yesterday – *adv.* – *ayer*

young man – *n.* – *el muchacho, el joven*

young woman – *n.* – *la muchacha, la joven*

CHAPTER 4

SPANISH TO ENGLISH DICTIONARY

Chapter 4

SPANISH TO ENGLISH DICTIONARY

a veces – adv. – sometimes

abogado – n. – (m.) lawyer

abrigo – n. – (m.) coat

abuela – n. – (f.) grandmother

abuelo – n. – (m.) grandfather

aburrido – adj. – boring

acción – n. – (f.) action

aceituna – n. – (f.) olive

acera (vereda) – n. – (f.) sidewalk

actor – n. – (m.) actor

actriz – n. – (f.) actress

adiós, hasta luego – good-bye

aerolinea – n. – (f.) airline

afeitar(se) – v. – shave

agricultor – n. – (m.) farmer

agua – n. – (f.) water

aguardar – v. – wait

águila – n. – (m.) eagle

alegría – n. – (f.) joy

algo – n. – something

alguien – n. – someone

almuerzo – n. – (m.) lunch

alpinismo – n. – (m.) mountain climbing

alquilar – v. – rent

amarillo – adj. – yellow

amor – n. – (m.) love

amorcito – n. – (m.) sweetheart

anillo – n. – (m.) ring

anoche – adv. – last night

anteojos – n. – (m.) eyeglasses

antes de – prep. – before

antiguo – adj. – ancient, old

aprender – v. – learn

apuntes – n. – (m.) notes, as those you take in class

árbitro – n. – (m.) referee

ardilla – n. – (f.) squirrel

arena – n. – (f.) sand

aroma – n. – (m.) aroma

arroz – n. – (m.) rice

artista – n. – (m./f.) artist

ascensor – n. – (m.) elevator

así – adv. – thus

asistir a – v. – attend

ataúd – n. – (m.) coffin

atlético – adj. – athletic

auditorio – n. – (m.) audience

auto – n. – (m.) car

autobús – n. – (m.) bus

automóvil – n. – (m.) car

avenida – n. – (f.) avenue

avión – n. – (m.) airplane

ayer – adv. – yesterday

azúcar – n. – (m.) sugar

azul – adj. – blue

bajar – v. – down (to go)

bajo – adj. – short

ballena – n. – (f.) whale

baño – n. – (m.) bathroom

barba – n. – (f.) beard

barca – n. – (f.) boat

barco – n. – (m.) boat

bastante – adv. – enough

beber (tomar) – v. – drink

bello – adj. – beautiful

bien – adj. – well

bisabuela – n. – (f.) great-grand-mother

bisabuelo – n. – (m.) great-grandfa-ther

blanco – adj. – white

boca – n. – (f.) mouth

bocacalle – n. – (f.) intersection

boda – n. – (f.) wedding

bonito – adj. – pretty

bote – n. – (m.) boat

brazo – n. – (m.) arm

bronquitis – n. – (f.) bronchitis

bucear – v. – snorkel

bueno – adj. – good

caballo – n. – (m.) horse

cabello (pelo) – n. – (m.) hair

cabeza – n. – (f.) head

cabra – n. – (f.) goat

cadera – n. – (f.) hip

caer(se) – v. – fall

café – n. – (m.) coffee

caja – n. – (f.) box

calcetín – n. – (m.) sock

callado – adj. – quiet

callar – v. – silent (to be)

calle – n. – (f.) street

callejón – n. – (m.) alley

cama – n. – (f.) bed

cambiar – *v.* – change

caminar (*andar*) – *v.* – walk

camisa – *n.* – (f.) shirt

campo – *n.* – (m.) field

cansado – *adj.* – tired

cansarse – *v.* – grow (get) tired

cantante – *n.* – (m.) singer

cara – *n.* – (f.) face

cargo – *n.* – (m.) responsibility

carne – *n.* – (f.) meat

caro – *adj.* – expensive

carro – *n.* – (m.) car

carta – *n.* – (f.) letter

cartero – *n.* – (m.) mailman

casa – *n.* – (f.) house

casamiento – *n.* – (m.) wedding

casi – *adv.* – almost

casona – *n.* – (f.) house (big)

catedral – *n.* – (f.) cathedral

centro – *n.* – (m.) downtown

cepillarse – *v.* – brush

cerca – *adj.* – near

cerdo – *n.* – (m.) pig

cerveza – *n.* – (f.) beer

césped – *n.* – (m.) turf, lawn, grass

chancho – *n.* – (m.) pig

chanza, chiste – *n.* – (f.) joke

chaqueta – *n.* – (f.) jacket

chico – *adj.* – small

chimenea (*hogar*) – *n.* – (f.) fire-place; chimney

choclo – *n.* – (m.) corn

ciego – *n.* – (m.) blind person

ciego – *adj.* – blind

ciervo (*venado*) – *n.* – (m.) deer

cine – *n.* – (m.) moviehouse, movie theater (cinema)

cineasta – *n.* – (m./f.) film director

cintura – *n.* – (f.) waist

cirujano – *n.* – (m.) surgeon

ciudad – *n.* – (f.) city

clavo – *n.* – (m.) nail

clima – *n.* – (m.) climate

coche – *n.* – (m.) car

cocina – *n.* – (f.) kitchen

codo – *n.* – (m.) elbow

colega – *n.* – (m.) colleague

colegio – *n.* – (m.) school (high)

collar – *n.* – (m.) necklace

colorado – *adj.* – red

comedor – *n.* – (m.) dining room

comer – *v.* – eat

cometa – *n.* – (m.) comet

cometa – *n.* – (f.) kite

cómoda (*el tocador*) – *n.* – (f.) dresser

comprar – *v.* – buy

conejo – n. – (m.) rabbit

conferencia – n. – (f.) lecture

confidencia – n. – (f.) secret

conocer – v. – know

consulta – n. – (f.) conference

contento – adj. – happy

correo – n. – (m.) mail

correr – v. – run

cortés – adj. – courteous

corto – adj. – short

crecer – v. – grow

creer – v. – believe

crisis – n. – (f.) crisis

cuadro – n. – (m.) painting

cuello – n. – (m.) neck

cultivar – v. – grow

cumpleaños – n. – (m.) birthday

cura – n. – (f.) cure

cura – n. – (m.) priest

curso – n. – (m.) course

deber – v. – owe

débil – adj. – weak

decepción – n. – (f.) disappointment

decir – v. – say (tell)

dedo – n. – (m.) finger

delito – n. – (m.) crime

demasiado – adv. – too much, too many

dependiente – n. – (m.) store clerk

deporte – n. – (m.) sport

descansar – v. – rest

desgracia – n. – (f.) misfortune

desmayo – n. – (m.) fainting

después de – prep. – after

detenerse (pararse) – v. – stop

día – n. – (m.) day

Día de Acción de Gracias – n. – (m.) Thanksgiving

diario – n. – (m.) newspaper

dibujo – n. – (m.) drawing

diente – n. – (m.) tooth

difícil – adj. – difficult

dinero – n. – (m.) money

Dios – n. – God

diploma – n. – (m.) diploma

disco duro – n. – (m.) hard disk

disco flexible – n. – (m.) floppy disk

divertido – adj. – funny

doctor (a) – n. – (m.) doctor, physician

dormir – v. – sleep

dormitorio (la alcoba) – n. – (m.) bedroom

drama – n. – (m.) drama

ducha – n. – (f.) shower

durazno – n. – (m.) peach

duro, difícil – *adj.* – hard

edificio – *n.* – (m.) building

elogio – *n.* – (m.) eulogy

embarazada – *adj.* – pregnant

emborracharse – *v.* – drunk (to get)

empezar – *v.* – begin

enfadarse (molestarse) – *v.* – angry (to get)

enfermera – *n.* – (f.) nurse

enfermo (a) – *n.* – (m.) sick person

ensalada – *n.* – (f.) salad

entonces – *adv.* – then

entrada – *n.* – (f.) entrance, lobby

entrar – *v.* – enter

enviar – *v.* – send

equipaje – *n.* – (m.) luggage

equipo – *n.* – (m.) team

escalera – *n.* – (f.) stair

escribir – *v.* – write

escritor (a) – *n.* – (m.) writer

escritorio – *n.* – (m.) desk

escuchar – *v.* – hear

escuela – *n.* – (f.) school

espalda – *n.* – (f.) back

espejo – *n.* – (m.) mirror

espejuelos – *n.* – (m.) eyeglasses

esperanza – *n.* – (f.) hope

esperar – *v.* – wait

espinaca – *n.* – (f.) spinach

esposa – *n.* – (f.) wife

esposo – *n.* – (m.) husband

estacionarse – *v.* – park

estrella – *n.* – (f.) star

estudiante – *n.* – (m./f.) student

éxito – *n.* – (m.) success

exterior – *adj.* – outer

fábrica – *n.* – (f.) factory

fácil – *adj.* – easy

familia – *n.* – (f.) family

fantástico – *adj.* – fantastic

feliz – *adj.* – happy

firma – *n.* – (f.) signature

físico – *n.* – (m.) physicist

flaco – *adj.* – thin

florero – *n.* – (m.) vase

foto – *n.* – (f.) photo

frágil – *adj.* – fragile

frase – *n.* – (f.) sentence

frente – *n.* – (f.) forehead

fresa – *n.* – (f.) strawberry

frío – *adj.* – cold

fuego – *n.* – (m.) fire

fuerte – *adj.* – strong

fumar – *v.* – smoke

fútbol – *n.* – (m.) soccer

gafas – *n.* – (f.) eyeglasses

gallina – n. – (f.) hen

gallo – n. – (m.) rooster

ganar – v. – win

gato – n. – (m.) cat

gente – n. – (f.) people

gordo – adj. – fat

grabadora – n. – (f.) tape recorder

grande – adj. – big

granja – n. – (f.) farm

grifo (la llave) – n. – (m.) tap

guagua – n. – (f.) bus

guapo – adj. – handsome

guía – n. – (f.) guide (book)

guía – n. – (m.) guide (person)

gustar – v. – like

hablar (conversar) – v. – talk

hacer – v. – make (do)

hacha – n. – (f.) hatchet

hambre – n. – (f.) hunger

heladera – n. – (f.) refrigerator

hembra – n. – (f.) female

hermana – n. – (f.) sister

hermano – n. – (m.) brother

hierba – n. – (f.) grass (tended, not wild)

hierro – n. – (m.) iron

hija – n. – (f.) daughter

hijo – n. – (m.) son

hombre de negocios – n. – (m.) businessman

hombro – n. – (m.) shoulder

hombrón – n. – man (big)

horno – n. – (m.) oven; furnace

humo – n. – (m.) smoke

idioma – n. – (m.) language

ignorar – v. – unaware (to be)

imagen – n. – (f.) image

impresora – n. – (f.) printer

ingeniero – n. – (m.) engineer

inteligente – adj. – intelligent

interesante – adj. – interesting

interior – adj. – internal

intoxicar – v. – poison

ir de compras – v. – shopping (to go)

irse – v. – leave

jabalí – n. – (m.) boar

jamón – n. – (m.) ham

jardín – n. – (m.) garden

jarrón – n. – (m.) vase

jefe – n. – (m.) boss

juez – n. – (m./f.) judge

jugador (a) – n. – (m.) player

jugar – v. – play

labio – n. – (m.) lip

lámpara – n. – (f.) lamp

lápiz – n. – (m.) pencil

largo – *adj.* – long

lavatorio – *n.* – (m.) sink

leche – *n.* – (f.) milk

lechuga – *n.* – (f.) lettuce

lectura – *n.* – (f.) reading

leer – *v.* – read

legumbre – *n.* – (f.) vegetable

lejos – *adj.* – far

lengua – *n.* – (f.) tongue

levantar – *v.* – raise, lift

levantarse (pararse) – *v.* – up (to get)

librería – *n.* – (f.) book store

libro – *n.* – (m.) book

limpio – *adj.* – clean

llegar – *v.* – arrive

llevar – *v.* – carry

locutor – *n.* – (m.) announcer

luego – *adv.* – later

luna – *n.* – (f.) moon

luz – *n.* – (f.) light

macho – *n.* – (m.) male

madera – *n.* – (f.) wood

madre – *n.* – (f.) mother

maíz – *n.* – (m.) corn

maleta – *n.* – (f.) suitcase

malo, mal – *adj.* – bad

mañana – *n.* – (f.) morning

mandar – *v.* – send

manejar (conducir, guiar) – *v.* – drive

mano – *n.* – (f.) hand

mantel – *n.* – (m.) tablecloth

mantener – *v.* – keep

mantequilla – *n.* – (f.) butter

manzana – *n.* – (f.) apple

mapa – *n.* – (m.) map

máquina – *n.* – (f.) machine

mar – *n.* – (m.) sea

maravilloso – *adj.* – marvelous

marido – *n.* – (m.) husband

marrano – *n.* – (m.) pig

marrón (pardo) – *adj.* – brown

más – *adv.* – more

mayor – *adj.* – older

mecánico – *n.* – (m.) mechanic

mecanógrafa – *n.* – (f.) typist

media – *n.* – (f.) sock

médico – *n.* – (m.) physician

mejor – *adj.* – better

menos – *adv.* – less

mercado – *n.* – (m.) market

merienda – *n.* – (f.) snack

mesa – *n.* – (f.) table

microondas – *n.* – (m.) microwave oven

miedo – *n.* – (m.) fear

mirar – *v.* – look at

molestar – v. – bother

montaña – n. – (f.) mountain

morado (violeta) – adj. – purple

morir – v. – die

moto – n. – (f.) motorcycle

mover(se), mudarse – v. – move

muchacha, joven – n. – (f.) young
    woman

muchacho, joven – n. – (m.) young
    man

muchedumbre – n. – (f.) crowd

muerte – n. – (f.) death

mujer – n. – (f.) wife, woman

muñeca – n. – (f.) wrist

músculo – n. – (m.) muscle

muslo – n. – (m.) thigh

nacer – v. – born (to be)

nacimiento – n. – (m.) birth

nada – nothing

nadar – v. – swim

nariz – n. – (f.) nose

Navidad(es) – n. – (f.) Christmas

necesitar – v. – need

negocio – n. – (m.) business

negro – adj. – black

nieta – n. – (f.) granddaughter

nieto – n. – (m.) grandson

niño – n. – (m.) boy

noche – n. – (f.) night

nombre – n. – (m.) name

nuera – n. – (f.) daughter-in-law

nunca – adv. – never

observar – v. – watch

odiar – v. – hate

oficio – n. – (m.) occupation

oír – v. – hear

ojo – n. – (m.) eye

ola – n. – (f.) wave

olvidar – v. – forget

ómnibus – n. – (m.) bus

orden – n. – (f.) order (do some-
    thing)

orden – n. – (m.) order (public
    order)

ordenador – n. – (m.) computer

oreja – n. – (f.) ear

oro – n. – (m.) gold

otoño – n. – (m.) autumn

oveja – n. – (f.) sheep

padre – n. – (m.) father

pagar – v. – pay

pájaro – n. – (m.) bird

pala – n. – (f.) shovel

pan – n. – (m.) bread

pantalón – n. – (m.) pants

papa (patatas) – n. – (f.) potato

Papa – n. – (m.) Pope

papel – n. – (m.) paper

paracaidismo – *n.* – (m.) parachuting

pararse – *v.* – stand

párpado – *n.* – (m.) eyelids

partido – *n.* – (m.) game

partir – *v.* – leave

pasajero (a) – *n.* – (m.) passenger

pasaporte – *n.* – (m.) passport

patio – *n.* – (m.) yard

pavo – *n.* – (m.) turkey

pecho – *n.* – (m.) chest

pedir – *v.* – order, ask

peinarse – *v.* – comb (one's hair)

peinilla – *n.* – (f.) comb

película – *n.* – (f.) film

pensar – *v.* – think

peor – *adj.* – worse

pequeño – *adj.* – small

pera – *n.* – (f.) pear

perder – *v.* – lose

periódico – *n.* – (m.) newspaper

periodista – *n.* – (m.) journalist

perro – *n.* – (m.) dog

pesadilla – *n.* – (f.) nightmare

pescado – *n.* – (m.) fish

pescar – *v.* – fish

pestañas – *n.* – (f.) eyelashes

pez – *n.* – (m.) fish

pinchar – *v.* – to prick, wound

pirámide – *n.* – (f.) pyramid

plata – *n.* – (f.) silver

plátano – *n.* – (m.) banana, plantain

playa – *n.* – (f.) beach

plaza de estacionamiento – *n.* – (f.) parking lot

plaza – *n.* – (f.) square

poco – *adj.* – little (not much)

poema – *n.* – (m.) poem

poeta – *n.* – (m.) poet

policía – *n.* – (m./f.) *el policía* – policeman / *la policía* – the police

político – *n.* – (m.) politician

pollo – *n.* – (m.) chicken

ponerse de pie – *v.* – stand

postre – *n.* – (m.) dessert

precio – *n.* – (m.) price

preferir – *v.* – prefer

preparar – *v.* – prepare

presencia – *n.* – (f.) presence

pretender – *v.* – aspire to

problema – *n.* – (m.) problem

profesor (a) – *n.* – (m.) teacher

profeta – *n.* – (m.) prophet

prójimo – *n.* – (m.) fellow human being

propina – *n.* – (f.) tip

puerco – *n.* – (m.) pig

puerta – *n.* – (f.) door

querer – *v.* – want

queso – *n.* – (m.) cheese

química – *n.* – (f.) chemistry

químico – *n.* – (m.) chemist

radio – *n.* – (m.) radio

ratón – *n.* – (m.) mouse

razón – *n.* – (f.) reason

recordar – *v.* – remember

refrigerador – *n.* – (m.) refrigerator

regresar – *v.* – return

reina – *n.* – (f.) queen

reloj – *n.* – (m.) watch

revista – *n.* – (f.) magazine

rey – *n.* – (m.) king

rico – *adj.* – rich

río – *n.* – (m.) river

rodilla – *n.* – (f.) knee

rojo – *adj.* – red

ropa – *n.* – (f.) clothing

rosa (rosado) – *adj.* – pink

ruido – *n.* – (m.) noise

sábana – *n.* – (f.) sheet

saber – *v.* – know

saco – *n.* – (m.) coat

sala – *n.* – (f.) living room

salida – *n.* – (f.) departure

salir – *v.* – out (to go)

salud – *n.* – (f.) health

saludar – *v.* – greet

sandía – *n.* – (f.) watermelon

sano – *adj.* – healthy

sastre – *n.* – (m.) tailor

sed – *n.* – (f.) thirst

señora – *n.* – (f.) wife, Mrs.

sensible – *adj.* – sensitive

sentarse – *v.* – sit down

serie – *n.* – (f.) series

siempre – *adv.* – always

silla – *n.* – (f.) chair

sillón – *n.* – (m.) couch

sistema – *n.* – (m.) system

sobre – *n.* – (m.) envelope

sobrina – *n.* – (f.) niece

sobrino – *n.* – (m.) nephew

sociedad – *n.* – (f.) society

soez – *adj.* – mean, vile

sofá – *n.* – (m.) sofa

sol – *n.* – (m.) sun

soldado – *n.* – (m.) soldier

soñar – *v.* – dream

sonrisa – *n.* – (f.) smile

soportar – *v.* – tolerate

subir – *v.* – to come up (to go)

subterráneo (*metro*) – *n.* – (m.) subway

suceso – *n.* – (m.) event

sucio – *adj.* – dirty

sueño – *n.* – (m.) dream

suerte – *n.* – (f.) luck

superior – *adj.* – superior

talón – *n.* – (m.) heel

tarde – *adv.* – late

torta – *n.* – (f.) cake, tart

taza – *n.* – (f.) cup

techo – *n.* – (m.) roof; ceiling

teclado – *n.* – (m.) keyboard

técnico – *n.* – (m.) technician

televisión – *n.* – (f.) television

tema – *n.* – (m.) theme

temperamento – *n.* – (m.) temperament

temprano – *adv.* – early

tía – *n.* – (f.) aunt

tiburón – *n.* – (m.) shark

tienda – *n.* – (f.) store

tina – *n.* – (f.) bathtub

tío – *n.* – (m.) uncle

toalla – *n.* – (f.) towel

tobillo – *n.* – (m.) ankle

tocadiscos – *n.* – (m.) record player

tocino – *n.* – (m.) bacon

todavía – *adv.* – still

toro – *n.* – (m.) bull

torre – *n.* – (f.) tower

tortuga – *n.* – (f.) turtle

trabajar – *v.* – work

traer – *v.* – bring

tranvía – *n.* – (m.) trolley

tren – *n.* – (m.) train

triste – *adj.* – sad

uña – *n.* – (f.) fingernail

uva – *n.* – (f.) grape

vacaciones – *n.* – (f.) vacation

vaca – *n.* – (f.) cow

valiente – *adj.* – courageous

vaso – *n.* – (m.) glass

vecindario – *n.* – (m.) neighborhood

vecino – *n.* – (m.) neighbor

velador – *n.* – (m.) night table

vendedor – *n.* – (m.) salesman

vender – *v.* – sell

ventana – *n.* – (f.) window

ver – *v.* – see

verde – *adj.* – green

verdura – *n.* – (f.) vegetable

vestirse – *v.* – dress (oneself)

vez – *n.* – (f.) time

viajar – *v.* – travel

viejo – *adj.* – old

viento – n. – (m.) wind

vigilar – v. – watch

vino – n. – (m.) wine

volar – v. – fly

volver – v. – return

vuelo – n. – (m.) flight

vulgar – adj. – vulgar

yerno – n. – (m.) son-in-law

zapato – n. – (m.) shoe

PRACTICE TEST 1

TEST 1
Section I:
LISTENING COMPREHENSION

(Answer sheets appear in the back of this book.)

TIME: 30 Minutes
50 Questions

Part A

Directions: For this section of the test, you will hear a number of conversations or parts of conversations. After each dialogue, you will hear four answer choices, identified as (A), (B), (C), and (D). When you have heard all four answer choices, choose the one that best completes or continues the conversation. Fill in the corresponding oval on your answer sheet. Neither the answer choices nor the conversations will be printed in your test booklet, so you must listen very carefully. Insert our CD No. 1 into your CD player.

Note: The Listening portion of the actual CLEP Spanish exam will be presented on audiotape.

---

1. Mark your answer on your answer sheet.

2. Mark your answer on your answer sheet.

3. Mark your answer on your answer sheet.

4. Mark your answer on your answer sheet.

5. Mark your answer on your answer sheet.

6. Mark your answer on your answer sheet.

7. Mark your answer on your answer sheet.

8. Mark your answer on your answer sheet.

9. Mark your answer on your answer sheet.

10. Mark your answer on your answer sheet.

11.   Mark your answer on your answer sheet.

12.   Mark your answer on your answer sheet.

13.   Mark your answer on your answer sheet.

14.   Mark your answer on your answer sheet.

15.   Mark your answer on your answer sheet.

16.   Mark your answer on your answer sheet.

17.   Mark your answer on your answer sheet.

18.   Mark your answer on your answer sheet.

Part B

> **Directions:** Now you will hear a series of selections, including narratives, news reports, announcements, and dialogues. Listen very carefully to each selection, as they are spoken only once. For each selection, one or more questions will be printed in your test booklet, each with four answer choices. The questions and answers will not be spoken. Choose the best answer to each question and fill in the corresponding oval on your answer sheet. You are given 12 seconds to answer each question.

19.   ¿Cuál es el deporte más popular en Estados Unidos?

(A) El soccer   (C) El fútbol americano

(B) El béisbol   (D) El baloncesto

20.   ¿Cuántos niños estadounidenses llegan a formar parte de las ligas universitarias?

(A) Una minoría   (C) Una elite

(B) Ninguno   (D) Muchos

21.   ¿Cómo considera el fútbol americano la narradora?

(A) Como un simple deporte

(B) Como un espectáculo

(C) Como el día de Acción de Gracias

(D) Como un gran negocio del espectáculo y una arraigada tradición

22. ¿Qué le succidió a Benito?

    (A) Se quedó dormido y llegó tarde.

    (B) No pudo dormir y llegó tarde.

    (C) Se quedó despierto y fue más temprano.

    (D) Fue despedido por quedarse dormido.

23. Los rios Tumuma y Viele aportan _____.

    (A) transporte y riego   (C) riquezas minerales

    (B) aguas potables   (D) destrucción ecológica

24. La tala de árboles provoca _____.

    (A) contención de las inundaciones

    (B) cambio de clima

    (C) sequía

    (D) mayor absorción de agua en la región

25. Chinichex la paga a su cliente _____.

    (A) la diferencia entre el precio de lo comprado y el precio del mismo objeto en otro lugar

    (B) la diferencia entre el precio de lo comprado en otro lugar y el número de boleta

    (C) el número de boleta multiplicado por el precio del artículo adquirido

    (D) el número de boleta multiplicado por la diferencia más la diferencia

26. ¿Por qué no pudo conocer el país del hielo el hombre?

    (A) Él estaba borracho.

    (B) El pueblo estaba encantado.

    (C) Su abuelo le había mentido.

    (D) No tenía brújula.

27. ¿Cómo lo llamaban a Elvis Presley?

   (A) El Rey   (C) Gran Manzana

   (B) E. P.   (D) Chubby

28. El periodista es _____.

   (A) humilde y generoso   (C) simplemente descriptivo

   (B) irónico y despectivo   (D) demasiado serio

29. Para encender el Sonoflex-flow hay que _____.

   (A) comprar el modelo Gold

   (B) esperar que titile la luz amarilla

   (C) tener paciencia

   (D) vaciar el compartimiento C

30. La presidenta ha decidido _____.

   (A) que se vengará con todos sus recursos

   (B) que los hechos violentos merecen ser respondidos con las mismas armas

   (C) que responder con violencia la es un error

   (D) que los seres violentos no merecen castigo

31. La chica de la canción _____.

   (A) ha traicionado al cantante

   (B) ha sido traicionada por el cantante

   (C) ha sido olvidada por el cantante

   (D) era calma y pacífica

32. Los concursantes deben _____.

   (A) ser calvos indefectiblemente

   (B) ser calvos o afeitarse la cabeza

   (C) llevar un traje de poliester

   (D) gritar: "Soy el más parecido al capitán Picard."

33. La señora que escucha este reporte debe _____.

    (A) abrigar bien a sus hijos a pesar de ser primavera

    (B) abrigar bien a sus hijos porque es invierno

    (C) poner ropa ligera a sus hijos para que no sufran por la sensación térmica

    (D) poner ropa ligera a sus hijos porque el invierno cesó de golpe

34. ¿Qué pasó al final?

    (A) Juan pasa a buscar a Carina a las diez en punto.

    (B) Carina pasa a buscar a Juan a las diez en punto.

    (C) Se encuentran en el laboratorio de fotografías a las once.

    (D) Se encuentran en el centro comercial a las once.

35. ¿Cuál es el punto principal del diálogo?

    (A) El trabajo es de dominio público.

    (B) Luis se niega a decir la naturaleza del trabajo.

    (C) Luis no puede decir la naturaleza del trabajo.

    (D) Luis promete explicar el secreto dos días despues.

36. El señor Guillermo Rodriguez _____.

    (A) ha decidido no ir al teatro

    (B) ha acceptado tres entradas en una ubicación peor ubicada

    (C) ha dejado a la tercera persona fuera de la función del día

    (D) ha decidido ceder su ticket a la tercera persona

37. ¿Cuál afirmación es correcta?

    (A) Un socio puede visitar a su hermano empleado en el club en sus habitaciones.

    (B) Algunos empleados del club pueden fumar en el club.

    (C) El invitado de un socio puede visitar a su novia empleada en el club.

    (D) Los empleados que tienen familiares socios del club carecen de privilegios.

38. La gloquilla es un animal _____.

    (A) subterráneo   (C) ciego

    (B) antártico   (D) volcánico

39. ¿Cuál es el problema?

    (A) El abuelo tiene mala memoria.

    (B) La oficina de correos se ha quedado con el paquete.

    (C) El nieto es mentiroso.

    (D) Al abuelo le importa mucho la edad que tiene.

40. El clinte _____.

    (A) tiene un gusto exquisito

    (B) tiene pretensiones desmedidas

    (C) tiene un gran amor por la música clásica

    (D) le gusta la música aburrida

41. Según el telegrama, ¿cuál es verdad?

    (A) Fue mucha gente y aplaudieron.

    (B) Fue mucha gente e hicieron mucho dinero.

    (C) La prensa aclamó la obra.

    (D) El autor no está conforme con la actuación.

42. ¿Cómo se caracteriza mejor las plantas del desierto?

    (A) Los tubérculos acumulan agua en sus tejidos.

    (B) Las cactáceas pierden las hojas en la estación seca.

    (C) Las plantas crecen arracimadas para compartir la facultad de absorción.

    (D) En algunos arbustos las ramas sintetizan la luz del sol.

43. ¿Cuál es un hecho histórico de la ciudad de Ushuaia?

    (A) Los aventureros desaparecieron diezmados por la enfermedad.

    (B) A todos los indígenas y buscafortunas los pusieron en una cárcel especial.

    (C) Todos los prisioneros de la cárcel de Ushuaia habían cometido crimenes más de una vez.

    (D) Ushuaia es un santuario de vida silvestre.

44. ¿Cuál es más probable?

    (A) El amigo se equivocó de cigarrillos.

    (B) El amigo trajo otra cosa a propósito.

    (C) No había cigarrillos para comprar.

    (D) Fumaran los de chocolate como si fueran reales.

45. De los tres apartamentos, ¿Qué se puede decir?

    (A) El segundo es el más caro.

    (B) El tercero es el más chico.

    (C) El primero es el más aireado.

    (D) El tercero lo vende directamente el dueño.

46. Según este horóscopo, para la gente de Virgo es una semana _____.

    (A) Auspiciosa y positiva   (C) De predicciones dudosas

    (B) Llena de esperanza   (D) De crecimiento espiritual

47. El hombre es _____.

    (A) un asesino a suelo   (C) un arquitecto

    (B) un cocinero   (D) un veterinaro

48. Según la conversación, ¿cómo se describe la chica con la pierna malherida?

    (A) Se rompió la pierna por culpa de los patines.

    (B) La madre le rompió la pierna al sentarse sobre ella.

    (C) Está completamente sana.

    (D) El yeso produce inhibición en el habla.

49. ¿Qué es muy obvio?

    (A) Quique es un excelente cantante.

    (B) Ricardo es pobre.

    (C) Todas las camisetas de Ricardo están hechas por él mismo.

    (D) Melba dice lo que piensa.

50. Según el narrador, ¿qué sucedió?

    (A) El titanic chocó contra el hielo.

    (B) El titanic fue atacado y explotaron sus motores.

    (C) Los miembros de la orquesta se salvaron de morir ahogados.

    (D) El equipo del titanic tenía todo bajo control.

This is the end of the audio section of Practice Test 1. Please go to the Reading section on the next page.

Section II: READING

TIME: 60 Minutes
80 Questions

Part A

Directions: This section contains several incomplete statements, each having four completion choices. Select the most appropriate answer and fill in the corresponding oval on your answer sheet.

51. El taxi se encuentra en _____ de aquellas dos calles.

    (A) la esquina   (C) la alfombra

    (B) el techo   (D) el rincón

52. El hombre que nos atiende en una tienda se llama _____.

    (A) mercancía   (C) cliente

    (B) dependiente   (D) parroquiano

53. ¿Cuándo vas a _____ este libro a la biblioteca?

    (A) regresar   (C) retornar

    (B) devolver   (D) volver

54. Voy a acostarme porque tengo _____.

    (A) sed   (C) calor

    (B) hambre   (D) sueño

55. Cuando el autobús llegó al fin de la trayectoria, _____ delante del Museo Arqueológico.

    (A) dejó de   (C) paró

    (B) cesó   (D) terminó

56. Julio dijo que _____ ayudarnos con la tarea.

(A) ensayaría   (C) probaría

(B) trataría de   (D) se quedaría

57. Mañana voy a pagar _____ de la casa.

(A) los cuentos   (C) las cuentas

(B) los boletos   (D) los billetes

58. ¿Qué piensas _____ estas pinturas?

(A) de   (C) a

(B) en   (D) con

59. Hoy he estudiado demasiado y _____ la cabeza.

(A) me hace daño   (C) me daña

(B) me hiere   (D) me duele

60. Mucha gente lleva abrigo cuando _____.

(A) hace calor   (C) corre

(B) llueve   (D) hace frío

61. Antes de hacer el viaje voy a comprar _____.

(A) una maleta   (C) una multa

(B) una máquina de coser   (D) una muñeca

62 _____ es un lugar, muchas veces en el campo, donde hay muchos árboles.

(A) Una verdulería   (C) Una leña

(B) Una madera   (D) Un bosque

63. Felipe se cortó con el cuchillo y tiene _____ en el dedo.

(A) un anillo   (C) una herida

(B) una uña   (D) una oreja

Part B

Directions: In each paragraph below, numbered blanks indicate that phrases or words have been purposely omitted. Four possible completion choices are provided for each blank space. Carefully read the paragraph and select the answer choice containing the word or phrase that is most suitable in the context of the paragraph. Fill in the corresponding oval on your answer sheet.

Alrededor de 8.500 personas visitan la Biblioteca Nacional todos los meses. __(64)__, no todos quedan __(65)__ con __(66)__ encuentran en el enorme edificio ubicado en Agüero y Libertador, y __(67)__, decepcionados. Aunque los archivos __(68)__ algo más de __(69)__ ejemplares, casi todos son libros editados __(70)__ más de una década. Por eso, __(71)__ buscan información actualizada se ven totalmente frustrados. Por ejemplo, si alguien quiere consultar __(72)__ sobre el conflicto por las Islas Malvinas, no hay nada.

64. (A) Sin embargo
    (B) Sin novedad
    (C) Sin par
    (D) Sin recurso

65. (A) satisfecho
    (B) satisfaces
    (C) satisfechos
    (D) satisfacer

66. (A) lo que
    (B) lo cual
    (C) el cual
    (D) los que

67. (A) se irán
    (B) se vayan
    (C) se fueron
    (D) se van

68. (A) cuentan con
    (B) cuenten con
    (C) contar con
    (D) contan con

69. (A) uno millón de
    (B) millón de
    (C) un millión de
    (D) un millón de

70. (A) hacía   (C) hacen

    (B) hace   (D) hizo

71. (A) los que   (C) ellos que

    (B) quiénes   (D) esos que

72. (A) obsecuencias   (C) obradas

    (B) obras   (D) obradoras

Al día siguiente Juan ___(73)___ a hablar con el Obispo, y ___(74)___ le dijo que le ___(75)___ ___(76)___ evidencia de la aparición. Juan ___(77)___ comunicó ___(78)___ a la Señora, ___(79)___ le dijo que ___(80)___ por la mañana y le daría evidencias que ___(81)___ al Obispo.

73. (A) volvió   (C) volviera

    (B) vuelve   (D) volver

74. (A) aquel   (C) esto

    (B) éste   (D) ése

75. (A) trajo   (C) traiga

    (B) trajera   (D) traerá

76. (A) algún   (C) ningún

    (B) ninguna   (D) alguna

77. (A) la   (C) les

    (B) le   (D) lo

78. (A) eso   (C) ese

    (B) ése   (D) éso

79. (A) quién   (C) quien

    (B) a quien   (D) de quien

80. (A) regrese   (C) regresar

    (B) regresara   (D) regresa

81. (A) convencerían   (C) convencieron

    (B) convenzan   (D) convencieran

Las reformas sociales en beneficio de los zapateros fueron __(82)__ tema central de los cinco años que fue Gobernador de Oaxaca. Abrió cincuenta escuelas nuevas y __(83)__ por la educación de las mujeres. Construyó caminos y abrió un puerto en la costa pacífica que había __(84)__ __(85)__ durante casi __(86)__ años. Logró __(87)__ las deudas del estado y dejó la tesorería estatal en __(88)__ condiciones cuando terminó __(89)__. Jamás se aprovechó del cargo público __(90)__ sacar beneficio propio.

82. (A) el   (C) nothing needed

    (B) la   (D) otra

83. (A) abogó   (C) abrazó

    (B) abonó   (D) abrigó

84. (A) permanecida   (C) permaneciendo

    (B) permanecido   (D) permanecer

85. (A) cerrado   (C) cerrando

    (B) cerrada   (D) cerrar

86. (A) trescientas   (C) trececientos

    (B) trescien   (D) trescientos

87. (A) pagar   (C) pagado

    (B) pagando   (D) pagadas

88. (A) buenos   (C) buenas

    (B) buen   (D) buena

89. (A) mancebo   (C) mandil

    (B) mandato   (D) manchón

90. (A) por   (C) porque

    (B) nothing needed   (D) para

Part C

Directions: Read each of the passages below. Each passage is followed by questions or incomplete statements. Choose the best answer
according to the text and fill in the corresponding oval on your answer
sheet.

La casita de Lencho estaba en el cerro. Desde allí se veía el campo de
maíz y el frijol en flor. Todo prometía una buena cosecha. Pero para ello
se necesitaba mucha lluvia.

Desde temprano por la mañana Lencho examinaba el cielo hacia el
noreste.

—¡Ahora sí que lloverá!

Su esposa asintió:

—Lloverá si Dios quiere.

Al mediodía, mientras la familia comía, grandes gotas de lluvia
comenzaron a caer. Enormes nubes negras avanzaban hacia el noreste. El
aire estaba cada vez más fresco y dulce, y Lencho observaba sus campos
con placer. Pero, de pronto, sopló un viento fuerte y comenzó a granizar.

Durante una hora cayó el granizo sobre todo el valle. Lencho se iba
angustiando cada vez más y cuando la tempestad pasó dijo con vos triste a
sus hijos:

—Ésto fue peor que las langostas; el granizo no ha dejado nada. No
tendremos ni maíz ni frijoles este año.

Sólo guardaban una esperanza en el corazón los habitantes del valle:
la ayuda de Dios.

Lencho pensaba en el futuro. Aunque era un hombre rudo, él sabía
escribir. Así es que decidió escribir una carta a Dios:

"Dios, si no me ayudas, pasaré hambre con toda mi familia durante
este año. Necesito cien pesos para volver a sembrar y vivir mientras viene
la cosecha, porque el granizo . . . "

Escribió "A DIOS" en el sobre. Le puso un sello a la cara y la echó
en el buzón.

Un empleado de correo la recogió más tarde, la abrió y la leyó, y, riéndose, se la mostró al jefe de correos. El jefe también se rió al leerla, pero muy pronto se puso serio y exclamó:

—¡La fe! ¡Qué fe tan pura! Este hombre cree de veras y por eso le escribe a Dios.

Y para no desilusionar a un hombre tan puro, el jefe de correos decidió contestar la carta.

El jefe pudo reunir sólo un poco más de la mitad del dinero pedido por Lencho. Metió los billetes en un sobre dirigido a Lencho y con ellos una carta que consistía en una palabra: DIOS.

Una semana más tarde Lencho entró en el correo y preguntó si había carta para él. Sí, había, pero Lencho no mostró la menor sorpresa. Tampoco se sorprendió al ver los billetes, pues él tenía fe en Dios y los esperaba. Pero al contar el dinero se enfadó. En seguida se acercó a la ventanilla, pidió papel y tinta, y se fue a una mesa escribir:

"Dios, del dinero que te pedí sólo llegaron a mis manos sesenta pesos. Mándame el resto, porque lo necesito mucho, pero no me lo mandes por correo porque todos los empleados de correo son ladrones. Tuyo,

LENCHO."

[Adapted from: "Carta a Dios," by Gregorio López y Fuentes, in Selecciones Españoles, *A Basic Spanish Reader, ed. Angel Flores (1967: Bantam Books, Inc., 271 Madison Ave., New York, NY 10016), pp. 26–30.]*

91. ¿Por qué se entristeció Lencho?

   (A) Sus hijos se murieron.

   (B) Llovió demasiado.

   (C) Las langostas destruyeron su sembrado.

   (D) El granizo arrasó su cultivo.

92. ¿Qué trabajo hacía Lencho?

   (A) Era cura.   (C) Era cartero.

   (B) Era agricultor.   (D) Era escribano.

93. ¿Por qué escribió Lencho su primera carta a Dios?

   (A) Para pedirle que le ayudara

   (B) Para quejarse de su mala suerte

(C) Para denunciar irregularidades en el correo

(D) Para rogarle que le diera una buena cosecha

94. Luego de leer la carta de Lencho, ¿qué hizo el jefe de correos?

(A) Se rió nada más.

(B) Regaño al empleado por abrir una carta ajena.

(C) Juntó dinero para auydarle a Lencho.

(D) Le devolvió la carta a Lencho sin dinero.

95. ¿Cómo reaccionó Lencho al recibir la respuesta a su carta?

(A) Se sorprendió.

(B) Se rió a carcajadas.

(C) Perdió la esperanza.

(D) No mostró ninguna sorpresa.

96. ¿Qué pensaba Lencho de los empleados de correo?

(A) Que eran hombres honrados

(B) Que eran deshonestos

(C) Que eran muy generosos

(D) Que eran muy bondadosos

97. ¿Qué sintió Lencho al ver la lluvia en sus campos?

(A) Placer

(C) Enojo

(B) Desesperación

(D) Angustia

El cacao no debe confundirse ni con el coco ni con la coca, fuente de la cocaína. Los árboles crecen en los trópicos, y por eso no pueden ser cultivados en los Estados Unidos. El cacao y su derivado, el chocolate, pueden ser auxiliares digestivos, estimular el flujo sanguíneo al corazón y ayudar a las personas con pecho congestionado a respirar mejor.

Una vez recolectados los granos del cacao, se tuesten y muelen para producir el licor de cacao. A ese líquido se le agrega cantidades minúsculas de lejía para intensificar su sabor. Se continúa el proceso para eliminar su grasa, conocida como manteca de cacao. El producto final, el chocolate, es una combinación del polvo de cacao desgrasado con un poco de su misma manteca que se le vuelve a añadir.

El polvo al que llamamos cocoa es simplemente licor de cacao seco, quizá con un poco de azúcar. El chocolate de pastelería es licor de cacao procesado sin azúcar. Al chocolate amargo se le añade un poco de azúcar; al chocolate semidulce un poco más, y al chocolate de leche todavía más—además de leche para hacerlo cremoso.

Los europeos desconocían la existencia del cacao hasta 1519, cuando el conquistador español Hernán Cortés vio al emperador azteca Moctezuma tomar una bebida llamada *chocolatl* en un tazón de oro. Cortés se interesó más en el tazón que en su contenido, hasta que los aztecas le informaran que la bebida se elaboraba de granos tan valiosos que cien podían comprar un esclavo en buen estado de salud.

Cortés introdujo el agasajo azteca a la corte española, donde resultó una sensación. Los españoles trataron de mantener el chocolate en secreto y lo lograron por más de cien años, pero para 1660 se había extendido por toda Europa. El chocolate adquirió especial popularidad en Inglaterra y Holanda, donde la amarga bebida se enriqueció y endulzó con leche y azúcar. Por extraño que parezca, hasta el siglo XIX el chocolate era sólo una bebida, en ocasiones amarga, a veces dulce, pero siempre líquida. No fue hasta hace uno 150 años que se elaboró en las barras y dulces que nos gustan tanto.

[Adapted from: Las Hierbas que Curan, *por Michael Castleman (1991, Rodale Press, 33 East Minor St., Emmaus, PA), pp. 123, 124, 127.]*

98. ¿A qué se refiere "el agasajo azteca"?

   (A) A la actitud del emperador Moctezuma con respecto a los conquistadores

   (B) Al tazón de oro del cual bebía Moctezuma

   (C) A la bebida *chocolatl* que Cortés llevó a España

   (D) A la destrucción del Imperio Azteca por los expañoles

99. ¿Dónde se cultivan los árboles de cacao?

   (A) En los Estados Unidos

   (B) En las zonas tropicales

   (C) En España

   (D) En Inglaterra y Holanda

100. ¿Qué hizo la corte española cuando supo del cacao?

(A) Difundío las noticias de inmediato al resto de Europa.

(B) Armó un escándalo, pues no le gustó la bebida amarga.

(C) Empezó a hacer chocolate en barra para exportar.

(D) Procuró que nadie más se enterara.

101. ¿De qué forma mejoraron la bebida de cacao los ingleses y los holandeses?

(A) Le echaron azúcar y leche.

(B) La sirvieron helada en vez de caliente.

(C) Le agregaron lejía para intensificar su sabor.

(D) Le quitaron toda la grasa.

102. Además de molerlos para elaborar una bebida, ¿qué otro uso les daban a los granos de cacao los aztecas?

(A) Los usaban como armas para hacer la guerra.

(B) Los echaban al mar para tener buena suerte.

(C) Los utilizaban para envenenar a sus enemigos.

(D) Los empleaban como dinero.

103. Según este pasaje, el cacao _____.

(A) no tuvo mucho éxito fuera de México

(B) tiene cierto valor medicinal

(C) carece de valor nutritivo

(D) se asemeja al coco y la coca

Blas de Santillana, mi padre, después de haber servido muchos años en los ejércitos de España, se volvió al pueblo donde había nacido. Allí se casó con una aldeana, y yo nací al mundo diez meses después que se habían casado.

De Santillana pasaron mis padres a vivir a Oviedo donde ambos encontraron trabajo. En Oviedo vivía un hermano mayor de mi madre, llamado Gil Pérez, el cual era sacerdote. Éste me llevó a su casa cuando yo era niño, y me enseño a leer; más tarde me envió a la escuela del doctor Godínez, el maestro más hábil que había en Oviedo, para estudiar la lengua latina.

Aprendí tanto en esta escuela, que al cabo de cinco o seis años entendía un poco los autores griegos, y bastante bien los autores latinos. Estudié, además, la lógica, que me enseñó a pensar y argumentar sin término. Me gustaban mucho las disputas, y detenía a los que encontraba por la calle, conocidos o desconocidos, para proponerles cuestiones y argumentos.

De esta manera me hice famoso en toda la ciudad, y mi tío estaba muy orgulloso de mí. Un día me dijo:

—Gil Blas, ya no eres niño; tienes dicisiete años, y Dios te ha dado habilidad. Voy a enviarte a la universidad de Salamanca, donde con tu clara inteligencia llegarás a ser un hombre de importancia. Para tu viaje te daré dinero y una buena mula que podrás vender en Salamanca.

Mi tío no podía porponerme cosa más de mi gusto, porque yo tenía ganas de ver el mundo; pero no mostré mi gran alegría. Al contrario, cuando llegó la hora de partir, puse una cara tan triste que mi tío me dio más dinero del que me habría dado si hubiese mostrado alegría.

Antes de montar en mi mula fui a dar un abrazo a mi padre y a mi madre, los cuales me dieron no pocos consejos. Me repitieron muchas veces que viviese cristianamente, y sobre todo no tomase jamás lo ajeno contra la voluntad de su dueño, y que no engañase a nadie. Después de haberme hablado largamente, me dieron la única cosa que podía esperar de ellos: su bendición. Inmediatamente monté en mi mula y salí de la ciudad.

[From: Aventuras de Gil Blas, *retold and edited by Carlos Castillo and Colley F. Sparkman,* Graded Spanish Readers, Book Four *(New York: D.C. Heath and Company, 1936 and 1937), pp. 1–2.]*

104. ¿Cómo se llama el narrador del relato?

(A) Blas de Santillana   (C) Gil Pérez

(B) Gil Blas   (D) el doctor Godínez

105. ¿Cómo aprendió a leer Gil Blas?

(A) Su tío se lo enseño.

(B) Lo aprendió en la escuela del doctor Godínez.

(C) Se lo enseñaron en la universidad.

(D) Sus padres se lo enseñaron.

106. ¿Por qué Gil Blas abandonó Oviedo?

(A) Queríair a vivir con su tío.

(B) Pensaba volver a su pueblo natal.

(C) Sus padres lo echaron de la casa.

(D) Iba a estudiar en la universidad.

107. ¿De quién fue la idea de que Gil Blas fuera a Salamanca?

(A) Gil Pérez   (C) sus padres

(B) el doctor Godínez   (D) Gil Blas

108. Antes de que Gil Blas se fuera a Salamanca, sus padres le dieron
_____.

(A) una mula y dinero para el viaje

(B) un abrazo y muchos consejos

(C) un caballo negro y una espada

(D) un traje nuevo y varios libros

109. ¿Cómo reaccionó Gil Blas a la idea de ir a Salamanca?

(A) No le gustó para nada.   (C) Le gustó mucho.

(B) Se encolerizó.   (D) Empezó a llorar.

A Rafael López, vecino del barrio de Santa Cruz, le ha tocado el gordo de la lotería de Navidad. Antes, el joben sevillano soñaba con ser cantante de música folklórica y hacerse rico y famoso. Mientras tanto, según nos ha contado el propio López, para ganarse la vida, pertenecía a un conjunto musical en el cual tocaba el tambor, pero sólo cuando faltaba alguien. Ahora ya no está apurado y por encima de todo no hay nadie que le desconozca en toda España.

110. ¿Cuál de las oraciones a continuación *no* resulta falsa?

(A) El joven se hizo cantante popular.

(B) El sevillano fingía ser cantante popular.

(C) Ahora, al joven le hace falta dinero para vivir.

(D) El joven sevillano quería ser cantante.

111. Rafael _____.

(A) ganó un premio musical

(B) servía de sustituto en una banda

(C) era pertinente

(D) tenía su propio conjunto

112. Rafael ganó _____.

(A) un viaje

(B) un conjunto musical

(C) mucho dinero

(D) un tambor

113. El joven sevillano _____.

(A) es célebre ahora

(B) tiene por qué llorar

(C) sigue careciendo de dinero

(D) tiene prisa

Ya son las diez y media. El tren rápido para Fulango salió hace hora y cuarto y llegará a su destino dentro de hora y media. El tren correo salió para la misma ciudad media hora antes que el rápido y todavía tardará dos horas más en llegar a Fulango.

114. ¿A qué hora salió el tren rápido para Fulango?

(A) A las diez y media   (C) A las doce

(B) A las nueve y cuarto   (D) A las nueve menos cuarto

115. ¿A qué hora salió el tren correo?

   (A) A las nueve menos cuarto

   (B) A las dos

   (C) A las doce y media

   (D) A las nueve y cuarto

116. ¿Cuándo ha de llegar el tren más lento?

   (A) A las nueve menos cuarto

   (B) A las dos

   (C) A las doce y media

   (D) A las nueve y cuarto

Ayer por la tarde hubo un atraco en un sucursal del Banco Nacional situado en las afueras de la capital. Los reos enmascarados huyeron del lugar del crimen llevándose una cantidad de dinero todavía por determinar y sin ser identificados. Los agentes de la policía armada rodearon el barrio, hicieron una redada y, a las cinco de la tarde, tuvieron éxito en su búsqueda. Se enteraron de que se trataba de una pareja campesina temporalmente radicada en la capital.

117. ¿Cuál de las contestaciones está bien?

   (A) Los policías salieron del barrio a las cinco de la tarde.

   (B) Los criminales todavía quedan libres.

   (C) Se sabe cuánto dinero fue robado.

   (D) La policía ha encontrado a los ladrones.

118. El asalto del banco fue llevado a cabo _____.

   (A) a las cinco de la tarde

   (B) en el centro de la ciudad

   (C) alrededor del barrio

   (D) por dos campesinos

119. El Banco Nacional _____.

    (A) cierra a las cinco de la tarde

    (B) está situado en el centro de la capital

    (C) fue robado ayer por la tarde

    (D) es el banco más grande de la ciudad

120. Los guardias _____.

    (A) trataron de impedir una rebelión

    (B) tuvieron que perseguir a los criminales al campo

    (C) supieron quiénes eran los reos

    (D) llegaron sin fusiles

121. Los criminales eran _____.

    (A) dos chicos del pueblo vecino

    (B) dos personas del extranjero

    (C) disfrazados

    (D) los policías armados

En algunas partes de la América Latina la situación económica va de mal en peor a causa de las deudas internacionales que no pueden pagar muchos gobiernos. A esto hay que agregar el aumento del costo de la vida y el paro forzoso.

Teniendo en cuenta la situación inestable de las bolsas internacionales, la bajada del valor del dólar y el desequilibrio de la balanza de pagos, se han reunido los representantes de los poderes más influyentes del mundo económico a fin de llegar a un acuerdo que evite un posible derrumbamiento financiero, para cuyo efecto habrá que obrar con cautela.

122. ¿Cuál de las frases describe mejor la situación?

    (A) Suben los precios, hay bastante trabajo y a los gobiernos les falta dinero.

    (B) Bajan los precios, hay demasiado trabajo y a los gobiernos les sobra dinero.

(C) Suben los precios, hay mucho desempleo y a los gobiernos les falta suficiente dinero.

(D) Suben los precios, hay mucho paro y los gobiernos consiguen pagar sus deudas.

123. Los delegados de las varias naciones _____.

(A) quieren estabilizar la economía internacional

(B) apenas se dan cuenta de la seriedad del problema

(C) niegan la gravedad de la situación

(D) van a bajar el valor de la moneda

124. Se entiende que _____.

(A) el resultado será eficaz

(B) será necesario proceder con cuidado

(C) se efectuará el fin deseado

(D) se logrará el propósito de la conferencia

Hoy en día la ciencia médica aconseja que el hombre siga un régimen alimenticio de legumbres, frutas frescas y cereales. En cambio, la comida típica del norteamericano medio se basa en el consumo excesivo de alimentos grasientos, carne roja y carbohidratos, lo cual puede conducir, si no al cáncer o a problemas cardíacos, a severos casos de obesidad.

A causa de la manía del adelgazamiento y el horror a la obesidad, ciertos médicos han advertido lo peligroso que puede ser perder mucho peso en poco tiempo, lo cual es posible si seguimos ciertas dietas que actualmente se han puesto muy de moda. Tales regímenes, a lo mejor, ayudan a uno a enflaquecer en seguida pero van en contra de las leyes naturales del cuerpo humano.

125. Según el artículo, comer muchos alimentos grasientos, carne roja y carbohidratos _____.

(A) ayuda a adelgazar

(B) puede conducir a problemas de sobre peso

(C) sube la hemoglobina

(D) es el régimen que aconseja la ciencia médica hoy en día

126. Según el artículo, ¿cuál de las comidas sería la más saludable?

    (A) sopa de pescado, rosbif, leche y pastel

    (B) ensalada de lechuga, pescado asado, una naranja

    (C) pan con mantequilla, pollo asado, patatas fritas

    (D) chuleta de puerco, arroz, helado

127. El artículo menciona que _____.

    (A) la ciencia médica aconseja que el hombre siga un régimen alimenticio de legumbres solamente

    (B) el régimen más efectivo es el más popular

    (C) la leche es la mejor bebida para las dietas

    (D) los norteamericanos comen demasiados alimentos grasientos

128. Los que quieren adelgazar deben _____.

    (A) seguir los regímenes que tengan resultado rápido

    (B) tener cuidado de no perder peso de prisa

    (C) seguir los regímenes que sean más populares

    (D) entender que las dietas más recientes son las mejores

Questions 129–130

Registro del Vehículo de Motor

Los residentes tienen que titular y registrar sus vehículos antes de conducir en las vías públicas.

Los residentes nuevos tienen que titular y registrar su vehículo dentro de un término de 60 días (o antes de que venza el registro de otro estado, lo que ocurra primero).

Este capítulo cubre el registro de su vehículo.

También discute las tabllas o placas, las inspecciones de seguridad del vehículo, y el seguro de responsabilidad civil.

Tablillas O Placas

En el momento en que usted registre su vehículo, usted recibirá dos tablillas (una para los vehículos remolcados o trailers, bicicletas motorizadas y motocicletas).

Hay que fijar una de las tablillas en la parte delantera y la otra en la parte trasera del vehículo.

Deben colocarse por lo menos a 12 pulgadas, pero a menos de 48 pulgadas, sobre el suelo.

Ambas tablillas tienen que ser limpias y visibles.

La tablilla de la parte posterior tiene que estar alumbrada para poder verse de noche a una distancia de 50 pies, aunque tenga tablillas reflectores.

---

129. Para conducir en las vías públicas, hay que _____.

(A) vivir en el estado por lo menos 60 días

(B) tener menos de 17 años de edad

(C) titular y registrar el vehículo con seguro

(D) tener el vehículo titulado y registrado con seguridad

130. Es muy importante que las tablillas _____.

(A) estén colocadas en la parte enfrente y delantera

(B) sean visibles con tablillas reflectores

(C) estén no sólo visibles sino bien colocadas

(D) se reemplacen cuando se compra un nuevo vehículo

TEST 1

ANSWER KEY

Listening Comprehension

1. (D)	14. (C)	27. (A)	40. (B)
2. (B)	15. (C)	28. (B)	41. (A)
3. (A)	16. (C)	29. (C)	42. (D)
4. (C)	17. (D)	30. (C)	43. (C)
5. (A)	18. (A)	31. (A)	44. (B)
6. (A)	19. (C)	32. (B)	45. (D)
7. (B)	20. (A)	33. (A)	46. (C)
8. (B)	21. (D)	34. (D)	47. (B)
9. (A)	22. (C)	35. (C)	48. (C)
10. (C)	23. (A)	36. (A)	49. (D)
11. (B)	24. (B)	37. (D)	50. (A)
12. (B)	25. (D)	38. (D)	
13. (B)	26. (B)	39. (C)	

Reading

51. (A)	71. (A)	91. (D)	111. (B)
52. (B)	72. (B)	92. (B)	112. (C)
53. (B)	73. (A)	93. (A)	113. (A)
54. (D)	74. (B)	94. (C)	114. (B)
55. (C)	75. (B)	95. (D)	115. (A)
56. (B)	76. (D)	96. (B)	116. (C)
57. (C)	77. (B)	97. (A)	117. (D)
58. (A)	78. (A)	98. (C)	118. (D)
59. (D)	79. (C)	99. (B)	119. (C)
60. (D)	80. (B)	100. (D)	120. (C)
61. (A)	81. (D)	101. (A)	121. (C)
62. (D)	82. (A)	102. (D)	122. (C)
63. (C)	83. (A)	103. (B)	123. (A)
64. (A)	84. (B)	104. (B)	124. (B)
65. (C)	85. (A)	105. (A)	125. (B)
66. (A)	86. (D)	106. (D)	126. (B)
67. (D)	87. (A)	107. (A)	127. (D)
68. (A)	88. (C)	108. (B)	128. (B)
69. (D)	89. (B)	109. (C)	129. (C)
70. (B)	90. (D)	110. (D)	130. (A)

DETAILED EXPLANATIONS
OF ANSWERS

Section I: Listening

Part A

1. **(D)**   The correct answer is D. "At what time does the 5:00 train leave?" (D) is the only logical answer because the 5:00 o'clock train could not be a 6:00 o'clock train (A), nor can a place — the train station (B) — be a time. The same is true of the directions given in (C). So, therefore, the answer has to be "soon" (D).

2. **(B)**   The correct answer is (B). "How did Mr. Ramirez do that?" The question asks how something was done. (A) "Well, thank you" is a response to a greeting. "Delicious" (C) is an illogical response that doesn't explain how and (D) refers to the spelling of a word but is nonsensical in this context. (B) "Carefully" answers the question, How?

3. **(A)**   The correct answer is (A). "What did it take to realize the problem?" "More than I would have imagined." The question doesn't ask about quantities of money as (B) and (C) suggest. The quantity referred to in the question concerns effort and is not measurable in this context. (D) "I studied math" does not refer to the problem either.

4. **(C)**   The correct answer is (C). The question asks who is sending a letter, not a place as (A) suggests and not a way of doing it as (B) states. It certainly can't be sent by a bird (D). Therefore, (C) "It was my girlfriend who sent the letter" is the most logical response.

5. **(A)**   The correct answer is (A). "How long has it been since he began to paint?" (A) is the correct answer, "two years." (B) cannot be the answer, because it can't be tomorrow, a reply in the future to a question asked of the past. (C) is an amount of money, so it is not strictly time. Quantities referred to in (D) refer to colors and a paintbrush, not time.

6. **(A)** The correct answer is (A). "Am I in Plaza San Martin?" asks the question. The person responding says it is indeed that square, and wonders about the blindness of the person who asks since he/she is in front of a sign which clearly indicates the name. (B) explains who San Martin is, an Argentinean hero, but that's not the answer to the question. (C) refers to a banking situation, in Spanish this could have referred to the benches of a plaza or park, but it wouldn't be referred to as a bank situation. "What's the room number?" (D) is nonsensical too. A plaza is a square, clearly not a hotel, so asking the room number is irrelevant. If it were a hotel's name, it would be El Plaza, of the masculine genre, because hotel in Spanish is masculine and "plaza" is feminine.

7. **(B)** The correct answer is (B). "What did they take out of the car?" is the question. "Sacar brillo" in Spanish is to make something shine, so, it could have been, but it wouldn't be written with the article *del*, but rather *al*. So it is something they took from the car. "Aunt Eudora's luggage" is the correct answer (B). "Maximum speed" (C) is not used with the verb *sacar*. The same is true for choice (D).

8. **(B)** The correct answer is (B). The question is "Why did they run so quickly?" Choice (A) is not correct. You don't run if you are early. You would run if the house were on fire (B), the correct answer. If you are paralyzed by anguish you can't run, so (C) is wrong. And if you are slow with no hope at all (D), you certainly don't run and you do not run quickly either.

9. **(A)** The correct answer is (A). "Who came later?" is the question. (A) says "Nobody came," but it is the correct answer. "Later on" (B) can't be correct because the answer is not about time. The end is a condition, not a noun, therefore, (C) can't be correct. And late Roberto is dead, so he couldn't go anywhere (D). So, who went? No one.

10. **(C)** The correct answer is (C). Juan Carlos can't bring the book to the person asking him for it. The four answer choices agree on that much. Response (A), not having money, couldn't be true. You don't need money to reach a book. You can't argue that the book is too hot to reach; at least it is difficult to find a book that is too hot to be handled. (C) is the answer. It is too high to be reached. (D) is not a logical response since you may not like physics but you could touch the book.

11. **(B)** The correct answer is (B) "I'm happy for the two of you." What he says in (A) is nonsense, changing the numbers of the original

sentence from two to three. In (B) the response makes sense, but he includes himself. In (C) he thanks her, but his remark that his friend is happy is absurd. (D) plays again with numbers and happiness, but the response would be insulting: "Don't be happy since we aren't at all."

12. **(B)** The correct answer is (B). If the summer were long, then it would not be cold and there is no need for a sweater (A). But you wouldn't make a geographical statement. You might respond to your mother by saying "But Mom, it's a spring day!" You can't argue you are not using a sweater because it is snowing and therefore cold. (C) You would use it then. And you can't agree as if you were told the contrary, as (D) does.

13. **(B)** The correct answer is (B). "That would be difficult since we will never see each other again" (B) is the only logical response to Alejandra's threat that she will do harm to Maria Jose if he ever crosses her path again. (A) is only possible if Maria Jose thinks he is going to be killed by a car. The response (C) that he has friends who are doctors is sarcastic but implies that he will need medical attention which is very unlikely. "I'll help you to cross the street" (D) is illogical and uses the figurative meaning of "camino" as street not "path" as used in this context.

14. **(C)** The correct answer is (C). The correct answer is Julio, not July, the month, but rather a person since it is capitalized. So (A) is incorrect. Julio may be precious but cannot be bought (B). You can't lie if you are asking a question (D). (C) is the most logical response "Especially his little face."

15. **(C)** The correct answer is (C). (A) "If you come during the day" is an illogical response to the question "Can I come to your house tonight?" You wouldn't agree and then say you won't be home (B). (C) is correct since the response "Sure, as long as you are punctual" is logical. (D) refers to the solid construction of the house, and, of course, it is interesting if you have an earthquake during the meeting, but totally irrelevant.

16. **(C)** The correct answer is (C). To be paid fairly is the hope of the speaker. If it is late, nothing will change (A). The suggestion of going away is not a logical response (B). (C) is correct: "They will only pay the minimum." And (D) "Justice is so" is an ambiguous remark as well as an illogical response to "I hope they pay us fairly."

17. **(D)**. The correct answer is (D). "Would we be capable of forgetting this disgrace?" You wouldn't take something to improve your memory if

you wanted to forget (A). To be a great worker or even a workaholic wouldn't necessarily guarantee that one would forget (B). Insurance may pay for everything but won't cure the persistence of a memory (C). (D) is a common expression in this context: "Time cures everything indeed."

18. **(A)** The correct answer is (A). If the person being spoken about loses their attention all the time, (A) is a very good answer. "What are you saying?" implies he/she is not listening. (B) "That's nothing, you should see how well I iron" is an illogical response. The reason alluded to in (C) is that the person studies to improve his/her concentration, but it is unlikely that he/she would study engineering to remedy an attention deficit or inability to concentrate. And loving is meritory (D) but doesn't explain why he/she is not paying attention.

Section I: Listening

Part B

19. **(C)** The correct response is (C) football. Choices (A), (B), and (D) are mentioned as sports which, although they are important, do not have as many fans as football.

20. **(A)** The most fitting answer is (A) a minority. Option (B) none is false, while (C) many is not suitable because it is too wide, and (D) an elite is not suitable since it is too restrictive, according to what the narrator explained.

21. **(D)** The correct answer is (D) as a spectacular and a revered tradition. Choice (A) simply as a sport is not correct because the passage makes it clear that it is more than a sport. Choices (B) as a show and (C) like Thanksgiving Day are only partially true, and are not as complete as (D).

22. **(C)** The correct answer is (C). Benito says he couldn't sleep that night and went to work early in order to keep his job, even if he is sleepy. He was not fired (D). He hasn't been late after sleeping too much (A). He hasn't been unable to sleep, having arrived late to work (B). So, the correct answer is (C); he remained awake and went to work earlier than usual.

23. **(A)** The correct answer is (A). We are not talking about water to drink (B) or mineral goods (C), and wind destruction is not the issue (D). The rivers serve as transportation, and water is good for the growth of the vegetation.

24. **(B)** The correct answer is (B). If the trees are cut, the weather changes because vegetation regulates the climate. A flood is not caused by the cutting of the trees (A), nor is a drought created (C). Absorption of water has diminished, not increased, due to the cutting of the forests (D).

25. **(D)** The correct answer is (D). It is true that Chinichex will pay the number of the receipt multiplied by the difference of the amount plus that difference. It is not only the difference of prices (A) or the difference between the number of the receipt and the amount of the purchase from a competitor's store (B). It is not the number of the receipt multiplied by the amount of the article being bought (C).

26. **(B)** The correct answer is (B). It is a fable about an enchanted town mysteriously protected by a forest. The man is not drunk (A), his grandfather has told him the truth, he didn't lie (C), and it wasn't the lack of a compass that bewitches the place and makes him go back every time (D).

27. **(A)** The correct answer is (A). He was called "The King"; even though E. P. are his initials, he was not called E. P. by the public. Those are the initials sewn on his underwear (B). The Big Apple is the name that refers to New York City, not the King (C). Chubby (D) was the name of the couple mentioned in the article, not the name of The King.

28. **(B)** The correct answer is (B). The journalist is ironic indeed. By saying apparently nice words about the star, he is being cruel and insulting to her. So, he is not kind (A). He is not only descriptive (C), there are a lot of personal subjective statements made by the journalist reflecting his opinion. And (D), no, he is not too serious. He has a fine sense of humor, although it is a sarcastic sense of humor.

29. **(C)** The correct answer is (C). You have to be enormously patient to make this device work. (A) is almost true. You have to buy the Gold model to have real success using the machine. But it is not absolutely necessary to buy the Gold model to get results. When a yellow light flashes (B), you have to begin from zero, so this is not the correct choice. If you empty the C space you will take out the battery and nothing will work; therefore, (D) is not the correct answer.

30. **(C)** The correct answer is (C). The president of the neighborhood watch organization has decided not to take revenge on some violent acts that happened. (A) is not true; she will not take violent decisions as a reply. She doesn't think violent actions deserve some other violent actions as an answer (B). She does not think that violent human beings shouldn't have any punishment. She thinks they should be punished but not necessarily in the same way they behave (D).

31. **(A)** The correct answer is (A). The girl the singer refers to in the song has betrayed him (A). The singer adored her and she "dressed in fire" and burned him, wounding him and leaving him to despair. The opposite, (B), is not true, that she has been the one betrayed by the singer. He has not yet forgotten her (C), and she was hardly a calm, peaceful acting person (D), at least not according to the scorned lover and singer.

32. **(B)** The correct answer is (B). The contest for those who look like *Star Trek's* Captain Picard is not only for those naturally bald (A) but for those bald in general, by their own means or by some other act (B). The polyester suit is not a condition to be in the contest, it is one of the prizes (C). There's no need to shout "I'm just like Captain Picard!" If you are going to join the contest, you just have to act like him and look like him a bit (D).

33. **(A)** The correct answer is (A). This weather report says that even when it is not expected, a cold front could come and the wind chill factor could change the weather unexpectedly. Therefore, a mother listening to this weather report should dress her children with sweaters. (B) is not correct since it is not winter. Cold weather would not be unusually strange in winter. (C) is illogical; you can't fight cold weather using summer clothes. Winter has not yet ceased, (D) rather it has yet to begin.

34. **(D)** The correct answer is (D). They are not meeting at 10:00 because they assume Carina will not be punctual. So (A) and (B) are not good choices. Carina will pick up Juan, so (A) has another inaccuracy. They are not meeting at the photo lab (C). Only Carina will go there. The correct answer is (D), they will meet at the mall at 11:00.

35. **(C)** The correct answer is (C). The secret is so secret it can't be public knowledge. So (A) is not possible. Luis is not refusing to tell the nature of the job (B). The job is so secret that Luis doesn't know its nature, so he can't divulge it (C). He is not promising to tell the secret two days later (D); they are supposed to find out within two days, before the holiday.

36. **(A)**   The correct answer is (A). Guillermo has canceled all the reservations because they couldn't add a third person close to the two already reserved seats. He decided not to go to the theater at all. He was offered three tickets in a poor location, but he refused to accept them. Therefore, (B) is incorrect. The third person is not out of the plan; they are all out of it. (D) Guillermo hasn't given his ticket to the third person; this is also false.

37. **(D)**   The correct answer is (D). This club has its complications. (A) is not correct; a member of the club cannot visit his brother's room because it is forbidden without exception to visit the fourth floor where the employees live; and this brother works at the club. Only the employees who have a member as part of the family can smoke, and only on the third floor, but all employees are forbidden to go onto the third floor, so no employee can smoke in the club (B). (C) is also incorrect. If guests are under the same limitations, then no guest can visit his girlfriend if she is an employee of the club. No employees, then, are entitled to special treatment (D).

38. **(D)**   The correct answer is (D). The gloquilla is prepared by mother nature to resist its habitat. So it can't live underground (A), and certainly not in the Arctic (B) because it has skin and eyes that resist bright light and high temperatures. It is not blind, because it has the ability to see in intense light, (C). It must be an animal living in a volcanic zone (D).

39. **(C)**   The correct answer is (C). The grandson is obviously trying to get some money from his grandfather. We have to suppose that his grandfather doesn't have a bad memory; he didn't want to send his grandson a present. Therefore, (A) is incorrect. The mail office hasn't kept the present. The present doesn't exist. So the grandson is only trying to find a way to get what he wants. (B) is wrong, and therefore, (C) is right. He is lying. The grandfather doesn't care about his own age; it is just an excuse that he uses to be free of sending him a present.

40. **(B)**   The correct answer is (B). (A) is incorrect; the customer doesn't have exquisite taste. He just wants to sleep listening to music that must bore him, but it has to be first rate. He is indeed pretentious (B). He doesn't love classical music. He loves its category (C). He doesn't like boring music; he just needs it to sleep (D).

41. **(A)**   The correct answer is (A). The play was a success because a lot of people went and applauded. It wouldn't be a success because of opin-

ions from the newspapers — the critics didn't like the play. Since the play was free, it was not a financial success (B). (C) is incorrect; the press was not pleased. (D) is not a correct statement; the author is very pleased and "satisfied with everything" as he states in the telegram.

42. **(D)**   The correct answer is (D). (A) is incorrect; the cactus is the plant that retains water. (B) is wrong, since a cactus has no leaves. Plants grow far away from one another to collect more water, (C) not close together. (D) is accurate; some branches adapt themselves to pick up the sun's energy and process it as leaves do.

43. **(C)**   The correct answer is (C). (A) is incorrect; those who died from illness were the Indians and the religious who went to evangelize them. (B) is also incorrect; those who were in jail were criminals who had committed another crime after already being in jail (C) is correct. (D) cannot be true; Ushuaia, even though it has wildlife and is an interesting research site, is not a special wildlife sanctuary like some other places in the South.

44. **(B)**   The correct answer is (B). The friend asked to buy cigarettes was so kind that he didn't. Instead, he bought chocolate cigarettes because he doesn't want his friend to smoke so much. Therefore, he was not distracted (A). He brought chocolates on purpose (B). There were real cigarettes to bring home, but he just didn't bring any, (C). They won't smoke the chocolate ones, (D) they're going to eat them, so (B) is the correct choice.

45. **(D)**   The correct answer is (D). (A) is incorrect. The second apartment that Mimi may rent is not the most expensive one. In fact, it may be the cheapest of the three possible apartments. The third is not the smallest. It has two bedrooms and a garden, more space than the other two (B). The first one has no terrace or garden, so it can't be the one with the most fresh air of the three (C). (D) is the only possibility; no fee is needed, because the owner sells the third one.

46. **(C)**   The correct answer is (C). Virgos are not born in May. So everything written in the horoscope is different. (A) says it's positive; it would be for those born on May, not for those of Virgo. (B) says it is full of hope for Virgo males but everything it predicts is terrible. (C) is the correct choice since this horoscope is doubtful. (D) predicts spiritual growth but this is not stated.

47. **(B)** The correct answer is (B). They are talking about something being cooked. It is not a professional killer (A), but rather a cook (B), making a joke about the fish he is cooking. An architect has nothing to do with this dialogue (C). A vet wouldn't cook his patients (D).

48. **(C)** The correct answer is (C). Many things happened to her, but her leg is not broken at all. So (C) is the right answer. (A) is wrong, since her skates were not the cause of any harm. (B) is incorrect; her mother sat on her leg but nothing happened. (D) is also incorrect, she talks and talks and talks without any inhibition.

49. **(D)** The correct answer is (D). (A) is incorrect; for Ricardo's birthday, Quique should not sing because he is a horrible singer. (B) is also wrong. Ricardo is not poor. Because he has so many things, they are having problems choosing something to make him for a present, something he may not have. (C) is incorrect. They are all signed. Autographs in Spanish means that they are not self-made. (D) is correct; Melba had no problem telling Quique he is a terrible singer. She says what she thinks, even if she causes harm.

50. **(A)** The correct answer is (A). The Titanic crashed into a glacier. It was destroyed by the solidified water only. It wasn't attacked, (B), and sadly the members of the orchestra were not saved and died there, (C). The Titanic crew had everything under control, so (D) is not true.

Section II: Reading

Part A

51. **(A)** "Esquina" means the corner or outer side of an angle formed for example, by two streets which meet or intersect each other. In the list of choices there appears the word "rincón," which is not appropriate in this case, although it does mean "corner," but in another sense: the inner side of an angle such as that formed by two walls which meet to form a corner of a room. Obviously, the other two possible answers given ("techo" = "roof" and "escalera" = "staircase") would not logically be used when talking about streets.

52. **(B)** "Dependiente" means clerk. This word also has a feminine form which is "dependienta." "Atender" (ie) means "to wait on."

"Mercancía" means "merchandise." "Cliente" and "parroquiano" both signify "customer."

53. **(B)** "Developer" means "to return" in the sense of "to give back." The other three possible choices also mean "to return," but only in the sense of "to come or go back." Of these three, "retornar" is the least frequently used.

54. **(D)** "Tengo sueño" signifies I am sleepy. The verb "acostarse" means "to go to bed." Hence, the other three answers would not apply. Notice how the verb "tener" is frequently used in Spanish to form idiomatic expressions: "tener sed" (to be thirsty), "tener hambre" (to be hungry), "tener calor" (to be hot). To this list, we might add other expressions such as "tener frío" (to be cold), "tener razón" (to be right), "no tener razón" (to be wrong), "tener vergüenza" (to be ashamed), "tener ganas de" + infinitive (to feel like doing something), "tener celos" (to be jealous), etc.

55. **(C)** All four of the answers mean "stopped," but the verb "parar" refers to a moving object which comes to a physical halt and *movement* ceases. "Dejar de" means to stop doing something ("Dejé de estudiar a las once" = I stopped studying at 11:00). Observe that this expression is *always* followed by an infinitive. "Cesar" and "terminar" also have this meaning. ("Cesó la lluvia a las nueve" = The rain stopped at 9:00. "La fiesta terminó a la medianoche" – The party ended/stopped at midnight.) The word "trayectoria," in this case, means "route."

56. **(B)** The first three verbs all have to do with the idea of "try," but each is used under very particular circumstances. "Tratar de" + infinitive is used when we want to say "to try to do something." "Ensayar" and "probar" mean "to try" or "to try out," but they are generally not followed by infinitives, but rather by nouns. For example, "Voy a probar el agua" (I'm going to try out the water). "Ensayar" can also be used to mean "to rehearse," as for a play. In addition, it can occasionally mean to try on, as with clothing, but the most common verb we use in this instance is the reflexive form of "probar," i.e., "probarse": "Voy a probarme esta blusa" (I'm going to try on this blouse). Remember that "probar" can also mean "to prove": "Me probaron que no tenía razón (They proved to me that I was wrong). "Quedarse" (to remain) would be entirely illogical syntactically in this case because it would have to be followed by the preposition "para" (in order to), which would be obligatory in front of the infinitive.

57. **(C)** Both "boletos" and "billetes" are tickets, for the theater or the train, for example, and would not fit in here with the word "casa" (house). "Cuentos" and "cuentas" look rather alike except for the difference in gender. The first means "story," or in a literary sense, "short story"; the second means "bills," and would therefore make sense within the context of the sentence.

58. **(A)** Normally, the only two prepositions which appear directly after "pensar" are "de" and "en." "Pensar de" is most often used in questions to ask for an opinion: "¿Qué piensas de este examen?" (What do you think about this test?). "Pensar en" means "to think about" in the sense of concentrating or meditating upon something or someone: "Pienso mucho en mi familia" (I think about my family a lot, i.e., my family is often on my mind). Remember that when "pensar" is followed directly by an infinitive (with no intervening preposition), the meaning is "to intend" or "to plan on" doing something: "Pienso ir al cine mañana" (I intend to go to the movies tomorrow).

59. **(D)** When a part of the body is causing pain, we use the verb "doler" (ue) preceded by the proper form of the indirect object pronoun (me, te, le, nos, os, les), which refers to the person feeling the pain. The subject of the verb "doler" is the part(s) of the body mentioned. Consequently, "doler," in any tense, will normally be used only in the third person singular and the third person plural. Compare the following sentences: "Le duelen los ojos" (His eyes hurt him), "Te dolía una muela" (Your tooth was hurting you, i.e., you had a toothache). "Dañar" and "hacer daño" mean "to hurt" in the sense of "to damage" or "harm": "El gato hizo daño a las cortinas" (The cat damaged the curtains). "Herir" (ie, i) is related to the noun "herida" (wound), and obviously means "to wound."

60. **(D)** To answer properly here, it is important to know the meaning of "abrigo" (overcoat). This helps us associate the sentence with cold weather and the word "frio" (cold) in the correct answer. Notice that with many weather expressions we use the third person singular of the verb "hacer." Other common expressions of this type are "hacer calor" (to be hot), "hacer mal tiempo" (to be bad weather), "hacer buen tiempo" (to be good weather), "hacer viento" (to be windy), and "hacer fresco" (to be cool). Two common verbs pertaining to weather which do *not* use "hacer" are "llover" (ue) which means "to rain" and "nevar" (ie), "to snow." Notice the vowel change in "llover" as it appears in choice (B). When it rains you wear a "raincoat," "un impermeable" or "una gabardina." The verb "correr" (to run) does not make much sense as a response for this item.

61. **(A)** Choosing the right answer here depends first on understanding the expression "hacer un (el) viaje" which means "to take a (the) trip." Of the four possibilities suggested, only "una maleta" (a suitcase) has a direct bearing on travel. "Una máquina de coser" is "a sewing machine." "Una multa" means "a fine." "Una muñeca" signifies either "a wrist" or "a doll."

62. **(D)** Answering correctly in this case can be aided if you recognize the words "lugar" (place), "árboles" (trees), and "campo" (countryside). A place in the countryside where there are many trees is logically a woods. A stand of trees is a "bosque." The word "madera" means "wood" as a building material, for example. "Leña" has a very specific meaning: "firewood" or "kindling wood." "Verdulería," although it suggests the idea of "verde" (green), actually means "green grocery," a place where one can buy green vegetables.

63. **(C)** Key words in the statement are "se cortó" (cut himself), "cuchillo" (knife), and "dedo" (finger). "Anillo" (ring) and "uña" (fingernail) can be related to "finger," but they seem to have no relationship to the idea of Felipe's cutting himself. "Oreja" (ear) would also be out of place here. "Herida" (wound), on the other hand, can be related to the idea of cutting oneself. Notice how, in this case, the verb "cortar" is used in its reflexive form "cortarse." Reflexive verbs can often be used to show an action which the subject does to itself: "Se sentó: (He sat down, i.e., he sat himself down) and "Me miré en el espejo" (I looked at myself in the mirror). In our sentence we did not use the possessive adjective "su" in front of the word "dedo" because in most cases we simply use the definite articles (el, la, los, las) with the parts of the body and clothing.

Section II: Reading

Part B

64. **(A)** "Sin embargo" is correct. It means nevertheless and makes sense in this context. (B) means "as usual," (C) means "without equal," and (D) means "without remedy."

65. **(C)** "Satisfechos" is correct. The masculine plural adjective form of satisfacer (to satisfy) is needed to match the noun "todos." (A) is incorrect because it isn't plural. (B) is conjugated in the present tense (he satisfies) and (D) is the infinitive (to satisfy).

66. **(A)** "Lo que" is correct. In context the translation needed here is "that which" or "what." "Lo cual" does not share this same translation, which makes (B) incorrect. Response (C) is incorrect because it is the masculine relative pronoun which could mean who, which or he who. Choice (D) is the plural relative pronoun meaning "those who."

67. **(D)** "Se van" is correct. The present tense predominates throughout this paragraph. Therefore, choices (A) the future tense (they will go), (B) the present subjunctive (they may go), and (C) the preterit tense (they went) are incorrect.

68. **(A)** "Cuentan con" is correct. Again, the present tense is called for in keeping with the meaning of this paragraph. (B) is incorrect because there is no reason for a subjunctive in this statement. (C) is the infinitive. (D) is incorrectly written and would require the stem change to be correct.

69. **(D)** "Un millón de" is correct. (A) is incorrect because the word "uno" must be apocopated before a masculine singular noun, in this case "millón." (B) is missing the "un." (C) is misspelled.

70. **(B)** "Hace" is correct. "Hace" followed by a period of time means "ago." No other tense will render this meaning which makes (A) the imperfect and (D) the preterit incorrect. (C) is incorrect because it is plural.

71. **(A)** "Los que" is correct. The translation "those who" is required in this context. (B) would also mean "those who" if it weren't accented. (C) and (D) are written incorrectly.

72. **(B)** "Obras" is correct. "Obras" are written works. (A) means "compliances," (C) refers to physical work (in farming), and (D) means "female workers."

73. **(A)** "Volvió" is correct. In the context of this paragraph, the preterit is required. Therefore, choices (B) the present tense and (C) the past subjunctive are incorrect. Choice (D) is the infinitive and a conjugated verb is required here.

74. **(B)** "Éste" is correct. Accented forms of "éste" not only mean this one/these but also may be translated as "the latter," which is the correct translation in this sentence. (A) is incorrect because it is the masculine

singular adjective form meaning "that far away." (C) is neuter and choice (D), although accented, can only mean "that one."

75. **(B)** "Trajera" is correct. The subjunctive is required as part of the noun clause introduced by a form of "decir" (dijo), an indirect command verb. The past subjunctive is required to follow the sequence. (A) the preterit, (C) the present subjunctive, and (D) the future are, therefore, incorrect.

76. **(D)** "Alguna" is correct. "Alguna" is the feminine singular adjective meaning "some," which matches the noun "evidencia." No negatives are called for since this statement is affirmative. Therefore, (B) and (C) are incorrect. (A) is incorrect because it is the masculine singular form that would precede a masculine singular noun.

77. **(B)** "Le" is correct. The verb "comunicó" would require an indirect object pronoun, in this case, to match up with "a la Señora." Choices (A) and (D) are direct object pronouns. Choice (C) is the plural indirect object pronoun.

78. **(A)** "Eso" is correct. The neuter form of the demonstrative is used to refer to previously mentioned events, occurrences, or happenings. In this case, Juan is communicating to the Virgen the information given to him by the Bishop. Because both (B) and (C) have gender, they are incorrect. Choice (D) is incorrect since no neuter pronouns require accent marks.

79. **(C)** "Quien" is correct. "Quien" is the relative pronoun referring to "Señora." No accent is required, which would make (A) incorrect. (B) "whom" and (D) "of whom" are incorrect translations in this context.

80. **(B)** "Regresara" is correct. Again, subjunctive is required in this noun clause prompted by the verb "dijo." To follow sequence, the past subjunctive is used. (A) is the present subjunctive, (C) is the infinitive, and (D) is the present indicative.

81. **(D)** "Convencieran" is correct. This adjective clause requires a subjunctive because its antecedent "evidencias" is indefinite. To follow sequence, the past subjunctive is required. (A) the conditional, (B) the present subjunctive, and (C) the preterit are incorrect.

82. **(A)** "El" is correct. "Tema," although it ends in "a," is masculine and would require a masculine singular article. Therefore, (B) and (D),

which are feminine, are incorrect. Obviously, since an article is needed, choice (C) is incorrect.

83. **(A)** "Abogó" is correct. "Abogó por" means "advocated for." (B) means "approved by," (C) means "embraced by," and (D) means "bundled up."

84. **(B)** "Permanecido" is correct. The past participle is required after the form of "haber" and is invariable. (A) is incorrect because it is feminine. (C) is the present participle and (D) is the infinitive.

85. **(A)** "Cerrado" is correct. "Cerrado" is the past participle used here as an adjective modifying "puerto." Therefore, (B) the feminine participle, (C) the present participle, and (D) the infinitive are incorrect.

86. **(D)** "Trescientos" is correct. (A) is incorrect because it is the feminine form of the number. Numbers from 200 to 900 are never apocopated, which makes (B) incorrect. (C) is not spelled correctly.

87. **(A)** "Pagar" is correct. After the conjugated verb "logró" an infinitive is required. (B) is the present participle, (C) is the past participle, and (D) is the feminine plural form of the past participle which is used as an adjective.

88. **(C)** "Buenas" is correct. The feminine plural form is required here to match the nouns "condiciones." (A) is the masculine plural form, (B) is the masculine singular apocopated form, and (D) is the feminine singular form.

89. **(B)** "Mandato" is correct. In this context (B), which means "mandate or command," is correct. (A) means "young man,"(C) means "apron," and (D) means "large stain."

90. **(D)** "Para" is correct. "In order to" is expressed by "para" before an infinitive. Therefore, (A), which does not have this translation, and (C), which means "because," are incorrect. (B) is incorrect for obvious reasons.

Section II: Reading

Part C

91. **(D)** Choice (D) is the correct answer. Lencho became sad because a hailstorm had destroyed his crop of beans and corn. The story tells us: "... cuando la tempestad pasó dijo con voz triste a sus hijos: ... el granizo no ha dejado nada" (when the hailstorm was over he told his children with a sad voice: ... the hail has left nothing). (A) is not a good choice, since nothing is said in the narrative about his children dying. (B) is not correct; we are told that a lot of rain was needed to ensure a good harvest. What saddened Lencho was not too much rain, but that the storm also brought hail. (C) is not the best choice. Lencho mentions the locusts ("langostas") only to say that the damage done by the hail was much worse than what a cloud of locusts might have caused.

92. **(B)** Choice (B) is the best answer. In the letter he wrote to God, he said, "Necesito cien pesos para volver a sembrar y vivir mientras viene la cosecha" (I need 100 pesos to sow again and to live on while the harvest comes). This, as well as other statements in the text, make it clear that he was a farmer ("agricultor"). That means (A) priest ("cura"), (C) postman ("cartero"), and (D) notary, court clerk ("escribano") are all incorrect.

93. **(A)** Choice (A) is the correct answer. The story tells us that Lencho had faith in God, so he wrote him a letter asking for 100 pesos to replant his crop and to live on until harvest time. (B) is incorrect, because Lencho never complained about his bad luck. (C) is not the best answer, because in his first letter to God, he does not mention any irregularities in the post office. In his second letter, at the end of the narrative, he indicates that he thinks the postal workers stole part of the money God sent him. (D) is not a good choice; in his letter Lencho does not ask God to give him a good harvest.

94. **(C)** Choice (C) is correct. After reading Lencho's letter, the postmaster was impressed by Lencho's faith, so he decided to collect some money to help him. (A) is not a good choice; while the postmaster's initial reaction to the letter was laughter, he did not "just laugh," but rather took steps to help Lencho. (B) is not right, because in the story the postmaster does not scold the employee for opening someone else's mail. (D) cannot be correct, because we are told that the postmaster collected money and answered Lencho's letter; he did not simply give the letter back to him without any money.

95. **(D)** Choice (D) is the best choice. The story tells us that Lencho showed no surprise at all when he received the letter from God. He was not surprised to see the money either, because he had faith and was expecting it. (A) is not correct, since we are told that he was not surprised in the least ("no mostró la menor sorpresa"). (B) is not a good choice; he did not "roar with laughter." (C) is incorrect, because he did not "lose hope" when he received the letter.

96. **(B)** Choice (B), "dishonest," is the correct answer. When Lencho got the money "from God," there was only 60 pesos in the envelope, and he had asked for 100. Lencho assumed God had sent the 100 pesos as requested, and that the postal workers had stolen some of it. In his second letter, he asks God to send the rest of the money, but advises him not to send it through the post office, because "all the postal employees are thieves" ("todos los empleados de correo son ladrones"). (A) is incorrect, because Lencho did not believe the postal workers were "honest" ("honrados"), but rather dishonest. (C) is not a good choice; although the postmaster was very generous, Lencho did not know it, and in fact suspected that the postal workers had stolen part of the money God had sent for him. (D) is not the best choice, since there is no information in the narrative that would indicate that Lencho thought the post office employees were "bondadosos" (kind, good-natured).

97. **(A)** Choice (A) is the best answer. Since a lot of rain was necessary for a good harvest, Lencho was pleased that it was raining. The story tells us: ". . . Lencho observaba sus campos con placer" (Lencho watched his fields with pleasure). (B) is not a good choice, because his reaction to the rain was not "despair (or desperation)." (C) "Anger" does not accurately express what Lencho felt when he saw the rain falling on his crops, so it is not the best choice. (D) cannot be correct; Lencho did not feel "anxiety" ("angustia") when the rain came. The story indicates that he began to feel that way when it started hailing.

98. **(C)** (C) is the correct answer. In the context in which it is used in the passage, "agasajo" means "gift" or "present," and clearly refers to "chocolatl," the drink the aztecs made from ground cacao beans. (A) is not an appropriate answer, since Moctezuma's attitude toward the conquistadors is not mentioned in the selection. Although (B) fits in with the concept of a gift, the "tazón de oro" (large golden cup) from which Moctezuma drank the "chocolatl" is only mentioned in passing, and the context excludes it as the antecedent of "agasajo." Since the destruction of

the Aztec Empire by the Spaniards is not dealt with in this passage, (D) is not a good choice.

99. **(B)** Choice (B) correctly answers the question, "Where are the cacao trees cultivated?" The text states that they grow in the tropics. (A) is not a good choice, because the information given in the passage indicates that cacao trees do not grow in the U.S. (C) is incorrect; since cacao was unknown in Europe until Cortés brought it from Mexico, and Spain is not in the tropics, it is logical to conclude that cacao trees are not cultivated in Spain. (D) is not a logical choice; while England and Holland are mentioned as having made improvements on the cacao drink, the European climate precludes the cultivation of cacao trees in those countries.

100. **(D)** Choice (D) is the best answer, since the passage reveals that the Spanish court tried to keep cacao, and the drink made from it, a secret, and managed to for more than 100 years. (A) is not a good choice, since Spain did not immediately spread the news to the rest of Europe. (B) is not correct, because although the passage relates that "chocolatl" caused a sensation in the Spanish court, it mentions nothing of the members of the court kicking up a scandal because they did not like the bitter drink. Choice (C) cannot be right; we are told in the reading that chocolate was only a drink up until 150 years ago when the process for making solid bar chocolate was developed.

101. **(A)** Choice (A) is correct, since the passage tells us that they sweetened it and made it richer by adding sugar and milk to it. (B) is not a good choice, since the text mentions nothing at all about whether the cacao drink was served hot or cold. (C) is incorrect; the passage states that a miniscule amount of lye ("lejía") is added to the liquid cacao during processing to intensify its flavor, but that has nothing to do with making the drink. (D) makes reference to another step in the refining process, the removal of cocoa butter, which has no connection with the early improvements made to the cacao drink by the English and Dutch.

102. **(D)** Choice (D) is the correct answer. Besides grinding the cacao beans to make the drink "chocolatl," the Aztecs used them as a form of money. The passage reveals that 100 beans could buy a healthy slave. (A) is not a good choice, because nothing is said in the reading about the beans being used as weapons to wage war. Since the text does not mention throwing beans into the sea for good luck, (B) is eliminated as a correct response. (C) cannot be right; since the Aztecs themselves make

"chocolatl" from the cacao beans, it is not logical that they would use the same beans to poison their enemies.

103. **(B)** Choice (B) is the best answer. The first paragraph of the passage tells us that "cacao and its derivative, chocolate, can aid in digestion, stimulate blood flow to the heart, and help people with chest colds breathe better," all of which would come under the heading of "medicinal value" ("valor medicinal"). (A) is incorrect, since the information given in the text indicates that cacao became very popular in Europe, making the statement that it "was not very successful outside of Mexico" false. (C) is not the best response; the passage does not take up cacao's nutritional value. (D) is not a good choice; in the first sentence of the passage we are told that "cacao should not be confused with coconut (*coco*) or coca, the source of cocaine," so the assertion that cacao "resembles coconut and coca" cannot be right.

104. **(B)** Choice (B) is the correct answer. The story is told in the first person, and we do not know the narrator's name until his uncle addresses him in the fifth paragraph. (A) is not a good choice, since the passage indicates that Blas de Santillana is the narrator's father. (C) is not correct, because we are told that Gil Pérez is the narrator's uncle. (D) is incorrect; Dr. Godínez was Gil Blas's school teacher in Oviedo.

105. **(A)** Choice (A) is the best answer. The second paragraph of the passage tells us that Gil Blas's uncle, Gil Pérez, taught him how to read. (B) is not a good choice, since according to the text, Gil Blas already knew how to read when he went to Dr. Godínez's school. (C) is incorrect, because although the passage indicates that he is setting off for the University of Salamanca, it also tells us that his uncle taught him to read when he was very young. (D) is not the best choice; it was his uncle, not his parents, who taught him to read.

106. **(D)** Choice (D) is correct. According to the story, Gil Blas was leaving Oviedo to go to the University of Salamanca. (A) is not a good choice; Gil Blas could not leave Oviedo to go live with his uncle, because his uncle lived in Oviedo. (B) is incorrect, because Gil Blas was leaving Oviedo to go study at the University of Salamanca, not because he was planning to return to his hometown (Santillana). (C) is not correct, since Gil Blas was not leaving Oviedo because his parents threw him out of the house.

107. **(A)**   Choice (A) is the best answer; it was his uncle, Gil Pérez, who told Gil Blas that he was sending him to the University of Salamanca, because he was intelligent and could become an important man. (B) is not the best answer, because the passage says nothing of Dr. Godínez suggesting that Gil Blas go to the university. (C) is not a good choice, since the text indicates that it was Gil Pérez's idea for his nephew to go to the university. (D) is not correct; we are told that Gil Blas liked the idea, but it originally came from his uncle, Gil Pérez.

108. **(B)**   Choice (B) is the best answer; the narrator tells us that when he went to say good-bye to his parents, all they were able to give him were a hug and a lot of advice. (A) is not a good choice, since it was his uncle who gave him a mule and some money for the trip. (C) is not correct, since the passage never mentions anyone giving him "a black horse and a sword." (D) is incorrect, because nothing is ever said about "a new suit and several books."

109. **(C)**   Choice (C) is the best answer. The narrator tells us that his uncle could not have proposed anything more to his liking, because he was anxious to see the world. ("Mi tío no podía proponerme cosa más de mi gusto, porque yo tenía ganas de ver el mundo.") (A) The statement "he did not like it at all" is not a good choice, because the text indicates that Gil Blas liked the idea of going to the University of Salamanca. (B) "He got angry" does not correctly describe Gil Blas's reaction to the idea of going to Salamanca. (D) is not a good choice. Although Gil Blas "put on a sad face" when he was setting out on his trip, he did not "start to cry."

110. **(D)**   The expression "soñar con" means "to dream about" and, in the context of the paragraph, implies a desire on Rafael's part. Consequently, the answer containing the verb "querer" is the most appropriate. Choice (A) would be wrong because "se hizo" means "became," but Rafael did not become a singer. In choice (B), "fingía" means "pretended," but the youth did not pretend he was a singer of popular music. Choice (C) is incorrect because "hacer falta" signifies "to need" (to be necessary), but López doesn't need money now that he has won the first prize in the Christmas lottery. In fact, he no longer has any financial problems, we are told. Note the use of the verb "tocar" in the first sentence of the paragraph. When it is preceded by an indirect object, as here, it may be translated as "to win something."

111. **(B)** The idiom "servir de" signifies "to serve as." We know that Rafael served as a substitute in a band because we are told that he worked with the band "sólo cuando faltaba alguien" (only when someone was missing). Here the verb "faltar" has the special meaning of "to be absent." Rafael did not win a musical prize, as (A) says, but rather the Christmas lottery. Choice (C) would be incorrect because the word "pertinente" (relevant) has nothing to do with the subject. One might be tempted to choose it because of its similarity to the expression "pertenecer a" (to belong to). Choice (D) tells us that Rafael had his own group ("su propio conjunto"), but the expression "pertenecer a" again indicates that he merely belonged to the group, not that it was his own.

112. **(C)** To choose the correct answer, one must know that "ganó" is the past tense of "ganar" and that it means "(he, she) won." As we are told in the first sentence, ". . . le ha tocado el gordo de la lotería de Navidad," he has won the Christmas lottery. Therefore, he has won a lot of money, which corresponds to choice (C), "mucho dinero." Note that "el gordo" is the name given to the grand prize in the yearly lottery drawn during Christmastime in Spain. Choice (A) would not be appropriate since there is no mention of a trip (un viaje) in the passage. Choice (B), "un conjunto musical," refers to the band he plays in and has nothing to do with Rafael winning the lottery. Choice (D), "un tambor," is just referring to the drum, and it is totally irrelevant to the question.

113. **(A)** Getting the right answer here is dependent on knowing that "célebre" means "famous." The last sentence of the reading says that "no hay nadie que le desconozca." The verb "desconocer" means "not to know or recognize." If there is no one who does not know Rafael, then he is famous. Notice that we have used the present subjunctive of the verb "desconocer." This is necessary because the "que" refers back to a person whose identity is unknown ("nadie"). Whenever the relative pronoun "que" refers back to someone or something unknown or non-existent, the verb following the "que" appears in the subjunctive. Compare these two sentences: "No hay nadie que sepa más que tú" (There is no one who knows more than you); "Hay muchos que saben más que yo" (There are many who know more than I). In the first sentence, we use the subjunctive of "saber" because the relative pronoun refers back to the word "nadie," a non-existent entity. In the second sentence we use not the subjunctive, but the indicative of "saber" because the relative pronoun refers back to actual existing people, "muchos" (many). Choice (B) would be incorrect because of the verb "llorar" (to cry). Notice the particular use of "por qué" in choice (B). Here it means "motive" or "reason," but Rafael has little to cry

about! To know that (C) is wrong, you must recognize the idiom "carecer de" + noun, which means "to be lacking (something)." It is used here in the present progressive tense with the auxiliary verb "seguir" (to continue), and means "continues to lack (need)" money. We know that this is untrue because Rafael has gotten rich from the lottery. Choice (D) uses the idiomatic expression "tener prisa" (to be in a hurry), which does not pertain to the situation.

114. **(B)**   To answer correctly, it is helpful to know that "rápido" means "fast." "El tren rápido" then would be "the fast train." You must also be familiar with the "hace" + time expression. The passage specifies that it is now 10:30 and the "tren rápido" left (salió) an hour and fifteen minutes ago (hace hora y cuarto). Therefore, one must subtract the times to arrive at the correct response, which is (B), "a las nueve y cuarto" (9:15). Choices (A) 10:30, (C) 12:00, and (D) 8:45 are then obviously incorrect.

115. **(A)**   The key to arriving at the correct answer is an understanding of "hace" + time expression. If this is used in conjunction with a past tense, in this case the preterit ("salió"), then the meaning is "ago." We are told that it is now 10:30 and the "tren rápido" left an hour and fifteen minutes ago, in other words, at 9:15. We also know that the "tren correo" left a half-hour before the "tren rápido," i.e., at 8:45 ("a las nueve menos cuarto"). Remember that in telling time, after the half-hour we start subtracting minutes from the following hour, hence the use of "menos." The word "cuarto" is synonymous with "quince" in telling time.

116. **(C)**   To answer correctly, it is helpful to know that "lento" means "slow." "El tren más lento," then, would be "the slower train," which, in this case, is the "tren correo." In the question, "haber de" + infinitive means "to be supposed to." We know that it is now 10:30. We are told that the mail train will take two hours more in arriving ("tardará dos horas más en llegar"). Hence, it will arrive at 12:30 ("a las doce y media"). "Tardar" + time expression + "en" + infinitive means "to take (time) in doing something."

117. **(D)**   "Reo" is a synonym for "ladrón" (thief). We know that after the hold-up at the branch office ("sucursal") of the National Bank, the criminals escaped ("huyeron") with an undetermined amount of money, "una cantidad de dinero todavía por determinar." "Todavía por determinar" means "yet to be determined." The policemen surrounded ("rodearon") the district, made a sweep of the area ("hicieron una redada") and were successful in their search ("búsqueda"). In other words, they

found the thieves. Crucial in choosing the right answer is the idiomatic expression "tener éxito (en)," which has nothing to do with exits or leaving, but rather means "to succeed (in)" doing something.

118. **(D)** The word "asalto" is a synonym of "atraco" (holdup), which appears in the first sentence of the reading. The expression "llevar a cabo" means "to realize" or "accomplish." It is used here in the passive voice to mean "was carried out." One finds the clue to the right answer in the phrase "por una pareja campesina temporalmente radicada en la ciudad." "Una pareja" means "a pair," "two," "a couple." We know that these individuals were not from the city, but rather the countryside because of the adjective "campesina." The verb "radicar," whose past participle, "radicado," is used as an adjective here means "to be located." We know, consequently, that the pair was temporarily ("temporalmente") living in the city. Therefore, they were strangers there. Notice that we have used the word "campesinos" in (D), not "extranjeros" because the latter would erroneously imply that they were from a foreign country and not just from a different part of the same country. Choice (A) would be wrong because the reading does not say when the holdup took place. (B) is not right since the crime occurred in the outskirts of the city ("las afueras") and not downtown ("en el centro de la ciudad"). (C) is incorrect because "alrededor de" means "around" in the sense of "surrounding."

119. **(C)** "Fue robado" means "was robbed," another way of conveying the idea of "hubo un atraco." It is used here in the passive voice. "Ayer por la tarde" means "yesterday afternoon," and appears in the first sentence of the reading. Therefore, the bank was robbed yesterday afternoon. (C) is the correct response according to this first sentence. Choice (A), "cierra a las cinco de la tarde," is incorrect, since there is no mention of the closing time of the bank in the reading. Choice (B) says the bank is located in the downtown area of the capital, which is incorrect, since the opposite is mentioned in the first sentence of the reading: ". . . situado en las afueras de la capital." The expression "en las afueras" means "in the outskirts." Choice (D) is also incorrect since the actual size of the bank is never discussed in the passage. "Sucursal del Banco Nacional" means "a branch of the National Bank," which may or may not be the largest bank in the city.

120. **(C)** The word "guardias" can mean "guards," but here it is used in a more general sense to signify "policemen." In answer (C), we have used the preterit tense of "saber," which can often mean "found out," rather than simply "knew." We see at the end of the story that the police captured

the "reos" (criminals) and identified them as a couple from the country. The policemen did not try to prevent a rebellion, as (A) indicates. The word "radicada" does not refer to "radical." (See explanation 118.) We know that the two criminals were from the countryside, but the police did not have to follow them into the countryside, as (B) says. "Perseguir" means "to pursue" or sometimes "to persecute." We know that the police force was armed ("armada"). Therefore, choice (D) is wrong because it says that they arrived without "fusiles" (guns).

121. **(C)** We are told in the story that the criminals were "enmascarados" (masked). Another way of saying this would be "disfrazados" (disguised), as in choice (C). Choice (A) does mention that the criminals are out of towners, but nowhere in the reading does it say that they are kids. Choice (B) is incorrect because "del extranjero" means "from abroad," in other words, "foreigners." Choice (D) is also an inappropriate response because we know it is not the policemen ("la policía") who robbed the bank.

122. **(C)** We learn from the reading that the economic situation in Latin America is going from bad to worse ("va de mal en peor") because of international debts ("deudas internacionales") which many governments are unable to pay, the increase in the cost of living ("el aumento del costo de la vida") and layoffs ("el paro forzoso"). Consequently, governments are lacking sufficient money ("a los gobiernos les falta suficiente dinero"), prices are rising ("Suben los precios"), and there is much unemployment ("desempleo"). Choosing the correct answer here can be aided by a clear understanding of certain other vocabulary and grammatical constructions: the difference between "subir" (to go up or rise) and "bajar" (to go down or fall"), "bastante" (enough) and "demasiado" (too much). Notice also the use of the verbs "faltar" (to be lacking to) and "sobrar" (to be more than enough). Both of these verbs follow the pattern of "gustar," i.e., they are normally used in only the third person singular or plural and are preceded by an indirect object pronoun. If the thing lacking is singular, then the verb will be singular; if it is plural, then the verb will be plural: "Nos falta tiempo" (We are lacking time); "Nos faltan amigos" (We are lacking friends). The same holds true for the verb "sobrar": "Nos sobra tiempo" (We have more than enough time); "Nos sobran amigos" (We have more than enough friends).

123. **(A)** The delegates ("delegados") to the international economic conference are concerned by the unstable situation on international stock markets ("la situación inestable de las bolsas internacionales"), the drop in

the value of the dollar ("la bajada del valor del dólar"), and the lack of balance in international trade ("el desequilibrio de la balanza de pagos"). They seek to arrive at an agreement ("llegar a un acuerdo") which will avoid a possible financial collapse ("que evite un posible derrumbamiento"). Consequently, they are trying to stabilize ("estabilizar") the international economy. The verb "evitar" means "to avoid." We have used it in the present tense of the subjunctive because the relative pronoun "que" refers back to an agreement ("acuerdo") which is still in doubt, one which will perhaps be arrived at sometime later during the conference. (B) is wrong because "apenas," meaning "scarcely," would imply that the delegates barely realize ("se dan cuenta de") the seriousness ("la seriedad") of the problem. Because of the verb "negar" (ie), "to deny," in choice (C), the statement would be contradictory to what we know. The delegates are not meeting to deny the seriousness ("la gravedad") of the problem, but rather to remedy it. Choice (D) is also wrong; the conferees are not necessarily going to devalue or lower the value ("bajar") of currency ("la moneda"). In fact, they have not yet decided what they must do.

124. **(B)**   "Se entiende" is the reflexive form of the third person singular of the present tense of "entender" (ie), "to understand." Remember that this form of the reflexive can mean "one" does something. It is often used as a substitute for the true passive voice. Here it means "It is understood." Choice (A) tells us that the result ("el resultado") will be effective "eficaz," but there is no certainty of that. Choice (C) says that the desired goal ("el fin deseado") will be carried out ("se efectuará"); we have no assurance of that either. In (D) "propósito" means "purpose," and the future tense of "lograrse" signifies "will be accomplished," which is also a shaky assumption. In (B), the correct answer, "será necesario proceder con cuidado" means "it will be necessary to proceed with care." "Haber que" + infinitive, which appears in the third person singular of the future tense in the last sentence of the reading, means "to be necessary to . . . ," and is synonymous to "ser necesario." The verb "obrar," which appears in the same sentence, means "to work," and "con cautela" signifies "with caution," and represents the same ideas as "con cuidado" (with care or carefully).

125. **(B)**   In the article, we are told that eating greasy foods ("alimentos grasientos"), red meat ("carne roja"), and carbohydrates ("carbohidra-tos") can lead to obesity ("obesidad"). Choice (B) mentions that these foods can lead to "problemas de sobre peso," which is another way of referring to an overweight problem. Thus, choice (B) is the correct answer. Choice (A) says that these foods help you lose weight ("adelgazar"), which is, of course, an incorrect response. Choice (C) is also incorrect because no-

where in the reading are the effects of these foods on a person's hemoglobin ("hemoglobina") mentioned. The article also mentions that the latest medical science reports recommend vegetables ("legumbres"), fresh fruits ("frutas frescas"), and cereals ("cereales") for a healthy diet. Choice (D), on the other hand, expresses the opposite.

126. **(B)** Choosing the right answer is facilitated by understanding certain vocabulary: "aconseja" (advises), "régimen" (diet), "alimenticio" (nutritional), "en cambio" (on the other hand), "grasiento" (greasy), "carbohidratos" (carbohydrates), "conducir" (to lead), "cardíacos" (pertaining to the heart), "obesidad" (the characteristic of being overweight), and "saludable" (healthful). If medical science advises that we eat vegetables, fruits and cereals and we wish to avoid the ailments mentioned in the paragraph, we would choose the menu containing lettuce salad, baked fish, and an orange. Vocabulary from the other suggested menus is as follows: "sopa de pescado" (fish soup), "rosbif" (roast beef), "leche" (milk), "pastel" (pie), "pan con mantequilla" (bread and butter), "pollo asado" (roast chicken), "patatas fritas" (French fries), "chuleta de puerco" (pork chop), "arroz" (rice), and "helado" (ice cream). Notice in the first sentence of the paragraph the use of the subjunctive of the verb "segure" (siga). This is necessary here because of the verb "aconseja" (advises), which implies an indirect command. After verbs of volition or commanding, we generally use a subjunctive in the following clause. Finally, the expression "lo cual," used in the second sentence, is a relative pronoun, i.e., a pronoun that refers back to something previously mentioned in the sentence. In this case, we are not referring back to any specific word, but rather to the whole idea expressed in the previous clause. Ideas do not have gender, are not masculine or feminine. Consequently, we do not use "el cual," "la cual," etc., but rather the neuter form "lo cual." We could have also said "lo que," which means the same thing.

127. **(D)** According to the article, Americans include too many greasy foods in their diet. Therefore, choice (D), "los norteamericanos comen demasiados alimentos grasientos," is the correct answer. Choice (A) says that medical science reports recommend a diet of vegetables "solamente." The key here is knowing that "solamente" means "only." Thus, it is an incorrect response, since it is not recommended that the diet be composed of only vegetables, but rather that vegetables be included in a balanced diet with other elements. Choice (B) is also incorrect because the most popular diets are not always the most effective diets. Choice (C) is unacceptable, since milk ("leche") is never mentioned in the article.

128. **(B)** In our sentence, we use the verb "adelgazar" meaning "to grow thin," and the third person plural of the present of "deber" ("should" + infinitive). The reading tells us that we should not "lose weight" ("perder peso") in little time and that, in fact, such a procedure can be dangerous. Consequently, choice (A), which says that we should "follow diets which have quick results" ("seguir los regímenes que tengan resultado rápido"), would be wrong. Choices (C) and (D) refer not to tried-and-true methods of weight loss, but rather to fads and perhaps unproven diets: "los más populares" (the most popular), "las dietas más recientes" (the most recent diets). A doctor, however, would say that those who wish to slim down "should be careful not to lose weight too quickly" ("deben tener cuidado de no perder peso demasiado de prisa"). Notice the idiomatic expressions "tener cuidado de" + infinitive ("to be careful" + infinitive) and "de prisa" (quickly or hurriedly).

129. **(C)** The correct answer is (C). In order to drive on public roads, you must register your vehicle with insurance. (B) is incorrect because it is not necessary to live in the state for 60 days before registering your vehicle, but you must do so within 60 days if you are a new resident. You must be at least 17 years of age, not less than 17 years of age in order to register (B). It is incorrect to say that you must have the vehicle titled and registered with "security" (seguridad) rather than "seguro" (insurance), as choice (D) states.

130. **(A)** The correct answer is (A). It is very important for the license plates to be visible and placed correctly. (C) is incorrect since both "enfrente" and "delantera" refer to the front of the vehicle, not the front and back. It is not necessary for the license plates to be visible by using "reflecting plates" (B). The reading states that although you have reflecting plates, they must also be illuminated in order to be seen at a distance of 50 feet. It is not necessary to replace your license plates when you buy a new vehicle since you may transfer them (D).

PRACTICE TEST 2

TEST 2
Section I:
LISTENING COMPREHENSION

(Answer sheets appear in the back of this book.)

TIME: 30 Minutes
50 Questions

Part A

> **Directions**: For this section of the test, you will hear a number of conversations or parts of conversations. After each dialogue, you will hear four answer choices, identified as (A), (B), (C), and (D). When you have heard all four answer choices, choose the one that best completes or continues the conversation. Fill in the corresponding oval on your answer sheet. Neither the answer choices nor the conversations will be printed in your test booklet, so you must listen very carefully. Insert our CD No. 2 into your CD player.
>
> **Note:** The Listening portion of the actual CLEP Spanish exam will be presented on audiotape.

1.   Mark your answer on your answer sheet.

2.   Mark your answer on your answer sheet.

3.   Mark your answer on your answer sheet.

4.   Mark your answer on your answer sheet.

5.   Mark your answer on your answer sheet.

6.   Mark your answer on your answer sheet.

7.   Mark your answer on your answer sheet.

8.   Mark your answer on your answer sheet.

9.   Mark your answer on your answer sheet.

10.   Mark your answer on your answer sheet.

11.   Mark your answer on your answer sheet.

12.   Mark your answer on your answer sheet.

13.   Mark your answer on your answer sheet.

14.   Mark your answer on your answer sheet.

15.   Mark your answer on your answer sheet.

16.   Mark your answer on your answer sheet.

17.   Mark your answer on your answer sheet.

18.   Mark your answer on your answer sheet.

Part B

> **Directions:** Now you will hear a series of selections, including narratives, news reports, announcements, and dialogues. Listen very carefully to each selection, as they are spoken only once. For each selection, one or more questions will be printed in your test booklet, each with four answer choices. The questions and answers will not be spoken. Choose the best answer to each question and fill in the corresponding oval on your answer sheet. You are given 12 seconds to answer each question.

19.   ¿Cómo clasifica Spielberg's "Parque Jurásico"?

   (A)   Como un laragometraje

   (B)   Como una película de ciencia ficción

   (C)   Como una película de ciencia

   (D)   Como un ejemplo de cine fantástico

20.   ¿Cuál es la profesión de Michael Crichton, según el texto?

   (A)   Cineasta   (C)   Científico

   (B)   Escritor de best-sellers   (D)   Profesor

21.   ¿Cómo ha conseguido Crichton grandes beneficios?

   (A)   Escribiendo novelas

   (B)   Creando clónicamente especies extinguidas a partir del ADN

(C) Rodando películas

(D) Vendiendo los derechos cinematográficos de sus novelas

22. ¿Sobre qué tema quería escribir Crichton desde hace mucho tiempo?

(A) Sobre dinosaurios

(B) Sobre ciencia

(C) Sobre los problemas de la ciencia

(D) Sobre las películas

23. ¿Qué quiere decir al empleado?

(A) Le desea buen viaje.

(B) Lo echan del trabajo.

(C) Lo ascienden a un puesto mejor.

(D) Lo asignan a otro país.

24. ¿Cómo se describe la comida criolla?

(A) La comida criolla es un plato de componentes revueltos.

(B) La comida criolla tiene muchas especias.

(C) La comida criolla no tiene nada que ver con la comida europea.

(D) La comida criolla es un exponente del cruce cutural.

25. ¿Cuál es el punto principal de la narración?

(A) Los indígenas vinculaban al sol con el origen.

(B) Desde que apareció el primer automóvil se perdió el sentido de la tierra.

(C) El pan ya no se hace con trigo.

(D) Los pueblos indígenas tenían una relación más directa y respetuosa con el mundo.

26. ¿Qué cuenta el escritor de la postal?

(A) La foto de la postal es del hotel en el que reside.

(B) Él vive en un lugar con la más amplia variedad de frutas.

    (C) Él lleva regalos para sus amigos y familia.

    (D) Hasta ahora no ha salido del hotel.

27.   ¿Cómo se responde?

    (A) Que pena.

    (B) Que maravilloso.

    (C) ¿Cuánto le debo?

    (D) Buen viaje.

28.   ¿Qué dice el narrador del plato que comío?

    (A) Le encanta la crema.

    (B) Es su plato favorito.

    (C) Hace un cumplido obligado por las circumstancias.

    (D) Le parece intragable.

29.   ¿Qué explicación da la persona que compra el televisor?

    (A) Debe pagar la primera cuota para llevarse el aparato.

    (B) Cubrirá todos los pagos en 13 meses.

    (C) Todas las cuotas tienen diez por ciento de interés.

    (D) Hay un adelanto inmediato.

30.   ¿Cómo se caracteriza la película?

    (A) La película es parte de una historia egipcia adaptada a México.

    (B) La película es parte de una historia mexicana escrita por un egipcio.

    (C) La película es parte de una historia mexicana siguiendo la tradición extranjerizante del director.

    (D) La película no es popular en absoluto.

31.   ¿Cómo se caracterizan a los jóvenes?

    (A) Los jóvenes toman trabajos convencionales.

(B) Los jóvenes adoran tener tareas rutinarias.

(C) Los jóvenes toman trabajos en los que desean quedarse para siempre.

(D) Los jóvenes toman trabajos inusuales para mantenerse mientras estudian.

32. ¿Qué se propone la narración?

(A) Somos seres primitivos.

(B) El vidrio es un material no convencional.

(C) Sólo los artesanos pueden hacer decoraciones manuales.

(D) Todos podemos hacer trabajos de artesanía.

33. ¿Qué se propone la lectura en cuánto al alcoholismo?

(A) Todas las personas depresivas toman alcohol.

(B) Todas las personas alcohólicas están perdidas para siempre.

(C) Es posible salir del hábito destructivo.

(D) Lo mejor es no pedir auxilio a alguien confiable.

34. ¿Qué trabajo se solicita?

(A) El puesto era de chofer.

(B) El puesto era de camarero.

(C) El puesto era de contable.

(D) El puesto era de operador de computadora personal.

35. ¿Comó se caracteriza la emisora?

(A) La emisora siempre hacía programas musicales.

(B) La emisora no adelantó sus planes a sus empleados.

(C) La emisora tenía un gran éxito.

(D) La emisora sigue transmitiendo su programación habitual.

36. ¿Cuál es la opinión del narrador?

(A) La intolerancia es muy buena para todos.

(B)   Vertiente es lo mismo que segregación.

(C)   Las culturas se enriquecen entre si.

(D)   Las culturas se corrompen entre si.

37.   ¿De que se trata el diálogo?

(A)   Se odian.

(B)   Él quiere algo a cambio del préstamo.

(C)   Ella no tiene dinero para almorzar.

(D)   A él le incomoda invitarla a almorzar.

38.   Al final de la conversación, ¿qué pasa?

(A)   El operador del diario está enojado.

(B)   El operador del diario quiere la bicicleta.

(C)   El que pone el aviso es muy exigente.

(D)   El aviso clasificado costó mucho.

39.   ¿Qué se exige?

(A)   Necesita que el comprador tenga bienes inmobiliarios.

(B)   Necesita que tenga un permiso del estado.

(C)   Necesita que el viaje sea seguro.

(D)   Necesita que haya un tercero respaldando la compra.

40.   ¿Cómo se caracteriza el tango?

(A)   El tango es música nativa de América.

(B)   El tango fue desde el principio música popular.

(C)   El tango ya no es popular.

(D)   El tango tuvo un origen humilde.

41.   ¿Cuál es la relación entre los deportistas y el dinero?

(A)   En el deporte no se gana dinero.

(B)   Los deportistas trabajan sólo por dinero.

(C) Que los deportistas trabajen sólo por dinero es un peligro.

(D) Que los deportistas pierdan el espíritu deportivo no es un peligro.

42. ¿Cuál es la verdad?

(A) Los dos están aprendiendo ajedrez.

(B) Ambos tienen ganas de jugar ajedrez.

(C) Uno de ellos es campeón colegial de ajedrez.

(D) Juegan por obligación.

43. ¿Cuál es la opinión correcta?

(A) A uno de ellos no le gustan los edificios.

(B) A uno de ellos le parece que las gárgolas no son clásicas.

(C) A uno de ellos le gusta sólo el de forma tubular.

(D) Ambos creen que parecen gigantes vigilando.

44. ¿Qué nos dice la notica?

(A) Varios cajeros robaron el banco.

(B) Un cajero salvó al banco de ser robado.

(C) Un lugar seguro ha sido robado facilmente.

(D) Se perdieron quince millones de dólares.

45. ¿Qué se puede deducir de la Historia?

(A) La Historia está fuera de duda.

(B) La Historia del indio no es tan precisa como la del conquistador.

(C) La Historia tiene distintos puntos de vista.

(D) La Historia tiene un solo punto de vista.

46. ¿Cuál es la responsabilidad del delegado?

(A) El delegado impone su opinión el curso que representa.

(B) El delegado es elegido por sucesión.

(C) El delegado debe defender los interéses de un grupo.

(D) El delegado asume sólo si lo vota una minoría.

47. ¿Cómo se hace un dibujo animado?

(A) Por cada movimiento del personaje hay que dibujar de nuevo el escenario.

(B) Por cada movimiento del personaje hay que dibujar un nuevo cuadro.

(C) Por cada cambio de escenario hay que dibujar personajes distintos.

(D) Por cada personaje distinto hay que dibujar un nuevo escenario.

48. ¿De la conversación, que se puede inferir?

(A) Hay luna llena.

(B) Tienen hambre.

(C) Están mirando una película.

(D) Discuten lo que van a comer en la casa.

49. ¿Cómo es el canario?

(A) El canario es electrónico.

(B) El canario canta más de una hora diaria.

(C) Cuando llueve, el canario duerme.

(D) El dueño del canario es muy distraído.

50. ¿Qué se puede deducir?

(A) Lo hará.

(B) Ellos no pueden hacerlo.

(C) No lo hará aunque pueda.

(D) Ellos aceptaron sus condiciones.

This is the end of the audio section of Practice Test 2. Please go to the Reading section on the next page.

Section II: READING

TIME: 60 Minutes
         81 Questions

Part A

> **Directions:** This section contains several incomplete statements, each having four completion choices. Select the most appropriate answer and fill in the corresponding oval on your answer sheet.

51. Las ovejas producen _____.

    (A) lana   (C) jamón

    (B) seda   (D) papas

52. Es _____ comer para vivir.

    (A) preciso   (C) precario

    (B) precioso   (D) precoz

53. Tú _____ antes de salir a la calle.

    (A) te viste   (C) te pusiste

    (B) te vestiste   (D) te pones

54. Todos vamos a _____ en el coche.

    (A) caber   (C) empacar

    (B) empujar   (D) dejar

55. Al fin de su discurso el general _____ que estaba dispuesto a morir por la patria.

    (A) sometió   (C) agregó

    (B) sumó   (D) encargó

56. Quisiera _____ al profesor Alvarez.

    (A) introduce   (C) conozco

    (B) presentarte   (D) saber

57. Hay un _____ en una cámara del piso cuarto.

    (A) incendio   (C) nevada

    (B) huracán   (D) fogata

58. La comida ha sido buenísima; vamos a dejarle una propina al _____.

    (A) cenicero   (C) camarero

    (B) acero   (D) bombero

59. ¿Por qué tienes _____ la pierna?

    (A) puesta   (C) devuelta

    (B) abierta   (D) rota

60. Se han apagado todas las luces. Estamos _____.

    (A) leyendo   (C) a la luz

    (B) a oscuras   (D) a tiempo

61. Anoche _____ a las doce pero no pude dormir.

    (A) soñé   (C) me desperté

    (B) me acosté   (D) me levanté

62. Enrique y Angela se casaron el sábado. Esta semana fueron _____.

    (A) a las estrellas   (C) de miel de abeja

    (B) de luna de miel   (D) de luna llena

63. Me cuesta trabajo captar la letra de esta _____.

    (A) sinfonía   (C) baile

    (B) telegrama   (D) canción

64. No me siento bien; tengo un _____.

    (A) reloj   (C) resfriado

    (B) enfermedad   (D) uña

65. El ruido de esa sirena _____.

    (A) me tranquiliza   (C) es rojo

    (B) me molesta   (D) me da celos

Part B

Directions: In each paragraph below, numbered blanks indicate that phrases or words have been purposely omitted, Four possible completion choices are provided for each blank space. Carefully read the paragraph and select the answer choice containing the word or phrase that is most suitable in the context of the paragraph. Fill in the corresponding oval on your answer sheet.

Según Yannover, no es posible efectuar cambios ni __(66)__ de los últimos __(67)__ tecnológicos si los __(68)__ nunca llegan. "Los mecanismos para conseguir dinero son eternos, puede pasar __(69)__ un año, y para __(70)__ tiempo ya se acabó el entusiasmo." Aunque no __(71)__ completamente justo comparar la biblioteca local con otras, vale la pena __(72)__ a __(73)__ Madrid, cuyo director tiene la dicha de manejar directamente un presupuesto anual de __(74)__ dólares.

66. (A) se aprovecha   (C) aprovecharse

    (B) se aprovechan   (D) se aproveche

67. (A) avances   (C) avanzados

    (B) aumentos   (D) adelantados

68. (A) fondos   (C) fondistas

    (B) fondillos   (D) folletos

69. (A) más que   (C) más de

    (B) más   (D) más de que

70. (A) eso   (C) ése
    (B) esa   (D) ese

71. (A) es   (C) será
    (B) ser   (D) sea

72. (A) echar un vistazo   (C) echar un terno
    (B) echar un trago   (D) echar un piropo

73. (A) al de   (C) la de
    (B) ella de   (D) el de

74. (A) millón de   (C) milliones de
    (B) millónes de   (D) millones de

Una tarde de lluvias primaverales, cuando viajaba sola hacia Barcelona ___(75)___ un automóvil alquilado, María de la Luz Cervantes sufrió ___(76)___ en el desierto de los Monegros. ___(77)___ una mexicana de veintisiete años, bonita y seria, que años antes había tenido un cierto nombre como actriz de variedades. Estaba casada con un prestidigitador de salón, con ___(78)___ iba a reunirse aquel día después de ___(79)___ a unos parientes en Zaragoza. Al cabo de una hora de señas ___(80)___ a los automóviles y camiones de carga que pasaban ___(81)___ en la tormenta, el conductor de un autobús destartalado se compadeció de ___(82)___. ___(83)___ advirtió, eso sí, que no iba muy lejos.

75. (A) conducir   (C) conduzca
    (B) conducía   (D) conduciendo

76. (A) una avería   (C) una ruptura
    (B) un colapso   (D) una interrupción

77. (A) Era   (C) Fue
    (B) Estaba   (D) Estuvo

78. (A) que   (C) la que
    (B) quien   (D) quién

79. (A) visitando   (C) visita

     (B) visitara   (D) visitar

80. (A) desesperado   (C) desesperada

     (B) desesperadas   (D) desesperando

81. (A) rayados   (C) raudos

     (B) raucos   (D) rayanos

82. (A) ella   (C) él

     (B) la   (D) lo

83. (A) Lo   (C) Le

     (B) Se   (D) La

Marcelo se extrañó de que Alfredo Zambrano __(84)__ acompañado aquella mañana a Cristina, su esposa. __(85)__ en la mirada del hombre un __(86)__ de odio, enfado, __(87)__, algo que le pusiera sobre aviso de que estaba enterado de sus __(88)__ con ella. En vano. La __(89)__ del industrial español, glauca, pasiva, __(90)__ por miles de resacas alcohólicas y __(91)__ no reflejaba nada que __(92)__ inquietarle.

84. (A) hubiera   (C) haya

     (B) había   (D) habría

85. (A) Busqué   (C) Observó

     (B) Buscó   (D) Veo

86. (A) artículo   (C) indicio

     (B) sentido   (D) sensorio

87. (A) amistad   (C) curiosidad

     (B) deseo   (D) enemistad

88.   (A) hijos   (C) negocios

     (B) relaciones   (D) obligaciones

89.   (A) estatura   (C) mirada

     (B) emoción   (D) vista

90.   (A) vidriada   (C) calmada

     (B) luminosa   (D) oscura

91.   (A) existencialismo   (C) existencial

     (B) existenciales   (D) existencialas

92.   (A) pueda   (C) podría

     (B) podía   (D) pudiera

Part C

> **Directions:** Read each of the passages below. Each passage is followed by questions or incomplete statements. Choose the best answer according to the text and fill in the corresponding oval on your answer sheet.

Desde hace dos días la familia Rodríguez gozaba de la anticipación del viaje que iba a hacer a Tijuana. Los dos niños expresaban su entusiasmo no sólo con sus preguntas, sino también con la nerviosidad que demostraban incesantemente. La abuelita, aunque sentía la misma exitación, por ser mayor hacía todo lo posible por esconderla. Siempre le gustaba ir a Tijuana. Decían algunos que era ciudad fea, pero para ella era México. Era ocasión de comprar tortillas, pan, jícama, vainilla, hierbas medicinales y lo más importante — estar en México donde todos hablaban español y ella no se sentía extranjera. Los padres de los niños compartían los mismos sentimientos.

93.   Calculen cuántos iban a Tijuana.

     (A) Dos   (C) Cuatro

     (B) Tres   (D) Cinco

94. La abuelita era _____.

    (A) venezolana   (C) de Nevada

    (B) mexicana   (D) de Nueva York

95. Una razón por la cual le gustaba Tijuana a la abuela era que _____.

    (A) se sentía como en su casa

    (B) algunos hablaban español

    (C) no vendían nada allá

    (D) era ciudad fea

96. Le gustaba a la abuela _____.

    (A) salir de Tijuana   (C) poder gastar su dinero

    (B) quedarse en Tijuana   (D) hablar inglés

No sé cómo me enfermé. La comida sí era diferente, pero ha sido sabrosa y yo tenía un hambre atroz. Puede ser que haya comido demasiado. De todos modos esta mañana me atacó un retortijón de tripas insoportable que duró casi una hora. Apenas podía yo respirar por el dolor. Hablé con el gerente del hotel cuando pude para que me pusiera en contacto con un médico. Grande fue la sorpresa mía cuando me anunció sin emoción ninguna que aquí en este pueblo no hay médico. Sólo hay un homeópata, pero es bueno y sabe curar. ¿Qué iba yo a hacer? Tenía que ir con él. Después de indicarle las síntomas, me dio ciertas hierbas indicándome cómo hacer el té que debiera tomar. Milagro de milagros. Después de tomar el té, comencé a sentirme mejor y en dos días estaba como nuevo.

97. ¿Dónde se encontraba la persona del cuento?

    (A) En una ciudad grande   (C) En un pueblo chico

    (B) En un hospital   (D) En su casa

98. La persona sufrió de _____.

    (A) una jaqueca

    (B) dolores fuertes de los intestinos

(C)   un resfriado

(D)   pies planos

99.   El homeópata era _____.

(A)   bueno para curar   (C)   el gerente del hotel

(B)   un matasanos   (D)   profesor de escuela

100.   La persona debiera hacer el té y _____.

(A)   aplicarlo al lugar del dolor

(B)   respirar el vapor

(C)   tomarlo

(D)   mirarlo

101.   Recobró la salud después de _____.

(A)   consultar con el homeópata

(B)   hacer el té

(C)   sufrir otros dolores

(D)   tomar el té

Dicen que las playas de la Costa Brava son unas de las mejores del mundo. Turistas de todas partes del mundo se dirigen a ésas durante todo el año, pero especialmente durante el verano. Se oye un babel de lenguas y el español que se habla entre ellos representa docenas de acentos. Naturalmente, el clima es muy agradable y los españoles son sumamente hospitalarios. Con razón España es el banco de gran parte de los turistas, especialmente los ingleses, los alemanes, los franceses y los suecos.

102.   Los turistas van a la Costa Brava por muchas razones; una de ellas es _____.

(A)   el buen tiempo

(B)   que todos hablan español

(C)   la distancia

(D)   la multiplicidad de acentos

103.   El español por naturaleza es _____ .

   (A) tacaño   (C) un esnob

   (B) descortés   (D) amigable

104.   La mayoría de los turistas vienen _____ .

   (A) del norte de Africa   (C) de España misma

   (B) del norte de Europa   (D) de Latinoamérica

Llovía a cántaros y era la medianoche. El tren seguía su trayectoria como de costumbre aunque el ingeniero no podía ver nada, ni las vías. Era fuerte el ojo ciclópico del monstruo de hierro, pero no servía de nada. Era tanta la lluvia que hasta goteaba por el techo de los coches. Unos pasajeros se mojaban, especialmente los que estaban dormidos. Otros, de menos fe en el ingeniero, miraban por las ventanas tratando de penetrar la oscuridad o se daban miradas de sospecha. El tren iba rápidamente, pero ahora comenzaba a caminar más despacio. Eso daba más razón de dudar a los preocupados que demostraban más inquietud como si anticiparan un desastre o algo semejante. Después de un rato no era tanta la velocidad del tren. De pronto el tren se paró. Los pasajeros que dormían se despertaron y por todos los coches se oía el bullicio de comentarios y preguntas. Todos querían saber lo que pasaba.

El ingeniero va delante del tren con su linterna, dijo uno que se asomaba por una ventana.

Esto causó más exitación. Después de unos minutos corrían por todo el tren estas noticias: ¡El ingeniero ha descubierto que la mucha agua ha llevado gran parte de las vías. ¡El tren volverá atrás a la última estación!

105.   Llovía y _____ .

   (A) era de noche

   (B) soplaba mucho el viento

   (C) brillaba el sol

   (D) hacía un frío terrible

106.   Confiaban en el ingeniero del tren _____ .

   (A) unos niños   (C) unos pasajeros

   (B) todos los pasajeros   (D) sus hijos

107. Después de examinar las vías, el ingeniero _____.

    (A) decidió seguir adelante

    (B) mandó repararlas

    (C) decidió no mover el tren

    (D) decidió regresar a la última parada

108. La mucha agua había _____.

    (A) mojado a todos los pasajeros

    (B) llevado el tren de la vía

    (C) impedido el progreso del tren

    (D) apagado la luz

109. Unos de los pasajeros _____.

    (A) estaban nerviosos

    (B) no pagaron el pasaje

    (C) tenían hambre y comenzaron a comer

    (D) bajaron del tren

110. El tren tenía _____.

    (A) unas ruedas rotas

    (B) una luz fuerte en frente

    (C) un coche, nada más

    (D) un pasajero, nada más

111. Los pasajeros no dormidos _____.

    (A) soñaban con los ángeles

    (B) caminaron al lado del tren

    (C) hablaron con el ingeniero

    (D) se sentían intranquilos

—No, no quiero confesarme. No sé por qué me tienen preso. No quiero que usted ni nadie me moleste. Lo que sí quiero es vivir y no morir. No me nieguen la vida, es mía y no quiero que me la quiten. Si ustedes son cristianos, ¿por qué me la quieren quitar? Yo quiero vivir. Soy joven y tengo una novia que me quiere mucho, igual que mis padres. Yo sé que usted me dirá que la muerte es la puerta para la vida eterna, pero ésta es la que me vale. No quiero dejar esta vida, ¿me entiende usted? La vida para mí es bella. Si fuera cosa de morir en guerra, eso sería diferente. En ese caso uno moriría con respeto, luchando por una causa honrada y por principios. Eso vale la pena, pero morir ante el paredón, ¡no! Eso no lo entiendo. No tiene sentido morir así. Hasta sería una vergüenza para mí, para la familia, para mi novia y para la humanidad. Es inhumano morir de esta forma.

112. ¿Dónde estará el joven?

    (A) Con su novia   (C) Sentado a la mesa

    (B) En la iglesia   (D) En la cárcel

113. ¿Quién vino a estar con él?

    (A) Un sacerdote   (C) Su familia

    (B) Un amigo   (D) El verdugo

114. ¿Dónde preferería morir?

    (A) Cerca de la novia

    (B) En el campo de batalla

    (C) En el hospital

    (D) Con la familia

Cuando el marinero se despertó, se encontraba solo y tirado en una playa extensa.
— ¿Sería isla? se decía. — ¿Y dónde están los otros?
Él era el único sobreviviente del bergantín naufragado. Él se acordaba de la tempestad violenta y la eminente destrucción del barco y luego esa ola inmensa que lo llevó al mar. Con sus últimos esfuerzos pudo agarrar una tabla suelta. Luego se había despertado adolorido y cansado, pero vivo y pudo ponerse de pie para mirar a su alrededor, buscando otro

ser viviente — pero no había nadie. ¿Qué iba a hacer él? ¿Cómo podría vivir? ¿Qué comería? ¿Cómo podría protegerse de la intemperie? ¡De repente se oye un rugido fuerte! El náufrago quedó petrificado.

115.   Llegó a la playa _____.

    (A)   cantando   (C)   flotando

    (B)   nadando   (D)   andando

116.   Le molestaba _____.

    (A)   la soledad   (C)   la mucha arena

    (B)   el tráfico   (D)   el sol caliente

117.   Estaba preocupado por _____.

    (A)   su familia   (C)   la ropa manchada

    (B)   la tripulación   (D)   su situación física

Hoy en día florecen las agencias de publicidad. Vivimos bajo un sistema que fomenta el consumo por parte del público de una gran variedad de productos, sean los naturales o los que se hacen a mano o en serie en las grandes fábricas. A las empresas mercantiles les hace falta enterarnos, por medio de la televisión o en los diarios y revistas, de las virtudes de lo que nos quieren vender.

Para el que quiera seguir la carrera publicitaria, abundan las escuelas de dibujo que ofrecen el entrenamiento preciso para conseguir un puesto como diseñador. Pero, en la capital, ninguna como la nuestra para brindarle entrada libre y fácil a este campo, cuyas posibilidades no parecen tener límite. Requisitos mínimos. Matrícula razonable. Pagos a plazos. Llame 39–43–82 o venga a nuestras oficinas: 7 Avenida del Inca.

118.   Este pasaje _____.

    (A)   critica el sistema capitalista

    (B)   ofrece empleo en una escuela de dibujo

    (C)   parece muy optimista

    (D)   promete un sueldo alto

119. Según el pasaje, _____.

    (A) hay más plazas en el campo que en la ciudad

    (B) sólo los grandes negocios se preocupan por la publicidad

    (C) la escuela es muy exigente

    (D) es fácil encontrar puesto como dibujante

120. Este pasaje es _____.

    (A) un cuento   (C) una advertencia

    (B) un anuncio   (D) un brindis

En la actualidad, sigue pendiente el dilema del desarme, sobre todo entre los dos grandes poderes que poseen la mayoría de las armas. ¿Quién sabe si en algún tiempo lejano se planteará de firme la posibilidad de abolir este peligro para la vida? De vez en cuando han surgido propuestas para realizar este sueño pero hasta el momento escasos han sido los resultados.

Los partidarios del desarme opinan que el desarrollo de bombas de rendimiento cada vez más grande podría acarrearnos una catástrofe de dimensiones increíbles. Los informes más recientes vienen apoyando tal teoría. Por otra parte, hay los que están en contra del desarme, creyendo que el enemigo no es de fiar, a no ser que se permita la inspección, la cual presentaría tal vez inconvenientes insuperables para los dos lados. Según los proponentes del desarme, la inspección podría llevarse a cabo contando con una organización internacional como las Naciones Unidas.

Lo obvio es que tenemos que hacer algo a favor de la paz y la supervivencia de la humanidad a la cual pertenecemos todos, amigos y adversarios.

121. ¿Cuál de las respuestas es falsa?

    (A) Hay mucho desacuerdo en cuanto a la cuestión del desarme.

    (B) Es posible que en el porvenir se resuelva la cuestión del desarme.

    (C) De veras, ya se ha solucionado el problema de las armas.

    (D) Ya se han sugerido soluciones al problema del desarme.

122. Los que se oponen al desarme _____.

    (A) son de otra parte

    (B) desconfían de la buena voluntad del adversario

    (C) son aversos a la supervivencia

    (D) apoyan la guerra

123. Los que favorecen el desarme _____.

    (A) rechazan la idea de la inspección internacional

    (B) temen abolir las armas

    (C) tienen confianza en el enemigo

    (D) están por la inspección internacional

124. Siempre va aumentando _____.

    (A) la escasez de propuestas

    (B) la realización de nuestras metas

    (C) la potencia de las bombas

    (D) el número de nuestros enemigos

Catalina Levine, joven norteamericana que pasa el verano estudiando en la Universidad Autónoma, ha concedido a este corresponsal una entrevista acerca de sus experiencias durante sus primeras semanas aquí en México. Nos dijo que antes de llegar, no se daba cuenta de lo importante que es el mestizaje en la cultura mexicana. Respecto a esto, hay que constatar que Catalina tiene la cabellera más rubia que el oro. No obstante, en vez de sentirse como una curiosidad entre nosotros, se ha adaptado bien en poquísimo tiempo a una sociedad que antes le era totalmente desconocida.

Viene ella dispuesta a sumergirse en la cultura nuestra puesto que piensa hacerse maestra de español en su propio país y en esta temporada sigue clases en esta materia. A lo mejor, algún día sacará el doctorada en idiomas. Ya ha tenido examen en su clase de literatura colonial. "Cuánto duró!" dijo ella, soltando una carcajada, "pero valió la pena."

125. ¿Quién ha hablado con Catalina?

    (A) Un payaso   (C) Un mestizo

    (B) Un profesor   (D) Un periodista

126. Catalina _____.

    (A) se parece a los mexicanos

    (B) no se siente como extranjera

    (C) busca un puesto

    (D) cuenta con el apoyo mestizo

127. Catalina cree que su examen _____.

    (A) fue largo   (C) fue difícil

    (B) fue fácil   (D) fue mejor

128. _____ Catalina al hablar de su examen.

    (A) Murmuró   (C) Gritó

    (B) Se rió   (D) Lloró

129. Cuando vino a México, Catalina _____.

    (A) entrevistó a los mestizos

    (B) no quería tener nada que ver con los mestizos

    (C) se tiñó el pelo

    (D) no entendía la cultura mexicana

Questions 130–131

GUIA SOBRE EL RECICLAJE-O-REUSO

LOS SIGUIENTES ARTICULOS DE RECICLAJE SE DEBEN PONER AL BORDE DE LA ACERA EN RECIPIENTES FUERTES Y REUSABLES ANTES DE LAS 7:00 AM. DEL DIA DE SU RECOGIDA ESPECIAL Y ENTRARLOS ANTES DE LAS 7:00 PM.

- **TARROS DE COMIDA DE ALUMINIO/LATA, ENVASES DE VIDRIO DE COMIDA Y BEBIDA/EMPAQUES DE COMIDA (TRANSPARENTES, CAFE Y VERDE SOLAMENTE) Y EMPAQUES PLASTICOS:**

  Preparación - lave los envases, quite y descarte las tapas y ponga todos los materiales en un tarro normal de basura de 30 galones que no pese más de 30 libras.

  Ejemplos Aceptables - tarros de cerveza, soda jugo, te helado, comida para animales, cafe, frutas, sopas, vegetales, y leche de bebé, botellas y empaques plásticos.

  Materiales Inaceptables - tablas de forro, papel de aluminio, sartenes desechables de alumino, platos de tortas, tarros de pintura, tarros de aerosol, cerámicas, espejos, materas de flores de greda, cristal, ampolletas, vidrio de ventanas, vasos de tomar, y tubos plásticos.

- **PAPEL MIXTO/REVISTAS Y CARTÓN CORRUGADO:**

  Preparación - estos articulos se deben amontonar, aplastar y amarrar firmemente con cordel/o cuerda fuerte o colocar sueltos en un tarro normal de basura de 30 galones. La cantidad total no debe exceder 30 lbs. por montón o por tarro.

  Materiales Aceptables - circular de descuento, cartones de envio, revistas, hojarascas de correo, sobres, cupones de descuento, papel blanco y de colores, avisos de correro directo, papel del fascimil, archivos plegadores de manila, plegadores pendaflex (saquele la barra metalica), cartulina (las cajas de cereal).

  Materiales Inaceptables - bolsas plásticás o de papel café, cartones cubiertos con cera, cajas de piza, librós de tapas duras, libros de bolsillo, guias telefónicas, papel carbón y copias heliográficas.

- **PERIÓDICOS: ESTOS INCLUYEN LOS ANUNCIOS DE LAS TIENDAS Y CUPONES QUE VIENEN DENTRO DEL PERIÓDICO.**

  Preparación - amarrelos con un cordel en paquetes de hasta 12 pulgadas de altura.

  No Se Aceptan - periódicos en bolsas de papel o en bolsas plásticás.

- **ARTICULOS PESADOS COMO NEVERAS, ESTUFAS, LAVADORAS, SECADORAS:**

  Preparación - Se debe comprar una etiqueta o "sticker" en el departamento de sanidad. No se recogerá ningún articulo que no tenga la etiqueta apropiada del departamento de sanidad.

- **MUEBLES Y OTROS ARTICULOS:**

Preparación - Se debe comprar una etiqueta de $5.00 por cada articulo, en el departamento de sanidad, y sacar el articulo al borde de la acera en el día regular en que recogen su basura.

Ejemplo - Alfombras, televisores, muebles, colchones, sofas, sillas, etc.

- **DESPERDICIOS O DESECHOS DEL PATIO:**

Preparación - Usar las bolsas de papel desechables de venta a $2.00 por diez bolsas; o se pueden usar zafacones.

Ejemplo - El pasto y hojas

No Se Aceptan - Ramas, piedras, bolsas plásticas, ni cualquier otro desperdicio

- **RECOGIDA DE LAS HOJAS EN EL OTOÑO:**

Preparación - Usar las bolsas de papel desechables de venta a $2.00 por diez bolsas o amontonarlas y dejarlas a la orilla de la acera para que la aspiradora las recoja.

Nota - Las hojas las puede llevar al centro de reciclaje en las bolsas de papel desechables. Que no contengan ramas, pasto, piedras, u otros objetos. Sólo para los residentes con identificación.

No Se Aceptan - Desperdicios o desechos del patio.

AVISO! NO SE ACEPTARAN PALILLOS, RAMAS, PLÁSTICO U OTRO DESPERDICIO, ADENTRO DE LAS BOLSAS DE DESPERDICIO DE PATIO. SE DESCONTINUARÁ EL USO DE BOLSAS DE DESPERDICIO DE PATIO, SI, ES QUE SE ENCUENTRA ALGUNO DE ESTOS MATERIALES EN ESTAS BOLSAS.

---

130. ¿Dónde se debe colocar los artículos de reciclaje?

   (A) En bolsas de papel

   (B) En tarros de patio

   (C) En recipientes débiles de plástico

   (D) En la acera al lado de la calle

131. Según el guía, ¿cuáles artículos no son aceptables?

    (A) Mezclar envases de vidrio con cartón corrugado

    (B) Pasto y hojas

    (C) Periódicos sueltos en tarros de basura

    (D) Máquinas domésticas con etiquetas

TEST 2

ANSWER KEY

Listening Comprehension

1. (D)	14. (C)	27. (B)	40. (D)
2. (C)	15. (C)	28. (C)	41. (C)
3. (B)	16. (C)	29. (B)	42. (B)
4. (D)	17. (B)	30. (A)	43. (B)
5. (D)	18. (A)	31. (D)	44. (D)
6. (C)	19. (C)	32. (D)	45. (C)
7. (D)	20. (B)	33. (C)	46. (C)
8. (C)	21. (D)	34. (B)	47. (B)
9. (A)	22. (A)	35. (B)	48. (B)
10. (B)	23. (B)	36. (C)	49. (B)
11. (D)	24. (D)	37. (B)	50. (C)
12. (B)	25. (D)	38. (B)	
13. (D)	26. (C)	39. (D)	

Reading

51. (A)	72. (A)	93. (D)	114. (B)
52. (A)	73. (C)	94 (B)	115. (C)
53. (B)	74. (D)	95. (A)	116. (A)
54. (A)	75. (D)	96. (C)	117. (D)
55. (C)	76. (A)	97. (C)	118. (C)
56. (B)	77. (A)	98. (B)	119. (D)
57. (A)	78. (B)	99. (A)	120. (B)
58. (C)	79. (D)	100. (C)	121. (C)
59. (D)	80. (B)	101. (D)	122. (B)
60. (B)	81. (C)	102. (A)	123. (D)
61. (B)	82. (A)	103. (D)	124. (C)
62. (B)	83. (C)	104. (B)	125. (D)
63. (D)	84. (A)	105. (A)	126. (B)
64. (C)	85. (B)	106. (C)	127. (A)
65. (B)	86. (C)	107. (D)	128. (B)
66. (C)	87. (D)	108. (C)	129. (D)
67. (A)	88. (B)	109. (A)	130. (D)
68. (A)	89. (C)	110. (B)	131. (A)
69. (C)	90. (A)	111. (D)	
70. (D)	91. (B)	112. (D)	
71. (D)	92. (D)	113. (A)	

DETAILED EXPLANATIONS OF ANSWERS

Section I: Listening

Part A

1. **(D)** The correct answer is (D). Having money and going to the Greek Islands is the secret desire of the speaker. He doesn't have money, so going to a closer place is a good option (D). Therefore, the response of going there in a month is not logical (A). The response to ask for a loan if the person has limited funds is illogical. Maybe the Greek Islands are the most beautiful place on earth, as (C) says, but the response is illogical, especially if you begin the sentence with "Better yet."

2. **(C)** The correct answer is (C). If you've spent the entire day on the Internet, you haven't been in a physical place but a virtual place, so it couldn't be hot (B). Also, not being home would be an impossible inference. It is not an open space outdoors, so (D) is incorrect. Therefore, (C), inquiring about having found interesting things on the Internet, is the best response.

3. **(B)** The correct answer is (B). The speakers comment that they could ski if they had what they needed, infers that they are in need of equipment, so "my brother's skis" is a good answer (B). A car is not required to ski (C) nor are beverages (A). "I can't leave home" (D) is not a logical response because it has nothing to do with the subject of having or not having equipment.

4. **(D)** The correct answer is (D). "This dog might bite you if you come closer." This dog is neither tame, docile, or friendly as (A) implies. To invite the dog owner to come closer to hug (B) is not a good idea unless you are trying to get bitten. To feed the dog if he bites you is not a logical response. (D) "This dog is well-trained indeed" is a logical response if the person believes that a well trained protective dog should protect its owner by biting anyone who gets too physically close.

5. **(D)**   The correct answer is (D), "I sigh each time you look at me." You might be in love but not with a stomachache as (A) implies and not with a problem in your eyes as (B) states. It can't be my hairstyle that frightens and amazes you (C) is not complementary. "The same happens to me" (D) would be a logical response.

6. **(C)**   The correct answer is (C), "I will do it again if they call me." (volver + infinitive = to do something again). Asking for something from a place you are talking about is abrupt and not logical (A). The phone not working is never implied (B). The response that it seems like a good idea to do what you know how to do best is a logical reply (C). "It's always good to start something new" is an illogical response since it is not the beginning of something new but a repetition of something already done.

7. **(D)**   The correct answer is (D), The speaker invites Gabito to talk finally about something that has been eluded. The response that one can't speak because they are mute shows that they are in fact quite capable of speaking (A). The response that it's a lie is not a logical response to a request but rather to a statement (B). Music as the topic of the discussion is never implied (C). (D) is a logical response because it expresses interest, "Go ahead, I'm listening."

8. **(C)**   The correct answer is (C), because among the ambiguities, it is possible to consider that there is something positive being said about the boss despite the speaker's opinion that he is unbearable. (A) is not possible because you cannot forget the unforgettable. (B) is not correct because you cannot infer from the sentence that the boss has no virtues at all. (D) is incorrect because even though the speaker's comment may suggest that there are positive aspects of his employment, the assumption that it is a comfortable place to work is presumptuous.

9. **(A)**   The correct answer is (A). The speaker asks for directions to the hotel Miramar. The correct response is (A) "Yes, on the next street." "Don't stand in front of the hotel" (B) doesn't answer the question nor does (C) "Yes, I'm a tourist." (D) "I can't accompany you there now" is illogical since only the directions were requested.

10. **(B)**   The correct answer is (B). The speaker asks Margarita to do a favor. The most logical response is (B) "I'm sorry, but I'm exhausted." "Yes, I thank you very much" (A) is illogical since Margarita is the one who will be doing the favor and receiving the thanks. Nor would she say

"You're welcome" (C) or "It would be unfortunate" (D) as a response to a request for a favor.

11. **(D)** The correct answer is (D), "How long until the event begins?" The response "five blocks" answers the question of distance, not time (A). It is not asking about the price of the ticket (B). And even though the word "falta" means "a sin," in this case, "hacer falta" refers to the length of time remaining until the event begins. (D) is the correct response, "It should have already begun."

12. **(B)** The correct answer is (B). The travel agent is making a reservation for two rooms during Holy Week. So, (A) asking for three weeks is a misunderstanding that the person makes, referring to two rooms rather than two weeks. (B) asks for only one room, instead of two. (C) is wrong because the respondent confuses "reservation" with "reserve." (D) is an illogical response because there is no previous mention of an arrival date.

13. **(D)** The correct answer is (D). The speaker suspects he has a mysterious sickness since January and tells this to his doctor. The doctor would not make the assumption that the patient has only one month to live based solely on the patient's fears, (A). Nor would he say that the patient must take an aspirin and go away, (B). In (C) the question "Why are you so sure?" is a possible response, but there is a contradiction here. The doctor assumes the patient is sure about the statement, but the patient expresses that he has only a vague suspicion. In (D) the doctor asks about the symptoms. This is closer to a doctor's logical response given the patient's statement.

14. **(C)** The correct answer is (C). The buyer is asking for paper to write his family some letters. (A) assumes he is the one that has been written to. (B) asks about the color of the ink but the speaker is buying paper. (C) is the correct response, "With lines or without?" since it refers to paper. (D) asks if they do it for the money which is an illogical response.

15. **(C)** The correct answer is (C). The speaker asks for verification of Luisa's birthday. (A) refers to the place of birth and (B) refers to her saint's day which is distinct. (D) refers to the day of the celebration, which is not necessarily the same day as her birthday. Therefore, (C) "my date of birth" is the only logical response to the question.

16. **(C)** The correct answer is (C). The speaker is imagining what he would do if he had a motorcycle, (A), asking for postcards is non-related as is the question "Aren't you afraid of heights?" (B). The coast where the speaker wants to go cannot be above the sea level. (C) is a logical response which expresses the respondent's belief that motorcycles are dangerous. (D) suggests to the speaker what the speaker has already said by stating that it would be better if he went.

17. **(B)** The correct answer is (B). The statement suggests that the spring air is dryer than that of autumn but the summer climate is stifling. (A) autumn cannot be more humid than summer nor can summer be drier than autumn (C). It would be erroneous to infer that winter is the most humid season. Therefore, the only logical statement to be inferred is that if spring is dry, then autumn is more humid than spring (D).

18. **(A)** (A) Asks for a pen to sign the check. This would be a logical response to the speaker's request that the check can only be cashed with a signature on the back. (B) Not accepting those conditions is silly since a signature is always required. You are not told that you can't have the money, so there is no need to react desperately about the instructions (C). You are not asked to fill out a form but rather to sign a check on the back side of the check (D).

Section I: Listening

Part B

19. **(C)** The correct answer is (C), as a science movie. Choice (A) as a long footage ("largometraje") is incorrect as it does not include any specification, and is not a valid classification. Neither (B) as a science fiction movie nor (D) as an example of a fantasy movie are correct, according to the explanation given in the narration.

20. **(B)** The correct answer is (B), writer of best-sellers. (A) Cineasta would not be correct because the text gives us to understand that he had been one in the past, but no longer was, by defining him as a former "cineasta." (C) Scientist and (D) teacher are false.

21. **(D)** The correct answer is (D), selling the cinema rights of his novels. Choice (A) writing novels is only partially correct. Choices (B) and (C) are false.

22. **(A)** The accurate answer is (A), on dinosaurs. (B) on science and (C) on the problems of science would be, according to the text, secondary themes in relation to the main theme of dinosaurs. They are therefore not complete answers like (A). Finally, choice (D) on movies is false.

23. **(B)** The correct answer is (B). He is being fired from his job. So (A) is not true. They are not wishing him a nice trip, so (B) is the correct choice. (C) is not correct since he is not being promoted, and (D) is also wrong. He is not assigned to some other country; he just lost his job.

24. **(D)** The correct answer is (D). "Creole food is a mixture of European and American influences." (A) is not correct; it's not scrambled elements. (B) is not correct; we are not talking about how many spices it has. (C) is incorrect. European food has a lot to do with Creole food. (D) is the best response; Creole food is a result of cultural crossing.

25. **(D)** The correct answer is (D). (A) is not correct; Indians venerate the earth as the origin, mostly because of food coming from the ground. (B) is an inaccurate statement; cars are not the reason for the loss of a sense of origin. (C) is incorrect; bread is made with wheat but we forget the process quite often. (D) is the best choice; the relation with mother earth was stronger and more respectful in times past.

26. **(C)** The correct answer is (C). (A) is incorrect. The photography on the postcard is of a hotel, but not the one where the author is staying. (B) is also incorrect. He is eating a greater variety of fruit, but not in a place with the greatest variety known. (C) is correct, he is bringing presents for friends and family. (D) is a contradiction. If he is suntanned he surely has been out of the hotel.

27. **(B)** The correct answer is (B). "What a pity" (A) is not an answer for a person who has won a trip to Hawaii. (B) "It is a wonderful thing" is correct. (C) is incorrect. If it is a prize you don't owe money to anyone. The one who won the trip can't say "Have a nice trip" to the rest (D).

28. **(C)** The correct answer is (C). Even though she doesn't like milk products, we can't say she loves cream. (A) is incorrect. (B) is incorrect. This is not her favorite plate; this is the first time she has tried this one.

She is trying not to be too tough and uses ambiguous commentaries, but she doesn't really like it. (C) is the best choice. (D) is incorrect; if it were so bad she wouldn't eat two times.

29. **(B)**   The correct answer is (B). (A), she has no need to pay the first payment to bring the TV home, is not true. (B) is true; she must cover all payments in 13 months. (C) is incorrect; each payment has more than ten percent on it. (D) is also not true; there's no need for an advanced payment.

30. **(A)**   The correct answer is (A). The Egyptian story of Mahfuz is adapted to Mexico. (B) is incorrect; it is not a Mexican story narrated by an Egyptian. (C) is incorrect; it is not a foreign point of view of Mexico. (D) is incorrect; the movie tries to be popular and based on tradition.

31. **(D)**   The correct answer is (D). The main point is that students take jobs that have unusual and unconventional hours. They do not accept conventional jobs (A), nor do they like having routine work assignments (B). Their jobs are usually transitional and, therefore, they do not wish to remain forever (C).

32. **(D)**   The correct answer is (D). Everyone can create arts and hand-made crafts. (A) is incorrect; we are not all primitive beings. (B) is not true; glass is not an unconventional raw material. (C) is not true; craftmakers are not the only ones who can do manual decorations.

33. **(C)**   The correct answer is (C). (A) is untrue. Not all depressed people drink. (B) is also false; alcoholics are not lost forever. People can recover from alcoholism; therefore, (C) is the most accurate statement. (D) is incorrect; it states that the best thing to do is to not ask for help from someone you trust, when in fact, just the opposite is true.

34. **(B)**   The correct answer is (B). (A) is incorrect; since the applicant couldn't work as a driver in a bar. (B) is the best response; he was supposed to work as a waiter. (C) is incorrect; the position was not for an accountant. (D) is also incorrect; even though he could have used the computer position, the job offered was for a waiter only.

35. **(B)**   The correct answer is (B). (A) is incorrect; the FM Latina had much more than music. (B) is correct; the workers at the radio station were not paid yet. (C) is false; they were not having any success which is the reason for the recent change. (D) is also a false statement; the radio station

has completely changed its programming to attract a wider audience. Now it is only music.

36. **(C)** The correct answer is (C). (A) is wrong; intolerance is always bad. (B) is wrong; to segregate is not to look at the origins. (C) is right; different cultures enrich each other. (D) is also incorrect; cultures do not destroy each other.

37. **(B)** The correct answer is (B). (A) is not true. They do not hate each other; they are just talking about what to sell, lend, and borrow. (B) is true; he wants something in exchange for his lending his camera and/or selling other items. (C) is incorrect. She wants to be invited to lunch, but she has money to pay for her lunch if he doesn't invite her. (D) is incorrect. He is delighted about taking her to lunch. He doesn't feel uncomfortable about that at all.

38. **(B)** The correct answer is (B). (A) is incorrect. He is not angry; they just discuss the terms of a possible classified ad. (B) is correct. He wants the bicycle, so he offers the owner of the bike a puppy that he has. (C) is incorrect. He's not very demanding since he has many choices to exchange his bike for. He is not demanding a difficult thing for it. (D) is untrue. They arranged a barter exchange themselves. The classified wasn't even necessary, so it wasn't expensive.

39. **(D)** The correct answer is (D). The buying won't be possible unless the buyer has a guarantee. (A) is not true; he is not requested to have real estate. (B) is incorrect; permission by the government is not needed. (C) is incorrect; they are not talking about traveling.

40. **(D)** The correct answer is (D). (A) is incorrect; tango is not American native music. It came from Europe; and after having its contact in lower class circles, it adopted its final form. (B) is untrue. Tango wasn't popular from the very beginning; it was said to be the music of the worst people of society and it was therefore rejected. (C) is not correct. Tango is still very popular all around the world. (D) is correct; tango origins came from the lower classes and very poor people.

41. **(C)** The correct answer is (C). (A) is incorrect. You can indeed earn a lot of money in sports. (B) is also incorrect. Sportsmen not only work for money, but they also love what they do, in general. (C) is correct. If this were so it would be dangerous if athletes played only for the money earning potential, but it states that it is, in fact, dangerous. Therefore, (C)

is the most accurate statement. (D) is incorrect. If sportsmen lose their spirit, it is dangerous. Sports are the expression of freedom and strength of the human spirit.

42. **(B)** The correct answer is (B). (A) is incorrect. One of them already knows chess very well. They just want to play chess for a while, so (B) is the correct answer. (C) is almost correct. One of them was a school champion once, and for a long time, but he isn't any more. (D) is incorrect. Nobody is obligating them to play chess; they just want to.

43. **(B)** The correct answer is (B). (A) is wrong. Both of them love buildings; they are watching and talking about them. (B) is correct. One of them thinks that the gargoyles they are talking about are not classic. (C) is incorrect. The one who likes the tubular building doesn't like only that one. (D) is incorrect. Only one of them thinks of those buildings as watching giants.

44. **(D)** The correct answer is (D). (A) passive voice is used. As in English, the passive voice in Spanish puts first what has to be more important in what is said. (A) is incorrect; only one employee of the bank did it, not many. (B) is incorrect. No employee of the bank saved the bank from being burglarized, on the contrary. (C) is incorrect. It took a lot of effort to rob the bank; it wasn't easy. (D) is the correct choice; 15 million dollars was stolen.

45. **(C)** The correct answer is (C). (A) is incorrect. History is not beyond all doubt. Things are told with no complete objectivity. (B) is incorrect. None of the histories, the Indians being one, or the conquerors as one, are the best possible choices. (C) is the correct answer; history has several different possible points of view. (D) is incorrect. History does not have only one point of view.

46. **(C)** The correct answer is (C). The people are choosing a delegate for their class. (A) is not correct; this delegate shouldn't impose his opinions on the rest. (B) is incorrect. It is not a monarchy; the delegate has to be voted on. (C) is the correct answer; the delegate should fight for the group's interests. (D) is incorrect. The delegate cannot be chosen if only a small group votes for him.

47. **(B)** The correct answer is (B). Cartoons are done image by image. But the place where the characters move can be the same drawing for a while. So (A) is incorrect. For each movement of the character, you don't

need a new drawing of the place he is moving in. (B) is correct. Each movement of the character needs a new drawing. (C) is incorrect. If you change scenes, you don't need to change characters. (D) is incorrect. You don't need new scenery for each character.

48. **(B)** The correct answer is (B). It is not a full moon because it's not perfectly round. They say it looks like a croissant or a half-eaten pizza, so (A) is incorrect. (B) is the best choice. They are all hungry; they are all thinking about food, even when they are looking at the moon. They are not watching a movie as (C) states. (D) is also incorrect because they never discuss what they are going to eat; they only mention food metaphorically to discuss what the moon looks like.

49. **(B)** The correct answer is (B). (A) is incorrect; the bird is not an electronic one. Sometimes it is motivated by electronics, but that's not the same. (B) is correct; this bird sings more than an hour a day. When it rains the bird sings more, so he does not fall asleep (C). (D) is incorrect; the owner of the bird is very obsessive and doesn't miss a detail.

50. **(C)** The correct answer is (C). (A) is incorrect. He is not going to make what he is asked to make. He is demanding some conditions that are impossible for the ones who want him. (B) is incorrect. Nobody says they can't do it. (C) is the correct statement. He can do it but he won't do it. (D) is contradictory; they have not accepted his conditions.

Section II: Reading

Part A

51. **(A)** "Ovejas" are "sheep." They do not produce "seda" (silk), "jamón" (ham) or "papas" (potatoes), but rather "lana" (wool). The word "papas" is used in South and Central America. In Spain, the word for "potatoes" is "patatas."

52. **(A)** "Preciso" (necessary) is a synonym of "necesario," which could also be used in this sentence. The three other possible choices, although they look or sound somewhat like "preciso," are inapplicable here: "precioso" (precious, pretty), "precario" (precarious, dangerous), "precoz" (precocious). Clauses beginning with "Es preciso . . ." or "Es necesario . . ." are followed by the infinitive if they express a generali-

zation, as is the case in our sentence. If, however, the idea referred to a specific person, we would then be required to use a subjunctive clause, rather than simply the infinitive, for example, "Es preciso *que tú comas* para vivir" (It is necessary that you eat in order to live).

53. **(B)** To make the right choice for this item you need to know the difference between "vestirse" (to get dressed) and "ponerse" (to put on an article of clothing). Since no item of apparel is mentioned, the two forms of "ponerse" cannot be used; we must say "Tú te vestiste" (You got dressed). It could be easy to choose item (A) by mistake because it looks somewhat like several forms of "vestirse," but remember that "viste" is the second person singular of the preterit tense of "ver" (to see) and would make little sense here.

54. **(A)** The verb "caber" means "to fit." When we follow it by "en," as in our sentence, we mean "to fit into." "Empujar" (to push) and "empacar" (to pack) could be relevant to cars but they would not be followed by "en." Rather, they would require that "coche" be a direct object instead of the object of a preposition. In these two cases, we would have to say "Todos vamos a empujar el coche" (We are all going to push the car); "Todos vamos a empacar el coche" (We are all going to pack the car). "Dejar" means "to leave," not in the sense of "to depart," but "to leave behind." It also would not be followed immediately by "en" and would require that "coche" be a direct object, for example: "Vamos a dejar el coche aquí" (We are going to leave the car here).

55. **(C)** The verb "agregar" means "to add," often in the sense of making an additional statement, which, of course, is what we mean in our sentence. Although "sumó" means "he added," it would not apply here because it is used only in a mathematical sense, as in "Sumó la lista de números" (He added the list of numbers). Neither "someter" (to subject or force to surrender) nor "encargar" (to entrust or to order goods) would make logical sense in our sentence.

56. **(B)** In our sentence, "Quisiera" is the imperfect subjunctive of the verb "querer." This form is frequently used instead of "quiero," for example, to express a courteous statement or request, for it is considered more polite. It is appropriate here because we are dealing with a formal situation in which someone is introducing one person to another. For introductions we use the verb "presentar," not "introducir." "Introducir" would not work here anyway because we need an infinitive following "Quisiera." The "te," which is attached to "presentar" in (B), is the second person singular direct object pronoun and means "you" (familiar).

"Conozco" is also wrong because it is not an infinitive. For us to use "conocer" in the sentence we would have to say "Quisiera conocer al profesor Alvarez" (I would like to know Professor Alvarez).

This, however, would not refer to an introduction, but would instead simply state *my* desire to meet Professor Alvarez. In item (D), it is true that we have an infinitive, "saber," but we cannot use it here, for this verb means to know facts or information, not to know or meet a person.

57. **(A)** In our sentence, "cámara" means "room," and "del piso cuarto" signifies "on the fourth floor." It is unlikely that there would be either a hurricane ("huracán") or a snow storm ("nevada") at that location. "Fogata" means "bonfire," the kind we have outdoors at picnics. "Incendio" is a more general term for fire and is used to refer to buildings which are on fire. "Fuego," a synonym for "incendio," could also have been used in this case.

58. **(C)** "Propina" means "tip," the kind we leave for a waiter or waitress. The verb "dejar" signifies "to leave behind." One of the most common words for waiter is "camarero," (C). Possible synonyms are "mozo" and "mesero," which are used in parts of South and Central America. Choice (A) is incorrect; "cenicero" means "ashtray." The word "acero," in (B), means "steel." In (D), "bombero" is a "fireman." We don't normally give him a tip. Notice the word "buenísima" in our sentence. The *-ísimo* ending may be attached to most adjectives. It signifies "very." Therefore, "buen*ísima*" means "*muy* buena."

59. **(D)** Each of the possible answers is a feminine form of the past participle. When past participles are not preceded by some form of the verb "haber," they function as adjectives and, therefore, agree in number and gender with the word they modify. In other words, we are looking for an adjective which can logically describe the word "pierna" (leg). The only sensible response here would be "rota" (broken). This is the irregular form of the past participle of the verb "romper." The other possible answers would make little sense here: "puesta" (placed, put on), "abierta" (open), "devuelta" (returned, given back). In Spanish, if we want to say "Why is your leg broken?", we do not use the possessive adjective "tu." Instead, by employing the verb "tener" in the second person singular, we know that we are referring to the subject "tú." That person has his leg broken. Because of the verb "tener," we can then use "la" instead of "tu" in front of "pierna." In Spanish, when the meaning is clear, we use the definite article, rather than possessive adjectives, with parts of the body and articles of clothing.

60. **(B)** The verb "apagar" means "to turn off," as with lights, etc. It is used in our sentence in the present perfect tense and in the reflexive form. Here it literally means "All the lights have turned themselves off," i.e., "All the lights have been turned off." Notice how Spanish can avoid the use of the true passive voice by substituting the reflexive form of the verb as long as the doer of the action is not mentioned. In the true passive voice our sentence would read as follows: "Todas las luces han sido apagadas." If all of the lights have been turned off, the implication is that we are "in the dark" ("a oscuras"). Choice (A) is not right because it would say "We are reading," which would be unlikely in the absence of light. "Estamos leyendo" is the present progressive of the verb "leer." This tense is arrived at by using some present tense form of "estar" + the -*ndo* form of the verb. Other progressive tenses may be created simply by changing the tense of "estar" in this construction. The progressive tenses are used to place *particular emphasis* on the fact that the action is (was, etc.) in progress at a given moment. If it is not necessary to give this special emphasis, then we use the simple tenses (present imperfect, etc.) Choice (C) is wrong because "a la luz" (in the light) would be contrary to what we expect when the lights are extinguished. "A tiempo" (on time), in item (D), has no relation to the fact that the lights have been turned off.

61. **(B)** To answer this question correctly, it is necessary to pay particular attention to the second clause of our sentence. The word "pero" (but) is very important here. If you used choice (A), "soñé" (I dreamed), the sentence would be illogical because first you fall asleep, and then you dream, but the second clause says that you "failed to sleep." The preterit tense of "poder" in the affirmative form can mean "to succeed or manage to do something." If "poder" is used negatively in the preterit, as in our sentence, it means "to fail" to do something. We hope you didn't confuse "soñar" (to dream) with "tener sueño" (to be sleepy). Choice (C), "me desperté" (I awakened), will not work, also because of the word "pero." Item (D) is illogical. "Me levanté" means "I got up," and should not be confused with "me acosté" (I went to bed), the correct answer. Notice that in (B), (C), and (D) the verbs are reflexive because they all show actions which the subject does to itself.

62. **(B)** "De luna de miel" means "on their honeymoon," which is the only correct answer of the four choices because the first sentence tells us that "Enrique and Angela got married on Saturday." We place the preposition "de" in front of "luna de miel" when it is used with the verbs "ir" (to go) or "estar" (to be). This happens also with other expressions such as "ir de vacaciones" (to go on vacation) and "estar de vacaciones" (to be on

vacation). Choice (A) means "to the stars," which is highly improbable. In (C), "miel de abeja" means "honey." In (D), "luna llena" signifies "full moon." Observe that in our sentence the verb "casarse" (to get married) is reflexive. The only time this would not be true is when, for example, a father says "I married off my daughter" ("Casé a mi hija"). Here, not only is the verb not reflexive, but also we must use the personal "a" which precedes direct objects which refer to specific people. Remember that "to get married *to*" is "casarse *con*": "Enrique se casó *con* Angela" (Enrique married Angela).

63. **(D)** "Cuesta trabajo" is a synonym for "es difícil" (it is difficult). In any of the tenses, this expression is used only in the third person singular or third person plural, depending on the subject, which in this case is the infinitive "captar." The pronoun "me" is an indirect object meaning "to me" or "for me." In other words, "Me cuesta trabajo. . ." means "It is difficult for me . . ." "Costar trabajo" follows the pattern of the verb "gustar," which also is used only in the third person singular or plural and is also preceded by an indirect object pronoun. The verb "captar" means "to get" or "to catch," in the sense of "to hear clearly." The word "letra" here means "the words of a song." Consequently, "canción" (song) is the right response. Since a symphony ("sinfonía"), (A), and a dance ("baile"), (C), do not usually have words, these two choices are wrong. "Telegrama" will not fit in the sentence because it, like many words ending in -*ma, -pa,* and -*ta,* is masculine ("el telegrama," "el mapa," "el artista"). Also, telegrams are usually read, not heard.

64. **(C)** In this sentence, "me siento" comes from the verb "sentirse" (ie, i), which means "to feel." You should not confuse it with "sentarse" (ie) which means "to sit down." Remember that the first person singular of the present of these two verbs looks the same: "me siento." It is only from the context that we can tell which of the two verbs we are dealing with. If the speaker says "No me siento bien," followed by "tengo un . . . ," we must look for an ailment to place in the blank. Consequently, (A), "reloj" (clock), and (D), "uña" (fingernail), are incorrect. Granted, "enfermedad" means "illness," but it will not fit in the sentence because it is feminine, and the sentence gives us the masculine indefinite article "un." Normally, words ending in -*a, -dad, -tad, -tud, -íon,* and -*íe* are feminine. The word "resfriado" means a "cold," and fits logically and grammatically in the sentence.

65. **(B)** "Ruido" means "noise." Most people would agree that the sound of a siren tends to bother us. Therefore, we might expect to find

some form of "molestar" (to bother or upset) in the answer. The pronoun "me" is a direct object of the verb "molesta" in this case. Choice (A) is wrong because it says the opposite of what we would normally anticipate: "me tranquiliza" (calms me). Choice (C) is wrong because "rojo" means "red," and noise does not have color. "Me da celos" signifies "makes me jealous." Some form of the verb "dar" is often used in idiomatic expressions to convey the idea of "to make" in the sense of "to cause": "los perros me dan miedo" (Dogs make me afraid, i.e., frighten me), etc.

Section II: Reading

Part B

66. **(C)** "Aprovecharse" is correct. This infinitive along with the previous one "efectuar" are both linked to "es posible." Since there is no change in subject (which would require a subjunctive verb), the infinitive is used. Since (A), (B), and (D) are all conjugated verb forms, they are incorrect.

67. **(A)** "Avances" is correct. In this context "avances" means advances. (B) is a word indicating increase in price or value. (C) is the adjective form meaning "advanced." (D) is the plural adjective meaning "anticipated."

68. **(A)** "Fondos" is correct. "fondos" means funds (as in monetary). "Fondillos" (B) means the "seat of trousers." (C) means "innkeepers" and (D) means "brochures."

69. **(C)** "Más de" is correct. In front of numbers, "more than" is expressed with "más de" rather than "más que." This would make (A) incorrect since it is written with "que" and (B) since it is missing the equivalent of "than" completely. (D) is incorrectly written.

70. **(D)** "Ese" is correct. The masculine singular demonstrative adjective is needed to modify the noun "tiempo." (A) is neuter, (B) is the feminine adjective, and (C) is accented which makes it the pronoun form of the demonstrative.

71. **(D)** "Sea" is correct. In this adverbial clause beginning with the conjunction "aunque," subjunctive is required since speculation and uncer-

tainty are intimated. (A) is the present indicative, (B) is the infinitive, and (C) is the future tense.

72. **(A)** "Echar un vistazo" is correct. (A) means "to glance at." (B) which means "to take a drink," (C) which means "to swear," and (D) which means "to flatter" do not make sense in the context of this sentence.

73. **(C)** "La de" is correct. "La de" refers to the previously mentioned "biblioteca" and means "that of." It is not necessary to repeat the noun each time; the repetition of the article is all that is necessary. (B) means "she of" and makes no sense. (A) is the masculine article combined with "a" but a feminine article is required here. (D) is simply the masculine article form.

74. **(D)** "Millones de" is correct. The word for million in Spanish has two forms, singular and plural. Since it precedes a plural number (30), "millónes" is required here. This would make choice (A) incorrect. Although choice (B) is plural, it does not require an accent mark. Choice (C) is misspelled.

75. **(D)** "Conduciendo" is correct. In translation one would need the present participle for this verb form. Also, in Spanish the verb form which commonly follows verbs of motion ("viajaba") is the present participle. This would eliminate choice (A) the infinitive, choice (B) the imperfect tense, and (C) the present subjunctive.

76. **(A)** "Una avería" is correct. An "avería" refers to the breakdown of a motor. "Un colapso" (B) refers to a breakdown in one's health. Choice (C) refers to a breakdown in negotiations. (D) refers to an interruption in service.

77. **(A)** "Era" is correct. A form of "ser" is required since "mexicana" indicates nationality. This would eliminate choices (B) and (D) which come from "estar." The imperfect is preferred since this indicates a characteristic which is ongoing. This would eliminate choice (C) which is the preterit of "ser."

78. **(B)** "Quien" is correct. Expressing "whom" after a preposition in Spanish requires the use of "quien." This would eliminate (A) which cannot be used to refer to persons after a preposition. (C) is the relative pronoun which would be used to refer to a feminine antecedent. (D) is accented and would be used as an interrogative.

79. **(D)** "Visitar" is correct. In Spanish the only correct verb form after a preposition ("después de") is the infinitive. Therefore, (A) the present participle, (B) the past subjunctive, and (C) the present indicative are incorrect.

80. **(B)** "Desesperadas" is correct. The past participle is being used here as an adjective and must agree with the noun "señas." Therefore, choices (A) and (C) are incorrect because they have the wrong gender. (D) is the present participle.

81. **(C)** "Raudos" is correct. In this context (C), which means "rapid," is correct. (A) means "striped," (B) means "raucous," and (D) means "contiguous."

82. **(A)** "Ella" is correct. After the preposition "de" the prepositional pronoun must be used. In this case the pronoun is referring to María, on whom the driver took pity. (B) is the feminine singular direct object pronoun; (C) is the subject pronoun meaning "he"; and (D) is the masculine singular direct object pronoun.

83. **(C)** "Le" is correct. The indirect object pronoun "le" meaning "to her" is used with verbs such as this one. One gives advise "to" another. Therefore, choices (A) and (D) which are direct object pronouns and (B) the reflexive pronoun are incorrect.

84. **(A)** "Hubiera" is correct. The subjunctive is required in the noun clause when the main clause states wishing/wanting, emotion, indirect command, doubt/denial or is an impersonal expression. The verb in the main clause "se extrañó" (wondered at) would indicate doubt. The past subjunctive is required to follow the sequence established in the main clause (the preterit). Therefore, (B) the imperfect, (C) the present subjunctive, and (D) the conditional tenses are incorrect.

85. **(B)** "Buscó" is correct. Because the subject is Marcelo and the action is completed, the third person singular of the preterit is needed. Although (C) would also fit this explanation, it doesn't fit in the context of this sentence. Therefore, (A) preterit (I looked for) and (D) present (I see) are incorrect.

86. **(C)** "Indicio" is correct. The translation "He looked for in the man's glance a sign of hatred, etc." indicates that "indicio" is the proper choice. The translations for (A) "articulo" (item), (B) "sentido" (sense), and (D) "sensorio" (sensory) do not fit in this context.

87. **(D)** "Enemistad" (hatred) is correct. The two nouns preceding this choice ("odio"-hatred, "enfado"-anger) indicate negative qualities. Choices (A) "amistad" (friendship), (B) "deseo" (desire), and (C) "curiosidad" (curiosity) do not fit in this context.

88. **(B)** "Relaciones" is correct. Within the context of this paragraph and this particular sentence, the word for "relationship" is most logical. [Marcelo looked for in the man's glance a sign of hatred, anger, something that would put him on guard that he (Alfredo) was aware of his "relationship" with her.] Therefore, (A) "hijos" (children), (C) "negocios" (business), and (D) "obligaciones" (obligations) are incorrect.

89. **(C)** "Mirada" is correct. Because it is the man's "glance" and not his (A) "height," (B) "emotion," or (D) "sight" that is described as "glauca, pasiva" (pale green and passive) because of alcoholic hangovers, answer (C) is the correct choice.

90. **(A)** "Vidriada" is correct. This is another adjective that describes his glance (as a result of hangovers) which means "glazed vision." Therefore, (B) "luminosa" (shining), (C) "calmada" (calm), and (D) "oscura" (obscure) are incorrect.

91. **(B)** "Existenciales" is correct. The plural adjective form of existential is required here to modify the previously mentioned noun "resacas." This would make (C) incorrect because it is singular. There is no specific feminine form for this adjective, making (D) incorrect. Choice (A) is the noun form meaning "existentialism."

92. **(D)** "Pudiera" is correct. The subjunctive is required in an adjective clause with a negative antecedent ("nada"). To maintain proper sequence, the past subjunctive is needed ("reflejaba" is in the imperfect tense). Therefore, (A) the present subjunctive tense, (B) the imperfect tense, and (C) the conditional tense are incorrect.

Section II: Reading

Part C

93. **(D)** Counting the people mentioned, we find five people were going to Tijuana — the parents (2), the grandmother (1), and the children (2).

94. **(B)** The story indicates the grandmother's love for Mexico and the fact that she doesn't feel like a foreigner ("extranjera") there; therefore, she is most likely Mexican.

95. **(A)** Choices (B) "some people spoke Spanish," (C) "nothing was sold there," and (D) "it was an ugly city" are not appropriate in the context of the passage.

96. **(C)** The story indicates that the grandmother takes the opportunity "to buy" many things while in Mexico. She did not necessarily like (A) "leaving Tijuana," (B) "staying in Tijuana," or (D) "speaking English."

97. **(C)** The story indicates there is no doctor available. A large city or a city of any size would probably have had a doctor, so choice (C) is the correct choice. Choice (B) has no basis. Choice (D) is incorrect since the protagonist is speaking with the hotel manager.

98. **(B)** The text indicates the illness as "un retortijón de tripas." One only needs to know that "tripas" has its cognate in the English word "tripe," and not necessarily that "retortijón" means "cramps" or "griping." The word "tripe" should suggest "intestine." None of the other indications is appropriate.

99. **(A)** Choice (B), a "quack," is not suitable, neither are (C) and (D). The quick cure was evidence of the homeopath's ability to cure, or at least his inability to do more harm.

100. **(C)** The "tomarlo" of the correct answer is infinitive, just like the verb "hacer" following the verb "debiera." They are in parallel usage. Naturally, the answer is that after making the tea, one should drink it. The other choices do not correspond in any way — "applying it to the painful area," "breathing the vapor," or "looking at it."

101. **(D)** After a preposition, the verb is always in infinitive form, and the cure came as a result of drinking the tea, not simply making it, as choice (B) indicates.

102. **(A)** "El buen tiempo" — the good weather, is indicated in the text ("el clima es muy agradable") as one of the reasons tourists go to the Costa Brava.

103. **(D)** "Stingy," "discourteous," or "snobbish" are not characteristics of the Spanish people, according to the reading. They are "friendly" however.

104. **(B)** The cooler countries of northern Europe provide most of Spain's tourists. These countries are mentioned in the text.

105. **(A)** "Medianoche" is certainly at night and there is nothing in the text about "wind" or that "it was cold." Choice (C) is impossible, since the sun does not shine at midnight.

106. **(C)** The expression "como si anticiparan un desastre o algo semejante" indicates that some of the passengers were worried; therefore, (B) is incorrect. On the other hand, some of the other passengers were asleep, indicating their confidence in the engineer.

107. **(D)** The text itself indicates that the train returned to the last station. The word "parada" (stop) indicates then that (D) is the correct answer.

108. **(C)** The train was unable to proceed, so its progress was impeded. It was not, however, removed from the track, as (B) indicates.

109. **(A)** Some of the passengers demonstrated their uneasiness by anticipating some kind of disaster, as stated in the reading.

110. **(B)** The train's cyclopic eye is a metaphorical expression for (B), "a strong light in front." Most trains have one front light. The other choices are implied nowhere in the text.

111. **(D)** Those passengers that were not asleep at midnight were uneasy, so (D) is the appropriate answer. The other choices, (A) "dreaming about the angels," (B) "walking beside the train," and (C) "talking with the engineer," do not fit the occasion.

112. **(D)** The correct answer is "en la carcel." Even though the word "carcel" never appears, it is mentioned that he is "preso" (imprisoned). The other choices are, therefore, incorrect. He is not "with his girlfriend," nor "in the church," and we have no knowledge of his position (sitting).

113. **(A)** The correct answer is "un sacerdote." We know this because the protagonist insists that he does not want to "confesarme" (to confess myself). The priest has obviously come to give him the Last Rites. The other choices are not acceptable, since there is no indication of "his friend," "his family," or "the executioner" visiting him.

114. **(B)** The correct answer is "en el campo de batalla" (the battlefield). We know this because he mentions that he could take dying "en guerra" (at war). Thus, the other choices are incorrect.

115. **(C)** The text indicates that the ship-wrecked sailor was able to grab a plank. Therefore, it is supposed that he floated ashore.

116. **(A)** Questions regarding how he would live, what he would eat, and how he could protect himself indicate that he was concerned about his physical needs. But, his first tragic thought was "there wasn't anyone."

117. **(D)** Naturally he was concerned about his ability to stay alive. The necessities of life were not evident anywhere and this concerned him.

118. **(C)** The word "pasaje" means "passage." It "seems very optimistic" ("parece muy optimista"). It is obviously an advertisement for a school which trains people to be artists and designers for advertisements in the media, and offers "free and easy access" ("entrada libre y fácil") to a "field" ("campo") "whose possibilities seem limitless" ("cuyas posibilidades no parecen tener límite"). The reader is given the impression that simply by attending this school, he will be guaranteed a job. Notice that the adjective "optimista" ends in -*a*, even though it modifies a masculine noun ("pasaje"). This happens with all adjectives which end in -*ista* (e.g., "pesimista," "oportunista," etc.). Choice (A) "critica el sistema capitalista" (criticizes the capitalistic system) is wrong; in reality, the school is part of the capitalistic system and is encouraging others to join that system. (B) "ofrece empleo en una escuela de dibujo" (offers employment in a school of design) is in error; the advertisement does not offer employment. Rather, it is seeking students to study at the school. (D), "promete un sueldo alto" (it promises a high salary), is also incorrect because no mention is made about what the graduates of the school might make.

119. **(D)** The advertisement implies that "it is easy to find a position as a designer" ("es fácil encontrar puesto como dibujante"). The first sentence tells us that "Nowadays publicity agencies are flourishing" ("Hoy en día florecen las agencias de publicidad"). Furthermore, the school, we are told, offers "free and easy access" ("entrada libre y fácil") to the field of advertising. In choice (A) "hay más plazas en el campo que en la ciudad" (there are more positions in the country than in the city), the word "campo" means "field of endeavor," rather than "country." Not "just large businesses are concerned with publicity" ("sólo los grandes negocios se preocupan por la publicidad"), as choice (B) would have us believe. The ad also speaks about products which even "are made by hand" ("se hacen a mano") but are also advertised. We know that (C) "la escuela es muy exigente" (the school is very demanding) is wrong because we are told that their "requirements" ("requisitos") are "minimal" ("mínimos").

120. **(B)** We can tell by the way this passage is written that it is not (A) "un cuento" (a short story). Remember that the feminine form of this word, "una cuenta," means "a bill" (such as you pay when leaving a restaurant). The passage is "an advertisement" ("un anuncio"). You should not have chosen (C) "una advertencia" (a warning or remark), just because it looks somewhat like the English word "advertisement." The word "brindis," which appears in (D), means a "toast" (as when one makes a toast to someone's health). It is related to the verb "brindar," which usually means "to make a toast." This verb, as it appears in the passage, has the special meaning of "to offer."

121. **(C)** We know that (C) "De veras, ya se ha solucionado el problema de las armas" (In truth, the problem of arms has already been solved) is false. In the first sentence, we read that "the dilemma of disarmament is still pending" ("sigue pendiente el dilema del desarme"). Remember that both "problema" and "dilema" are masculine words in Spanish. Choice (A) "Hay mucho desacuerdo en cuanto a la cuestión del desarme" (There is much disagreement concerning the question of disarmament) is true because the article speaks of the controversy between "the supporters of disarmament" ("los partidarios del desarme") and "those who are against disarmament" ("los que están en contra del desarme"). (B) is also true: "Es posible que en el porvenir se resuelva la cuestión del desarme" (It is possible that in the future the problem of disarmament will be solved). Notice that in this sentence we have had to use the subjunctive of "resolverse" (ue) because of the expression "Es posible que," which implies doubt. "El porvenir" is a synonym for "el futuro." (D) is also true: "Ya se han sugerido soluciones al problema del desarme" (Solutions have

already been suggested for the problem of disarmament). We know this because we are told that "han surgido propuestas para realizar este sueño" (proposals have arisen to realize this dream). The verbs "sugerir" (ie, i) (to suggest) and "surgir" (to arise or appear) should not be confused.

122. **(B)** Those who oppose disarmament are "suspicious of" ("desconfían de") the good will of the adversary. Note here the vocabulary used to indicate the same meaning: "no es de fiar" ("is not to be trusted") is the same as "desconfían de" ("mistrust"). Choice (A) is incorrect. The reader could confuse the statement "son de otra parte" ("they are from elsewhere") with the line in the text "Por otra parte" which means "on the other hand." Choices (C) and (D) have no basis in fact. There is no mention made that "those opposed to disarmament ("los que se oponen el desarme") are adverse ("aversos") to "survival" ("la supervivencia"). Nor is there any mention made of "supporting war" ("apoyan la guerra") in reference to either side. The last paragraph would support the opposite for "both sides" ("amigos y adversarios") in that "we have to do something" ("tenemos que hacer algo") in favor of peace and the survival of humanity ("a favor de la paz y la supervivencia de la humanidad").

123. **(D)** Those who favor disarmament ("los proponentes del desarme") are in favor of international inspection if it could be carried out ("si podría llevarse a cabo") counting on an international organization like the U.N. ("contando con una organización internacional como las Naciones Unidas."). An important part of understanding this choice is knowing the idiom "estar por," which means "to be in favor of." This would then make answer (A), stating that they "reject ("rechazan") the idea of international inspection," incorrect. Choice (B) states that they "fear abolition of arms" ("temen abolir las armas"). The opposite is true. In the second paragraph it states that "the supporters of disarmament ("los partidarios del desarme") opine that the development of more powerful bombs ("el desarrollo de bombas de rendimiento cada vez más grande") would bring about a catastrophe of incredible proportions ("podría acarrearnos una catastrofe de dimensiones indreíbles."). Choice (C) is not valid. There is no direct statement indicating that "those who are in favor of disarmament" ("Los que favorecen el desarme") "have confidence in the enemy" ("tienen confianza en el enemigo"). The "lack of trust in the enemy" ("el enemigo no es de fiar") is attributed to "those who are against disarmament" ("los que están en contra del desarme").

124. **(C)** The potency of the bombs is gradually increasing. In the first sentence of the second paragraph there is a reference to "the development of bombs with greater and greater force/output" ("el desarrollo de

bombas de rendimiento cada vez más grande"). Choice (A) is false. On the contrary, "proposals have surged" ("han surgido propuestas"). It is the "results" that have been "lacking" ("escasos han sido los resultados"). Choice (B) is false. "The realization of our goals" ("la realización de nuestras metas") to abolish this danger ("abolir este peligro") has met with little success ("escasos han sido los resultados"— literally, "few have been the results"). Choice (D) is not valid. Only the "two great powers" ("los dos grandes poderes") who "possess the majority of arms" ("poseen la mayoría de las armas") are mentioned at the beginning of the reading. There is no mention made about the "number" of enemies increasing.

125. **(D)** The first sentence of the reading tells us that Catalina "has granted" ("ha concedido") "an interview" ("una entrevista") to a "correspondent" ("corresponsal"). Therefore, we know that "un periodista" (a journalist) has spoken with her. (A) "un payaso" is "a clown." (B) "un profesor," of course, means "a teacher" or "a professor." (C) "un mestizo" signifies "a person of mixed blood" (both Indian and Caucasian).

126. **(B)** Catalina does not feel like a foreigner. The last sentence of the first paragraph says that "instead of feeling like a curiosity" ("en vez de sentirse como una curiosidad"), "she has adapted herself well" ("se ha adaptado bien") "in very little time" ("en poquísimo tiempo") "to a society which before was totally unknown to her" ("a una sociedad que antes le era totalmente desconocida"). Choice (A) "se parece a los mexicanos" claims that Catalina "resembles the Mexicans." This is untrue because we know that she is blonde ("rubia"). Choice (C) "busca un puesto" would have us believe that Catalina "is looking for a job," but she is just a student now. We know that sometime later she would like to become a Spanish teacher ("piensa hacerse maestra de español"), but not now. Choice (D) says that Catalina "is counting on the support of the mestizos" ("cuenta con el apoyo mestizo") which has no bearing whatsoever on the reading. Several important expressions appear in relation to this question. "Sentirse" (ie, i) is often followed by an adjective, e.g., "Me siento cansado" (I feel tired). Notice that it is reflexive. "Parecerse a" means "to look like" or "to count on" or "to rely on." Note that in choice (C), the verb "buscar" means "to look for." Do not use "por" or "para" after it. Also, "hacerse" means "to become." It is used with professions and with the words "pobre" and "rico."

127. **(A)** In the last sentence of the reading, Catalina says "¡Cuánto duró!" when speaking of her "test" ("examen"). This means "How long it lasted!" "Duró" is the third person singular preterit of the verb "durar" (to

last). It should not be confused with the adjective "duro" which means "hard" or "difficult." For that reason, you should not have chosen (C) "fue difícil" (it was difficult). Choice (B) "fue fácil" (it was easy) and choice (D) "fue mejor" (it was better), have no relation to what the reading says.

128. **(B)** "Soltar una carajada" means "to burst out laughing." The verb "soltar" (ue) literally means "to let loose" or "to free." A "carcajada" is a "raucous laugh." The verb "reírse" (i) also means "to laugh." It may be used either reflexively or non-reflexively. "Murmuró" in (A) means "muttered." In (C), "Gritó" signifies "shouted." In (D), "Lloró" is "cried."

129. **(D)** We know that, upon her arrival in Mexico, Catalina knew little, if anything, about the country because the writer says beforehand that "society" ("sociedad") "was totally unknown to her" ("le era totalmente desconocida"). Choice (A) says that Catalina "interviewed the mestizos" ("entrevistó a los mestizos"). She did not interview anyone; she herself was interviewed by the "corresponsal" (correspondent). (B) claims that she "didn't want to have anything to do with the mestizos" ("no quería tener nada que ver con los mestizos"), which is untrue. (C) says that she "tinted her hair" ("se tiñó el pelo"), which cannot be substantiated on the basis of the reading. The verb "teñir" (i) means "to tint or dye." See how we have used it reflexively in (C) to show that this was an action which she did to herself. Consequently, we need not use the possessive adjective "su" (her) in front of "pelo." It must have been her own hair that she tinted if she performed the action on herself, as reflexive verbs often indicate. Note the idiomatic expression "no tener nada que ver con" in (B). This means "not to have anything to do with." Its contrary, "tener algo que ver con," signifies "to have something to do with" or, sometimes, "to be related to."

130. **(D)** The correct answer is (D). Recyclable articles should be placed on the sidewalk by the side of the street. These articles should not be placed in paper bags (A) nor in "yard cans" (B), but rather in "strong reusable containers" such as garbage cans. Therefore, choice (C) "weak plastic containers" are also not acceptable.

131. **(A)** The correct answer is (A). According to the guide, mixing bottles and corrugated paper is not acceptable. All of the other materials are acceptable, viz., grass and leaves (B), loose newspapers in trash cans (C), and domestic appliances with stickers attached (D).

PRACTICE TEST 3

TEST 3
Section I:
LISTENING COMPREHENSION

(Answer sheets appear in the back of this book.)

TIME: 30 Minutes
            50 Questions

Part A

Directions: For this section of the test, you will hear a number of conversations or parts of conversations. After each dialogue, you will hear four answer choices, identified as (A), (B), (C), and (D). When you have heard all four answer choices, choose the one that best completes or continues the conversation. Fill in the corresponding oval on your answer sheet. Neither the answer choices nor the conversations will be printed in your test booklet, so you must listen very carefully. Insert our CD No. 2 into your CD player.

Note: The Listening portion of the actual CLEP Spanish exam will be presented on audiotape.

1.   Mark your answer on your answer sheet.

2.   Mark your answer on your answer sheet.

3.   Mark your answer on your answer sheet.

4.   Mark your answer on your answer sheet.

5.   Mark your answer on your answer sheet.

6.   Mark your answer on your answer sheet.

7.   Mark your answer on your answer sheet.

8.   Mark your answer on your answer sheet.

9.   Mark your answer on your answer sheet.

10.   Mark your answer on your answer sheet.

11.   Mark your answer on your answer sheet.

12.   Mark your answer on your answer sheet.

13.   Mark your answer on your answer sheet.

14.   Mark your answer on your answer sheet.

15.   Mark your answer on your answer sheet.

16.   Mark your answer on your answer sheet.

17.   Mark your answer on your answer sheet.

18.   Mark your answer on your answer sheet.

Part B

Directions: Now you will hear a series of selections, including narratives, news reports, announcements, and dialogues. Listen very carefully to each selection, as they are spoken only once. For each selection, one or more questions will be printed in your test booklet, each with four answer choices. The questions and answers will not be spoken. Choose the best answer to each question and fill in the corresponding oval on your answer sheet. You are given 12 seconds to answer each question.

---

19.   ¿Dónde está el señor?

(A)   En una tienda de ropa para caballeros

(B)   En una tienda de ropa para mujeres

(C)   En una tintorería

(D)   En un mercardo al aire libre

20.   ¿Quién va a cumplir años mañana?

(A)   El cliente   (C)   El amigo del cliente

(B)   El hermano del cliente   (D)   El hijo del cliente

21.   ¿Por qué es tan cara la camisa?

(A)   Porque es producto nacional.

(B)   Porque es de una tela especial.

    (C)   Porque es la última mode importada.

    (D)   Porque es la última de ese estilo.

22.   ¿Qué quiere el pasajero?

    (A)   Quiere hacer tiempo y pasear en auto.

    (B)   Quiere ir urgentemente al museo.

    (C)   Quiere ir al baño.

    (D)   Quiere hacer ejercicio.

23.   ¿Qué está prohibido?

    (A)   Se prohibe tener hijos.

    (B)   Se prohibe cortar el artículo comprado.

    (C)   Se prohibe transcribir partes del libro.

    (D)   Se prohibe manejar en estado de ebriedad.

24.   ¿Cómo se caracteriza la termita madre?

    (A)   La termita madre pone huevos todo el tiempo.

    (B)   La termita madre se mueve sin parar

    (C)   La termita madre es enorme y torpe.

    (D)   La termita madre mantiene el té caliente por varias horas.

25.   ¿Quién es Paula?

    (A)   La hermana de Rosa   (C)   La hermana de Chepe

    (B)   La tía de Rosa   (D)   La mamá de Rosa

26.   ¿Por qué está preocupada Rosa?

    (A)   Porque su tía no tiene teléfono.

    (B)   Porque a Chepe no le interesa su problema.

    (C)   Porque no quiere a su hermana.

    (D)   Porque no quiere que su mamá se preocupe por ella.

27.   ¿Qué le sugiere Chepe a Rosa?

   (A)   Que le encargue un recado a Paula.

   (B)   Que le escriba una carta a su mamá.

   (C)   Que hable con su mamá por teléfono.

   (D)   Que vuelva a su casa de inmediato.

28.   Con respeto al producto, ¿cuál es verdad?

   (A)   El producto no ha sufrido cambios.

   (B)   El producto es igual de seguro que antes.

   (C)   El producto es ahora más seguro.

   (D)   El producto disminuye el error humano.

29.   ¿Cuál es un hecho del jugo de naranja?

   (A)   El jugo de naranja se usa para la limpieza de trajes pequeños.

   (B)   El jugo de naranja ataca los virus.

   (C)   El jugo de naranja aumenta la fortaleza del organismo.

   (D)   El jugo de naranja aumenta sus efectos en invierno.

30.   ¿Cuál es el problema?

   (A)   No tiene mas mercadería.

   (B)   Tiene poca mercadería.

   (C)   El proveedor olvidó llevarle más cantidad.

   (D)   El proveedor le llevó mercadería, pero poca cantidad.

31.   ¿Cómo se resuelve el problema?

   (A)   No quedan más chocolates.

   (B)   Se los va a pagar cuando vuelva.

   (C)   Le va a comprar otros chocolates.

   (D)   Se los comió un amigo de Uruguay.

32.   ¿Cuál es una descripción correcta?

   (A)   Los dedos del perro son parte de su pelo.

   (B)   La piel del perro viene de sus uñas.

   (C)   El perro suda por las uñas.

   (D)   Las uñas del perro son parte de su piel.

33.   ¿Bajo cuál condicíon surge el miedo?

   (A)   El miedo surge ante cualquier amenaza.

   (B)   El miedo surge cuando no se puede enfrentar una amenaza.

   (C)   El miedo surge ante lo que nos hace frente.

   (D)   El miedo surge cuando uno se siente poderoso.

34.   Con respeto al faro, ¿cuál es verdad?

   (A)   Todos visitan el faro.

   (B)   El faro sólo es visitado por algunos.

   (C)   Nunca lo visitan durante febrero.

   (D)   El mar cubre el faro durante febrero.

35.   ¿Por qué debe hacer el desayuno Felisa?

   (A)   Felisa debe hacer el desayuno porque no hizo las camas.

   (B)   Felisa debe hacer el desayuno porque está castigada.

   (C)   Felisa debe hacer el desayuno porque Esteban no está.

   (D)   Felisa debe hacer el desayuno porque le toca hoy.

36.   ¿Por qué estarán contentos los alumnos?

   (A)   Los alumnos estarán contentos porque el viernes no habrá clases.

   (B)   Los alumnos estarán contentos porque deberán hacer doble tarea.

   (C)   Los alumnos estarán contentos porque se conmemora la fecha.

   (D)   Los alumnos sorprenden a todo el mundo.

37. ¿Por qué pregunta la mujer por la señora?

   (A) Quiere encontrarse con la señora.

   (B) Está persiguiendo a la señora.

   (C) No quiere encontrarse con la señora.

   (D) Quiere perderse en la ciudad.

38. Los vegetarianos según el carnivoro de esta conversación
   _____.

   (A) tienen mal aliento

   (B) son mentirosos por comer verdura

   (C) tienen problemas dentales

   (D) carecen de energía fisica suficiente

39. La escritora ha vivido _____.

   (A) una infancia en el mar y una adolescencia en las montañas

   (B) una infancia en las montañas y una adolescencia en el mar

   (C) una niñez en la nieve y una adolescencia en el mar

   (D) una adolescencia en la nieve y una niñez en el mar

40. Para la escitora lo real es _____.

   (A) también lo imaginario

   (B) sobre todo lo imaginario

   (C) lo vivido en el mundo material

   (D) el pasado

41. ¿Qué hora es?

   (A) Las 8 de la mañana   (C) Las 7 de la noche

   (B) Las 12 de la tarde   (D) Las 11 de la noche

42. ¿Por qué trae mala cara Luis?

   (A) Porque ha tenido examen.

   (B) Porque el examen ha sido un desastre.

(C) Porque no se le da bien la política.

(D) Porque no le gustan las ciencias naturales.

43. ¿Cuánto tiempo llevaba Luis preparando para el examen?

(A) Más de dos meses   (C) Dos meses

(B) Dos semanas   (D) Dos días

44. Con respeto al auto, ¿cuál es verdad?

(A) Se compró un auto nuevo.

(B) Tuvo el auto sólo un día.

(C) Lo estacionó junto a un bar.

(D) Llama "cafetería" a su auto, cariñosamente.

45. ¿Qué se puede deducir?

(A) La tercera persona está vestida de rojo.

(B) El perseguido es policía.

(C) El que lo persigue está disfrazado.

(D) El perseguido está un poco loco.

46. ¿Qué sucedió?

(A) Los ladrones quedaron atrapados en el sótano de la joyería.

(B) Los ladrones no pudieron vaciar las cajas de seguridad.

(C) La alarma sonó apenas abrieron la primera caja de seguridad.

(D) Los ladrones no pudieron escapar.

47. ¿Dónde están las Islas Canarias?

(A) En las costas de la Península Ibérica

(B) En el desierto del Sáhara

(C) Junto a las costas africanas

(D) Muy lejos de España

48. ¿Cómo eran los guanches, físicamente?

(A) Altos, rubios y de ojos claros

(B) Bajitos, morenos y de ojos oscuros

(C) De características físicas similares a las de pueblos cercanos.

(D) Como la imagen prototipo que el mundo tiene de los españoles.

49. ¿Cuál es la explicación de este físico particular que dan algunos estudiosos?

(A) Que los guanches vienen del desierto del Sáhara.

(B) Que proceden de la Península Ibérica.

(C) Que son descendientes de los habitantes de la Atlántida.

(D) Que son descendientes de pueblos africanos.

50. ¿Qué afirman sobre las Islas Canarias los que apoyan esta teoría?

(A) Que son un pico que el agua nunca llegó a cubrir.

(B) Que son los picos que sobresalen de la Atlántida que se hundió en el mar.

(C) Que son un archipiélago español.

(D) Que son un archipiélago del Sáhara.

This is the end of the audio section of Practice Test 3. Please go to the Reading section on the next page.

Section II: READING

TIME: 60 Minutes
            80 Questions

Part A

> **Directions:** This section contains several incomplete statements, each having four completion choices. Select the most appropriate answer and fill in the corresponding oval on your answer sheet.

51. Para ser un buen cazador, hay que saber _____.

(A) comer   (C) dormir

(B) tirar   (D) nadar

52. Los Rodríguez van a hacer un viaje por Europa. Sería bueno si tuvieran _____.

(A) mucho sueño   (C) zapatos apretados

(B) veinte hijos   (D) un mapa

53. Ella es mi mejor amiga, por eso _____.

(A) me gusta estar con ella   (C) siempre se aleja de mí

(B) nunca le escribo a ella   (D) canta en voz alta

54. No puedo salir contigo porque no estoy _____.

(A) cansado   (C) enfermo

(B) vestido   (D) sonriendo

55. Él sí es más grande que yo. Con razón, _____.

(A) nunca hace nada   (C) va a todas partes

(B) siempre está a tiempo   (D) pesa más que yo

56. Los trenes corren por _____.

    (A) las vías   (C) las fronteras

    (B) los canales   (D) las carreteras

57. No me gusta tomar el sol porque siempre _____.

    (A) llueve   (C) me escribe la familia

    (B) me quemo   (D) me mojo

58. No puedo mover el brazo. Parece que está _____.

    (A) de mal humor   (C) paralizado

    (B) lejos de mí   (D) fuera de moda

59. Yo no sé cuál _____ escoger para llegar a Madrid.

    (A) carta   (C) oportunidad

    (B) fruta   (D) camino

60. Mi madre está orgullosa de mí, pues me dice que soy muy _____.

    (A) sobrino   (C) nieto

    (B) listo   (D) malo

61. Me gusta estar en la panadería por _____.

    (A) el olor   (C) la presión alta

    (B) la mucha gente   (D) lo mojado que está

62. Yo te ayudaré a _____ las maletas.

    (A) estudiar   (C) comer

    (B) hacer   (D) beber

63. Aquí tiene usted un peral, un manzano y un limonero. Todos son _____.

    (A) árboles   (C) bebidas

    (B) frutas   (D) iguales

Part B

Directions: In each paragraph below, numbered blanks indicate that phrases or words have been purposely omitted. Four possible completion choices are provided for each blank space. Carefully read the paragraph and select the answer choice containing the word or phrase that is most suitable in the context of the paragraph. Fill in the corresponding oval on your answer sheet.

Era julio y hacía un calor __(64)__ y no encontraba cómo refrescarme. Aquella noche salí con unos amigos que __(65)__ de los planes de ir a esquiar. Los escuché atentamente por unos minutos y no tenía la menor idea de adónde pensaban ir en agosto. Les __(66)__ adónde __(67)__ a esquiar en agosto. Al oír esto, __(68)__ y me contestaron "Bariloche." Sorprendida y __(69)__ me sentí verdaderamente estúpida. Uno de ellos me explicó que está en la Argentina, como si __(70)__ tonta. Al sur de Sudamérica en las __(71)__ de los Andes hay magníficas __(72)__ de esquiar.

64. (A) intoxicante (C) fresco
    (B) sofocante (D) encantador

65. (A) hablaban (C) hablaran
    (B) hablaron (D) hablen

66. (A) he preguntado (C) preguntaron
    (B) preguntaré (D) pregunté

67. (A) irían (C) iban
    (B) iría (D) iba

68. (A) se ríen (C) se reían
    (B) se rieron (D) se reirán

69. (A) confundida (C) en desorden
    (B) confusa (D) obscura

70. (A) fuera   (C) fui

     (B) sea   (D) era

71. (A) elevaciones   (C) colinas

     (B) cimas   (D) alturas

72. (A) pistas   (C) vistas

     (B) ciudades   (D) cortes

Pensé un momento y decidí ir con ellos. Por días sólo hablé del viaje, de mi __(73)__ que sólo la tenía en mi mente, pero al __(74)__ el día de salir en el largo viaje, me entraba una __(75)__ y un ataque de nervios que no __(76)__ podía controlar. Días antes __(77)__ decidí ser __(78)__ conmigo misma y admitir que el miedo me tenía __(79)__ un saco de nervios. Bueno, con todo fui y lo __(80)__ muy bien. Descansé y esquié un poco pero __(81)__ más importante fue que enfrenté mi miedo.

73. (A) llegada   (C) salida

     (B) emoción   (D) aventura

74. (A) acercándose   (C) acercarse

     (B) se acerca   (D) se acercaba

75. (A) ansiedad   (C) depresión

     (B) sonrisa   (D) alegría

76. (A) la   (C) las

     (B) lo   (D) los

77. (A) de salgo   (C) de salir

     (B) de salí   (D) de saliera

78. (A) controlada   (C) amistosa

     (B) honesta   (D) seria

79.   (A)   hecha   (C)   hacer

      (B)   hecho   (D)   haciendo

80.   (A)   pasé   (C)   pasaba

      (B)   pasó   (D)   pasaría

81.   (A)   el   (C)   los

      (B)   la   (D)   lo

Pasaría dos días ___(82)___ en las cabañas anaconda, un albergue de madera ___(83)___ sobre ___(84)___. ¿Por qué?, preguntas. Bueno, las tienen que construir así, si no, entran los animales de la jungla. Todo es muy rústico, no hay electricidad en las cabañas y el agua del baño ___(85)___ del río. Por la noche, uno puede oír los ___(86)___ únicos de la selva. Al día siguiente fue necesario que ___(87)___ con los otros en una expedición de la jungla pero como estaban en una isla tuvo que tomar unas lanchas y seguir ___(88)___ hacia el sur en el río hasta llegar a un área ___(89)___ por científicos. Empezó la caminata con un guía indio que llevaba un machete para abrir un ___(90)___ por la densa vegetación.

82.   (A)   alojando   (C)   alojados

      (B)   alojado   (D)   alojaba

83.   (A)   construido   (C)   construida

      (B)   construidos   (D)   construyó

84.   (A)   pilos   (C)   pilotes

      (B)   pilotos   (D)   pelados

85.   (A)   es transporta   (C)   transportada

      (B)   se transporta   (D)   transportan

86.   (A)   gritos   (C)   sueños

      (B)   ruidos   (D)   mullidos

87. (A) salga   (C) saliera

     (B) salgo   (D) salir

88. (A) caminando   (C) caminan

     (B) caminar   (D) a caminar

89. (A) conservado   (C) conservada

     (B) conservando   (D) conservó

90. (A) carril   (C) callejón

     (B) camino   (D) pasillo

Part C

Directions: Read each of the passages below. Each passage is followed by questions or incomplete statements. Choose the best answer according to the text and fill in the corresponding oval on your answer sheet.

Llegaba el día de su cumpleaños. En unos días ella tendría trece años. Iban a comenzar los años de casi una señorita, y ella ya sentía la nerviosidad de anticipación. Quería estar segura de que sus padres no se habían olvidado de lo que ella quería más que cualquier cosa en el mundo — un reloj de pulsera. Uno de esos de oro con manitas bien adornadas. Un reloj bien pequeño y delicado. Ella sabía que con ese reloj en su muñeca nadie dudaría que ella fuera señorita de verdad. Al pensar en el reloj, su corazón palpitaba más aprisa. ¿Podría ella esperar aquel día? Cada día sería un año, pero ella sería capaz de tener la paciencia necesaria.

Al fin llegó el día. Sus padres la despertaron cantando y present ándole un paquete chiquito envuelto en papel festivo y con un moño precioso. Ella, con manos temblorosas, abrió el paquete, quitando primeramente la cinta y luego el papel. Ella bien sabía que sería el reloj. Al abrir la cajita, ¿cuál cree que fue la sorpresa? Sí, era un reloj, pero no él que anticipaba, sino uno de Mickey Mouse.

91. La muchacha iba a _____.

   (A)   comprar un reloj   (C)   dormir tarde

   (B)   comer mucho pastel   (D)   cumplir años

92. La muchacha quería como regalo de su cumpleaños _____.

   (A)   un moño   (C)   un reloj de pulsera

   (B)   una muñeca   (D)   un rifle

93. Sus padres le presentaron _____.

   (A)   el desayuno en la cama

   (B)   una cajita artísticamente adornada

   (C)   diez dólares

   (D)   dos de sus mejores amigas

94. Al abrir la cajita, sus manos _____.

   (A)   temblaban

   (B)   la acariciaban

   (C)   quedaron paralizadas

   (D)   se chocaron

95. La muchacha recibió _____.

   (A)   un golpe tremendo

   (B)   el reloj que anticipaba

   (C)   otro reloj

   (D)   otro año de vida

   El verano pasado me tocó la buena suerte de estar en el estado de Nueva York, no en una ciudad grande, sino en las montañas del norte del estado donde abundan los árboles que cubren el paisaje. Fui con mi perro cazador y mi rifle porque me habían dicho que los animales de caza menor abundaban también. Yo había alquilado una cabaña solitaria y anticipaba dos semanas de completa distracción y descanso de la rutina de mi trabajo. Apenas podía yo dormir pensando en el gusto que me iba a dar estar solo con mi perro en este ambiente. Cuando llegaron las primeras luces del alba, mi perro, ya anticipando las aventuras del día, me despertó. Tan pronto como pude, me alisté y salí. La niebla agregaba algo misterioso a este evento. El perro iba adelante husmeando uno que otro tronco de árbol y algunas plantas. Después de dos horas yo no había encontrado ningún animal, y decidí volver a seguir mis pasos, pero no pude. Yo estaba perdido. Después de caminar más de una hora, nunca pude encontrar la vereda que venía de la cabaña. Por dicha, el perro comprendió la situación, y de instinto me dejó y fue en busca del rastro. Pronto volvió, meneando la cola. Gracias al perro pude volver a la cabaña. Como es de esperar, el día siguiente salí con menos entusiasmo y con más cuidado.

96. Este individuo quería gozar de _____.

    (A) los deportes de cancha

    (B) la cocina continental

    (C) las vacaciones al aire libre

    (D) estar con gente

97. El iba a pasar quince días _____.

    (A) casando   (C) cansando

    (B) cazando   (D) cantando

98. Su fiel compañero fue su _____.

    (A) perro   (C) rifle

    (B) animal de caza menor   (D) pájaro carpintero

99. El primer día se levantó _____.

    (A) tarde   (C) ya de noche

    (B) temprano   (D) y volvió a acostarse

100. Al salir de la cabaña, se dio cuenta _____.

    (A) de la lluvia

    (B) de que no llevaba zapatos

    (C) de la niebla

    (D) que cantaban los pájaros

101. Gracias al perro _____.

    (A) pudo encontrar de nuevo el camino

    (B) se llenó de pulgas

    (C) espantó a todos los animales

    (D) pasó la noche al fresco

102. Ya que los perros husmean casi todo, se puede decir que tienen _____.

    (A) cola larga   (C) buen olfato

    (B) buenas patas   (D) hocico grande

    – Pero Carlos, decía su amigo Rafael, – no puede ser mapa original del tesoro de los piratas, el papel no es viejo.

    – Naturalmente, contestó Carlos, – es una copia. Pero sí es verídico, y mañana saldremos para los cayos. ¿Nos acompañas?

    – Pues, no debería, pero sí me interesa el proyecto. La mañana siguiente Carlos, Rafael y dos amigos más salieron para *Cayo Hueso*. Llevaban palas, provisiones y una carpa, todo lo necesario para buscar el famoso tesoro del pirata Bracamontes.

    Al llegar, primero pusieron la carpa y como tenían hambre, comenzaron con la preparación de la comida también. Todos cooperaron y pronto se quedaron satisfechos.

    Uno sugirió que con el calor sería mejor esperar hasta más tarde para empezar la búsqueda. Todos estaban de acuerdo y pronto todos gozaron de los brazos de Morfeo.

    Después de la siesta, ya ansiosos por encontrar el lugar indicado en el mapa, alguien preguntó,

    – ¿Dónde está el mapa?

    Nadie sabía y todos se pusieron a buscarlo. Abrieron todo, hasta revisaron en lugares imposibles, pero no encontraron el mapa. Todos se quedaron estupefactos y se preguntaron,

    – ¿Es posible que hayamos dejado el mapa en casa?

    Bueno, así era el caso. El viaje fue en vano y todos se sentían estúpidos. Pero, no fue un desastre completo. Todos gozaron de la anticipación de la aventura y ahora podrían fijar otra fecha para el gran descubrimiento.

103. El mapa del pirata que tenían era _____.

    (A) original   (C) de seda

    (B) falso   (D) copia

104. Se fueron al cayo _____.

    (A) en un día de campo

    (B) para las olimpiadas

    (C) a conocer la playa

    (D) a buscar lo indicado en el mapa

105. Cuando llegaron al lugar indicado, _____.

    (A) comenzaron a escarbar

    (B) pusieron la carpa y comieron

    (C) se bañaron en el sol

    (D) se bañaron en el mar

106. ¿Dónde estaba el mapa?

    (A) Carlos lo había dejado en casa.

    (B) Lo perdieron.

    (C) Alguien se lo comió.

    (D) Lo rompieron.

107. ¿Qué sentimiento tenían ellos al darse cuenta de que no tenían el mapa?

    (A) Se bañaron en el mar.

    (B) Comenzaron a cantar.

    (C) Se sentían estúpidos.

    (D) Llamaron a la casa.

En Sevilla, España, junto a la catedral, hay una torre muy alta de piedra tallada. Antiguamente, servía de minarete para los musulmanes que ocuparon aquel lugar y gran parte de España por más de siete siglos. Lleva esta torre por nombre *La Giralda*. Dicen los sevillanos que la torre es tan alta que a mediodía, cuando pasa el sol en su zenit, la torre tiene que doblarse para que pase. Es una idea exagerada, sí, pero da una idea de cuánto respetan los locales a su famosa torre. Encima hay un ángel que antes guiaba a los navegantes que subían el río. Sevilla era el centro del comercio entre España y el Nuevo Mundo, y actualmente los archivos de las Américas se encuentran ahí. Desde lo alto de la torre se ve toda la extensión de la ciudad y sirve, como algunos dicen, como vigilante constante. Con razón, Sevilla está orgullosa de su torre.

108. La torre fue construida por los _____.

    (A) íberos   (C) romanos

    (B) españoles   (D) musulmanes

109. *La Giralda* es ahora _____.

    (A) la torre de una iglesia

    (B) defensa contra los enemigos

    (C) el edificio más alto de España

    (D) en ruinas

110. Era importante la torre para los _____.

    (A) soldados   (C) marineros

    (B) curas   (D) estudiantes

111. Para consultar algo referente a los archivos de las Américas, hay que ir a _____.

    (A) *La Giralda*   (C) Madrid

    (B) Santo Domingo   (D) Sevilla

Déjenme explicarles cómo es la selva amazónica del Perú, a ustedes que nunca han salido de la capital. Me imagino que algo habrán oído de los mosquitos y víboras y el calor pegajoso que no deja a uno tranquilo. Pero es fácil acostumbrarse a esto, y pronto uno se empieza a fijar en otras cosas, como las increíbles especies do monos que se ven entre las ramas, las orquídeas y las mariposas de colores brillantes. Esto no significa que no sea buena idea llevar un botiquín con medicinas, pero lo que les quiero decir es que no hay que dejarse intimidar por los peligros de la selva. En realidad, creo que lo más peligroso es el vuelo de Lima a Iquitos, la única ciudad importante de la amazonía peruana. El tiempo es turbulento por lo general, y los aviones que hacen el trayecto parecen tener muy poca confianza en sus capacidades mecánicas. De Iquitos uno puede adentrarse en la selva a pie o tomar el río, pero en cualquier caso conviene contratar a un guía. Les pido que si alguna vez vienen a la selva amazónica no cometan el error de algunos turistas americanos que andan preguntando por todos lados dónde quedan las ruinas incaicas más cercanas.

112. ¿A quién se dirige el narrador?

(A) A viajeros experimentados en los peligros de la selva

(B) A los turistas americanos

(C) A los habitantes amazónicos

(D) A los habitantes de la capital

113. ¿Cuáles son los atractivos de la selva que el narrador destaca?

(A) Los monos y las orquídeas

(B) El calor pegajoso

(C) El viaje en avión

(D) Los turistas americanos

114. ¿Qué es Iquitos?

(A) Una ciudad selvática importante

(B) La ciudad donde viven los turistas americanos

(C) La línea aérea que vuela desde Lima

(D) Unas famosas ruinas incaicas

115. ¿Qué recomienda el narrador a quienes se adentran en la selva?

(A) No pisar las orquídeas

(B) Contratar a un guía

(C)   Contratar a un turista americano

(D)   Dejar el botiquín médico en casa

¿Por qué lee la gente libros de viajes? Probablemente porque todos queremos viajar pero no podemos, y tenemos que contentarnos con los relatos de otro. Claro que no queremos viajar sólo por viajar, sino que deseamos conocer lugares exóticos. Y justamente la mayoría de los libros de viaje transcurren en lugares alejados y remotos, y muchas veces peligrosos. En realidad, la pregunta que me parece más interesante y difícil de contestar es por qué se escriben los libros de viajes. Y también cuándo se escriben: si durante el viaje mismo o después, en un momento de reflexión. Si el viajero ya ha viajado o mientras viaja, ¿por qué se preocupa de organizar un relato que no podrá ser más emocionante que el viaje en sí? ¿Para recordar los detalles más tarde? ¿Para analizar el significado de la experiencia? ¿O para revivirlo para el lector que no pudo ir de viaje? Esta última razón parece la más probable porque también explica el por qué se leen los libros de viaje. Cuando los leemos, somos el viajero que en la realidad no pudimos ser. Además hay otra cosa. Los libros de viaje son generalmente más interesantes que los viajes que emprendemos en la realidad. ¿Por qué es esto? ¿Acaso los autores que viajan y luego escriben su viaje son más interesantes que los lectores? Yo creo que no. Lo que pasa es que los autores de estos libros saben antes de viajar que van a escribir un libro de viaje, y hacen lo posible por seguir una ruta llena de aventuras. Viajan por las regiones menos visitadas del país, viajan por tierra y no por aire o mar, y hablan frecuentemente con los lugareños.

116.   ¿Por qué se leen tanto los libros de viaje?

(A)   Porque traen interesantes recetas de cocina

(B)   Porque traen buenos consejos sobre cómo vivir nuestra vida

(C)   Porque los lectores son viajeros frustrados

(D)   Porque cuestan poco dinero

117.   ¿Dónde se ubican los libros de viaje?

(A)   Sobre todo en las ciudades

(B)   En lugares peligrosos y remotos

(C)   En los momentos de reflexión

(D)   En sitios con muchos animales

118. ¿Por qué se escriben libros de viajes?

(A) Para transmitir conocimientos antropológicos

(B) Para que el lector envidie al autor que ha viajado

(C) Para establecer contacto con los pueblos visitados

(D) Para que el lector viva la experiencia del autor

119. ¿Por qué es el autor de libros de viaje más interesante que el lector?

(A) Porque conoce más mundo

(B) Porque escribe mejor

(C) El autor de libros de viajes no es más interesante que el lector.

(D) Porque conoce más y mejores recetas de cocina

La salud es una preocupación natural de todo ser humano, pero en nuestra sociedad contemporánea se ha convertido casi en una obsesión o en un culto. Los síntomas de este problema se ven en todas partes: la insistencia maniática en tomar sólo alimentos considerados sanos y naturales; la necesidad de ejercitarse hasta el dolor y el agotamiento; el fanatismo de los no fumadores y su agresividad contra quienes gustan de fumar (o lo hacen por vicio), etc. ¿A qué se debe esta situación? Sin duda el puritanismo tradicional de nuestra sociedad — para el cual la higiene es un principio capital — tiene mucho que ver con la obsesión contemporánea con la salud. Pero también parece existir entre mucha gente hoy en día un temor al cuerpo, una inseguridad que traduce un miedo a la muerte. Al cuerpo no hay que mimarlo tanto como se hace hoy. Por supuesto tampoco hay que abusarlo, y si uno vive con moderación no hace falta privarse de todos los alimentos calóricos ni correr hasta la fatiga. Claro que hay una razón más inmediata que explica el culto de la salud en nuestra sociedad, y es la amplia disponibilidad de todos los alimentos y bebidas imaginables. Frente a esta avalancha de cosas deseables hay que saber controlarse. Un último factor que puede ser considerado es la creación de una verdadera industria de la salud, desde los fabricantes de vitaminas y minerales hasta los dueños de gimnasios particulares para correr y jugar tenis en un ambiente de lujo.

120. ¿Qué piensa el autor de los que hacen demasiado ejercicio?

   (A) Que demuestran síntomas de una preocupación excesiva con la salud

   (B) Que son buenos amantes

   (C) Que son muy religiosos

   (D) Que comen demasiado

121. ¿Cómo se relaciona el puritanismo al culto de la salud?

   (A) Porque la gente reza para tener buena salud

   (B) Porque el puritanismo enfatiza la higiene

   (C) No se relaciona porque los puritanos desaparecieron hace tiempo.

   (D) Porque la tradición puritana prohíbe la carne

122. ¿Significa nuestra actual obsesión con la salud una afirmación del cuerpo?

   (A) Sí, el cuerpo es todo lo que verdaderamente poseemos y tenemos que desarroyarlo

   (B) Sí, porque el que cree en la salud cree en el cuerpo

   (C) No, porque los que se preocupan demasiado de su salud son gente enfermiza que morirá pronto

   (D) No, porque preocuparse demasiado de la salud significa desconfiar del cuerpo y temer a la muerte

123. ¿Tiene la abundancia de comida y bebida en nuestra sociedad un efecto negativo sobre la salud?

   (A) No, porque la mayoría de la gente no puede darse el lujo de comprar muchas cosas de comer y de beber

   (B) Sí, si uno no sabe moderarse

   (C) No, porque toda comida y bebida es buena

   (D) Sí, porque fumar hace daño

124. ¿Por qué existe una industria de la salud?

   (A) Porque el gobierno busca el bien de los ciudadanos

   (B) Para mejorar la economía de las áreas deprimidas

   (C) Porque existe una demanda poderosa de objetos saludables

   (D) Para competir con productos importados del Japón

Las diferencias culturales entre la América Latina y los Estados Unidos se reflejan en los deportes preferidos por las masas: el fútbol-soccer en la América del Sur y el fútbol americano en el Norte. De modo que si podemos analizar estos deportes desde un punto de vista cultural, obtendremos información más general sobre estas sociedades. Hay por lo menos dos diferencias importantes entre el fútbol sudamericano y el norteamericano. En primer lugar, aquél premia el individualismo y la espontaneidad mientras éste está fundado sobre el espíritu de equipo y la planificación de las jugadas. Así también, las sociedades latinoamericanas son más individualistas (más caóticas, dirían sus detractores) que la norteamericana, donde los principios comunitarios se respetan con mayor facilidad, y donde la entidad económica dominante es la corporación, cuyo héroe es el "team-player." La otra diferencia importante es el uso o medición del tiempo en el fútbol americano, que siempre se descuenta, se mide desde arriba para abajo. O sea, a los dos equipos se les da 60 minutos (un capital de tiempo), que gastan con mayor o menor beneficio. Los espectadores y jugadores están siempre conscientes de que FALTAN tantos minutos, no de que han pasado tantos otros. En cambio, en el fútbol sudamericano el tiempo se acumula. No se dice que faltan 20 minutos por jugar, sino que se llevan jugados 25. El tiempo PASA en el fútbol suda-mericano, no se agota. (Además, muchas veces los partidos duran más de los 90 minutos reglamentarios, lo cual sería impensable en el fútbol norteamericano. Ahí siempre se juegan 60 minutos, aunque el tiempo real que pasa es a veces 3 horas y media.) ¿Qué puede significar esta diferencia en la concepción del tiempo entre los deportes mencionados?

125. ¿Cuál es el deporte preferido de los latinoamericanos?

   (A) Remar en bote

   (B) El fútbol americano

   (C) El análisis cultural

   (D) El fútbol-soccer

126. ¿Qué virtudes son importantes para triunfar en el fútbol-soccer?

   (A) El espiritu de equipo

   (B) La espontaneidad

   (C) El ser miembro de una corporación importante

   (D) La habilidad de analizar culturalmente al adversario

127. ¿Cómo se mide el tiempo en el fútbol americano?

   (A) Restándolo

   (B) Desde adentro para afuera

   (C) Con relojes nucleares

   (D) Sumándolo

128. De acuerdo a este análisis de los deportes, ¿Cuál es un rasgo de la sociedad norteamericana?

   (A) El caos

   (B) La imposibilidad de saber qué hora es

   (C) El individualismo

   (D) El orden y la planificación

Questions 129–130

> ## SU HIJO/A TIENE QUE USAR UN CASCO PARA MONTAR BICICLETA.

Ha llegado la época de las bicicletas y su hijo/a está ansioso/a por salir a montar. Seguramente usted ya ha inspeccionado las cadenas y los neumáticos de la vieja bicicleta o quizás este año esté pensando comprar una BMX nueva. Está muy bien que se prepare, pero si su hijo/a va a salir a montar bicicleta, usted debe recordar un detalle muy importante:

EL CASCO

La persona que maneja bicicleta sin ponerse casco, simple y llanamente no está bien preparada. Por lo tanto, no permita que su hijo/a salga a montar bicicleta sin ponerse casco.

ES IMPORTANTE QUE USTED SEPA QUE:

- Todos los años ocurren más de 3.000 accidentes de bicicletas entre los niños y adolescentes menores de 14 años de edad, según informes del Departamento de Vehículos Motorizados.

- Más de tres cuartas partes de esas muertes fueron ocasionadas por lesiones en la cabeza.

¿POR QUÉ SE TIENE QUÉ USAR CASCO?

- Si los jugadores de fútbol americano, de hockey e inclusivo de baloncesto se ponen cascos protectores, los ciclistas también deben protegerse contra riesgos.

- Con los cascos se puede evitar que la cabeza sufra lesiones o se puede aminorar la gravedad de las lesiones en la cabeza que generalmente son el principal peligro para los ciclistas.

- Las bicicletas pueden ir a velocidades que fácilmente llegan a las 20 millas por hora o más, inclusivo cuando las manejan los niños pequeños.

- Si se piensa en el costo humano y económico de las lesiones en la cabeza, los casos son una protección de bajo costo.

¿QUÉ CLASE DE PROTECCIÓN DA UN CASCO?

Cuando una persona se golpea la cabeza contra el suelo, el cráneo sufre un golpe seco, pero el cerebro tarda unos instantes en chocar contra las paredes del cráneo. Los cascos están hechos para absorber el impacto y evitar o reducir el choque del cerebro contra el cráneo. Además, por lo general tienen colores llamativos y franjas fosforescentes para que se pueda ver bien a los ciclistas en las calles y los caminos.

¿EN QUÉ DEBO FIJARME CUANDO COMPRO UN CASCO?

Compre solamente cascos aprobados por el Instituto Americano de Normas o por Snell Memorial Foundation. Ambas instituciones someten a pruebas los tradicionales cascos duros y los "cascos blandos" que recientemente salieron a la venta, para comprobar si cumplen con las normas de seguridad establecidas.

Los cascos deben estar hechos de poliestireno firme u otro material que absorba choques y se abolle con impacto para absorber el choque producido por una caída y proteger el cerebro de posibles daños. Muchos cascos llevan almohadillas de espuma en su interior para que las personas que los usan se sientan más cómodas y para que se ajusten mejor a la cabeza, pero no ofrecen protección.

129. El casco es necesario porque _____.

    (A) impide accidentes serios

    (B) corre un gran peligro sin ella

    (C)   es aprobado por el Instituto Americano de Normas

    (D)   no es solo para los niños sino para los adultos también

130. ¿Aparte del casco, que más se recomienda para protegerse?

    (A) Una campana, luces y chaleco brillante

    (B) Una bocina fosforescente

    (C) Franjas que absorban choques

    (D) Una capa iluminante

TEST 3

ANSWER KEY

Listening Comprehension

1.	(C)	14.	(C)	27.	(C)	40.	(A)
2.	(B)	15.	(A)	28.	(C)	41.	(A)
3.	(A)	16.	(D)	29.	(C)	42.	(B)
4.	(C)	17.	(B)	30.	(B)	43.	(A)
5.	(B)	18.	(C)	31.	(C)	44.	(B)
6.	(D)	19.	(A)	32.	(D)	45.	(D)
7.	(D)	20.	(B)	33.	(B)	46.	(D)
8.	(B)	21.	(C)	34.	(B)	47.	(C)
9.	(A)	22.	(A)	35.	(D)	48.	(A)
10.	(C)	23.	(C)	36.	(B)	49.	(C)
11.	(B)	24.	(C)	37.	(C)	50.	(B)
12.	(A)	25.	(A)	38.	(D)		
13.	(D)	26.	(D)	39.	(A)		

Reading

51.	(B)	71.	(D)	91.	(D)	111.	(D)
52.	(D)	72.	(A)	92.	(C)	112.	(D)
53.	(A)	73.	(D)	93.	(B)	113.	(A)
54.	(B)	74.	(C)	94.	(A)	114.	(A)
55.	(D)	75.	(A)	95.	(C)	115.	(B)
56.	(A)	76.	(D)	96.	(C)	116.	(C)
57.	(B)	77.	(C)	97.	(B)	117.	(B)
58.	(C)	78.	(B)	98.	(A)	118.	(D)
59.	(D)	79.	(B)	99.	(B)	119.	(C)
60.	(B)	80.	(A)	100.	(C)	120.	(A)
61.	(A)	81.	(D)	101.	(A)	121.	(B)
62.	(B)	82.	(B)	102.	(C)	122.	(D)
63.	(A)	83.	(A)	103.	(D)	123.	(B)
64.	(B)	84.	(C)	104.	(D)	124.	(C)
65.	(A)	85.	(B)	105.	(B)	125.	(D)
66.	(D)	86.	(B)	106.	(A)	126.	(B)
67.	(C)	87.	(C)	107.	(C)	127.	(A)
68.	(B)	88.	(A)	108.	(D)	128.	(D)
69.	(B)	89.	(C)	109.	(A)	129.	(B)
70.	(A)	90.	(B)	110.	(C)	130.	(A)

DETAILED EXPLANATIONS
OF ANSWERS

Section I: Listening

Part A

1. **(C)** is the correct choice. "One dollar" answers the question "How much money do you have?" All other answer choices are incorrect; they have the wrong tense.

2. **(B)** is the correct choice. "He is at work" answers the question, "Where is your dad?" The other answer choices (A) "His name is Pepe," (C) "I ate it," and (D) "He is tall and thin" are not logical responses to the question.

3. **(A)** is the correct choice. "Bread and coffee" answers the question "Did you have breakfast?" The other answer choices (B) "I eat," (C) "I'm not hungry," and (D) "I went to the movies" are not appropriate answers to the question.

4. **(C)** is the correct choice. "At 7:15" answers the question "At what time did you get up?" Choices (A) "He got up early," (B) "I didn't get up," and (D) "Much early" are incorrect.

5. **(B)** is the correct choice. "We went to dinner and the movies" answers the question "Did you go out with your boyfriend last night?" All other answer choices do not apply to the question.

6. **(D)** is the correct choice. "With my sister" answers the question "Who did you go shopping with?" All other answer choices do not apply to the situation.

7. **(D)** is the correct choice. "Would you like to see my office?" implies that he is the principal. All other answer choices do not answer the question.

8. **(B)** is the correct choice. "After we eat" answers the question "Are we going to the pool today?" Choices (A) "We went yesterday," (C) "There is no pool," and (D) "I'm going in a moment" do not answer the question.

9. **(A)** is the correct choice. *"The Modern Woman"* answers the question "What magazine are you reading?" Answer choice (B) is a fairy tale, and (C) and (D) are books.

10. **(C)** is the correct choice. "No, they belong to Paul" answers the question "Are those your books?" Choices (A) "They are his books," (B) "It belongs to Manuel," and (D) "They are your books" do not answer the question.

11. **(B)** is the correct choice. "My grandmother passed away" answers the question "Why are you sad?" Choices (A) "I got an A on my exam," (C) "I'm not sad," and (D) "I'm very hungry" do not logically answer the question.

12. **(A)** is the correct choice. "In an hour" answers the question "Will we arrive today?" Choices (B) "You arrived today," (C) "They today," and (D) "They arrived yesterday" do not answer the question.

13. **(D)** is the correct choice. "I never miss a game" answers the question "Do you like football?" Choices (A) "What football?" (B) "I never play," and (C) "He likes it a lot" do not answer the question.

14. **(C)** is the correct choice. "It's ugly" answers the question "What do you think of this skirt?" All other choices are incorrect.

15. **(A)** is the correct choice. "It's my cousin" answers the question "Who is that guy?" Choice (B) "He is handsome" is a description, so (B) does not answer the question. Choices (C) "It's far away" and (D) "I'm Maria" do not make sense in this dialog.

16. **(D)** is the correct choice. "No, turn left" answers the question "I go straight, right?" Choices (A) "Yes, I go straight," (B) "Let's not continue," and (C) "Yes continue to the right" are incorrect.

17. **(B)** is the correct choice. "In Mexico with my Aunt Elena" answers the question "Where do your grandparents live?" Choices (A) "They are

on vacation," (C) "They are not alive," and (D) "They are good" do not answer the question.

18. **(C)** is the correct choice. "On the tables" answers the question "Where do we put the lamps?" Choices (A) "In the oven," (B) "With the bed," and (D) "Inside the freezer" are wrong choices for this question.

Section I: Listening

Part B

19. **(A)** Choice (A) is the correct answer. The question asks: "Where is the man?" The dialogue is set in a men's clothing store, and the information given makes it clear that the customer is buying a shirt for his brother. This would preclude (B) as a possible answer, since one would not buy a man's shirt in a women's clothing store. (C) cannot be correct, because the clothes are not sold at the dry cleaner's shop (la tintorería). In the dialogue the customer asks to see the shirt in the shop window (el escaparate), and since you would not find one of those in an open air market, (D) cannot be the correct response.

20. **(B)** Choice (B) must be the correct response to the question: "Who is going to have a birthday tomorrow?" In the dialogue, the customer says that he is buying the shirt for his brother ("hermano"). This eliminates (A) the customer, (C) the customer's friend, and (D) the customer's son from being correct answers.

21. **(C)** Choice (C) correctly answers the question. When the customer asks the saleslady why the shirt is so expensive, she replies that it is the latest fashion imported from Paris ("la última moda importada de París"). Because of this (A) is automatically ruled out, since "producto nacional" refers to something made in the country, not imported. (B) is not correct, because the type of cloth from which the shirt is made is never even mentioned in the conversation, and (D) "la última de ese estilo" (the last one of that style) refers to information not contained in the dialogue, making it incorrect.

22. **(A)**   is the correct statement. He just wants to take a ride to kill time. (B) is incorrect if he were in such a hurry to go to the museum, he wouldn't ask for a long ride. (C) is incorrect; if he were so anxious to go to the restroom, he would go as soon as possible. (D) is incorrect; the passenger cannot work out traveling in a taxi.

23. **(C)**   The correct answer is (C). (A) is incorrect; it is not forbidden to have children. We are talking about a book, the copyright, and the limits on reproducing fragments of the material in the book. (B) is incorrect; the text is not talking about cutting out an article being bought. (C) is the most accurate expression; you cannot use the text of the book without permission. (D) is also incorrect; the prohibition has nothing to do with driving or drinking.

24. **(C)**   The correct answer is (C). The queen of the termites doesn't lay her eggs non-stop, so (A) is incorrect. She can't move easily, so (B) is incorrect. (C) is the most accurate statement. The queen of the termites is huge and not very graceful. (D) is incorrect. A termite is not a thermos.

25. **(A)**   Choice (A) correctly answers the question: "Who is Paula?" In the dialogue Rosa has left a message for her mother with her sister, Paula. Chepe first mentions her by name, then Rosa clarifies that she is her sister. (B) is incorrect, because the information given in the dialogue makes it clear that Rosa and Chepe are going to Rosa's aunt's house. The aunt is mentioned near the end of the conversation, and her name is not given. (C) Chepe addresses Rosa as "mi vida" (my darling), and she calls him "mi amor" (my love), which is a fair indication that they are not brother and sister. Since Paula is identified as Rosa's sister, she cannot be Chepe's. (D) According to the conversation, Rosa has given Paula (her sister) a message for their mother, making it impossible for Paula and "la mamá de Rosa" (Rosa's mother) to be the same person.

26. **(D)**   Choice (D) is the correct response. The question asks why Rosa is worried, and out of these four choices, this is the only one that is plausible according to the information given in the dialogue. Rosa states at the beginning of the conversation that she does not want her mother to worry on account of her. (A) Rosa is going to call her mother from her aunt's house, so the statement that her aunt doesn't have a phone cannot be correct. (B) The conversation is between Chepe and Rosa, and it is he who ultimately suggests that she use her aunt's phone to call her mother. The assertion that he does not care about her problem ("no le interesa su problema") is false. (C) Although it might be true that Rosa does not love

her sister, it is not an appropriate response because the dialogue makes it clear that she is worried about something else.

27. **(C)** Choice (C) is the correct response, because Chepe does suggest that Rosa use her aunt's telephone to call her mother. (A) is incorrect, because in the conversation Chepe asks Rosa if she left a message with Paula, but he never suggests that is what she should do. (B) Given Rosa's level of anxiety that her mother know her whereabouts and not worry about her, it is unlikely that Chepe would suggest that she write her mother a letter. (D) is not correct, because Chepe does not suggest Rosa return home immediately. He proposes that she call her mom from her aunt's house.

28. **(C)** The correct answer is (C). (A) is not true; the product suffered many changes. (B) is also untrue; the product is not as safe as it was before but the product is much safer now than before. Therefore, (C) is correct. (D) is incorrect; human error is not diminished by the product. The error will still exist, but the effects of human error are diminished.

29. **(C)** The correct answer is (C). (A) is incorrect; orange juice is not a cleaning product. (B) is incorrect. Orange juice doesn't attack viruses; its vitamins defend the human organism against them. (C) is the correct statement; orange juice improves human strength. (D) is incorrect; orange juice is not essentially better in winter.

30. **(B)** The correct answer is (B). (A) is incorrect; he still has some merchandise to sell. He does not have much left, but some, so (B) is correct. (C) is incorrect. The forgotten thing is some other merchandise. (D) is also incorrect, since it states that a small amount of merchandise was delivered to the store rather than none.

31. **(C)** The correct answer is (C). (A) is false; there are no more chocolates that a friend from Uruguay brought, but there are others. (B) is untrue; he is not going to pay her for those chocolates. (C) is correct; he is going to buy some others. (D) is false; the friend from Uruguay hasn't eaten the chocolates, he brought them.

32. **(D)** The correct answer is (D). (A) is incorrect. The dog's paws are not part of his fur, but his nails, so (D) is the right choice. (B) is incorrect because his skin is not coming from his nails. Dogs do not sweat from their nails, (C).

33. **(B)** The correct answer is (B). (A) is untrue. Fear does not appear due to any given threat. (B) is correct; fear appears when the threat seems to be stronger than us. (C) is incorrect; fear does not appear when something faces us. (D) is also incorrect. When you feel powerful, you may feel fearful, but it is not a rule that being powerful induces fear.

34. **(B)** The correct answer is (B). (A) is untrue; it is not so easy for everybody to visit the lighthouse. (B), therefore, is the right choice. The lighthouse is only visited by some people. (C) is incorrect. February is a good month to visit the lighthouse. (D) is false; the sea doesn't cover the lighthouse at all.

35. **(D)** The correct answer is (D). (A) is incorrect. Felisa must have breakfast done for everybody because those are the rules. Nobody is punished in the house, so (B) is incorrect. She did not have the beds done yesterday, and she was supposed to. It was her turn to make breakfast today, so (C) is incorrect. Although Esteban is not at home, his turn to make breakfast was yesterday; therefore, (D) is the correct answer.

36. **(B)** The correct answer is (B). (A) is incorrect. Pupils won't be happy because they'll have their Friday off. (B) is correct. Pupils will be happy because they'll have double homework. (C) is incorrect because the date is not a reason for them to be happy. (D) is also incorrect. These pupils do not surprise anybody there. They all know they are uncommon already.

37. **(C)** The correct answer is (C). (A) is false. He doesn't want to meet the lady. (B) is untrue. He is not following the lady. (C) is correct. He wants to find her. (D) is incorrect. He doesn't want to get lost in the city.

38. **(D)** The correct answer is (D). Vegetarians are not said to have bad breath here, however, the meat-eaters do. (A) and (B) are incorrect. There is a joke about purity, vegetarians and lies, but it does not imply that people lie because they are vegetarians. (C) is right about those who eat meat in this dialogue, at least. But it is not an accurate generalization about all vegetarians. (D) is the correct choice. Vegetarians are accused by the meat-eater of not having enough physical strength.

39. **(A)** The correct answer is (A). The writer has lived her childhood by the seaside and her adolescence in the mountains. She recalls the absence of the sea as a teenager. So (B) is not possible. She reminisces

about his memories of snow from her childhood (C), but she is talking about a dream she had. She doesn't make any mention of snow during her adolescence (D).

40. **(A)** is the best answer. The speaker actually says reality is what you imagine it to be. She is not saying what you imagine is actually more important than anything else, (B). The writer is not saying that the fact that you live in the physical world is the most important thing (C). She is not putting the past above all else (D).

41. **(A)** The correct answer is (A). It's probably 8 AM, because they are ordering breakfast. The woman said good night to everybody, but that's why she is asked if she feels alright. She's probably still half asleep; that's why she is corrected and greeted with "good morning."

42. **(B)** The correct answer is (B) because the exam was a disaster. Choice (A) because he has had an exam would be only partially correct. (C) because he doesn't like politics and (D) because he doesn't like natural sciences are false according to the content of the dialogue.

43. **(A)** The correct answer is (A) more than two months. Options (B), (C), and (D) are incorrect because they are less than the time the woman specified that Luis spent preparing for the exam.

44. **(B)** The correct answer is (B). (A) is incorrect; it wasn't a new car that he bought, but an old one. (B) is correct. He had the car only one day. (C) is incorrect. The car is in a bar but he didn't put it there. (D) is incorrect. Even though in Spanish you can say an old car is a "cafetera" (coffeemaker), the fact is that he changed the broken car in the bar, and they gave him a coffeemaker for it.

45. **(D)** The correct answer is (D). (A) is wrong; the third person mentioned has a yellow dress, not a red one. (B) is incorrect; the person being followed is not a policeman, of course. He wouldn't be asking for help because he is being followed. (C) is incorrect; the person following this one cannot be changing his costumes each block. It rather seems that this one being followed is a little bit crazy (D). So (D) is the correct answer.

46. **(D)** The correct answer is (D). (A) is incorrect. The thieves weren't trapped in the basement of the jewelry store they were stealing in. They were trapped in the basement of the building next to it. (B) is incorrect. They could open and take all from the boxes in the store. (C) is also

incorrect. The alarm began to ring after they stole everything. (D) is correct. They couldn't make it out because they were trapped in the tunnel.

47. **(C)** The correct answer is (C), "Junto a las costas africanas." (A), "En las costas de la Península Ibérica," and (B), "En el desierto del Sáhara," are wrong. (D), "Muy lejos de España," is not correct, either, because the narrator explains that the Canary Islands are part of Spain.

48. **(A)** The guanches were tall, blonde, and with blue or green eyes, so the correct answer is (A). (B) and (D) are exactly the opposite image of the guanches, according to the narrator. (C), "De características físicas similares a las de pueblos cercanos," is wrong, too, because it is said in the text that no other people nearby looked like them.

49. **(C)** The explanation is (C), "Que son descendientes de los habitantes de la Atlántida." The rest of the options are false, according to the narrator. (A) is false because the Canary Islands are near the Sahara desert, but the guanches didn't come from there. (B) is false, too, because the Canary Islands are far from the Iberian Peninsula and the guanches didn't come from there either. (D) is incorrect because the Canary Islands are near the African coast, but the narrator doesn't mention that the guanches are descended from African tribes.

50. **(B)** The correct answer is (B), "Que son los picos que sobresalen de la Atlántida que se hundió en el mar." (A), "Que son un pico que el agua nunca llegó a cubrir," is partially true, but it's not as complete as (B). (C), "Que son un archipiélago español," is true, but it is not the correct answer to this specific question. Finally, (D), "Que son un archipiélago del Sáhara," is false.

Section II: Reading

Part A

51. **(B)** One must know the idiom "hay que" and that "saber" also means "to know how" in order to complete the sentence properly. All the answers are in the infinitive, but only "tirar" has anything to do with being a "cazador," a "hunter."

52. **(D)** It is important to recognize the imperfect subjunctive form of "tener," "tuvieran." The only answer appropriate for travelers is "un mapa," "a map." The other answers are not logical, especially (C), tight shoes.

53. **(A)** The "por eso" idiom must be understood to choose "I like to be with her," the only suitable answer to complete the sentence because she is my best friend. Choices (B), (C), and (D) are obviously unsuitable. Choice (C) means "to keep her distance."

54. **(B)** An understanding of all possible answers is necessary to connect "I can't go out with you" with "I am not dressed."

55. **(D)** The comparative "taller" or "bigger" requires "él pesa más que yo." The "sí" in this sentence can be translated as "really," and "con razón" as "naturally."

56. **(A)** None of the other answers fits the word "trenes," except the word for rails ("vías"); (B) and (D) are routes of other types of travel.

57. **(B)** The use of "gustar" is to be translated as "to be pleasing," rather than as in English, "to like." When two verbs are used together, the first is conjugated, and the second is generally in the infinitive. Sun bathing can produce a burn. Note the use of the reflexive "quemarse." None of the other answers can be correct.

58. **(C)** Again, two verbs are used together: the first is conjugated, and the second is in the infinitive or sometimes the gerund. "Mover" is a cognate of "to move," as is the proper answer, "paralizado." Students should take advantage of proper cognate recognition, but should remember too that there are also false cognates.

59. **(D)** "Cuál" may be used with a feminine or masculine noun, so the choice of answer must depend on knowing the meaning of "llegar" connected with "Madrid." One gets to Madrid by a road. The other choices are unrelated to the subject.

60. **(B)** One must understand the word "orgullosa" in order to answer correctly. If my mother is "proud" of me, then she will most likely tell me I am "listo" (clever). None of the other choices makes sense.

61. **(A)** The *ía* ending on nouns usually indicates "shop," and in this

case a "bakery." The only logical connection with any of the possible answers is "the smell." All the other choices are unpleasant.

62. **(B)**   One must understand that "hacer" is used with "maleta" as an idiomatic expression for "to pack." The other choices are irrelevant to the subject.

63. **(A)**   Although these words all resemble names of fruits, they are actually names for fruit trees. The fruits from these trees are pears, apples, and lemons, consecutively.

Section II: Reading

Part B

64. **(B)**   "Sofocante" is correct. It means "to impede respiration," which is what the air was doing to him. (A) means "intoxicating or poisonous." (C) means "cool, fresh" and (D) means "charmer."

65. **(A)**   "Hablaban" is correct. It means "they were talking." Although this is an adjective clause modifying the antecedent "amigos," no subjunctive is required because the antecedent is definite. This would eliminate choices (C) and (D) which are both subjunctive. Choice (B) is the preterit which is incorrect since a continuous past action is being intimated.

66. **(D)**   "Pregunté" is correct. Again, the completed past action is required since the act of asking the question was not a repeated past action. (A) means "I have asked," (B) means "I will ask," and (C) means "they asked."

67. **(C)**   "Iban" is correct. (B) and (D) must be eliminated because they are singular. The indirect object pronoun "les" (to them) which precedes pregunté indicates that the subject of this verb is plural. (A) is incorrect since it means "they would go" and the translation should be "they were going."

68. **(B)**   "Se rieron" is correct. The preterit is called for since the action is locked into a specific point in time in the past with the statement "al oír esto" (upon hearing this). Therefore, (A) the present tense (they laugh),

(C) the imperfect tense (they were laughing), and (D) the future tense (they will laugh) are all incorrect.

69. **(B)** "Confusa" is correct. The correct translation for this item is "confused." This would eliminate choices (C) and (D). In most cases the past participle of verbs acts as an adjective. There are, however, some verbs whose past participle and adjective forms are different. This is one of those types. Choice (A) is the past participle or verbal form while choice (B) is the adjective form.

70. **(A)** "Fuera" is correct. The past subjunctive is required after "como si" (as if). Therefore, (B) the present subjunctive, (C) the preterit, and (D) the imperfect are all incorrect.

71. **(D)** "Alturas" is correct. It means "heights." The other choices (A) "elevations," (B) "summits," and (C) "hills" do not make sense in this context.

72. **(A)** "Pistas" is correct. It means "trails." Choices (B) "cities," (C) "views," and (D) "courts" make no sense in this context.

73. **(D)** "Aventura" is correct. Here the correct translation is needed in context. Choice (D) means "adventure." Choice (A) "arrival," (B) "emotion," and (C) "departure" do not translate well in this context.

74. **(C)** "Acercarse" is correct. "Al" followed by an infinitive means "upon." In this case, the translation is "Upon approaching the day of departure . . ." Item (A) the present participle (approaching), (B) the present tense (it approaches), and (D) "it was approaching" are conjugated and cannot follow "Al."

75. **(A)** "Ansiedad" is correct. The choices given here have to make sense when translated. In the context of this statement, the person is referring to a nervous attack. Choice (A) "anxiety" fits well. Choice (B) "smile," (C) "depression," and (D) "happiness" are incorrect in this context.

76. **(D)** "Los" is correct. The masculine direct object pronoun is a redundant reference to the previously mentioned compound direct object already stated (an anxiety and nervous attack). It is common in Spanish, when the direct object precedes the verb, to use a direct object pronoun to

refer back to it. Choices (A), (B), and (C) are direct object pronouns but are incorrect in gender and number.

77. **(C)** "De salir" is correct. "Antes de" is a preposition and, in Spanish, the only correct verb form that may directly follow a preposition is the infinitive. In English we use a present participle in this structure. Because choices (A), (B), and (D) are all conjugated verb forms, they are not acceptable.

78. **(B)** "Honesta" is correct. A translation of this sentence would indicate that choice (B) "honest" makes the most sense. Choices (A) "controlled," (C) "friendly," and (D) "serious" are not logical in this context.

79. **(B)** "Hecho" is correct. This past participle is being used as an adjective to refer back to the previously mentioned noun "miedo" which is masculine singular. This would eliminate choice (A) which is feminine. (C) the infinitive and (D) the present participle are incorrect verb forms in this context.

80. **(A)** "Pasé" is correct. The subject (yo) is given in the first verb. The completed past (preterit) is required also. Therefore, choice (B) "it passed," (C) "it was passing," and (D) "it would pass" are incorrect.

81. **(D)** "Lo" is correct. "Lo" used with an adjective or adverb is translated "part or thing." In this case this means "the most important thing/part was . . ." Choices (A), (B), and (C) are all definite articles.

82. **(B)** "Alojado" is correct. Because "alojado" (lodged, housed) refers to the "joven" (young man), it must be masculine singular. Verb forms used as adjectives are expressed using the past participle. (A) is the present participle (lodging); (C) is the plural form of the adjective; and (D) is the imperfect tense (he was lodging).

83. **(A)** "Construido" is correct. The past participle, which acts as an adjective here, is modifying "albergue" which is masculine singular. (B) is incorrect because it is masculine plural and (C) because it is feminine singular. (D) is incorrect because it is the third singular of the preterit tense (he constructed).

84. **(C)** "Pilotes" is correct. It means wood "pilings" upon which a structure is built. (A) is a medicinal shrub; (B) means "pilots"; and (D) is a masculine plural adjective meaning "bald."

85. **(B)** "Se transporta" is correct. In a passive construction (in this case "is transported") where the subject is a thing ("agua"), in Spanish it is most common to use the "reflexive substitute" for the passive voice. This structure requires the pronoun "se" placed before the third singular or plural of the verb (determined by the noun). (A) is incorrect because there are two conjugated verbs in a row. (C) is the feminine singular past participle (transported), and (D) is the third plural of the present tense (they transport).

86. **(B)** "Ruidos" is correct. It means "noises." (A) means "shouts"; (C) means "dreams"; and (D) is the soft filling used in cushions.

87. **(C)** "Saliera" is correct. A subjunctive verb form is required because this noun clause is introduced by the impersonal expression ("fue necesario") and there has been a change in subject from "it" to "he." The past subjunctive is required to follow sequence since the main verb is in the preterit ("fue"). (A) is the present subjunctive (he leave), (B) the present indicative (I leave), and (D) the infinitive (to leave).

88. **(A)** "Caminando" is correct. The present participle (the verb form ending in –ing) is required after "seguir" and "continuar" (to continue), verbs of motion, and "estar." (B) is the infinitive (to walk), and (D) is the infinitive preceded by an "a."

89. **(C)** "Conservada" is correct. The past participle used as an adjective here must agree in number and gender with the noun it modifies ("área"). Although this word is preceded by "un," the masculine singular article, it is still a feminine word. Because "área" begins with a stressed "a" in the first syllable, masculine articles are used for pronunciation's sake. The noun is, however, still feminine. (A) is the masculine singular adjective; (B) is the present participle (conserving); and (D) is the preterit (he conserved).

90. **(B)** "Camino" is correct. It means "path" or "road." (A) means "track." (C) means "alley." (D) means "hallway."

Section II: Reading

Part C

91. **(D)** It should be rather easy to connect "cumplir años" with "cumple-años." Add to this the fact that she was going to be 13, and the only logical answer is (D).

92. **(C)** The word "pulsera" can be remembered because of the traditional location for taking the pulse. This was to be a special kind of wristwatch, a gold one with ornate hands. Alone, "pulsera" means "bracelet." "Un moño," in this context, means "bow," formed by "la cinta," "ribbon." It can also mean "bun" or "top knot," as in hairstyle. In the passage, "su muñeca" means "her wrist," but "una muñeca" can also mean "a doll."

93. **(B)** Notice the indirect object "le," indicating something to be given to her. Any of the choices fulfill this requirement; however, knowing the subject matter of the story makes the choice simple.

94. **(A)** The natural nervousness of the girl opening the hoped-for gift would make her hands tremble. Choice (D) uses the verb "chocar" which means "to hit together" or "to shake hands."

95. **(C)** Understanding the twist in the story makes answer (C) the correct choice.

96. **(C)** Notice that the word for "vacation" is always in the plural, "vacaciones." "In the open air" or "out of doors" is generally translated "al aire libre."

97. **(B)** Although these words may sound similar, they are very different in meaning. All are in the present participle form, used as nouns. It should also be noted that the expression "quince días" is another way of saying "two weeks." The fellow wanted to spend this time out of doors and hunting.

98. **(A)** The answer is his "faithful dog." Even though choice (C) could be a possibility, the information given in the story indicates that his dog was his important companion, not his gun.

99. **(B)** From the reading, "las primeras luces del alba" should be the clue that he awoke early, so choice (B) should be selected.

100. **(C)** The idiom "darse cuenta de" is always translated as "to realize" or "to become aware of." When used in front of a verb, "que" must precede the verb, which may never be in the infinitive form. "Niebla" is generally translated as "fog."

101. **(A)** "Al fresco" can also be translated as "out of doors." Occasionally, the expression "de nuevo" is used for "again." In this case, choice (A) is correct since the dog helped him to find the way back.

102. **(C)** One must know the verb "husmear," "to sniff out" or "to smell out." This then gives the clue to answer (C) "buen olfato" because of its cognate "olfactory." The word "hocico" is used for an animal's "mouth," "muzzle," or "snout."

103. **(D)** According to the text, the pirate's map was a copy.

104. **(D)** "Lo indicado" is the proper way to give a noun character to "indicado" and is translated as "that which is indicated." Note that the word "mapa," even though it ends in –a, is masculine.

105. **(B)** Despite the excitement of looking for the treasure, the boys first put up the tent and ate. The verb "escarbar," in choice (A), means "to dig."

106. **(A)** Carlos forgot the map at home. The expression "se lo comió" should be translated as "ate it up." And remember that the verb "romper" not only means "to break," but also "to tear."

107. **(C)** The boys felt a little stupid having left the treasure map at home. The question asks for "what feeling" the fellows had. This should make the answer choice easier.

108. **(D)** Although all the answers are grammatically correct, only (D) is accurate.

109. **(A)** The expression "junto a la catedral" indicates that it is now the church tower.

110. **(C)** The wind vane atop the tower helped sailors judge the direction of the wind.

111. **(D)** Sevilla is the location of the "Archivos de las Américas."

112. **(D)** The answer to this question is made explicit in the first sentence of the narrative, where the "ustedes" makes it clear that the narrator or speaker is addressing city folk who have never left the capital. If you chose (A) you may have missed much of the point of the passage and its tone, which is playful at the expense of those who know little or nothing about the jungle, especially the American tourists alluded to at the end. They are unaware of the great distances separating the Amazonian region of Peru from its Andean zone (where the Incas lived). It should be clear that these tourists are not being addressed by the speaker, which eliminates (B) as the correct answer. (C) is wrong because there is no mention of aboriginals in the passage.

113. **(A)** Choices (B) and (C) are clearly not tourist attractions, especially as the plane trip from the capital to the jungle is described as the most dangerous aspect of the experience. You'll choose (D) only if you are not paying attention and draw a facile connection between tourism and the attractions of an exotic place.

114. **(A)** By now you should find the references to American tourists disturbing and should realize that they are made in the same playful spirit as the original reference in the narrative passage. By now you should also have re-read the end of that passage carefully if only to figure out just what is going on with these recurrent tourists. If you've done this, then you probably didn't pick (B) as your answer, since you are likely to know that no particular city is mentioned in connection with the tourists. However, two cities are indeed mentioned, and one is Iquitos, about which it is explicitly stated that it is the only important Amazonian city in Peru. The other two available choices (C) and (D) are factually incorrect, though a careless reading of the passage could have been responsible for choosing either one or the other as the correct answer.

115. **(B)** The passage says "Conviene contratar un guía," and this is the phrase that supports (B) as the correct answer. (D) could not be it since it directly contradicts narrative information. (A) and (C) are fairly ludicrous choices, and you won't find the narrative passage consistent with either one of them.

116. **(C)** None of the incorrect choices are actually mentioned explicitly or implicitly in the passage, so if you chose any of them, you probably didn't read carefully. In fact, it's hard to imagine that anything in the

passage could be misinterpreted to coincide with any of the wrong answers, though (B) could be more easily arrived at by a process of distortion or overreading. The phrase that you needed to key on for the correct answer is "cuando los leemos, somos el viajero que en la realidad no pudimos ser."

117. **(B)** Here it helps to know the verb "ubicar" in the question, which can anyway be deduced from the several choices ("ciudades," "lugares," and "sitios" all suggest the idea of location or setting). Knowing this, and keying on the last two sentences of the narrative, you should have picked the right answer. The others are all plausible, but (A) contradicts the narrative information (which speaks of the less frequented regions of a country), (C) misunderstands the appropriate passage in the narrative (where it says that travel books might be written in moments of reflection), and (D) is an invention not supported by any textual evidence.

118. **(D)** The correct answer is explicitly stated in the narrative passage, which claims that travel books are probably written to revive the travel experience for the reader who couldn't go on a trip. The remaining choices are not totally implausible [except for (B)] but are not supported by the passage either.

119. **(C)** The key to this answer is not to believe what the question implicitly affirms, namely, that travel book authors are more interesting than their readers. The passage explicitly denies this hypothesis ("yo creo que no"), which makes the remaining choices irrelevant.

120. **(A)** There are certain references in the passage that might lead a careless reader to choose (C) or (D), such as the references to Puritanism and to the abundance of food in our society, but these allusions appear in a different context and refer to something else in the passage. [(B) would be a gratuitious answer since there are no references to sex at all]. (A), on the other hand, is the right choice because that passage explicitly states the link between over-exercising and a modern obsession with health.

121. **(B)** The passage defines Puritanism in terms of the capital principle of hygiene. Choices (A) and (C) are naive answers not supported by any textual evidence, and there is no reference to the Puritan religion forbidding meat anywhere in the passage.

122. **(D)** To choose the right answer you have to ask yourself what the passage states concerning the status of the body in a society obsessed by

health practices. And what it says is that our society's obsession with clean living represents a fear of the body and of death, an insecurity concerning our body which motivates overexercising and excessive dieting. This is essentially what (D) states. The other choices might be internally consistent but do not accord with the line of the argument.

123. **(B)**   This is the kind of question that requires a yes-or-no type of answer. So first you have to make up your mind what it is to be, and once you've decided that according to the logic of the passage abundance of food and drink is indeed deleterious to one's health, your next step is to choose between the two positive answers. (D) is the wrong choice not because it isn't internally consistent but because there is nothing said in the passage about smoking. (B), on the other hand, restates one of the points explicitly made in the passage (using a different vocabulary: "moderarse" instead of "controlarse" and "abundancia" instead of "disponibilidad").

124. **(C)**   The wrong choices might sound plausible to someone who hasn't read the passage, but the fact is that the latter makes the implicit connection between a general concern for health and the growth of a health industry, which is a kind of supply/demand connection. (The word "demanda" appears in the correct choice.)

125. **(D)**   This is a very simple question that refers you to the opening sentence of the paragraph. Choice (C) is deliberately mystifying, and (A) refers to nothing whatsoever in the passage.

126. **(B)**   Choices (A) and (C) could only be the product of a misreading, since these qualities apply to American football or to American society but not to soccer or to Latin American societies. (D) will not mystify those who have read the passage carefully and who know that in it soccer and spontaneity are linked together.

127. **(A)**   This is a more complicated question because it depends on your having followed a potentially ambiguous argument, namely, the whole question of the use of time in the two different sports at issue. The correct answer is (A) (subtracting it), which restates what the paragraph says about spending ("gastar") time in American football. The idea is that you are given a "capital" of time that you have to "invest" carefully and wisely, and that the time used is to be subtracted from the original total as an expenditure is from a sum total. You also have to know that in Spanish "restar" means "to subtract" (just as "sumar" means "to add"). Now you

know why (D) is wrong. (B) is a sort of pun on a phrase in the passage ("desde arriba para abajo"). You have to be careful here not to be misled by appearances. (C) is deliberate nonsense.

128. **(D)** (A) contradicts the information given in the passage, namely, that it is Latin American societies whose detractors refer to them as chaotic. By the same token, (C) is wrong because the passage makes the point that individualism is a trait of Latin American societies. (B), needless to say, is whimsical.

129. **(B)** The correct answer is (B). According to the advertisement, if you do not wear a helmet, you are at great risk. (A) states that the helmet "provides" rather than "prevents" a serious accident. (C) is incorrect because its approval by the American Institute of Norms does not make it necessary. Nor is it necessary because it is recommended for adults as well as children (D).

130. **(A)** The correct answer is (A). Aside from a helmet, the advertisement recommends that you also use a bell, lights, and reflectors as well as a brightly colored phosphorescent vest. A "phosphorescent speaker" is not mentioned (B) nor are "straps that absorb shocks" (C) and "a brightly lit hat" (D).

CLEP SPANISH TRANSCRIPTS TEST 1

CLEP SPANISH TRANSCRIPTS TEST 1

Listening Part A

> **Directions**: You will now hear short conversations, or parts of conversations, then four responses labeled (A)—(D). Choose the response that completes or continues the conversation. Listen carefully as neither the conversations, nor answer choices, will appear in your test booklet.

Número 1. **FEMALE** Disculpe, ¿a qué hora sale el tren de las cinco?

            MALE (A) A las seis.

                    (B) En la estación.

                    (C) Hacia el pueblo más cercano.

                    (D) Muy pronto.

Número 2. **FEMALE** ¿Cómo hizo eso, señor Ramírez?

            MALE (A) Bien, gracias.

                    (B) Con mucho cuidado.

                    (C) Estaba muy rico.

                    (D) Con zeta.

Número 3. **FEMALE** ¿Cuánto costó darse cuenta de este problema?

            MALE (A) Más de lo que hubiera pensado.

                    (B) 80 pesos.

                    (C) Un cheque a treinta días.

                    (D) Porque estudié matemáticas.

Número 4.   **FEMALE**   ¿Quién envió esa carta?

            MALE   (A) En el correo.

                          (B) Mi canario.

                          (C) Mi novia.

                          (D) Sin estampillas.

Número 5.   **MALE**   ¿Cuánto hace que empezó a pintar?

          FEMALE   (A) Dos años.

                          (B) Mañana.

                          (C) Doscientos dólares.

                          (D) Cuatro colores y un pincel.

Número 6.   **MALE**   ¿Estoy en la plaza San Martín?

          FEMALE   (A) Sí, ¿no ve el cartel?

                          (B) El procer argentino.

                          (C) Sí, está a tres cuadras de aquí.

                          (D) ¿Qué número de habitación?

Número 7.   **MALE**   ¿Qué sacaron del automóvil?

          FEMALE   (A) Brillar como el bronce.

                          (B) Las valijas y bolsas de tía Eudora.

                          (C) La máxima velocidad.

                          (D) 120 kilómetros por hora.

Número 8.   **MALE**   ¿Por qué corrían tan rápido?

          FEMALE   (A) Porque estaban llegando temprano.

                          (B) Porque había un incendio.

                          (C) Porque estaban paralizados de angustia.

                          (D) Porque eran lentos sin remedio.

Número 9.   **MALE**   ¿Quién vino despues?

                FEMALE   (A) Nadie.

                               (B) Más tarde.

                               (C) El final.

                               (D) El finado Roberto.

Número 10. **FEMALE**   ¿Juan Carlos, me alcanzas el libro, por favor?

                MALE   (A) No puedo, no tengo dinero.

                               (B) No puedo, está muy caliente.

                               (C) No puedo, está muy alto.

                               (D) No puedo, es de física cuántica.

Número 11. **FEMALE**   Luchi, me alegro por Ustedes dos.

                MALE   (A) -Yo le agradezco por Ustedes tres.

                               (B) -Gracias, yo me alegro por nosotros tres.

                               (C) -Gracias, es Usted muy feliz.

                               (D) -No se alegre que somos menos.

Número 12. **FEMALE**   Pónte el suéter que hace mucho frío.

                MALE   (A) El verano es muy largo.

                               (B) ¡Pero mamá, si es un día primaveral!

                               (C) No lo haré, nieva demasiado.

                               (D) Claro, mejor uso algo liviano.

Número 13. **FEMALE**   María José, si vuelves a cruzarte en mi camino te haré daño.

                MALE   (A) No puedes, ni siquiera sabes manejar.

                               (B) Difícil, no nos volveremos a ver jamás.

                               (C) Tengo amigos médicos.

                               (D) Bueno, prometo ayudarte cruzar la calle.

Número 14. **MALE** ¿Verdad que Julio es precioso?

 FEMALE (A) Prefiero agosto.

  (B) Demasiado caro.

  (C) Sobre todo su carita.

  (D) Mientes, como siempre.

Número 15. **MALE** ¿Puedo ir a tu casa esta noche?

 FEMALE (A) Si vienes de día, sí.

  (B) Bueno, pero no estaré.

  (C) Seguro, si eres puntual.

  (D) No creo, es de buena construcción.

Número 16. **MALE** Espero que nos paguen justamente.

 FEMALE (A) No creo, ya son las cinco.

  (B) Mejor vámonos.

  (C) Solo nos pagarán el mínimo.

  (D) La justicia es así.

Número 17. **MALE** ¿Seremos capaces de olvidar esta desgracia?

 FEMALE (A) Por eso yo tomo tónico para la memoria.

  (B) Por supuesto, tú eres muy trabajador.

  (C) El seguro se hará cargo.

  (D) El tiempo lo cura todo.

Número 18. **MALE** No nos dimos cuenta de lo distraído que eras.

 FEMALE (A) ¿Cómo dice?

  (B) Eso no es nada, viera lo bien que plancho.

  (C) Claro, claro, por eso estudio ingeniería.

  (D) Yo también te quiero.

This is the end of Test 1 Part A — Listening.
Continue with Test 1, Listening Part B.

CLEP SPANISH TRANSCRIPTS TEST 1

Listening Part B

Selección número 1.

FEMALE: Dicen que es el deporte que más dinero mueve en Estados Unidos y el que cuenta con más aficionados, por encima del béisbol y del baloncesto de la NBA. El fútbol americano (como lo llamamos los españoles para diferenciarlo del europeo, al qué ellos denominan "soccer") hace tiempo que dejó de ser un simple deporte para convertirse en un gran negocio del espactáculo y en una tradición tan arraigada a la cultura americana como el pavo asado del día de Acción de Gracias. Los niños estadounidenses sueñan con llegar a ser un día estrellas del fútbol americano, pero son una minoría los que llegan a formar parte de las ligas universitarias, y sólo una exclusiva elite de ellos tiene acceso a ese gran circulo de juego y dinero que es la NFL. Una vez alcanzada la liga profesional, el gran hito para un jugador es llegar a participar en un Super Bowl.

NARRATOR: Ahora contesten las preguntas 19, 20, y 21

[†] **Timing issues are somewhat different for the CBT. See page 6.**

Selección número 2.

FEMALE:	-¡Hola Benito, que extraño verlo aquí a esta hora!
MALE:	-Es que no pude dormir y vine mas temprano.
FEMALE:	-¡Pero no va a poder dormir hasta esta noche!
MALE:	-Lo sé, pero no quiero perder mi trabajo.

NARRATOR: Ahora contesten la pregunta 22

Selección número 3. **EL FLAGELO DEL RIO**

FEMALE: El límite Este de la región está formado por los ríos Tumuma y Viele, que le sirven como via de transporte y de poblamiento, y que aportan su humedad y con ella su riqueza al litoral, pero que también le causan periódicas catástrofes, como son las inundaciones. Si bien los sedimentos y los cambiantes niveles de esos ríos generan islotes alargados, cada cierta cantidad de años hay crecidas extraordinarias - las del 1983 y 1992, por ejemplo-que inundan vastísimas extensiones (convertidas entonces en rarísimas deltas) y cobran alto precio en vidas y perdidas económicas. Algo es cierto: se trata de una fuerza natural incontrolable. Pero también es cierto que el hombre la empeora: las monstruosas deforestaciones en el sur de Brenil y Baranuay redujeron la capacidad de absorción de agua en esos territorios, y son responsables sin duda, de agravar la situación a través de los cambios climáticos provocados también por esa tala indiscriminada que se traduce en tan inusuales como abrumadoras lluvias.

NARRATOR: Ahora contesten las preguntas 23 y 24

Selección número 4. **¡NADIE PUEDE COMPETIR CON CHINICHEX!**

MALE: Si todavia hacia falta una prueba más de lo imbatible que es Chinichex, le traemos la nueva oferta de primavera: ¡Lea bien! Si encuentra el artículo que nos ha comprado a un precio mas barato le pagamos la diferencia y además le pagamos esa diferencia multiplicada por el número que figura en la parte superior de la boleta de su compra en CHINICHEX. ¡Si! ¡Encuentre a Alguien que nos derrote con sus precios y tal vez gane mucho dinero! ¡Chinichex está tan seguro de sus gangas que no teme! ¡Venga y compre en Chinichex y luego vaya y busque otros precios! ¡Si lo consigue lo recompensaremos!

NARRATOR: Ahora contesten la pregunta 25

Selección número 5. ***FABULA***

MALE: En un oscuro pueblo rural al que misteriosamente un bosque impenetrable protegía de todo contacto con el exterior. Un hombre decidió que no podía vivir sin conocer el país del hielo del que había oído hablar a su abuelo. Asi que dejó de realizar su labor en el pueblo y ante el asombro de todos los demas dedicó su tiempo a la tarea de cruzar el bosque. Hizo numerosos intentos valerosos pero siempre que creía estar atravesando el tramo final hacia el otro lado, aparecía de nuevo en el perfil del pueblo natal.

NARRATOR: Ahora contesten la pregunta 26

Selección número 6. ***NOTICIA BREVE EN EL DIARIO***

FEMALE: Nueva York. Una prenda del celebre Elvis Presley fue sustraida ayer del museo Presley inaugurado hace una semana en la Gran Manzana por una pareja de mediana edad. El matrimonio, de apellido Chubby, aparentemente muy afecto al popular musico, planeó minuciosamente el hurto de una prenda íntima de seda blanca con bordado en plata con las iniciales E.P. que habría pertenecido al Rey.

NARRATOR: Ahora contesten la pregunta 27

Selección número 7. ***VISITANDO A LA ESTRELLA***

FEMALE: La diva número uno del país, Antonia, claro, nos recibe en su íntimo vestidor revestido en seda carmesí. Se deshace en sonrisas pero lo primero que nos advierte es que no hagamos ninguna mención a su avanzada edad o a sus numerosas intervenciones de cirugía estética, cosa que no haremos, por supuesto. Ante nuestra sorpresa por su inamovible sonrisa Antonia comenzó a hablarnos de sus amores celébres. Realmente la emoción no hacía temblar esa maravillosa dentadura postiza ni un milímetro. No sabemos si por el estupendo trabajo del dentista o porque Antonia domina las emociones como nadie. Cuando el reportaje iba a dar comienzo la Diva hizo sonar una campanilla y rapidamente tres serviciales señoritas nos trajeron unas bandejas muy generosas con té de jazmín y bizcochitos algo endurecidos por el paso del tiempo, como nuestra anfitriona.

NARRATOR: Ahora contesten la pregunta 28

Selección número 8. **INSTRUCCIONES**

MALE: Tómese la batería recargable y coloquésela en el compartimiento C. de la estructura base del Sonoflex-flow 7000. A la derecha del Orificio central podrá ver una perilla que activará la recarga cuando usted accione la perilla hacia la leyenda superior que dice: "SI." La recarga de la batería tardará unos veinte minutos aproximadamente. ¡Entonces estará listo para disfrutar del armado final del Sonoflex-flow 7000, versión beta! Una luz verde titilará en el frente del apáráto. SI fuera una luz amarilla la que titila recomience toda la instalación desde el principio (ver página 2). Si fuera una luz roja la que titila, deje caer el Sonoflex-flow rapidamente. Si hubiera luz pero no titilara llame a nuestro servicio técnico que lo atenderá gentilmente las 24 horas. Si no se enciende ninguna luz chequee la existencia de batería en el compartimiento C. ¡Si usted es el feliz poseedor del modelo Sonoflex-flow 7000 Gold accione el poder y disfrute del campo Sonoro! Si en cambio Usted posee el modelo normal, ¡no se preocupe! ¡Sonoflex le facilitará la posibilidad de acceder al Modelo Gold por una sensible diferencia económica!

NARRATOR: Ahora contesten la pregunta 29

Selección número 9. **FRAGMENTO DE UN DISCURSO DE LA PRESIDENTA DE AMIGOS DEL BARRIO**

FEMALE: "Me preguntan porqué no quiero vengarme de la gente que realizó esos actos de violencia que nos conmocionaron el fin de semana pasado. Muchos han sido víctima de estos abusos de violencia callejera a los que nos estamos acostumbrando casi con indiferencia, y eso me asusta. Y cuando por fin despertamos, tenemos sed de sangre. No, no, no.

No es que no crea que estos seres violentos no merezcan justicia. Pero creo que no está en nuestras manos hacernos cargo de ejercer esa justicia. Yo no he de utilizar violencia para atacar la violencia. Así habría triunfado una manera de pensar y de vivir que no es la que queremos para nuestras vidas. Es la que nos propone esta gente. Utilizar sobre ellos la misma vara sería un error, sería darles el triunfo, cederles el trono, concederles que sus leyes son las nuestras. Y no lo son. Yo digo que hemos de luchar hombro con hombro contra estos hechos desgraciados, pero con la fuerza de la convicción y la paz."

NARRATOR: Ahora contesten la pregunta 30

Selección número 10. **LETRA DE UNA BALADA DE ROCK**

MALE: "Nena, oh, yo te adoraba nena, sí.

Y te adoro, todavía, creo que sí.

Oh nena, sí.

Tú te vestiste de fuego y ardiste en mi ego,
Oh nena, tú.

Tú me has herido de nuevo y yo desespero,
nena, sí, oh nena, nena oh.

Y si bien eres mi tesoro

Ya nada de ti añoro

Salvo a ti, nena,
¿y? Entonces,

Oh nena,

Herido en mi destino al

Final del camino te

Olvidaré.

Uuuh, yeah.

Tú te vestiste de fuego y

Yo desespero,

Creo, sí.

Nena, sí. Oh nena

Ah. Solo tú."

NARRATOR: Ahora contesten la pregunta 31

Selección número 11. **INVITACIÓN**

FEMALE: El club de fans de Star Trek de Villa Insuperable convoca al concurso titulado: "Soy el mas parecido al capitán Picard." Como recordarán el actor que representa al capitán mencionado es calvo en un 80% de su craneo. Luego aquellos que se presenten al concurso con toda la cabellera serán eliminados automáticamente. También lo serán aquellos que solo pretendan concursar solo a partir de sus calvicies. Deberá existir una representación cuidadosa. El primer premio será un traje de la Confederación Estelar de puro poliester.

NARRATOR: Ahora contesten la pregunta 32

Selección número 12. **REPORTE METEOROLÓGICO**

FEMALE: Probables lluvias ligeras hacia el anochecer, con descenso de la temperatura. Un aire frío del sur se dirige nor-noreste con velocidad y podría sorprendernos con un inesperado invierno primaveral. La sensación térmica debida al viento haría que registremos una temperatura inédita para esta época del año.

NARRATOR: Ahora contesten la pregunta 33

Selección número 13.

FEMALE:	—Juan, te pasaré a buscar por el centro comercial despues de retirar unas fotografías del laboratorio y antes de pagar mi gimnasio.
MALE:	—Bien, Carina. ¿Pero sabes a qué hora exacta me pasas a buscar?
FEMALE:	—Juan, tú sabes que soy muy impuntual. Te propongo pasar a las diez, pero calcula una hora de atraso.
MALE:	—Muy bien. Pero paga tu gimnasio otro día.
NARRATOR:	Ahora contesten la pregunta 34

Selección número 14.

MALE:	—Buen día. Desde hoy trabajaremos juntos en un proyecto sumamente secreto. Debemos hablar pues dentro de dos días es feriado.
FEMALE:	—Oh, ¿y de que se trata?
MALE:	—No puedo decirlo, es secreto.
FEMALE:	—¿Pero yo trabajaría en él?
MALE:	—Correcto.
FEMALE:	—Entonces, ¿cómo voy a trabajar si tú no me dices nada?
MALE:	—Bueno, no lo sé.
FEMALE:	—¿No lo sabes?
MALE:	—No, nadie me lo explicó porque es extremadamente secreto.
FEMALE:	—¿Cómo? Pero, ¿cómo vamos a trabajar entonces? ¿Tenemos un superior que nos comunique que hacer?
MALE:	—Sí, pero tenemos prohibido comunicarnos con él.
FEMALE:	—¿Por qué?
MALE:	—Es para mantener el secreto bien guardado.
FEMALE:	—A esta altura no hay ni siquiera secreto que guardar.
MALE:	—Shhhhh, callémonos! Alguien puede estar escuchando.
NARRATOR:	Ahora contesten la pregunta 35

Selección número 15. **TICKETS**

MALE: —Buenas noches, tenemos dos tickets reservados y necesitamos uno más con una ubicación cercana a la de los otros dos.

FEMALE: —Como no. Veamos, ¿a nombre de quién están?

MALE: —Guillermo Rodríguez.

FEMALE: —Muy bien. Pero lamento informarle que no hay tickets cercanos a esta ubicación. ¿Podrá la tercera persona conformarse con otra?

MALE: —Mmm, lo lamento, pero es muy exigente. Creo que cancelaré los otros dos tickets. Si no vamos los tres no va nadie.

FEMALE: —Le puedo dar tres tickets en una ubicación mediocre.

MALE: —Bien, entonces. Le agradezco mucho pero cancele toda la transacción.

FEMALE: —Muy bien señor.

NARRATOR: Ahora contesten la pregunta 36

Selección número 16. **REGLAMENTACIÓN**

MALE:

1. Se prohibe a todo socio del club circular por el piso cuarto en el que residen los empleados del club, sin excepciones.

2. Los empleados del club no podrán tener acceso al piso tercero.

3. Los socios del club pueden traer invitados que están sujetos a la misma reglamentación que los socios.

4. Los empleados que tengan familiares que son socios del club podrán fumar en el piso tercero.

NARRATOR: Ahora contesten la pregunta 37

Selección número 17. **LOS OJOS DE LA GLOQUILLA**

FEMALE: Los ojos de la gloquilla presentan una particularidad asombrosa. El doble párpado superior, que le permite mediante una acción retráctil sumamente lubricada, mantiene el ojo preparado para soportar altísimos grados de luminosidad y también de calor. Si sumamos esto a la fortaleza de su piel, sólida y blanca, con capacidades de refracción térmica y reflexión luminosa, podemos decir que es un animal claramente preparado para vivir en el difícil entorno físico que le tocó.

NARRATOR: Ahora contesten la pregunta 38

Selección número 18. **UNA CARTÁ**

MALE: Querido abuelito;

Me ha sorprendido mucho que no me hayas hecho llegar mi regalo de cumpleaños, como de costumbre. Supongo que habrá habido algún problema en la oficina de correo, pues tú nunca olvidas. Ya que te escribo estas líneas te digo que si tienes dudas sobre que regalo darme pues no te preocupes tanto. Un cheque estará bien, yo me encargo de hacer las compras. Ya sé que me olvidé de tu cumpleaños el mes pasado, pero ha sido a propósito. Supuse que no querrías que te recordara la edad que tienes. ¡Eres tan coqueto!

Tu nieto

NARRATOR: Ahora contesten la pregunta 39

Selección número 19. **EN LA DISQUERÍÁ**

FEMALE: —¿Puedo ayudarlo en algo? Veo que busca música de Beethoven...

MALE: —No, solo busco algo de calidad indiscutible. Bach, Brahms, o algún compositor que me ayude a conciliar el sueño.

FEMALE: —Oh, ¿es Usted amante de la música clásica?

MALE: —No, tengo insomnio. Y si me aburro me duermo más rápido.

FEMALE: —Oh, entonces busca música aburrida.

MALE: —Sí, pero de primera calidad. No podría soportar dormirme con cualquier cosa. Tiene que ser de primera.

FEMALE: —Bien, señor. Pero tal vez empiece a descubrir que le gusta y sea peor para su problema de sueño.

MALE: —Correré el riesgo.

NARRATOR: Ahora contesten la pregunta 40

Selección número 20. **TELEGRAMA**

FEMALE: LLEGO´ HOY A LAS 22 HORAS - STOP - EL ESTRENO FUE UN EXITO - STOP - A LOS CRITICOS NO LES GUSTO´ LA OBRA - STOP - FUE BUENA IDEA NO COBRAR LA PRIMERA FUNCION - STOP - HARE MODIFICACIONES ENTRE LOS ACTORES - STOP - ME SIENTO MUY SATISFECHO CON TODO - STOP

NARRATOR: Ahora contesten la pregunta 41

Selección número 21. **PLANTAS DEL DESIERTO**

MALE: Casi todas las plantas de climas áridos desarrollan adaptaciones particulares para poder sobrevivir. Casi todas recurren a raíces muy extendidas y profundas para una mejor captación de la escasa agua disponible y están muy separadas una de otras para evitar la competencia por el agua, lo que produce una vegetación escasa. Algunas especies vegetales almacenan agua en sus tejidos, como las cactaceas, por ejemplo, o en ciertos órganos subterráneos, como los tuberculos. Para reducir la evaporación la mayoría de las especies leñosas pierde sus hojas durante la estación seca, y algunos arbustos transmiten la facultad fotosintética a las ramas o tallos.

NARRATOR: Ahora contesten la pregunta 42

Selección número 22. **LA CIUDAD MÁS AL SUR DEL MUNDO**

FEMALE: Ushuaia, la capital de Tierra del Fuego, es la ciudad ubicada más al sur que cualquier otra del mundo. Fundada en 1770 en el sur argentino, fue primero un puesto de evangelización de indígenas, pero fue devastada por la tuberculosis. Luego fue una parada de aventureros y buscafortunas. Más tarde su fama se oscureció por la existencia de una prisión para reincidentes levantada a fines del siglo pasado. Pero hoy la prisión es una base naval y la ciudad es un centro de pesca, turismo y fabricación de tecnología.

NARRATOR: Ahora contesten la pregunta 43

Selección número 23. **UN PEDIDO CUMPLIDO**

FEMALE: —¿Me has traido lo que te pedí?

MALE: —Bueno, sí te traje, pero no te traje.

FEMALE: —¿Cómo sí pero no? Mira que yo sin cigarrillos no puedo estar.

MALE: —Te traje cigarrillos, pero de chocolate.

FEMALE: —¿De chocolate? ¡No se pueden fumar!

MALE: —Como poder puedes, pero es complicadísimo.

FEMALE: —¿Lo has hecho a propósito?

MALE: —No, ¡es que la cajita se parece tanto!

FEMALE: —No puede haberte confundido. Lo hiciste a sabiendas.

MALE: —Bueno, sí. Pero es que, ¡me encanta el chocolate!

FEMALE: —Bueno, dáme uno.

MALE: —¿Lo vas a fumar?

FEMALE: —No, tonto. Lo voy a comer y no te dejaré ni uno.

NARRATOR: Ahora contesten la pregunta 44

Selección número 24. **EL DEPARTAMENTO DE MIMI**

MALE: —¡Hola Mimi! ¿Conseguiste departamento para comprar?

FEMALE: —Sí. Pero estoy confundida. Encontré tres. El primero tiene dos dormitorios pero le falta luz. El segundo tiene terraza pero sólo un dormitorio. El tercero tiene dos dormitorios y jardín.

MALE: —Bueno, entonces será el tercero, ¿verdad?

FEMALE: —No, no es tan fácil. Porque el primero queda cerca de mi trabajo, el segundo queda más cerca todavia y el tercero queda muy lejos.

MALE:	— ¡Caramba! ¿Y qué vas a hacer?
FEMALE:	—No sé porque el primero no es tan baráto como el segundo y el tercero es un poco caro pero no me cobran adelanto.

NARRATOR: Ahora contesten la pregunta 45

Selección número 25. **HORÓSCOPO**

FEMALE: Para los nacidos bajo el signo de Virgo:

Esta semana se presenta muy auspiciosa y positiva para aquéllos que hayan nacido en el mes de mayo. En el amor: una sorpresa horrible que estaba esperando va a llegar a su vida. En el trabajo: probablemente lo pierda a manos de un compañero envidioso. Tardará un poco en conseguir otro trabajo a pesar de sus conocimientos en el ramo que ejerce. Vida social: Como perderá amigos y todos pensarán que necesita dinero su vida social promete ser escasa. Salud: hágase un chequeo general, es muy probable que encuentre algo que no le va a gustar.

NARRATOR: Ahora contesten la pregunta 46

Selección número 26.

FEMALE:	— ¿Lo has hecho?
MALE:	—Sí, lo he hecho.
FEMALE:	— ¿Fue muy difícil?
MALE:	—No, no ofreció resistencia.
FEMALE:	— ¿Te costó hacerlo?
MALE:	—Y, me dio lástima.
FEMALE:	— ¿Lo hiciste al horno?
MALE:	—No, a la cacerola.
FEMALE:	— ¿Quedará bien?
MALE:	—No lo probé todavía.
FEMALE:	— ¿Se quejó?
MALE:	—No. Me miró como comprendiendo.
FEMALE:	— ¿Le pusiste unas papas?

MALE:	—Sí. Y otras cositas.
FEMALE:	—Y bueno, era su destino.
MALE:	—Y sí, pero siempre es difícil.

NARRATOR: Ahora contesten la pregunta 47

Selección número 27. **PIERNA MALHERIDA**

MALE:	— ¡Oh, estás con la pierna enyesada!
FEMALE:	—Sí, me lastimé el hueso.
MALE:	— ¿Cómo fue?
FEMALE:	—Y, venía patinando por la terraza cuando sonó el teléfono y salí corriendo y tropecé con una mesita.
MALE:	— ¿Y allí fue?
FEMALE:	—No sé, porque despues me incorporé y al bajar la escalera me resbalé y la mitad la bajé rodando.
MALE:	—Oh, y allí te rompiste...
FEMALE:	—No estoy segura porque justo tocaron el timbre en la puerta principal y me levanté para atender y cuando abrí la puerta seguí hacia la calle por el impulso y me golpeé contra el buzón de correo.
MALE:	—Ay, que dolor. ¿Y allí te rompiste?
FEMALE:	—No, como me dolía todo me acosté en el sofa de la sala y vino mamá sin darse cuenta y se sentó sobre mi pierna.
MALE:	— ¿Y entonces?
FEMALE:	—Entonces sonó un crac y vino la ambulancia.
MALE:	— ¿Y?
FEMALE:	—Y parece que no tenía nada en la pierna, que el crac fue otra cosa.
MALE:	— ¿Pero y el yeso?
FEMALE:	— ¡Me puse a llorar porque quería uno y tanto molesté que al final me lo pusieron!

NARRATOR: Ahora contesten la pregunta 48

Selección número 28.

MALE:	— ¿Qué le regalamos a Ricardo? ¡Tiene de todo!
FEMALE:	— ¿Qué opinas de un autito a control remoto, Quique?
MALE:	— ¡Tiene!
FEMALE:	—Pero uno lindo...
MALE:	—Tiene unos cuarenta.
FEMALE:	—Oh. Entonces algo de ropa, una camiseta con la cara de alguno de sus artistas preferidos.
MALE:	—Tiene, y todas autografiadas.
FEMALE:	—Oh. Bueno, entonces yo le hago una torta con mis propias manos.
MALE:	—Eso está bien, ¿pero yo que puedo hacer, Melba?
FEMALE:	—Lo que quieras, pero no le cantes, por favor.

NARRATOR: Ahora contesten la pregunta 49

Selección número 29. **EL HUNDIMIENTO DEL TITANIC**

MALE: Entonces se escuchó un ruido sordo y poco después se dio el aviso. El titanic se hundía. Algunos pensaron que habían sido atacados, otros que habrían explotado los motores. Pocos pensaron que podían chocar con un iceberg y hundirse. La gente fue abandonando el barco, pero no había suficientes botes salvavidas. Así que muchos se quedaron a bordo hasta el final. La pequeña orquesta del titanic siguió tocando hasta que el barco se hundió completamente.

NARRATOR: Ahora contesten la pregunta 50

This is the end of Test 1 — Part B Listening. Now begin the Reading portion of Test 1.

CLEP SPANISH TRANSCRIPTS TEST 2

CLEP SPANISH TRANSCRIPTS TEST 2

Listening Part A

> **Directions**: You will now hear short conversations, or parts of conversations, then four responses labeled (A)—(D). Choose the response that completes or continues the conversation. Listen carefully as neither the conversations, nor answer choices, will appear in your test booklet.

Número 1. **FEMALE** Si tuviera dinero, viajaría a las islas griegas.

MALE (A) Bueno, te veo allá el mes que viene.

(B) Bien, ¿me puedes prestar para comprar una televisión, entonces?

(C) Mejor, no hay lugar mas hermoso en la Tierra.

(D) Entonces confórmate con un lugar más cercano.

Número 2. **FEMALE** ¡Me pasé el día en el Internet!

MALE (A) ¿Hacía calor?

(B) ¡Con razón no te encontré en tu casa!

(C) ¿Encontraste algo interesante?

(D) Yo odio el aire libre.

Número 3. **FEMALE** Podremos esquiar si llevan con que hacerlo.

MALE (A) Bien, yo llevo las bebidas.

(B) Bien, tengo los esquíes de mi hermano.

(C) Bien, yo tengo automóvil.

(D) Bien, no puedo salir de casa.

Número 4.   **FEMALE**   Este perro te mordería si tú te me acercaras.

         MALE   (A)   ¡Ay, que mansito perrito!

                  (B)   Bueno, entonces abrázame.

                  (C)   Le daríamos de comer si sucediera.

                  (D)   ¡Qué bien enseñado está!

Número 5.   **MALE**   Cada vez que me miras no puedo evitar suspirar.

       FEMALE   (A)   Tengo pastillas para la acidez estomacal, si quieres.

                  (B)   Es que tengo una basurilla en el ojo.

                  (C)   Es que me asombra tu peinado.

                  (D)   A mi me pasa lo mismo.

Número 6.   **MALE**   Volveré a hacerlo si me llaman desde España.

       FEMALE   (A)   Tráeme algo típico de allá.

                  (B)   Pero el teléfono no funciona, entonces.

                  (C)   Me parece bien, pues es lo que sabes hacer.

                  (D)   Siempre es bueno comenzar con algo nuevo.

Número 7.   **MALE**   Gabito, debemos hablar de cierto tema.

       FEMALE   (A)   Imposible, soy mudo.

                  (B)   Mentira, mentira.

                  (C)   Siempre estoy listo para hablar de música.

                  (D)   Muy bien, te escucho, comienza tú.

Número 8.   **MALE**   Si mi jefe no fuera tan insoportable sería incomparable; pero de todas maneras es, sin duda, inolvidable.

       FEMALE   (A)   Mejor, así no te acuerdas más de él.

                  (B)   Es bueno saber que no tiene ninguna virtud.

                  (C)   Es bueno saber que tiene algo bueno a pesar de todo.

                  (D)   Es una fortuna trabajar en un sitio tan cómodo.

Número 9.   **FEMALE**   ¿Puede decirme dónde queda el Hotel Miramar?

           MALE   (A) Sí, está en la próxima calle.

                     (B) Ah no, no pare Ud. enfrente del hotel.

                     (C) Sí, soy turista.

                     (D) No te puedo acompañar ahora.

Número 10. **FEMALE**   ¿Me puedes hacer un favor Mario?

           MALE   (A) Sí, te lo agradezco mucho.

                     (B) Lo siento, pero estoy agotado.

                     (C) No hay de qué.

                     (D) Sí, sería una desgracia para mí.

Número 11. **FEMALE**   ¿Podría Usted decirme cuánto falta para el evento?

           MALE   (A) Faltan cinco cuadras.

                     (B) Con ocho pesos más tendrá la cantidad completa.

                     (C) Me lo impide el pecado.

                     (D) Ya debió haber comenzado, señorita.

Número 12. **FEMALE**   Le reservo dos habitaciones de lujo hasta Semana Santa.

           MALE   (A) No, mejor tres semanas.

                     (B) No por favor, sólo una.

                     (C) Dígame lo que tenga que decir sin reservas.

                     (D) Esa fecha de arribo no me conviene.

Número 13. **FEMALE**   Doctor, me parece, por lo que sospecho vagamente, tener síntomas de una enfermedad muy rara desde enero.

           MALE   (A) Tiene usted un mes de vida.

                     (B) Tome una aspirina y vuelva en un mes.

                     (C) ¿Por qué está tan segura?

                     (D) ¿Podrá Ud. decirme cuáles son esos síntomas?

Número 14. **FEMALE** Buenas tardes, quisiera papel para escribirle cartas a mi familia....

MALE (A) ¿Y le dan buenas noticias?

(B) ¿Tinta azul o tinta negra?

(C) ¿Con rayas o sin rayas?

(D) ¿Lo hacen por dinero?

Número 15. **FEMALE** Luis, el 5 de octubre es tu cumpleaños, ¿verdad?

MALE (A) Sí, es mi lugar de nacimiento.

(B) Sí, es mi santo.

(C) Sí, es mi fecha de nacimiento.

(D) Sí, es la fecha de la celebración.

Número 16. **MALE** Si me comprara una moto iría a visitar a mis parientes en la costa.

FEMALE (A) Adiós, ¡manda postales!

(B) ¿No le tienes miedo a las alturas?

(C) Yo gastaría ese dinero en otra cosa menos peligrosa.

(D) Y si tu vas, mejor.

Número 17. **MALE** El aire de primavera es más seco que el de otoño, pero en verano el clima es agobiante.

FEMALE (A) Entonces el otoño es más humedo que el verano.

(B) Entonces el otoño es más humedo que la primavera.

(C) Entonces el verano es más seco que el otoño.

(D) Entonces el invierno es la estación más humeda.

Número 18.   **MALE**   Usted puede cobrar este cheque si firma al dorso del mismo.

FEMALE   (A) Muy bien, ¿me presta un bolígrafo?

(B) ¡De ninguna manera aceptaré estas condiciones!

(C) ¡Pero señor, necesito ese dinero!

(D) Muy bien, déme el formulario y lo firmo de inmediato.

This is the end of Test 2 Part A — Listening. Continue with Test 2, Listening Part B.

CLEP SPANISH TRANSCRIPTS TEST 2

Listening Part B

Directions: You will hear a series of dialogues, news reports, narratives, and announcements. Listen very carefully, as each selection will only be spoken once. One or more questions with four possible answers are printed in your test booklet. They will not be spoken. After each selection has been read, choose the best answer choice for each question and fill in the corresponding oval on your answer sheet. You will be given 12 seconds to answer each question.[†]

Selección número 1.

FEMALE: Steven Spielberg asegura que "Parque Jurásico" no es ni un film de ciencia ficción ni un ejemplo de cine fantástico, sino una película de ciencia, a secas, porque lo que en ella se narra muy bien pudiera suceder hoy en día. También afirma que se han necesitado 65 millones de años para realizar el famoso largometraje, porque ése ha sido el tiempo que ha pasado desde que los gigantescos dinosaurios poblaron la Tierra hasta que los avances científicos han permitido especular con la creación clónica de especies extinguidas a partir del ADN. Michael Crichton, el autor de la novela en la que se basa el film, se ha convertido en uno de los más famosos escritores de "best-sellers" de los útimos años en Estados Unidos. Antiguo cienasta, el novelista ha conseguido suculentos beneficios vendiendo los derechos cinematográficos de sus obras a las grandes productoras de Hollywood. Crichton, a quien siempre le ha apasionado el tema de los dinosaurios, dijo que desde hace mucho tiempo tenía ganas de escribir algo sobre ellos, muy ligado con la ciencia y los problemas que ésta puede llegar a causar.

NARRATOR: Ahora contesten las preguntas 19, 20, 21, y 22

[†] **Timing issues are somewhat different for the CBT. See page 6.**

Selección número 2. **RAZONES**

FEMALE: Su trabajo es de primera calidad pero debo despedirlo porque la empresa ha decidido ampliar sus horizontes.

NARRATOR: Ahora contesten la pregunta 23

Selección número 3. **LA COMIDA CRIOLLA**

FEMALE: La comida criolla es una mezcla de influencias de comida europea y americana.

NARRATOR: Ahora contesten la pregunta 24

Selección número 4. **LA TIERRA**

MALE: Los pueblos indígenas en general solían tener un gran respeto por la naturaleza. Veneraban el sol, la lluvia y la tierra. A esta última sobre todo, pues la vinculaban con el cultivo y el sentido de origen. Esto se ha perdido en las culturas contemporáneas en las que uno ya no relaciona el primer motor de las cosas con el resultado final. Un pan viene de la panadería, ya no del trigo que otros hombres cultivaron. De la misma manera uno ya no pertenece a un sitio, ya no se identifica con un agua o un aire a menos que haga un esfuerzo cultural para lograrlo.

NARRATOR: Ahora contesten la pregunta 25

Selección número 5. **UNA POSTAL**

MALE: "Hola. Estoy muy bien aquí, en las playas. El hotel que se ve en la foto no es en el que estoy, pero como es el más lindo prefiero mandar esta postal y no otra. Me he bronceado y como mucha fruta muy exótica. Cuídenme a mi gata. Les mando saludos. Cuando vuelva les llevaré algunas cositas que compré de recuerdo. Hasta pronto."

NARRATOR: Ahora contesten la pregunta 26

Selección número 6. **PREMIO**

FEMALE: —Ha ganado Usted un viaje a Hawaii.

NARRATOR: Ahora contesten la pregunta 27

Selección número 7. **JUICIO GASTRONÓMICO**

MALE: Este plato está muy rico, un poco salado para mi gusto, pero las especias lo suavizan, como la crema. No soy muy amigo de los productos lácteos, pero en este caso no quedaba más remedio que utilizarlos para poder resistir lo fuerte que está sazonado. Pero como ves, me comí dos platos enteros.

NARRATOR: Ahora contesten la pregunta 28

Selección número 8. **COMPRANDO UN TELEVISOR**

MALE: Me puede pagar la primera cuota con un cheque a treinta dias y luego once cuotas de 25 con un interés del diez por ciento. No hay un adelanto inmediato, así que se lleva el aparato hoy mismo y no necesita preocuparse por pagos extras.

NARRATOR: Ahora contesten la pregunta 29

Selección número 9. **UNA PELÍCULA**

FEMALE: El director Jorge Fons abreva en la vertiente más tradicional del cine mexicano para construir con sencillez y emoción un tema genuinamente popular e inequivocamente localista, bajo la pluma del premio Nobel egipcio Naguib Mahfuz, adaptado a la región.

NARRATOR: Ahora contesten la pregunta 30

Selección número 10. **TRABAJOS DE LOS JOVENES**

MALE: Los trabajos pasajeros que la juventud ejerce son en general trabajos de horario insólito. Esto se debe a que a los jovenes no les molesta tener horarios fuera de lo común cuando buscan una ocupación que no sea rutinaria y que es una transición hacia otras actividades.

NARRATOR: Ahora contesten la pregunta 31

Selección número 11. **TODOS PODEMOS HACERLO**

MALE: Las tareas de decoración manual no son exclusividad de los artesanos. Uno tambien puede, con imaginación y elementos comunes construir por ejemplo marcos en papel maché, figuras en cartulina, adornos en cerámica, incluso trabajos en vidrio o plásticos y otros materiales no convencionales. El hombre primitivo fue el primer artesano. Y él vive en nosotros.

NARRATOR: Ahora contesten la pregunta 32

Selección número 12. **EL ALCOHOLISMO**

MALE: Hay personas que por falta de tratamiento o de auxilio no encuentran alivio a sus sufrimientos y sufren una depresión que a veces conduce al riesgo de caer en el alcoholismo. A medida que crece el hábito es más difícil salir del mismo. Lo mismo sucede con los psicofármacos. Lo principal en todos estos casos es realizar una consulta con alguien confiable que pueda orientar los problemas hacia una solución segura.

NARRATOR: Ahora contesten la pregunta 33

Selección número 13. **TRABAJO**

MALE: —¿Qué sabe hacer?

FEMALE: —Sé computación, toco la trompeta, escribo poemas, manejo contabilidad, sé conducir camiones y cocino magnificamente bien.

MALE: —¿Podrá tocar la trompeta mientras atiende a los clientes?

FEMALE: —No lo sé. ¿Cómo sostengo la bandeja, entonces?

MALE: —Mmm, ¿podrá conducir un camión mientras limpia las mesas?

FEMALE:	—No lo creo. No hay mucho espacio entre ellas.
MALE:	—Aja, entonces, tal vez pueda llevar la contabilidad en la computadora mientras cobra el servicio a los clientes.
FEMALE:	—Puedo, pero el cliente tiene que venir hasta la computadora. No puedo ir de lugar en lugar con ella.
MALE:	—¿Pero entonces?
FEMALE:	—¿No quiere que cocine?
MALE:	—Ya tengo una cocinera extraordinaria.
FEMALE:	—Bueno, me voy.
MALE:	—¡Vaya, escriba poesía!
NARRATOR:	Ahora contesten la pregunta 34

Selección número 14. **RADIO**

MALE:	Radio Latina FM Sur dejó de transmitir ayer su programación habitual. Locutores y operadores fueron avisados el último día. Los cambios fueron decididos por los socios de la empresa, que desde hoy emite programas solamente musicales. La emisora alude que ya no podía competir comercialmente con el resto del dial y que deben buscar un público más amplio.
NARRATOR:	Ahora contesten la pregunta 35

Selección número 15. **DECLARACIONES SOBRE MÚSICA Y NO SOLO SOBRE MÚSICA**

MALE:	"La intolerancia no le hace bien a nadie. Una cosa son las vertientes y otra la segregación. Esto es válido para la música -en lo que yo trabajo- como para todo. Si yo quiero poner una batería en mi agrupación de música tradicional, lo hago. Quienes piensan que no se puede enriquecer una cultura con agregados de otras culturas, se equivoca. Es por eso que los odios culturales tienen lugar, por miedo e ignorancia."
NARRATOR:	Ahora contesten la pregunta 36

Selección número 16. **PRESTAMOS**

FEMALE: —¿Me prestas tu mapa?

MALE: —Si tú me prestas tu cámara fotográfica.

FEMALE: —Caramba, no suelo prestar mi cámara fotográfica, pero puedo prestarte mi radio a cambio de tu mapa.

MALE: —No quiero tu radio, quiero sacar fotos y no puedo con una radio.

FEMALE: —Bueno, ¿me prestas el mapa?

MALE: —¿Me prestas la cámara?

FEMALE: —Bien, te presto la cámara pero además del mapa me tienes que invitar a almorzar.

MALE: —Muy bien. Encantado. ¿Qué te parece si vamos al cine, también?

FEMALE: —Me parece bien, pero dáme el mapa así sabemos donde ir.

NARRATOR: Ahora contesten la pregunta 37

Selección número 17. **PONIENDO UN AVISO CLASIFICADO**

MALE: — Quisiera poner un aviso en su diario.

FEMALE: —¿En qué rubro?

MALE: —Ventas o Canjes.

FEMALE: —¿Qué ofrece?

MALE: —Vendo o canjeo una bicicleta de cinco velocidades, negra, con todos los accesorios impecables.

FEMALE: — ¿Y qué querría Usted a cambio?

MALE: —100 pesos o bien, podría cambiarla por muchas cosas, veamos, un walkman, un televisor mediano, clases de natación, ropa, discos compactos si son de músicos que me gusten, libros interesantes -pero muchos-, ehhhh.

FEMALE: —Este aviso le va a costar caro.

MALE: —Oh, perdone Usted. Ponga que canjeo por cosas que me interesen.

FEMALE: —Bien, ¿le interesa un cachorro de doberman?

MALE: — ¿Cómo dice?

FEMALE: —Sí, me interesa su bicicleta y mi perra tuvo cachorros.

Son de pura raza.

MALE: —Me interesa, sí. Entonces, no ponga el aviso. ¿Cuándo puedo ir a ver al cachorrito?

NARRATOR: Ahora contesten la pregunta 38

Selección número 18. **CONDICIONES**

FEMALE: No aceptaré la transacción a menos que tenga un garante o sea otra persona que tenga buen crédito.

NARRATOR: Ahora contesten la pregunta 39

Selección número 19. **EL TANGO**

MALE: El tango se originó en la zona portuaria a partir de la inmigración masiva de fines de siglo pasado. Primero fue la música de las clases más bajas y el ambiente más sórdido. Luego accedió a otros círculos y fue adoptado por toda la sociedad. De ser mal visto pasó a formar parte de la identidad de la ciudad.

NARRATOR: Ahora contesten la pregunta 40

Selección número 20. **ESTRELLAS DEL DEPORTE**

MALE: Hoy en día las estrellas del deporte ganan fortunas jamás pensadas años atrás. Los jovenes con cualidades para el deporte son estimulados de todas las maneras posibles para que hagan carrera y fortuna en ese medio. Peligrosamente, pues el mundo del dinero cobra sitio cada vez más importante en el mundo del deporte, y se va perdiendo, a veces, el espíritu que dio lugar a su existencia. Cuando los jugadores solo jueguen por el dinero habrá terminado el deporte como tal. Por suerte no es así todavía, y sólo estamos hablando de un peligro que no tiene por qué concretarse.

NARRATOR: Ahora contesten la pregunta 41

Selección número 21. **AJEDREZ**

FEMALE: —Me gusta muchísimo el ajedrez. Lo he descubierto de nuevo.

MALE: —Que bueno. ¿Jugamos una partida?

FEMALE: —No sé, todavía no sé mucho. Podemos jugar si quieres.

MALE: —No sé, yo sé demasiado. He sido campeón colegial por mucho tiempo.

FEMALE: —Bueno, no importa. Gáname, pero juguemos por jugar.

MALE: —Bueno, ¿qué quieres, piezas blancas o negras?

FEMALE: —Me da lo mismo.

NARRATOR: Ahora contesten la pregunta 42

Selección número 22. **ARQUITECTURA**

FEMALE: — ¿Qué opinas de estos edificios enormes?

MALE: —Me gusta el de forma tubular, y me encanta aquél que tiene gárgolas plateadas.

FEMALE: —A mi en cambio me gusta la sencillez clásica de aquél de la derecha.

MALE: —Parecen gigantes vigilando, ¿no es cierto?

FEMALE: —Yo diría que parecen edificios, simplemente.

MALE: —Muy gracioso.

NARRATOR: Ahora contesten la pregunta 43

Selección número 23. **UN ROBO**

MALE: Quince millones de dólares han sido robados del Banco Nacional por uno de los cajeros que cuidaba el tesoro.

NARRATOR: Ahora contesten la pregunta 44

Selección número 24. **PUNTOS DE VISTA**

FEMALE: La historia no es siempre precisa. En general está contada por el bando ganador. Muy distinta sería la crónica si por ejemplo tuvieramos la perspectiva del indio frente a la del conquistador.

NARRATOR: Ahora contesten la pregunta 45

Selección número 25. **VOTANDO UN DELEGADO DEL CURSO**

MALE: —Tenemos que votar para elegir el delegado de nuestro curso.

FEMALE: —¿Y para qué queremos delegado?

MALE: —Él nos representará en nuestros deseos y defenderá nuestros problemas.

FEMALE: —¿Pero y si opina diferente?

MALE: —Él deberá asumir la opinión de todos nosotros.

NARRATOR: Ahora contesten la pregunta 46

Selección número 26. **DIBUJOS ANIMADOS**

FEMALE: Para hacer dibujos animados hay que dibujar escena por escena en cuadro tras cuadro. Se pueden superponer personajes a un mismo escenario, pero por cada ínfimo movimiento del personaje hay que hacer un dibujo completo. La sucesión de los mismos provoca la sensación de fluidez.

NARRATOR: Ahora contesten la pregunta 47

Selección número 27. **PIZZA**

MALE: —Miren, la luna parece una pizza gigante.

FEMALE: —Una pizza medio comida.

MALE: —No, parece una banana aplastada.

FEMALE: —O una medialuna de manteca.

MALE: —No, parece un pedazo de queso.

FEMALE: —¿Y si vamos a casa?

NARRATOR: Ahora contesten la pregunta 48

Selección número 28. **PÁJAROS**

MALE: Tengo un canario muy caprichoso. Sólo canta a las cuatro de la mañana, durante media hora; a las siete de la mañana, durante veinte minutos; a las cinco de la tarde, si le prendo el televisor o la radio, unos diez minutos; a las once de la noche, si le doy lechuga, durante quince minutos. Si llueve, extiende la duración del canto un 30 por ciento. Es un canario muy riguroso con sus horarios.

NARRATOR: Ahora contesten la pregunta 49

Selección número 29. **HACER**

FEMALE: Si quisiera lo haría - puedo fácilmente - si las condiciones que exijo no fueran imposibles para Ustedes.

NARRATOR: Ahora contesten la pregunta 50

This is the end of Test 2 — Part B Listening. Now begin the Reading portion of Test 2.

CLEP SPANISH TRANSCRIPTS TEST 3

CLEP SPANISH TRANSCRIPTS TEST 3

Listening Part A

Número 1. **FEMALE** ¿Cuánto dinero tienes?

            MALE (A) No tienes.

                     (B) Tienes mucho.

                     (C) Un dólar.

                     (D) Tenemos dinero.

Número 2. **FEMALE** ¿Dónde está tu papá?

            MALE (A) Se llama Pepe.

                     (B) En el trabajo.

                     (C) Me la comí.

                     (D) Es alto y delgado.

Número 3. **FEMALE** ¿Desayunaste?

            MALE (A) Pan y café.

                     (B) Si desayuno.

                     (C) No tengo hambre.

                     (D) Fui al cine.

Número 4. **FEMALE** ¿A qué hora te levantaste?

            MALE (A) Se levantó temprano.

                     (B) No me levanté.

(C) A las siete y cuarto.

(D) Mucho temprano.

Número 5. **MALE** ¿Saliste con tu novio anoche?

FEMALE (A) Salgo siempre.

(B) Fuimos a cenar y vimos una película.

(C) Salí con amigos.

(D) Salí a las ocho de la mañana.

Número 6. **MALE** Ayer compré un vestido. ¿Con quién fuiste de compras?

FEMALE (A) No compré nada.

(B) Compro comida.

(C) Voy sola.

(D) Con mi hermana.

Número 7. **FEMALE** Sr. Ramirez, ¿Es usted el director de la escuela?

MALE (A) Estudio aquí.

(B) Me llamo Raul Ramirez.

(C) El director no está.

(D) Le gustaría conocer mi oficina.

Número 8. **MALE** Mami, ¿Vamos a la piscina hoy?

FEMALE (A) Fuimos ayer.

(B) Después que comemos.

(C) No hay piscina.

(D) Voy en un momento.

Número 9. **MALE** ¿Qué revista estás leyendo?

FEMALE (A) La Mujer Moderna.

(B) Un cuento de Hadas.

       (C) La casa de Bernarda Alba.

       (D) Don Quijote de la Mancha.

Número 10. **FEMALE** Manuel, ¿Son esos tus libros?

     MALE (A) Son sus libros.

       (B) Es de Manuel.

       (C) No, son de Pablo.

       (D) Son tus libros.

Número 11. **MALE** Carlota, ¿Porqué estás triste?

    FEMALE (A) Saqué una "A" en el examen de química.

       (B) Mi abuelita falleció.

       (C) No estoy triste.

       (D) Tengo mucha hambre.

Número 12. **FEMALE** ¿Llegaremos, hoy?

     MALE (A) Después de una hora.

       (B) Llegaste hoy.

       (C) Hoy llegaron.

       (D) Llegaron ayer.

Número 13. **FEMALE** ¿Eres aficionado al fútbol?

     MALE (A) ¿Qué fútbol?

       (B) Nunca juego.

       (C) Sí, le gusta mucho.

       (D) Nunca me pierdo un partido.

Número 14. **MALE** Carmen, dime ¿Qué piensas de esta falda?

    FEMALE (A) No pienso.

       (B) Pienso de la falda.

       (C) Es muy fea.

       (D) No es caro.

Número 15.   **MALE**   Oye Maria, ¿Quién es ese chico?

                FEMALE   (A) Es mi primo.

                                    (B) Es guapo.

                                    (C) Está lejos.

                                    (D) Soy Maria.

Número 16.   **MALE**   Sigo derecho ¿verdad?

                FEMALE   (A) Sí, sigo derecho.

                                    (B) No sigamos.

                                    (C) Sí, sigue derecha.

                                    (D) No, dobla a la izquierda.

Número 17. **FEMALE**   ¿Dónde viven tus abuelos?

                MALE   (A) Están de vacaciones.

                                    (B) En Mexico con mi tia Elena.

                                    (C) No viven.

                                    (D) Son muy buenos.

Número 18.   **MALE**   Perdon Sra. ¿Dondé ponemos las lamparas?

                FEMALE   (A) En el horno.

                                    (B) Con la cama.

                                    (C) Sobre las mesitas.

                                    (D) Dentro del congelador.

This is the end of Test 3 Part A — Listening. Continue with Test 3 — Listening Part B.

CLEP SPANISH TRANSCRIPTS TEST 3

Listening Part B

> **Directions**: You will hear a series of dialogues, news reports, narratives, and announcements. Listen very carefully, as each selection will only be spoken once. One or more questions with four possible answers are printed in your test booklet. They will not be spoken. After each selection has been read, choose the best answer choice for each question and fill in the corresponding oval on your answer sheet. You will be given 12 seconds to answer each question[†].

Selección número 1.

FEMALE: Buenos días, señor. ¿En qué puedo servirle?

MALE: Buenos días. Quisiera ver esa camisa colorada que está en el escaparate.

FEMALE: Por supuesto. En seguida se la traigo (pausa breve). Aquí la tiene.

MALE: Ah, sí, me gusta mucho. ¿La tiene en talla 30?

FEMALE: ¡Cómo no!, pero me parece que le va a quedar chica.

MALE: No es para mí. Es para mi hermano. Mañana será su cumpleaños. ¿Cuánto cuesta?

FEMALE: Se la puedo dejar por 100 nuevos pesos.

MALE: ¡100 pesos! ¿Por qué tan cara?

FEMALE: Pues como ve, se trata de la última moda importada de París. Seguro que a su hermano le va a encantar.

MALE: A lo mejor tiene razón, pero no puede valer más de 70 pesos.

FEMALE: Bueno, señor, para Ud. se la dejo por 80, pero no se lo

[†] **Timing issues are somewhat different for the CBT. See page 6.**

vaya a decir a todo el mundo.

MALE: ¡De acuerdo! Aquí tiene los 80 pesos.

FEMALE: Muchas gracias, señor. Le aseguro que no se va a arrepentir. ¿Quiere que se la envuelva como regalo?

MALE: Sí, por favor.

NARRATOR: Ahora contesten las preguntas 19, 20, y 21

Selección número 2. **TAXI**

FEMALE: —Taxi, lléveme por el camino más largo al museo más cercano.

MALE: —¡Pero el museo más cercano queda a dos cuadras!

FEMALE: —Por eso mismo, hágame caso.

NARRATOR: Ahora contesten la pregunta 22

Selección número 3. **PROHIBIDO**

FEMALE: "Prohibida la reproducción total o parcial del contenido de este volumen, bajo pena de multas severas ordenadas por la ley de este país."

NARRATOR: Ahora contesten la pregunta 23

Selección número 4. **LA TERMITA REINA**

MALE: "La termita madre tiene las dimensiones de varios cientos de las termitas comunes. Se desplaza arrastrada por éstas."

NARRATOR: Ahora contesten la pregunta 24

Selección número 5.

FEMALE: Ay, Chepe, de veras debiera haber hablado con mi mamá antes de hacer este viaje tan precipitado. No quiero que se preocupe por mi cuenta.

MALE: Dale, Rosa, no tengas cuidado. ¿No dejaste un recado con Paula?

FEMALE: Pues, sí, pero no sé si hice bien. Tú sabes cómo es mi hermana. Es muy irresponsable, y además es capaz de no darle el recado a mi mamá por puro despecho.

MALE: Eso sí, Paula tiene fama de ser rencorosa. Pues, ni modo. Por el momento, sólo podemos esperar que cumpla.

FEMALE: ¿Y si no? ¿Qué hago? Mi mamá no va a saber por qué tardo ni dónde estoy, y se va a afligir mucho.

MALE: Puede ser, pero tú ya eres grande, y tu mamá sabe que eres muy responsable, y que puedes cuidarte a ti misma. ¿No crees?

FEMALE: Por supuesto, pero siempre le aviso si voy a tardar en llegar a casa.

MALE: Tranquilízate, mi vida. Cuando lleguemos a la casa de tu tía puedes llamarla por teléfono para explicarle todo y decirle que estás bien. Así sales de la duda de si Paula le comunicó el mensaje que le encargaste. ¿Qué te parece?

FEMALE: Pues, sí, mi amor, tienes toda la razón. Eso es lo que voy a hacer.

NARRATOR: Ahora contesten las preguntas 25, 26, y 27

Selección número 6. **EL PRODUCTO**

MALE: Este producto está garantizado por la empresa que lo ha diseñado para el mercado. Hemos incluido ahora un mecanismo que lo protege del polvo y que disminuye las chances de error por razones mecánicas. El nuevo y colorido envoltorio y detalles de terminación completamente novedosos lo hacen mas atractivo para el uso cotidiano. Inerte para la transmisión de energía eléctrica, puede usarse sin temor a accidentes de esa índole.

NARRATOR: Ahora contesten la pregunta 28

Selección número 7. **VITAMINAS Y NARANJAS**

MALE: Las vitaminas de la naranja aumentan las defensas del organismo humano contra algunos efectos de las bajas temperaturas y afecciones invernales. También restituye energía gastada en la vida diaria.

NARRATOR: Ahora contesten la pregunta 29

Selección número 8. ***PROVISION DE MERCADERÍA***

FEMALE: No tendré más que esto de esta mercadería hasta que se te ocurra traer nuevamente, si no te olvidas otra vez, como hoy.

NARRATOR: Ahora contesten la pregunta 30

*Selección número 9. **NOTA EN EL REFRIGERADOR***

MALE: Maria:

Me comí los chocolatitos que quedaban de los que te regaló tu amigo de Uruguay. Espero que no te enojes conmigo. Te los repongo esta noche cuando vuelva de la clase de dibujo. Un beso.

Antonio

NARRATOR: Ahora contesten la pregunta 31

*Selección número 10. **LAS PATAS DEL PERRO***

FEMALE: Las uñas y los dedos del perro son estructuras modificadas de la misma piel. La uña es una extensión de la epidermis. Lasalmohadillas inferiores de las patas poseen una epidermis protectora gruesa que contienen glándulas de sudor, que además ayudan a la limpieza de las patas. Es la parte menos sensitiva al calor y el frío del perro.

NARRATOR: Ahora contesten la pregunta 32

*Selección número 11. **EL MIEDO***

FEMALE: El miedo surge cuando la amenaza supera la capacidad de enfrentarla y uno se siente vulnerable.

NARRATOR: Ahora contesten la pregunta 33

Selección número12. **EL FARO**

FEMALE: Entre dunas y mar, rodeado por un paisaje silvestre y con una larga historia que lo enriquece, el Faro de la Punta Blanca es visitado por muchos curiosos. Es de difícil acceso hoy día, pero no son pocos los que atraidos por su belleza emprenden la travesía para contemplarlo de cerca. En el mes de febrero es más fácil acceder al faro desde el mar. Entonces es posible acercarse, pero no muchos saben este dato.

NARRATOR: Ahora contesten la pregunta 34

Selección número 13. **ORDEN EN LA CASA**

FEMALE: Hoy le toca preparar el desayuno a Felisa, porque ayer lo hizo Esteban y Guillermo no está en casa. Además Felisa no hizo las camas ayer, cuando le tocaba hacerlas. Y si bien Guillermo no las hizo hoy, como era su obligación, no es por castigo que Felisa debe hacer el desayuno, sino porque así son las reglas de la casa.

NARRATOR: Ahora contesten la pregunta 35

Selección número 14. **DEDUCCIÓN**

FEMALE: Con motivo de la fecha que se conmemora el viernes no habrá clases en todo el país. Debido a esta razón, los alumnos deberán hacer el doble de tarea en casa, y por conseccuencia, estarán muy contentos. Esto, por eso, no debe sorprender a nadie, nuestros alumnos son ejemplares.

NARRATOR: Ahora contesten la pregunta 36

Selección número 15. **BUSCANDO**

FEMALE: —Hola. ¿No vio pasar por acá una señora alta con rulos rojos y vestido verde?
MALE: —Sí, se fue por la izquierda.
FEMALE: —Entonces me voy por la derecha.

MALE:	—¿Pero no la está buscando?
FEMALE:	—Sí, pero para perderla.
MALE:	—¿Pero por qué se ríe?
FEMALE:	—Porque estoy contenta de haberla encontrado. ¡Hasta luego!

NARRATOR: Ahora contesten la pregunta 37

Selección número 16.

MALE:	—Pues si yo he de tener ese aliento que tu tienes por comer carne, me alegro de ser vegetariano!
FEMALE:	—Yo tengo mala una muela, ¡caramba!
MALE:	—¡Pues es hora de curarla!
FEMALE:	—¡Y si yo pierdo el aliento cada vez que corro dos metros, me alegro de no ser vegetariano!
MALE:	—¡Yo no he perdido el aliento en mi vida!
FEMALE:	—¡Ah, no sabía que un vegetariano, seres tan puros, podían ser tan mentirosos!
MALE:	—¡Y que puedo esperar yo de una persona que vive de animales sacrificados!
FEMALE:	—¡Momento, que yo tengo una muy alta opinión de las vacas!
MALE:	—¡Ya lo creo!

NARRATOR: Ahora contesten la pregunta 38

Selección número 17. **FRAGMENTO DE UN REPORTAJE**

MALE:	¿Qué le ha motivado a escribir este libro?
FEMALE:	—Un recuerdo de infancia relacionado con veraneos en un lugar de la costa. Más tarde, cuando ya era adolescente solo frecuentaba paisajes de montaña. Supe que la incomodidad de mi adolescencia estaba vinculada a la ausencia del sonido del mar. Y esto lo pensaba mientras miraba los altos picos y bajaba a los valles por el bosque de las laderas.
MALE:	—¿Es real la anécdota central de la historia?

FEMALE:	—Todo lo imaginario es real también, señor periodista.
MALE:	—Disculpeme, quería saber si la anécdota central le ocurrió o es fruto de su invención.
FEMALE:	—No estoy dispuesto a discutir sobre lo que es real y lo que no lo es. Para mi el vago resplandor de una ciudad nevada que vi en un sueño de mi niñez hace ya más de cuarenta años es más verdadero que este momento en el que hablo con usted de tonterías intelectuales.
MALE:	—Ya veo. ¿Podrá decirme entonces si haber escrito el libro lo ha liberado de su obsesión con el pasado?
FEMALE:	—Señor periodista, uno es presente porque uno es pasado. Y ese pasado que fue es un pasado que es ahora. Ahora es pasado, pero lo es ahora. Y doy por terminada esta entrevista. Buenas tardes.
NARRATOR:	Ahora contesten las preguntas 39 y 40

Selección número18.

FEMALE:	—Buenas noches, señor.
MALE:	—Buenos días señorita. ¿Se siente Usted bien?
FEMALE:	—Sí, claro. ¿Por qué lo dice?
MALE:	—Por nada, traiganos un desayuno americano, por favor.
NARRATOR:	Ahora contesten la pregunta 41

Selección número 19.

FEMALE:	¡Luis! ¡Vaya cara que traes! ¿Qué te pasa, hombre?
MALE:	Es que hoy he tenido examen de política y . . . ha sido un desastre.
FEMALE:	Pero si llevabas más de dos meses preparándote para esta prueba. ¿Cómo te ha ido tan mal?
MALE:	Yo al principio tampoco lo entendía. Cuando miré la hoja con las preguntas, no sabía contestar ninguna.
FEMALE:	Es extraño. A ti siempre te ha ido muy bien en política.

MALE:	Y me sigue yendo bien. Lo que pasó es que, cuando entregué el examen en blanco, me di cuenta de que. . . ¡estaba en la clase de ciencias naturales!
FEMALE:	¡Eres un auténtico despistado!
NARRATOR:	Ahora contesten las preguntas 42 y 43

Selección número 20. *AUTOMÓVIL*

MALE:	—Hoy me compré un automóvil usado muy bonito.
FEMALE:	—¿Estás contento?
MALE:	—Era el automóvil mas lindo del mundo.
FEMALE:	—¿Sucedió algo?
MALE:	—Ya no lo tengo. Dejó de funcionar a las veinte cuadras.
FEMALE:	—¡No me digas!
MALE:	—Pero fueron las veinte cuadras mas lindas del mundo.
FEMALE:	—¿Y dónde está ahora?
MALE:	—Lo usan de adorno en el bar que está frente a la plaza.
FEMALE:	—¡Oh!
MALE:	—Sí. Me lo pagaron con una cafetera usada. ¿No es bonita? ¿No es cierto que es la cafetera más bonita del mundo?
NARRATOR:	Ahora contesten la pregunta 44

Selección número 21. *AUXILIO*

FEMALE:	—¡Socorro, me persiguen! ¡Ayúdeme, por favor! Un hombre de camisa blanca, descalzo, con rulos abundantes y mirada de loco me viene siguiendo hace diez cuadras. Temo que haga una locura.
MALE:	—Yo no veo a nadie.
FEMALE:	—Fíjese bien, tiene un buzo azul y bufanda y es completamente calvo.
MALE:	—Yo sólo veo a una señora rubia paseando a su perro.
FEMALE:	—Eso, tal vez es ella. Seguro que es ella, claro. De vestido rojo.
MALE:	—No, no, tiene vestido amarillo.

FEMALE:	—Amarillo, claro. Quise decir amarillo. Entonces, ¿me va a ayudar, no? Me quiere matar.
MALE:	—No parece. Ella parece estar paseando al perro únicamente.
FEMALE:	—Es que tiene una gran habilidad para esconderse.
MALE:	—Ah. Ya veo.
NARRATOR:	Ahora contesten la pregunta 45

Selección número 22. **TÚNEL**

FEMALE:	Los ladrones entraron a la joyería haciendo un agujero por el sótano del edificio contiguo. La alarma sonó cuando ya habían vaciado las últimas cajas de seguridad. El sótano de origen del túnel era de un antiguo edificio en el que quedaron atrapados por no poder abrir la puerta.
NARRATOR:	Ahora contesten la pregunta 46

Selección número 23.

MALE:	Junto a las costas africanas, cerca del desierto del Sáhara, se hallan las Islas Canarias, un archipiélago que, pese a los kilómetros que lo separan de la Península Ibérica, forma parte de España. Los antiguos pobladores canarios, llamados guanches, rompían la imagen prototipo que el mundo tiene de los españoles, bajitos, de pelo moreno y ojos oscuros. Los guanches eran altos, con la piel bronceada por el sol, rubios y de ojos azules o verdes. Estas caracterítas físicas, tan distintas a las de cualquier otro pueblo cercano, son de difícil explicación, pero algunos estudiosos del tema afirman que eso se debe a que los guanches son descendientes de los habitantes de la legendaria Atlántida, un continente del que se dice que, hace muchos años, se hundió para siempre bajo el mar. Los que apoyan esta teoría afirman que las Islas Canarias son los picos de la Atlántida que el agua nunca llegó a cubrir.
NARRATOR:	Ahora contesten las preguntas 47, 48, 49, y 50

**This is the end of Test 3 — Part B Listening.
Now begin the Reading portion of Test 3.**

ANSWER SHEETS

CLEP Spanish
Practice Test 1

1. Ⓐ Ⓑ Ⓒ Ⓓ
2. Ⓐ Ⓑ Ⓒ Ⓓ
3. Ⓐ Ⓑ Ⓒ Ⓓ
4. Ⓐ Ⓑ Ⓒ Ⓓ
5. Ⓐ Ⓑ Ⓒ Ⓓ
6. Ⓐ Ⓑ Ⓒ Ⓓ
7. Ⓐ Ⓑ Ⓒ Ⓓ
8. Ⓐ Ⓑ Ⓒ Ⓓ
9. Ⓐ Ⓑ Ⓒ Ⓓ
10. Ⓐ Ⓑ Ⓒ Ⓓ
11. Ⓐ Ⓑ Ⓒ Ⓓ
12. Ⓐ Ⓑ Ⓒ Ⓓ
13. Ⓐ Ⓑ Ⓒ Ⓓ
14. Ⓐ Ⓑ Ⓒ Ⓓ
15. Ⓐ Ⓑ Ⓒ Ⓓ
16. Ⓐ Ⓑ Ⓒ Ⓓ
17. Ⓐ Ⓑ Ⓒ Ⓓ
18. Ⓐ Ⓑ Ⓒ Ⓓ
19. Ⓐ Ⓑ Ⓒ Ⓓ
20. Ⓐ Ⓑ Ⓒ Ⓓ
21. Ⓐ Ⓑ Ⓒ Ⓓ
22. Ⓐ Ⓑ Ⓒ Ⓓ
23. Ⓐ Ⓑ Ⓒ Ⓓ
24. Ⓐ Ⓑ Ⓒ Ⓓ
25. Ⓐ Ⓑ Ⓒ Ⓓ
26. Ⓐ Ⓑ Ⓒ Ⓓ
27. Ⓐ Ⓑ Ⓒ Ⓓ
28. Ⓐ Ⓑ Ⓒ Ⓓ
29. Ⓐ Ⓑ Ⓒ Ⓓ
30. Ⓐ Ⓑ Ⓒ Ⓓ
31. Ⓐ Ⓑ Ⓒ Ⓓ
32. Ⓐ Ⓑ Ⓒ Ⓓ
33. Ⓐ Ⓑ Ⓒ Ⓓ

34. Ⓐ Ⓑ Ⓒ Ⓓ
35. Ⓐ Ⓑ Ⓒ Ⓓ
36. Ⓐ Ⓑ Ⓒ Ⓓ
37. Ⓐ Ⓑ Ⓒ Ⓓ
38. Ⓐ Ⓑ Ⓒ Ⓓ
39. Ⓐ Ⓑ Ⓒ Ⓓ
40. Ⓐ Ⓑ Ⓒ Ⓓ
41. Ⓐ Ⓑ Ⓒ Ⓓ
42. Ⓐ Ⓑ Ⓒ Ⓓ
43. Ⓐ Ⓑ Ⓒ Ⓓ
44. Ⓐ Ⓑ Ⓒ Ⓓ
45. Ⓐ Ⓑ Ⓒ Ⓓ
46. Ⓐ Ⓑ Ⓒ Ⓓ
47. Ⓐ Ⓑ Ⓒ Ⓓ
48. Ⓐ Ⓑ Ⓒ Ⓓ
49. Ⓐ Ⓑ Ⓒ Ⓓ
50. Ⓐ Ⓑ Ⓒ Ⓓ
51. Ⓐ Ⓑ Ⓒ Ⓓ
52. Ⓐ Ⓑ Ⓒ Ⓓ
53. Ⓐ Ⓑ Ⓒ Ⓓ
54. Ⓐ Ⓑ Ⓒ Ⓓ
55. Ⓐ Ⓑ Ⓒ Ⓓ
56. Ⓐ Ⓑ Ⓒ Ⓓ
57. Ⓐ Ⓑ Ⓒ Ⓓ
58. Ⓐ Ⓑ Ⓒ Ⓓ
59. Ⓐ Ⓑ Ⓒ Ⓓ
60. Ⓐ Ⓑ Ⓒ Ⓓ
61. Ⓐ Ⓑ Ⓒ Ⓓ
62. Ⓐ Ⓑ Ⓒ Ⓓ
63. Ⓐ Ⓑ Ⓒ Ⓓ
64. Ⓐ Ⓑ Ⓒ Ⓓ
65. Ⓐ Ⓑ Ⓒ Ⓓ
66. Ⓐ Ⓑ Ⓒ Ⓓ

67. Ⓐ Ⓑ Ⓒ Ⓓ
68. Ⓐ Ⓑ Ⓒ Ⓓ
69. Ⓐ Ⓑ Ⓒ Ⓓ
70. Ⓐ Ⓑ Ⓒ Ⓓ
71. Ⓐ Ⓑ Ⓒ Ⓓ
72. Ⓐ Ⓑ Ⓒ Ⓓ
73. Ⓐ Ⓑ Ⓒ Ⓓ
74. Ⓐ Ⓑ Ⓒ Ⓓ
75. Ⓐ Ⓑ Ⓒ Ⓓ
76. Ⓐ Ⓑ Ⓒ Ⓓ
77. Ⓐ Ⓑ Ⓒ Ⓓ
78. Ⓐ Ⓑ Ⓒ Ⓓ
79. Ⓐ Ⓑ Ⓒ Ⓓ
80. Ⓐ Ⓑ Ⓒ Ⓓ
81. Ⓐ Ⓑ Ⓒ Ⓓ
82. Ⓐ Ⓑ Ⓒ Ⓓ
83. Ⓐ Ⓑ Ⓒ Ⓓ
84. Ⓐ Ⓑ Ⓒ Ⓓ
85. Ⓐ Ⓑ Ⓒ Ⓓ
86. Ⓐ Ⓑ Ⓒ Ⓓ
87. Ⓐ Ⓑ Ⓒ Ⓓ
88. Ⓐ Ⓑ Ⓒ Ⓓ
89. Ⓐ Ⓑ Ⓒ Ⓓ
90. Ⓐ Ⓑ Ⓒ Ⓓ
91. Ⓐ Ⓑ Ⓒ Ⓓ
92. Ⓐ Ⓑ Ⓒ Ⓓ
93. Ⓐ Ⓑ Ⓒ Ⓓ
94. Ⓐ Ⓑ Ⓒ Ⓓ
95. Ⓐ Ⓑ Ⓒ Ⓓ
96. Ⓐ Ⓑ Ⓒ Ⓓ
97. Ⓐ Ⓑ Ⓒ Ⓓ
98. Ⓐ Ⓑ Ⓒ Ⓓ
99. Ⓐ Ⓑ Ⓒ Ⓓ

100. Ⓐ Ⓑ Ⓒ Ⓓ
101. Ⓐ Ⓑ Ⓒ Ⓓ
102. Ⓐ Ⓑ Ⓒ Ⓓ
103. Ⓐ Ⓑ Ⓒ Ⓓ
104. Ⓐ Ⓑ Ⓒ Ⓓ
105. Ⓐ Ⓑ Ⓒ Ⓓ
106. Ⓐ Ⓑ Ⓒ Ⓓ
107. Ⓐ Ⓑ Ⓒ Ⓓ
108. Ⓐ Ⓑ Ⓒ Ⓓ
109. Ⓐ Ⓑ Ⓒ Ⓓ
110. Ⓐ Ⓑ Ⓒ Ⓓ
111. Ⓐ Ⓑ Ⓒ Ⓓ
112. Ⓐ Ⓑ Ⓒ Ⓓ
113. Ⓐ Ⓑ Ⓒ Ⓓ
114. Ⓐ Ⓑ Ⓒ Ⓓ
115. Ⓐ Ⓑ Ⓒ Ⓓ
116. Ⓐ Ⓑ Ⓒ Ⓓ
117. Ⓐ Ⓑ Ⓒ Ⓓ
118. Ⓐ Ⓑ Ⓒ Ⓓ
119. Ⓐ Ⓑ Ⓒ Ⓓ
120. Ⓐ Ⓑ Ⓒ Ⓓ
121. Ⓐ Ⓑ Ⓒ Ⓓ
122. Ⓐ Ⓑ Ⓒ Ⓓ
123. Ⓐ Ⓑ Ⓒ Ⓓ
124. Ⓐ Ⓑ Ⓒ Ⓓ
125. Ⓐ Ⓑ Ⓒ Ⓓ
126. Ⓐ Ⓑ Ⓒ Ⓓ
127. Ⓐ Ⓑ Ⓒ Ⓓ
128. Ⓐ Ⓑ Ⓒ Ⓓ
129. Ⓐ Ⓑ Ⓒ Ⓓ
130. Ⓐ Ⓑ Ⓒ Ⓓ

CLEP Spanish
Practice Test 2

1. Ⓐ Ⓑ Ⓒ Ⓓ
2. Ⓐ Ⓑ Ⓒ Ⓓ
3. Ⓐ Ⓑ Ⓒ Ⓓ
4. Ⓐ Ⓑ Ⓒ Ⓓ
5. Ⓐ Ⓑ Ⓒ Ⓓ
6. Ⓐ Ⓑ Ⓒ Ⓓ
7. Ⓐ Ⓑ Ⓒ Ⓓ
8. Ⓐ Ⓑ Ⓒ Ⓓ
9. Ⓐ Ⓑ Ⓒ Ⓓ
10. Ⓐ Ⓑ Ⓒ Ⓓ
11. Ⓐ Ⓑ Ⓒ Ⓓ
12. Ⓐ Ⓑ Ⓒ Ⓓ
13. Ⓐ Ⓑ Ⓒ Ⓓ
14. Ⓐ Ⓑ Ⓒ Ⓓ
15. Ⓐ Ⓑ Ⓒ Ⓓ
16. Ⓐ Ⓑ Ⓒ Ⓓ
17. Ⓐ Ⓑ Ⓒ Ⓓ
18. Ⓐ Ⓑ Ⓒ Ⓓ
19. Ⓐ Ⓑ Ⓒ Ⓓ
20. Ⓐ Ⓑ Ⓒ Ⓓ
21. Ⓐ Ⓑ Ⓒ Ⓓ
22. Ⓐ Ⓑ Ⓒ Ⓓ
23. Ⓐ Ⓑ Ⓒ Ⓓ
24. Ⓐ Ⓑ Ⓒ Ⓓ
25. Ⓐ Ⓑ Ⓒ Ⓓ
26. Ⓐ Ⓑ Ⓒ Ⓓ
27. Ⓐ Ⓑ Ⓒ Ⓓ
28. Ⓐ Ⓑ Ⓒ Ⓓ
29. Ⓐ Ⓑ Ⓒ Ⓓ
30. Ⓐ Ⓑ Ⓒ Ⓓ
31. Ⓐ Ⓑ Ⓒ Ⓓ
32. Ⓐ Ⓑ Ⓒ Ⓓ
33. Ⓐ Ⓑ Ⓒ Ⓓ

34. Ⓐ Ⓑ Ⓒ Ⓓ
35. Ⓐ Ⓑ Ⓒ Ⓓ
36. Ⓐ Ⓑ Ⓒ Ⓓ
37. Ⓐ Ⓑ Ⓒ Ⓓ
38. Ⓐ Ⓑ Ⓒ Ⓓ
39. Ⓐ Ⓑ Ⓒ Ⓓ
40. Ⓐ Ⓑ Ⓒ Ⓓ
41. Ⓐ Ⓑ Ⓒ Ⓓ
42. Ⓐ Ⓑ Ⓒ Ⓓ
43. Ⓐ Ⓑ Ⓒ Ⓓ
44. Ⓐ Ⓑ Ⓒ Ⓓ
45. Ⓐ Ⓑ Ⓒ Ⓓ
46. Ⓐ Ⓑ Ⓒ Ⓓ
47. Ⓐ Ⓑ Ⓒ Ⓓ
48. Ⓐ Ⓑ Ⓒ Ⓓ
49. Ⓐ Ⓑ Ⓒ Ⓓ
50. Ⓐ Ⓑ Ⓒ Ⓓ
51. Ⓐ Ⓑ Ⓒ Ⓓ
52. Ⓐ Ⓑ Ⓒ Ⓓ
53. Ⓐ Ⓑ Ⓒ Ⓓ
54. Ⓐ Ⓑ Ⓒ Ⓓ
55. Ⓐ Ⓑ Ⓒ Ⓓ
56. Ⓐ Ⓑ Ⓒ Ⓓ
57. Ⓐ Ⓑ Ⓒ Ⓓ
58. Ⓐ Ⓑ Ⓒ Ⓓ
59. Ⓐ Ⓑ Ⓒ Ⓓ
60. Ⓐ Ⓑ Ⓒ Ⓓ
61. Ⓐ Ⓑ Ⓒ Ⓓ
62. Ⓐ Ⓑ Ⓒ Ⓓ
63. Ⓐ Ⓑ Ⓒ Ⓓ
64. Ⓐ Ⓑ Ⓒ Ⓓ
65. Ⓐ Ⓑ Ⓒ Ⓓ
66. Ⓐ Ⓑ Ⓒ Ⓓ

67. Ⓐ Ⓑ Ⓒ Ⓓ
68. Ⓐ Ⓑ Ⓒ Ⓓ
69. Ⓐ Ⓑ Ⓒ Ⓓ
70. Ⓐ Ⓑ Ⓒ Ⓓ
71. Ⓐ Ⓑ Ⓒ Ⓓ
72. Ⓐ Ⓑ Ⓒ Ⓓ
73. Ⓐ Ⓑ Ⓒ Ⓓ
74. Ⓐ Ⓑ Ⓒ Ⓓ
75. Ⓐ Ⓑ Ⓒ Ⓓ
76. Ⓐ Ⓑ Ⓒ Ⓓ
77. Ⓐ Ⓑ Ⓒ Ⓓ
78. Ⓐ Ⓑ Ⓒ Ⓓ
79. Ⓐ Ⓑ Ⓒ Ⓓ
80. Ⓐ Ⓑ Ⓒ Ⓓ
81. Ⓐ Ⓑ Ⓒ Ⓓ
82. Ⓐ Ⓑ Ⓒ Ⓓ
83. Ⓐ Ⓑ Ⓒ Ⓓ
84. Ⓐ Ⓑ Ⓒ Ⓓ
85. Ⓐ Ⓑ Ⓒ Ⓓ
86. Ⓐ Ⓑ Ⓒ Ⓓ
87. Ⓐ Ⓑ Ⓒ Ⓓ
88. Ⓐ Ⓑ Ⓒ Ⓓ
89. Ⓐ Ⓑ Ⓒ Ⓓ
90. Ⓐ Ⓑ Ⓒ Ⓓ
91. Ⓐ Ⓑ Ⓒ Ⓓ
92. Ⓐ Ⓑ Ⓒ Ⓓ
93. Ⓐ Ⓑ Ⓒ Ⓓ
94. Ⓐ Ⓑ Ⓒ Ⓓ
95. Ⓐ Ⓑ Ⓒ Ⓓ
96. Ⓐ Ⓑ Ⓒ Ⓓ
97. Ⓐ Ⓑ Ⓒ Ⓓ
98. Ⓐ Ⓑ Ⓒ Ⓓ
99. Ⓐ Ⓑ Ⓒ Ⓓ

100. Ⓐ Ⓑ Ⓒ Ⓓ
101. Ⓐ Ⓑ Ⓒ Ⓓ
102. Ⓐ Ⓑ Ⓒ Ⓓ
103. Ⓐ Ⓑ Ⓒ Ⓓ
104. Ⓐ Ⓑ Ⓒ Ⓓ
105. Ⓐ Ⓑ Ⓒ Ⓓ
106. Ⓐ Ⓑ Ⓒ Ⓓ
107. Ⓐ Ⓑ Ⓒ Ⓓ
108. Ⓐ Ⓑ Ⓒ Ⓓ
109. Ⓐ Ⓑ Ⓒ Ⓓ
110. Ⓐ Ⓑ Ⓒ Ⓓ
111. Ⓐ Ⓑ Ⓒ Ⓓ
112. Ⓐ Ⓑ Ⓒ Ⓓ
113. Ⓐ Ⓑ Ⓒ Ⓓ
114. Ⓐ Ⓑ Ⓒ Ⓓ
115. Ⓐ Ⓑ Ⓒ Ⓓ
116. Ⓐ Ⓑ Ⓒ Ⓓ
117. Ⓐ Ⓑ Ⓒ Ⓓ
118. Ⓐ Ⓑ Ⓒ Ⓓ
119. Ⓐ Ⓑ Ⓒ Ⓓ
120. Ⓐ Ⓑ Ⓒ Ⓓ
121. Ⓐ Ⓑ Ⓒ Ⓓ
122. Ⓐ Ⓑ Ⓒ Ⓓ
123. Ⓐ Ⓑ Ⓒ Ⓓ
124. Ⓐ Ⓑ Ⓒ Ⓓ
125. Ⓐ Ⓑ Ⓒ Ⓓ
126. Ⓐ Ⓑ Ⓒ Ⓓ
127. Ⓐ Ⓑ Ⓒ Ⓓ
128. Ⓐ Ⓑ Ⓒ Ⓓ
129. Ⓐ Ⓑ Ⓒ Ⓓ
130. Ⓐ Ⓑ Ⓒ Ⓓ
131. Ⓐ Ⓑ Ⓒ Ⓓ

CLEP Spanish Practice Test 3

1. Ⓐ Ⓑ Ⓒ Ⓓ	34. Ⓐ Ⓑ Ⓒ Ⓓ	67. Ⓐ Ⓑ Ⓒ Ⓓ	100. Ⓐ Ⓑ Ⓒ Ⓓ
2. Ⓐ Ⓑ Ⓒ Ⓓ	35. Ⓐ Ⓑ Ⓒ Ⓓ	68. Ⓐ Ⓑ Ⓒ Ⓓ	101. Ⓐ Ⓑ Ⓒ Ⓓ
3. Ⓐ Ⓑ Ⓒ Ⓓ	36. Ⓐ Ⓑ Ⓒ Ⓓ	69. Ⓐ Ⓑ Ⓒ Ⓓ	102. Ⓐ Ⓑ Ⓒ Ⓓ
4. Ⓐ Ⓑ Ⓒ Ⓓ	37. Ⓐ Ⓑ Ⓒ Ⓓ	70. Ⓐ Ⓑ Ⓒ Ⓓ	103. Ⓐ Ⓑ Ⓒ Ⓓ
5. Ⓐ Ⓑ Ⓒ Ⓓ	38. Ⓐ Ⓑ Ⓒ Ⓓ	71. Ⓐ Ⓑ Ⓒ Ⓓ	104. Ⓐ Ⓑ Ⓒ Ⓓ
6. Ⓐ Ⓑ Ⓒ Ⓓ	39. Ⓐ Ⓑ Ⓒ Ⓓ	72. Ⓐ Ⓑ Ⓒ Ⓓ	105. Ⓐ Ⓑ Ⓒ Ⓓ
7. Ⓐ Ⓑ Ⓒ Ⓓ	40. Ⓐ Ⓑ Ⓒ Ⓓ	73. Ⓐ Ⓑ Ⓒ Ⓓ	106. Ⓐ Ⓑ Ⓒ Ⓓ
8. Ⓐ Ⓑ Ⓒ Ⓓ	41. Ⓐ Ⓑ Ⓒ Ⓓ	74. Ⓐ Ⓑ Ⓒ Ⓓ	107. Ⓐ Ⓑ Ⓒ Ⓓ
9. Ⓐ Ⓑ Ⓒ Ⓓ	42. Ⓐ Ⓑ Ⓒ Ⓓ	75. Ⓐ Ⓑ Ⓒ Ⓓ	108. Ⓐ Ⓑ Ⓒ Ⓓ
10. Ⓐ Ⓑ Ⓒ Ⓓ	43. Ⓐ Ⓑ Ⓒ Ⓓ	76. Ⓐ Ⓑ Ⓒ Ⓓ	109. Ⓐ Ⓑ Ⓒ Ⓓ
11. Ⓐ Ⓑ Ⓒ Ⓓ	44. Ⓐ Ⓑ Ⓒ Ⓓ	77. Ⓐ Ⓑ Ⓒ Ⓓ	110. Ⓐ Ⓑ Ⓒ Ⓓ
12. Ⓐ Ⓑ Ⓒ Ⓓ	45. Ⓐ Ⓑ Ⓒ Ⓓ	78. Ⓐ Ⓑ Ⓒ Ⓓ	111. Ⓐ Ⓑ Ⓒ Ⓓ
13. Ⓐ Ⓑ Ⓒ Ⓓ	46. Ⓐ Ⓑ Ⓒ Ⓓ	79. Ⓐ Ⓑ Ⓒ Ⓓ	112. Ⓐ Ⓑ Ⓒ Ⓓ
14. Ⓐ Ⓑ Ⓒ Ⓓ	47. Ⓐ Ⓑ Ⓒ Ⓓ	80. Ⓐ Ⓑ Ⓒ Ⓓ	113. Ⓐ Ⓑ Ⓒ Ⓓ
15. Ⓐ Ⓑ Ⓒ Ⓓ	48. Ⓐ Ⓑ Ⓒ Ⓓ	81. Ⓐ Ⓑ Ⓒ Ⓓ	114. Ⓐ Ⓑ Ⓒ Ⓓ
16. Ⓐ Ⓑ Ⓒ Ⓓ	49. Ⓐ Ⓑ Ⓒ Ⓓ	82. Ⓐ Ⓑ Ⓒ Ⓓ	115. Ⓐ Ⓑ Ⓒ Ⓓ
17. Ⓐ Ⓑ Ⓒ Ⓓ	50. Ⓐ Ⓑ Ⓒ Ⓓ	83. Ⓐ Ⓑ Ⓒ Ⓓ	116. Ⓐ Ⓑ Ⓒ Ⓓ
18. Ⓐ Ⓑ Ⓒ Ⓓ	51. Ⓐ Ⓑ Ⓒ Ⓓ	84. Ⓐ Ⓑ Ⓒ Ⓓ	117. Ⓐ Ⓑ Ⓒ Ⓓ
19. Ⓐ Ⓑ Ⓒ Ⓓ	52. Ⓐ Ⓑ Ⓒ Ⓓ	85. Ⓐ Ⓑ Ⓒ Ⓓ	118. Ⓐ Ⓑ Ⓒ Ⓓ
20. Ⓐ Ⓑ Ⓒ Ⓓ	53. Ⓐ Ⓑ Ⓒ Ⓓ	86. Ⓐ Ⓑ Ⓒ Ⓓ	119. Ⓐ Ⓑ Ⓒ Ⓓ
21. Ⓐ Ⓑ Ⓒ Ⓓ	54. Ⓐ Ⓑ Ⓒ Ⓓ	87. Ⓐ Ⓑ Ⓒ Ⓓ	120. Ⓐ Ⓑ Ⓒ Ⓓ
22. Ⓐ Ⓑ Ⓒ Ⓓ	55. Ⓐ Ⓑ Ⓒ Ⓓ	88. Ⓐ Ⓑ Ⓒ Ⓓ	121. Ⓐ Ⓑ Ⓒ Ⓓ
23. Ⓐ Ⓑ Ⓒ Ⓓ	56. Ⓐ Ⓑ Ⓒ Ⓓ	89. Ⓐ Ⓑ Ⓒ Ⓓ	122. Ⓐ Ⓑ Ⓒ Ⓓ
24. Ⓐ Ⓑ Ⓒ Ⓓ	57. Ⓐ Ⓑ Ⓒ Ⓓ	90. Ⓐ Ⓑ Ⓒ Ⓓ	123. Ⓐ Ⓑ Ⓒ Ⓓ
25. Ⓐ Ⓑ Ⓒ Ⓓ	58. Ⓐ Ⓑ Ⓒ Ⓓ	91. Ⓐ Ⓑ Ⓒ Ⓓ	124. Ⓐ Ⓑ Ⓒ Ⓓ
26. Ⓐ Ⓑ Ⓒ Ⓓ	59. Ⓐ Ⓑ Ⓒ Ⓓ	92. Ⓐ Ⓑ Ⓒ Ⓓ	125. Ⓐ Ⓑ Ⓒ Ⓓ
27. Ⓐ Ⓑ Ⓒ Ⓓ	60. Ⓐ Ⓑ Ⓒ Ⓓ	93. Ⓐ Ⓑ Ⓒ Ⓓ	126. Ⓐ Ⓑ Ⓒ Ⓓ
28. Ⓐ Ⓑ Ⓒ Ⓓ	61. Ⓐ Ⓑ Ⓒ Ⓓ	94. Ⓐ Ⓑ Ⓒ Ⓓ	127. Ⓐ Ⓑ Ⓒ Ⓓ
29. Ⓐ Ⓑ Ⓒ Ⓓ	62. Ⓐ Ⓑ Ⓒ Ⓓ	95. Ⓐ Ⓑ Ⓒ Ⓓ	128. Ⓐ Ⓑ Ⓒ Ⓓ
30. Ⓐ Ⓑ Ⓒ Ⓓ	63. Ⓐ Ⓑ Ⓒ Ⓓ	96. Ⓐ Ⓑ Ⓒ Ⓓ	129. Ⓐ Ⓑ Ⓒ Ⓓ
31. Ⓐ Ⓑ Ⓒ Ⓓ	64. Ⓐ Ⓑ Ⓒ Ⓓ	97. Ⓐ Ⓑ Ⓒ Ⓓ	130. Ⓐ Ⓑ Ⓒ Ⓓ
32. Ⓐ Ⓑ Ⓒ Ⓓ	65. Ⓐ Ⓑ Ⓒ Ⓓ	98. Ⓐ Ⓑ Ⓒ Ⓓ	
33. Ⓐ Ⓑ Ⓒ Ⓓ	66. Ⓐ Ⓑ Ⓒ Ⓓ	99. Ⓐ Ⓑ Ⓒ Ⓓ	

MAXnotes®

REA's Literature Study Guides

MAXnotes® are student-friendly. They offer a fresh look at masterpieces of literature, presented in a lively and interesting fashion. **MAXnotes®** offer the essentials of what you should know about the work, including outlines, explanations and discussions of the plot, character lists, analyses, and historical context. **MAXnotes®** are designed to help you think independently about literary works by raising various issues and thought-provoking ideas and questions. Written by literary experts who currently teach the subject, **MAXnotes®** enhance your understanding and enjoyment of the work.

Available **MAXnotes®** include the following:

Absalom, Absalom!
The Aeneid of Virgil
Animal Farm
Antony and Cleopatra
As I Lay Dying
As You Like It
The Autobiography of
   Malcolm X
The Awakening
Beloved
Beowulf
Billy Budd
The Bluest Eye, A Novel
Brave New World
The Canterbury Tales
The Catcher in the Rye
The Color Purple
The Crucible
Death in Venice
Death of a Salesman
The Divine Comedy I: Inferno
Dubliners
The Edible Woman
Emma
Euripides' Medea & Electra
Frankenstein
Gone with the Wind
The Grapes of Wrath
Great Expectations
The Great Gatsby
Gulliver's Travels
Handmaid's Tale
Hamlet
Hard Times
Heart of Darkness

Henry IV, Part I
Henry V
The House on Mango Street
Huckleberry Finn
I Know Why the Caged
   Bird Sings
The Iliad
Invisible Man
Jane Eyre
Jazz
The Joy Luck Club
Jude the Obscure
Julius Caesar
King Lear
Leaves of Grass
Les Misérables
Lord of the Flies
Macbeth
The Merchant of Venice
Metamorphoses of Ovid
Metamorphosis
Middlemarch
A Midsummer Night's Dream
Moby-Dick
Moll Flanders
Mrs. Dalloway
Much Ado About Nothing
Mules and Men
My Antonia
Native Son
1984
The Odyssey
Oedipus Trilogy
Of Mice and Men
On the Road

Othello
Paradise
Paradise Lost
A Passage to India
Plato's Republic
Portrait of a Lady
A Portrait of the Artist
   as a Young Man
Pride and Prejudice
A Raisin in the Sun
Richard II
Romeo and Juliet
The Scarlet Letter
Sir Gawain and the
   Green Knight
Slaughterhouse-Five
Song of Solomon
The Sound and the Fury
The Stranger
Sula
The Sun Also Rises
A Tale of Two Cities
The Taming of the Shrew
Tar Baby
The Tempest
Tess of the D'Urbervilles
Their Eyes Were Watching God
Things Fall Apart
To Kill a Mockingbird
To the Lighthouse
Twelfth Night
Uncle Tom's Cabin
Waiting for Godot
Wuthering Heights
Guide to Literary Terms

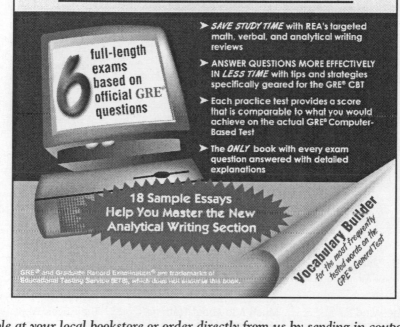

"The ESSENTIALS" of HISTORY

REA's **Essentials of History** series offers a new approach to the study of history that is different from what has been available previously. Compared with conventional history outlines, the **Essentials of History** offer far more detail, with fuller explanations and interpretations of historical events and developments. Compared with voluminous historical tomes and textbooks, the **Essentials of History** offer a far more concise, less ponderous overview of each of the periods they cover.

The **Essentials of History** provide quick access to needed information, and will serve as handy reference sources at all times. The **Essentials of History** are prepared with REA's customary concern for high professional quality and student needs.

UNITED STATES HISTORY

1500 to 1789 From Colony to Republic
1789 to 1841 The Developing Nation
1841 to 1877 Westward Expansion & the Civil War
1877 to 1912 Industrialism, Foreign Expansion & the Progressive Era
1912 to 1941 World War I, the Depression & the New Deal
America since 1941: Emergence as a World Power

WORLD HISTORY

Ancient History (4500 BC to AD 500)
The Emergence of Western Civilization
Medieval History (AD 500 to 1450)
The Middle Ages

EUROPEAN HISTORY

1450 to 1648 The Renaissance, Reformation & Wars of Religion
1648 to 1789 Bourbon, Baroque & the Enlightenment
1789 to 1848 Revolution & the New European Order
1848 to 1914 Realism & Materialism
1914 to 1935 World War I & Europe in Crisis
Europe since 1935: From World War II to the Demise of Communism

CANADIAN HISTORY

Pre-Colonization to 1867
The Beginning of a Nation
1867 to Present
The Post-Confederate Nation

If you would like more information about any of these books,
complete the coupon below and return it to us or visit your local bookstore.

"The ESSENTIALS" of LANGUAGE

Each book in the **LANGUAGE ESSENTIALS** series offers all the essential information of the grammar and vocabulary of the language it covers. They include conjugations, irregular verb forms, and sentence structure, and are designed to help students in preparing for exams and doing homework. The **LANGUAGE ESSENTIALS** are excellent supplements to any class text or course of study.

The **LANGUAGE ESSENTIALS** are complete and concise, with quick access to needed information. They also provide a handy reference source at all times. The **LANGUAGE ESSENTIALS** are prepared with REA's customary concern for high professional quality and student needs.

Available Titles Include:

French *Italian*

German *Spanish*

*If you would like more information about any of these books,
complete the coupon below and return it to us or visit your local bookstore.*

RESEARCH & EDUCATION ASSOCIATION
61 Ethel Road W. • Piscataway, New Jersey 08854
Phone: (732) 819-8880   **website: www.rea.com**

Please send me more information about your LANGUAGE **Essentials books**

Name _____

Address _____

City _____ State _____ Zip _____

REA's **Problem Solvers**

The "PROBLEM SOLVERS" are comprehensive supplemental textbooks designed to save time in finding solutions to problems. Each "PROBLEM SOLVER" is the first of its kind ever produced in its field. It is the product of a massive effort to illustrate almost any imaginable problem in exceptional depth, detail, and clarity. Each problem is worked out in detail with a step-by-step solution, and the problems are arranged in order of complexity from elementary to advanced. Each book is fully indexed for locating problems rapidly.

ACCOUNTING
ADVANCED CALCULUS
ALGEBRA & TRIGONOMETRY
AUTOMATIC CONTROL
    SYSTEMS/ROBOTICS
BIOLOGY
BUSINESS, ACCOUNTING, & FINANCE
CALCULUS
CHEMISTRY
COMPLEX VARIABLES
DIFFERENTIAL EQUATIONS
ECONOMICS
ELECTRICAL MACHINES
ELECTRIC CIRCUITS
ELECTROMAGNETICS
ELECTRONIC COMMUNICATIONS
ELECTRONICS
FINITE & DISCRETE MATH
FLUID MECHANICS/DYNAMICS
GENETICS
GEOMETRY
HEAT TRANSFER

LINEAR ALGEBRA
MACHINE DESIGN
MATHEMATICS for ENGINEERS
MECHANICS
NUMERICAL ANALYSIS
OPERATIONS RESEARCH
OPTICS
ORGANIC CHEMISTRY
PHYSICAL CHEMISTRY
PHYSICS
PRE-CALCULUS
PROBABILITY
PSYCHOLOGY
STATISTICS
STRENGTH OF MATERIALS &
    MECHANICS OF SOLIDS
TECHNICAL DESIGN GRAPHICS
THERMODYNAMICS
TOPOLOGY
TRANSPORT PHENOMENA
VECTOR ANALYSIS

If you would like more information about any of these books,
complete the coupon below and return it to us or visit your local bookstore.

REA's Test Preps
The Best in Test Preparation

REA's Test Prep Books Are The Best!

(a sample of the <u>hundreds of letters</u> REA receives each year)

" I am writing to congratulate you on preparing an exceptional study guide. In five years of teaching this course I have never encountered a more thorough, comprehensive, concise and realistic preparation for this examination. "

Teacher, Davie, FL

" I have found your publications, *The Best Test Preparation...*, to be exactly that. "

Teacher, Aptos, CA

" I used your *CLEP Introductory Sociology* book and rank it 99% — thank you! "

Student, Jerusalem, Israel

" Your GMAT book greatly helped me on the test. Thank you. "

Student, Oxford, OH

" I recently got the French SAT II Exam book from REA. I congratulate you on first-rate French practice tests."

Instructor, Los Angeles, CA

" Your AP English Literature and Composition book is most impressive."

Student, Montgomery, AL

" The REA LSAT Test Preparation guide is a winner! "

Instructor, Spartanburg, SC

(more on back page)

REA's Test Prep Books Are The Best!

(a sample of the <u>hundreds of letters</u> REA receives each year)

" Using [*The Best Review for the CLEP General Exams*]
with the companion book, *The Best Test Preparation for
the CLEP General Exams*, saved me from sitting in the classroom for a
whole semester. Provides sample tests, study tips — everything you
need to be successful. "

Student, Port Orchard, WA

" REA's CLEP Spanish practice test (listening section) was especially helpful....
A *must*! "

CLEP Spanish Test-Taker

" Your book was such a better value and was so much more complete than
anything your competition has produced — and I have them all! "

Teacher, Virginia Beach, VA

" Compared to the other books that my fellow students had, your book was
the most useful in helping me get a great score. "

Student, North Hollywood, CA

" Your book was responsible for my success on the exam, which helped me get
into the college of my choice... I will look for REA the next time I need help. "

Student, Chesterfield, MO

" Just a short note to say thanks for the great support your book gave me in
helping me pass the test... I'm on my way to a B.S. degree because of you! "

Student, Orlando, FL

(more on previous page)